POLICE ADMINISTRATION UNDER THE BRITISH RULE

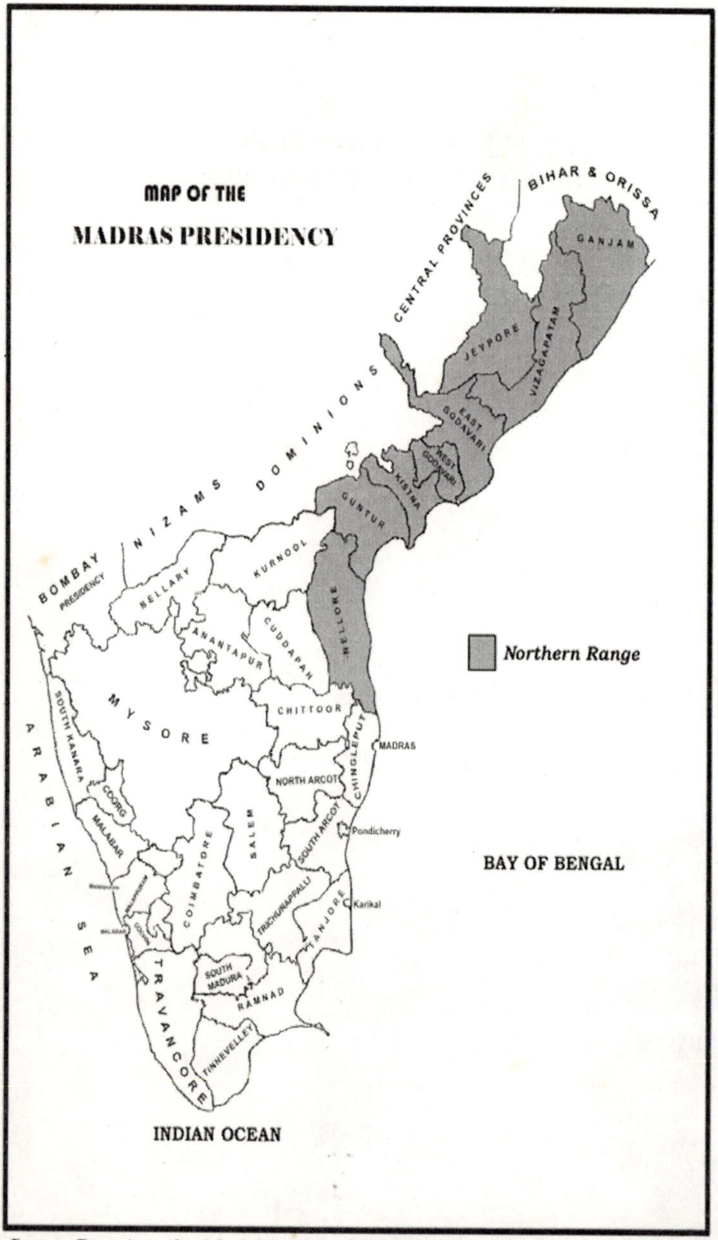

Source: Report on the Administration of the Police of the Madras Presidency 1929

POLICE ADMINISTRATION UNDER THE BRITISH RULE

In the Northern Range of the Madras Presidency 1924-47

Dr. B. Roja

M.A., M.Phil., Ph.D

GYAN

The Publication of this book has been financially supported by the ICHR and the responsibility for the facts stated or opinions expressed is entirely of the author and do not of the Council.

ISBN: 978-81-212-1257-1

First Published, 2015

Published by

Gyan Publishing House
23, Main Ansari Road
Daryaganj, New Delhi-110002
Phones: 23282060, 23261060
Fax : 91-11-23285914
E-mail: books@gyanbooks.com

Laser Typesetting: Rajender Vashist, Delhi

Printed at: G. Print Process, Delhi

Cataloging in Publication Data—DK
Courtesy: D.K. Agencies (P) Ltd. <docinfo@dkagencies.com>

Roja, B., author.
Police administration under the British rule : in the northern range of the Madras Presidency 1924-47 / Dr. B. Roja, MA, MPhil., Ph.D.
pages cm
Includes bibliographical references (pages) and index.
ISBN 9788121212571

1. Police administration—India—Madras (Presidency)—History—20th century. 2. India—History—British occupation, 1765-1947. I. Title.

DDC 363.2095482 23

Contents

Synopsys

The Northern range was one of the police divisions of the erstwhile Madras Presidency of the British India. It came into existence when the British government divided the Madras Presidency into police ranges for the police administrative convenience. It is situated between the Eastern Ghats and Bay of Bengal and it included the northernmost part of the present Andhra Pradesh state and southern part of Orissa state. The Northern range consisted of the districts of Ganjam, Jeypore, Vizagapatam, Godavari, Kistna, Guntur and Nellore.

The economy of the Northern range can be attributed to its flourishing agricultural land in most of the districts and paddy is the main crop cultivated. The seacoast of the Northern range with its harbours at Beemilipatnam, Vizagapatam, Coconada, Masulipatnam, and Krishnapatnam has created extensive sea trade. The ship building activity on the river systems had also encouraged the trade with Madras and other ports by employing a large number of native vessels and this had promoted immense trade and commerce. The railways system was well-connected among the districts and the railways terminus with its ports had opened large trade dealings overseas with Ceylon and Burma. The districts were famous for its textile industries and each area of the districts of the Northern range had specialised in a particular product — Masulipatnam of Kistna district for chintzes, Chicacole of Vizagapatam district for muslins, Tuni of East Godavari district for white long-cloth, Nellore for romals, and Peddapuram of East Godavari district and Berhampur of Ganjam district were known for silk. The roadways and waterways also helped in intra- and internal trade and commerce. These factors made the Northern range administratively important to the British government.

The police administration is complex and its dimensions are multi-faceted and varied. The police is the branch of the justice system that has a specific responsibility of maintaining law and order and combating the crime. The economic condition of this range demanded the attention of the British to develop a unified police administration. The British government had enacted the Madras Police Act of 1859, and the police of the Madras Presidency was organised under this Act. For a unified police administration, the British had enacted the Indian Police Act of 1861 on the recommendations of the Central Police Commission of 1860 and the police administration was reorganised on the model of the Irish Constabulary with a Superintendent for each district. Under the Section 4 of this Act, the Inspector General of Police was the chief of the police administration in the Madras Presidency. In the year 1902, the Police Commission was constituted by the orders of the Viceroy Curzon under the chairmanship of Fraser A.H.L to investigate into the state of police administration, and on its recommendations, the Madras Presidency was divided into ranges for the administrative convenience. Each range was placed under the charge of European Deputy Inspector General of Police. These ranges were further divided into districts under the charge of Superintendents and the districts were further divided into sub-divisions which consisted of police circles with a number of police stations. The police administration of the Northern range was under the in charge of Deputy Inspector General of Police. The police administration in the Northern range was organised by the British government as an instrument for the prevention and detection of crime and to maintain law and order.

The role of the police under the British was to protect the life and property of the people, and at the same time, to protect the British rule. The British organised unified police administration which was an important wing of the public and judicial administration and it continues to be more or less the same even after Independence. The police administrative set-up in the Northern ranges was conceived and constituted by the British. The police administration of the range, from the level of Deputy Inspector General of Police to the Constable and from the district police headquarters to the police station, formed a unit. Further, this study examines the police administration at various levels of the range and includes the organisational structure, police functions, crimes, Special Police Forces and police-public relationship with reference to selection, recruitment, training, discipline, dismissals, promotions, rewards, grave crimes and other offences in the Northern range within the overall framework of the Madras Presidency.

To administer the large acquired territories in this country and its diverse population, the British designed a police administrative system which played a key role in maintaining their dominance and hegemony. The police organisation, largely composed of natives, furthered the goals of colonial dominance through its functions of order, maintenance, crime control, and surveillance. This work further analyses the important role that the police played in maintaining British rule in the Northern range. It is also useful in evaluating the structure of the British police system and its characteristics of use of both force and consent. It provides a mechanism for understanding the disciplining and control of both the police administration and the public. The period 1924-47 under the British rule saw rapid changes in the law and order system. These efforts were largely through legislative measures, implementation of recommendations of commissions and implementation of new administrative rules. The administrative system developed during this period has had far-reaching impact on the police administration in India as the system has continued unchanged. The policing system existed before the advent of the British but a unified system of police administration was first organised by them.

The present work is on 'Police Administration under the British rule in the Northern range of Madras Presidency 1924-47.' The years 1924 and 1947 are significant in the history of the districts of the Northern range and also in India. The year 1924 is significant because partial induction of natives was started under the recommendations of the Lee Commission, and during the same year, the British government also introduced the Intelligence Agencies at the district level of administration. This year is also significant as the Criminal Tribal Act of 1924 was amended for the final time and was introduced in the Northern range as the range was inhabited by a number of criminal tribes. The year 1947 is significant in the annals of the Indian history as the country attained Independence from the British after a long freedom struggle. On 15th August, 1947, India achieved Independence and the Indian police officers continued to direct the police forces of the country and occupy the positions in the police administration. During the British rule, the main concerns of the police were maintenance of public peace and investigation of crimes that occurred despite their preventive efforts. After Independence, the police administration continued, and with changing circumstances, the police force was transformed into a police service. The present work is an attempt to bring to the light the police administration under the British rule in the Northern range of the Madras Presidency for the period 1924-47.

There are no written or published works on the police administration under the British rule in the Northern range of the Madras Presidency. Though there are a number of studies on the police administration such as Mehartaj Begum's work on "*District Police Administration, A Case Study of the Kurnool District*"; David Arnold's work on "*The Armed Police and Colonial Rule in South India*"; Ramaswamy P.N.'s, work on "*Development of Criminal Law in India*"; work by Sumiti Kumar Chatterjee on "*Indian Police*"; Misra KK's work on "*Police Administration in Ancient India*"; Durbashin P.R's work on "*Police in Independent India*"; Chande M.B.'s work on "*The Police in India*"; Giriraj Shah's work on "*Indian Police A Retrospect*". Though these works are all related to police administration in India, they are mainly focussed on the different problems and issues relating to the police in general. Since there are no systematic research studies in particular on police administration under the British in the Northern range during the period 1924-47, so, I have chosen this work to study at macro- level.

The present work is broadly divided into seven chapters, including introduction and conclusion chapters. The first chapter is 'Introduction'; it describes the geographical and historical background of the districts in the Northern range. The geographical features covering the hills, rivers, lakes, climate, rainfall, and soils are described along with the various dynasties that ruled at different periods of time. It also covers the police background, system of police, the organisation of provincial police forces and various related reforms. It also gives a brief description on the research area, topic and its significance, a survey of literature on police, the objective of the study and methodology.

The second chapter is 'Organisational structure of the Police Administration'; it details the police administration, constitution of the police at various levels of the range, their selection through examinations, recruitment method and the rate of recruits, sanctioned strength and actual strength, and the strength of literate and illiterates among the recruited police. The training of these recruits in the various Recruits Schools established in the Madras Presidency, the course of the training, methods of physical training, and the facilities provided for training are also dealt herein.

The third chapter is 'Functions of the Police Department'; it covers the powers and functions of the various cadres of police at different levels of the administration of the range. The detailed methods of discipline are explained with the statistics, the punishments of the police in their personal and official capacity with dismissals, black mark, reduction in scale and cadre, departmental promotion for their good performance, and rewards through titles and medals for encouragement.

The fourth chapter is 'Crimes and Offences', as crime is always committed in one form or another, and the type and the magnitude of crime, changes from place to place to which the Northern range was no exemption. This chapter analyses the different types of grave crimes along with few interesting cases, their motives and punishments meted out to the offenders, statistics, and the offences of the criminal tribes in the Northern range.

The fifth chapter is 'Special and Auxiliary Police Forces and their Services', it pertains to various branches of police administration at the rural and urban regions such as Criminal Investigation Department, Railway Police, Traffic Police, Port Police, Village Vigilance Committees, and Special Police Forces, like Armed Reserves, East Coast Special Police, Malabar Special Police, Civic Guards, and Presidency Emergency Police including services rendered by these foreces.

The sixth chapter is 'Police-Public relations'. The success and failure of the police is largely dependent on the cordiality of police-public relationship and the extent of co-operation the police acquires from the public in its day to day functions. This chapter explains the police role in preventive and punitive functions, public co-operation in the crime control, and rewards granted to the public in appreciation for their cooperation.

The seventh chapter is the 'Conclusion'. The conclusions are drawn in the light of the preceding chapters. In this chapter, the study has brought to light the important and positive role played by police administration in maintaining law and order and controlling crime in the Northern range, the largest range of the Madras Presidency in the context of growing population and rapid urbanisation.

The methodology chosen for this study is essentially scientific which implies collection, classification, analysis of data, and the method to an extent, is both analytical and descriptive. The study mainly depended on the archival source materials, like Annual and Administrative Reports of the Police Administration of the Madras Presidency, Government Acts, Government Letters, Government

Orders of the Home Department and Judicial Department, Collector's Standing Orders, Statistical Atlas, District Gazetteers, Manuals, Encyclopaedia, Pamphlets, Census Reports, Journals, Contemporary Newspapers, Criminal Investigation Department Reports of 1919, and published books. The source materials were collected from Andhra Pradesh State Archives, Hyderabad; Government of Andhra Pradesh Regional office of State Archives, Vishakhapatnam; Tamil Nadu State Archives, Chennai; Dr V.S. Krishna Memorial Library, Vishakhapatnam, and also from Andhra University Law Department Library, Vishakhapatnam.

Preface

The police administration is an important wing of the public and judicial administration. The British government had designed and organised the police administration under the Indian Police Act of 1861 for the preservation of stability and to ensure protection against disorder. The police was a crucial department of administration during the British rule in India and apart from maintaining law and order, it also served as an instrument of control by them. In the following work, I have made an attempt to study the police administration under the British rule in the Northern range of Madras Presidency from 1924 to 1947 with the help of archival source material. This study of the police administration brings forth the impact of the British rule in the districts of the range.

To administer the large acquired territories in the Northern range, the British police administrative system played a key role in maintaining their dominance and hegemony over the natives. The Northern range was one of the police divisions of the Madras Presidency and it came into existence when the British government divided the presidency into police ranges for administrative convenience. The Northern range is situated between the Eastern Ghats and Bay of Bengal and it included the northernmost part of the present Andhra Pradesh state and southern part of Orissa state. This range comprises the districts of Ganjam, Jeypore, Vizagapatam, Godavari, Kistna, Guntur, and Nellore.

This work analyses the important role played by the police, its characteristics use of both force and consent in maintaining the British rule in the Northern range. This study provides a mechanism for understanding the disciplining and control of both the police administration and the public. The police administration of the range, right from the level of Deputy Inspector General of Police to the Constable and from the district police headquarters down to the police station, formed an administrative unit. This study also highlights the police administration at various levels of the range and includes the organisational structure, police functions, crimes, special police forces, and police-public relationship with reference to selection, recruitment, training, discipline, dismissals, promotions, rewards, grave crimes and other offences in the Northern range within the overall framework of the Madras Presidency.

The Northern range was a part of the erstwhile Madras Presidency and the districts of this range were under the British from 1759-47. Hence, the police administration during the period of the study 1924-47 comes under the British rule. The two years, 1924 and 1947, of the period of the study are important; the year 1924 is significant because of partial induction of natives into the police superior cadres, the introduction of the Intelligence Agencies at the district level of administration, and for the introduction of the Criminal Tribal Amendment Act. While the year of the period of study 1947, is significant in the annals of the Indian history as the country attained Independence from the British in this very year. On attaining freedom, the Indian police officers continued to direct the police forces of the country and occupy the positions of the police administration which they formerly held. The police administration during the period 1924-47 has had far reaching impact on the police administration in India as the system has continued unchanged following the end of the British rule in 1947.

An attempt is made to review some of the important studies on police administration in India and their contributions. Some of these are, Mehartaj Begum's work on *"District Police Administration";* David Arnold's work on *"The Armed Police and Colonial Rule in South India"*; Ramaswamy P.N.'s work *"Development of Criminal Law in India";* Sumiti Kumar Chatterjee's work on *"Indian Police"*, and her another work *"The Police in Ancient India";* Misra K.K.'s work on *"Police Administration in Ancient India";* Durbashin P.R.'s work on *"Police in Independent India";* a work on *"The History of Andhra Pradesh Police, 1861-1961"*; Chande M.B.'s work on *"The Police in India";* Giriraj Shah's work on *"Indian Police — A Retrospect"* and her another work, viz. *"State Policing in India"*; Bhardwaj R.K.'s work on *"Indian Police Administration";* Naranaswamy K's work *"Policing in India";* Devi Dayal Aggrawal's, *"Central Bureau of Investigation and Policing in India";* and work on *"The History of the Madras Police, 1859-1959"*. All these works have focussed on the different problems and issues relating to the police, in general. Hitherto, there are no systematic research studies, in particular, on police administration in the Northern range. So, I have chosen to study police administration under the British rule in the Northern range of the Madras Presidency from the years 1924 to 1947.

The main objective of the study is to find out as to what extent the police administration under the British rule in the Northern range of the Madras presidency had functioned during the period. The crime was inevitable as this range was densely populated, urbanised and large Agency tracts were inhabited by numerous criminal tribes. So, I made an attempt to study various grave crimes of this range under socio-political, economic, and religious conditions and brought to light the effectiveness of the police administration.

The methodology chosen for this study entitled, "Police Administration under the British rule in the Northern range of the Madras Presidency 1924-47" is essentially scientific which implies collection, classification, analysis of data, and the method to an extent is descriptive. I have followed historical method which essentially includes interpretation of data from primary and secondary source material. Much of the data on the police administration have been obtained from various State Archives in India. The primary source materials were collected from Andhra Pradesh State Archives, Hyderabad; Government of Andhra Pradesh Regional Office of State Archives, Visakhapatnam; Tamil Nadu State Archives, Chennai: Dr V.S. Krishna Memorial Library, Vishakhapatnam; and also Andhra University Law Department Library, Vishakhapatnam. The collected source material in my research work are Annual and Administrative Reports of the Police Administration of the Madras Presidency for the years 1924-47, Criminal Investigation Department Reports of 1919, Reports on Crimes, Census Reports, Government Orders of the Home Department, Police (Public), Law and Judicial Department, Government Letters, Standing Orders, Regulations, Minutes of Consultations, Acts, District Gazetteers and Administrative Manuals, and Statistical Atlas and contemporary newspapers. The secondary source material consisted of published books, articles, journals, and unpublished works.

The present study has been divided into seven chapters, including the introduction and conclusion chapters. The first chapter is 'Introduction'; it describes the geographical, historical, and police background and also gives a brief description on the research area topic, its significance, review of literature, the objective of the study and methodology.

The second chapter is 'Organisational Structure of the Police Administration'; it details the police administration, constitution of the police at various levels of the range, their selection through examinations, recruitment method and the rate of recruits, sanctioned strength and actual strength, and the strength of literate and illiterates among the recruited police. The training of these recruits in the various Recruits Schools established in the Madras Presidency is also described thereunder .

The third chapter is 'Functions of the Police Department'; it covers the powers and functions of various cadres of police at different levels of the administration. The detailed methods of discipline are explained with the statistics, the punishments of the police in their personal and official capacity, and promotion and rewards for their performance through titles and medals for encouragement.

The fourth chapter is 'Crimes and Offences', which analyses the different types of grave crimes, such as murders, thefts, dacoities, robberies, communal disturbances, and labour unrests, among others along with few interesting cases with statistics. It also covers the criminal tribes and the offences committed by them in the Northern range.

The fifth chapter is 'Special and Auxiliary Police Forces and their Services'; it pertains to various branches of police administration at the rural and urban regions, such as Criminal Investigation Department, Railway Police, Traffic Police, Port Police, Village Vigilance Committees, and Special Police Forces like Armed Reserves, East Coast Special Police, Malabar Special Police, Civic Guards, and Presidency Emergency Police apart from describing services dealt by them.

The sixth chapter is 'Police-Public relations'. The success and failure of the police is largely dependent on the cordiality of police-public relationships and the extent of co-operation the police gets from the public in its day to day functions. This chapter explains the police role in preventive and punitive functions, public co-operation in crime control, and rewards granted to the public in appreciation for their cooperation.

The seventh chapter is the 'Conclusion.' The conclusions are drawn in the light of the preceding chapters. In this chapter, the study has brought to light the important and positive role played by police administration in maintaining law and order, and in controlling crime in the Northern range, the largest range of the Madras Presidency.

A map is attached in order to show the geographical territories and boundaries of the Northern range and also an appendix, glossary, and bibliography has been placed at the end of the book.

Dr. B. Roja

Glossary

Circar	:	Government or a province or a district or a division.
Chaukidar	:	A watchman or a policeman in a station.
Cholam	:	Sorghum, a type of foodgrain.
Cauvalry	:	Soldiers or warriors who fought mounted on horseback.
Doraga	:	Principal judicial clerk.
Fituri	:	Traitorous or a rebellious uprising.
Firman	:	A degree or order.
Ghat	:	Mountain pass or mountain range.
Harijan	:	A term coined by Gandhi for Dalits which means son of God.
Jaghir	:	The revenue of a given tract of land made over to a servant of the state.
Kaval	:	Watch, guard, protection, preservation, keeping, a typical South Indian institution.
Kabuli	:	A caste, whose profession was lending money.
Kamma	:	A caste in South Indian Hindu religion.
Kotwal	:	The chief officer of police for a city or town.
Komati	:	A caste in South India who consider themselves to be Vaisya.
Muffasil	:	Rural locality, an administrative division of a state.
Munisif	:	A civil judge in a court of law.
Manasabdar	:	Landlord.

Muttadar	: A person who holds a village or group of villages.
Naik	: Head of a small body of soldiers.
Nizam	: Governor.
Palegars	: A subordinate feudal chief.
Platoon	: Group.
Panchayat	: A village council or a caste council.
Ryot	: Farmer.
Sanad	: Commonly used in India as a diplomatic instruments of grant.
Satyagraha	: A policy of passive political resistance, advocated by Gandhi against British rule in India.
Sanyasi	: Name given to Hindus who have renounced the world.
Sepoy	: Name of Indian soldier in the period of British administration.
Sibbundy	: Officials or servants.
Subah	: A grand division of a country.
Subedar	: The governor of a subah.
Taluks	: Collector of different demonstrations and ranks.
Talaiyaris	: A Telugu word which means village watchman.
Tahsil	: Sub-division of a district.
Thanas	: Groups of petty states.
Thanadars	: Officers serving under deputy political agents.
Tahsildar	: The officer in charge of the collection of revenue.
Vakil	: Public Prosecutor.
Zamindar	: A land (zamin) holder (dar), landowner.

1

Introduction

The Northern range was one of the police divisions of the erstwhile Madras Presidency of the British India. This range included the Nnorthern most part of the present Andhra Pradesh state and the Southern part of Orissa state. The Northern range was a narrow region lying along the coast of the Western side of the Bay of Bengal from 15°40' to 20°17' North latitude and 79° 12' and to 85° 20' Eastern longitude. Its Northern border was contiguous with Orissa and the Southern border was with the districts of Chittoor and Chingleput. The Northern range included the districts of Ganjam, Jeypore, Vizagapatam, Godavari, Kistna, Guntur, and Nellore. The region was also known as Coastal Andhra region.

The Northern range came into existence when the British government divided the Madras Presidency into three police ranges, viz. the Northern range, the Central range, and the Southern range for the purpose of administrative convenience in police matters.[1] In each range, there were five to eight districts and each district was again sub-divided into taluks.[2] During the period of 1924-47, to which this study pertains, Madras Presidency consisted of four ranges, namely Northern range, Central range, Southern range and Western range.[3] In the Northern range during this period, the districts were re-organised. In the year 1925, the district of Godavari was bifurcated into two districts — West and East Godavari districts.[4] The Nellore district was transferred to the Central range in the year 1929 and was again incorporated back into the Northern range in the year 1936.[5] In the year 1936, the districts of Jeypore and Ganjam along with some parts of the Vizagapatam were transferred to the newly-formed Orissa Province.[6] The entire police administration of the Northern range was under the charge of Deputy Inspector General of Police, who was assisted by a number of police subordinates.[7] Mr George was the Deputy Inspector General of Police during the years 1924-25.[8] A brief description about the districts of the Northern range in the Madras Presidency follows.

Ganjam District

The district of Ganjam was one of the districts of the Northern range and it got its name from the word 'Ganj-i-am' which means 'granary of the world'. The district bore its name also after the old township which was situated on the northern bank of river Rushikulya and it served as its headquarters too. The area of the district was 8,311 square miles, of which, 5,205 square miles comprised vast agency tracts with a population of 2,168,456.[9] There was a struggle for amalgamation of Oriya tracts which culminated into organisation of the district of Ganjam.[10] Later, the district got separated from the Northern range of the Madras Presidency and became a part of the newly-formed state of Orissa Province with effect from 1st April, 1936.[11] During formation of Orissa Province, the taluks of Srikakulam, Sompeta, and Tekkali, and some portions of Parlakimidi, Ichapuram, and Berhampur taluks which formed parts of the Ganjam district were retained and added to Vizagapatam district.[12]

Vizagapatam District

Vizagapatam was one of the north-eastern districts of the Northern range.[13] This district was the largest and most populous with 2,566,571[14] people spread across an area of 17,222 square miles.[15] Vizagapatam was part of the Northern Circars — a region comprising Coastal Andhra and southern coastal Orissa. The British for the sake of administrative convenience separated the Agency tracts of Ganjam, Vizagapatam, and Godavari districts and constituted them into an Agency division in the year 1921. This division was later merged in the district of Vizagapatam after the year 1931. In the year 1936 when the Orissa Province was formed, a portion of Vizagapatam district and a major portion of Ganjam district were transferred to the Orissa Province. The remaining portions of these two districts were clubbed to constitute the enlarged Vizagapatam district with its headquarters as Vizagapatam. The portions of the district that were transferred to the Orissa Province were — the complete taluks of Bissam Cuttack, Jeypore, Koraput, Malkanagiri, Naurangapur, Pottangi, and Rayagada and segments of Gunupur,

Padwa, and Parvatipur taluks which were a part of the Agency portion of the Vizagapatam district. In the year 1946, the district of Vizagapatam was bifurcated into South Vizagapatam and North Vizagapatam.[16]

Jeypore District

Jeypore was one of the districts of the Northern range with an area of 8,757 square miles and a population of 625,658. The population was seemingly less when compared to that of the other districts of the range. The term 'Jeypore' means 'city of victory'[17] and this district consisted of the taluks of Aurada, Mahadeoputti, Naurangpur, and Malkangiri.[18] Jeypore district was surrounded by Eastern Ghats and the Aruku hills on its three sides. Oriya was the language predominantly spoken in this district with a significant population speaking Telugu and Hindi. In the year 1936 when the Orissa Province was formed, it was transformed so from the then Madras Presidency.[19]

Godavari District

Godavari district was one of the districts in the Northern range which was situated on the north-eastern coast of the Madras presidency. The north-western portion of the district was covered with Agency tracts. The river Godavari imparts its name to this district and with the construction of the Dowlaishwaram barrage by Sir Arthur Cotton, large tracts of land were brought under cultivation.[20] The British government, for purpose of administrative convenience, divided the Godavari district into East and West Godavari districts in the year 1925.[21]

East Godavari district, which was one of the divisions of the old Godavari district, has a major portion of the delta area with Coconada as its headquarters. The area of the East Godavari district was 6,221 square miles[22] with a population of 1,673,968.[23] It consisted of 13 taluks[24] and in the year 1942, the taluk of Polavaram was transferred to West Godavari district and nearly half of this district was covered by the Eastern Ghats.[25] This district was known as the 'Rice Bowl' or 'Rice Granary' of Andhra Pradesh state because of abundant paddy fields.[26] The river Yeleru and the river Rampa flow through this district but the Godavari river is the main river which contributes to the prosperity of this district.[27]

West Godavari district was carved out of the Godavari district and the Kistna district in the year 1925[28] and it was separately registered by this name.[29] As the western delta of the river Godavari lies in this district, it was rightly named so.[30] It has an area of 2,396 square miles and a population of 1,051,542.[31] The district headquarters was Eluru. The West Godavari district was divided into eight taluks and these were Eluru, Chintalapudi, Polavaram, Kovvur, Tadepalligudem, Tanuku, Narsapur, and Bheemavaram.[32] The taluk of Polavaram which was the largest agency area of the East Godavari district was transferred to this district in the year 1942 when it was made an independent sub-taluk.[33]

Kistna District

This district was then a part of the Northern range of the Madras Presidency formerly called as Masulipatnam district. It was situated on the coast of the Bay of Bengal at the mouth of the river Krishna and was named after it.[34] This district has an area of 3,511 square miles and a population of 1,081,772.[35] The coastal districts of Godavari and Nellore were situated on its north and south respectively. This district was formed in the year 1859[36] and it comprised entire Guntur district and the portion of the former Masulipatam district.[37] The execution of irrigation schemes on the Godavari and Krishna rivers had made this district prosperous and it was readjusted for administrative convenience. In the year 1904, few taluks were transferred from Godavari district to Kistna district when the latter was made a separate district with the district headquarters at Machlipatam.[38] There were no changes in the territorial delimitation of the district till the 15th of April 1925, when Krista district was bifurcated into Kistna and West Godavari district.[39]

Guntur District

Guntur district was then a part of the Northern range and was located on the east coast of the Bay of Bengal with the Krishna river forming north-eastern and eastern boundary of the district[40]. The district had a coastline of 100 kilometers. This district has an area of 5,735 square miles and a population of 1,809,574.[41] The Guntur district was formed in the year 1904 with Guntur as the district headquarters.[42] The districts Guntur and West Godavari were separated from Kistna District in the year 1904 and 1925 respectively.[43]

Nellore District

Nellore district which was then a part of the Northern range was the southern most coastal district with a costal length of nearly 160 kilometers and it was bounded by the Bay of Bengal on the east. Nellore was the district headquarters[44] and it consisted of thirteen taluks.[45] This district of Nellore covers an area of 7,973 square miles with a population[46] of 1,385,553 and was located on the banks of the Pennar river.[47] The district was once known as Vikrama Simhapuri but later it came to be referred to as Nellore. This district gets its name from the Tamil language word 'nellu' meaning paddy and 'ur' meaning town, as paddy crop was largely cultivated in this district.[48]

Geographical Features of the Northern Range

The topography and ecological factors usually play a significant role in moulding the economy, administrative system, law and order, and the judicial system of a region. Hence, it is necessary to understand the geographical features of the Northern range, such as the hills, rivers, lakes, climate, rainfall, and soils.

Most of the geographical areas of the districts in the Northern range consist of three natural divisions namely, the delta, the uplands and the agency tracts. The delta areas lies between the uplands and the agency areas. The delta areas of this range contained fertile lands in which paddy and other crops were cultivated. In the deltas, many permanent islands were formed due to the changing course of the river which were known as 'Lankas'[49] and these islets were very fertile. The upland area comprised the undulating and wooded plains, and in these upland areas, cereal crops were grown. The agency area consisted of the Eastern Ghats and these were densely covered with trees, foliage and thick forests with some scattered hills. The produce of the agency areas were teak, bamboo, honey, soap nuts, and tamarind.

Rivers and Lakes

The Northern range is criss-crossed with many rivers but the major rivers are Krishna, Godavari and Pennar. The other rivers of this range are Nagavali, Indravati, Saveri, Musi, Paleru, Munneru, Chandravanka, Naguleru, Sarada, Varaha, Yeleru, Tandava, Byneru, Yerrakaluva, Gunderu, Tammileru, etc. The river Godavari is compared to the river Nile and the Hindus also call this river as Dakshina Ganga.[50] The rivers Krishna and Godavari are considered as holy rivers and the Pushkaram festival is celebrated once in every twelve years. After the construction of anicuts on these river systems, provision was made for water supply for irrigation to this range all round the year and for navigation.

The canals in the Godavari and the Krishna deltas were made navigable and the Buckingham canal was connected from the city of Madras to the delta of the Krishna river at Peddaganjam. The Lankas were formed due to changing course of these rivers and they are fertile due to accumulation of silt brought down by the rivers.[51] The Pennar river and its tributaries supply water to numerous irrigation channels of the Nellore district. There was ship building activity on these river systems and the coastal trade with Madras and other ports employed a large number of native vessels. The produce from this range like, cotton stuffs, chintzes, carpets, muslin, silk, indigo were exported to Britain.

The lakes Kolleru and Pulicat are the two major lakes in the Northern range. The lake Kolleru is a natural sweet water lake. It is situated in the West Godavari district and served as a natural flood-balancing reservoir. A part of this lake also lies with the Kistna district.[52] The lake Pulicat is the largest salt water lake in the Northern range which is located near the village Pulicat in the border of the Nellore district.[53]

Hills and Soils

The main hill areas of the Northern range are a chain of ghats that run parallel to the coast. The Eastern Ghats were a major line of division in the topography of this region.[54] The ghats become more distinct towards the south and to the extreme north of the coast. The Eastern Ghat region is home to dense tropical forests and common shrub vegetation.[55] The other hill ranges were Kondapalle, Jammalavoidurgam, Mogalrajapuram, and Indrakiladri in the Kistna district.[56] The Eastern Ghats in the Nellore district are locally known as Veligondas.[57] In the East Godavari district, these ghats spread throughout the Agency sub-taluks of Rampachodavaram and Yellavaram.[58] The hills of Palakonda, Parvathipuram, and Salur taluk exist in the district Vizagapatam.[59] Most of the area of the Northern range was covered with the Agency tracts.

The main soils of this range are alluvial, black-regur, and red-ferruginous. Due to these varieties of soils, this range produces a number of crops like rice, maize, millet, oil seeds, sugar cane, chillies, indigo, cotton and tobacco. The Northern range has abundant mineral resources such as coal, graphite, limestone, mica, pyrite, chromite, etc.

Climate and Rainfall

The Northern range mostly has a tropical climate: the summers are very hot and humid with non-existent winters. The monsoon plays a major role in determining the climate in the districts of the Northern range. The summers last from March to June, and in the coastal plains, the summer temperatures are generally higher than that in the rest of the range with temperatures hovering between 20°C and 41°C. As this range has a long coastal belt, the winters are not very cold with temperatures generally ranging between 12°C to 30°C. The climate is warm and damp on the coast and it is drier in the interior region. The districts of the Northern range get rainfall from both the south-west and north-east monsoon and the highest rainfall is received in the Araku valley of the Vizagapatam district. During the months of October and November, the tropical cyclones which form in the Bay of Bengal along with the north-east monsoon also bring rains to the southern and coastal regions of this range.

Agriculture and Irrigation

The Northern range has rich agricultural land due to the deltas of the Pennar, Godavari and Krishna rivers. The prosperity of this range can be attributed to its flourishing agricultural land and abundant water supply from these major rivers. The main sources of irrigation are the canals from these rivers besides a number of tanks and wells. The major irrigation works by the British in this range were the Godavari anicut at Dowlaishwaram, Krishna anicut at Bezwada, and Sangam anicut at Nellore.[60] Most of the population of the Northern range was engaged in agriculture and paddy was the main crop. The other agricultural productions of this range were cotton, sugar, ragi, millet, maize, oil seeds, tobacco, spices, pulses, coffee, vegetables, and fruits and some small quantities of tea, jute, and indigo were also grown.[61]

Demography

The people who inhabited the Northern range can be classified into three categories — people living in the coastal areas, in the plains, and the people of agency areas. The Hindus constitute the majority of the population whereas Christians and the Muslims take the second and third positions respectively. The majority of the population of this range speaks Telugu language and the other languages such as Tamil, Oriya, Kannada, Gujarati, Hindi, Marathi, Urdu, Koya, Yerukalam, Lambadi, Relli, and Paky were also spoken.[62]

Commerce and Trade

The sea coast of the Northern range with its harbours at Vizagapatam, Coconada, Masulipatnam, and Beemilipatnam has created extensive opportunities sea-trade. The Western Railways terminus near Godavari with its ports had opened large trade dealings overseas with Ceylon and Burma. The exports from the districts of this range were hides, coffee, and raw cotton. Roadways and river systems also helped in intra and internal trade and commerce. The districts in the Northern range were well-connected with railways and the South Indian railways serves the extreme south with its terminus at Tuticorin and branches at Nellore district. The railways of the Madras and Southern Mahratta railway passed through all the Deccan districts. While the East Coast railways passing through the districts of the Northern range connected with Calcutta, Masulipatnam was one of the first ports in which the Europeans on the Coromandel operated and every European company had its administrative and office establishments.[63] The chief port of Nellore district was Krishnapatnam and this district was mainly a weaving area. Transport of goods was facilitated from Krishnapatnam through the river Pennar which formally exported blue chintzes.

Historical Background of the Northern range

The Northern range was ruled by various dynasties at different periods of time and some of the dynasties that ruled over this range were Mauryas, Satavahanas, Salankayanas, Vishnukundins, Western Chaulkyas of Badami, Eastern Chaulkyas of Vengi, Imperial Cholas, Velanati Cholas, Kakatiyas, Musunuri Chiefs, Reddis of Kondaveedu, Gajapatis of Orissa, Telugu Cholas of Eruva, Qutb Shahis, Mughals, Vijayanagaras, and Asif Jahis. The great Chinese traveller Hiuen Tsang visited the districts of this range and paid rich tributes to it in his travelogue.[64] With the advent of the Europeans, the course of history in the districts of the Northern range has become an important chapter in the annals of Indian history. In the Northern range, the commercial activities of the British started at Masulipatnam by establishing a factory in the year 1640.[65] The Europeans had established themselves in this range as merchants, as manifested by the English and Dutch settlements at Masulipatnam and the French settlement at Yanam. The Europeans acquired territories from the native rulers by way of grants and they tacitly secured supremacy later.

Acquisition of the Districts of the Northern Range

The geographical regions of Northern Circars came under the British rule during the years 1759-1802. The British made their first acquisition in Andhra during the course of the Third Carnatic war 1758-63. Robert Clive, at the request of Ananda Gajapati Raju of Vizianagram, sent a force under the command of Colonel Forde to the Northern Circars to expel the French forces. He defeated the

French forces and captured Masulipatnam in the year 1758. Thereupon, Salabat Jung, the Nizam of Deccan entered into an agreement with the British in the year 1759. He ceded Masulipatnam to the British and this was the first acquisition of the British in the Northern Circars. After the death of Ananda Gajapati Raju in the year 1760, the affairs in the Northern Circars became complicated. Salabat Jung's suzerainty over the Northern Circars was recognised by the Treaty of 1759 and he marched to Rajahmundry[66] to settle the disputed succession to the Vizianagram zamindary and proclaimed China Vijaya Rama Raju as the new raja of Vizianagram. In the year 1760, Nizam Ali Khan went to Bezwada, and with the help of the British waged war against the Marathas. In return, the Nizam granted Eluru and two other Circars to the British, which were at that time, governed by his Fauzdar, Hasan Ali Khan. He granted *sanads* for the five Circcars to the Madras government in the name of Nizam Ali Khan, who ousted Salabat Jung and then occupied the throne of Hyderabad in 1762. These *sanads* were sent to Masulipatnam and the British occupied the Circars.

At the time of the British conquest, the districts of the Northern range were under the management of local chieftains like rajas, zamindars, and poligars. The supremacy of the British over South Indian region culminated in 1763 with the decline of French authority. However, this did not immediately lead to the annexation of the territory of Northern Circars as most of the parts in Circars were under the direct rule of the Nizam of Hyderabad. In the year 1765, Robert Clive, the Governor of Bengal, could secure a *firman* from the Mughal emperor Shah Alam who gave away the Circar districts to the British.[67] In the following year, the Nizam unwillingly confirmed the cession of these areas through a treaty with the British. Under this treaty, the British acquired Chicacole, Rajahmundry, Eluru, Kondapalli, and Guntur. [68] These areas later formed the districts of Vizagapatam, Ganjam, Godavari, and Kistna. Under the Treaty of 1756, the East India Company was to get the control of Guntur circar after the death of Baslat Jung. However, in the year 1788, Lord Cornwallis obtained Guntur from the Nizam and this cession forms the second stage of the British acquisition of Northern Circars. In the year 1802, the Nawab of Carnatic was relieved of his *subah* and Nellore district was annexed to the British territory.[69] To sum up, in the year 1766, the districts of Vizagapatam, Ganjam, Godavari, and Kistna came under the British rule. In the year 1788, Guntur was acquired[70] and three years after the British got possession of the Northern Circars, Viziarama Raju wrote to the government of Madras claiming that in the year 1752, Salbat Jung, the subedar of the Deccan, had granted him Jeypore as a *jaghir* for a fixed annual payment. The British, considering the past services of the Vizianagram Raja, decided to confirm him the possession of the *jaghir* as long as he continued to be obedient to them. The British officers were first appointed in the Jeypore estate in the year 1863 and this place was made their headquarters, but in the year 1870, the headquarters was transferred to Koraput.[71]

In the year 1802, the British had acquired the district of Nellore, thus bringing all the districts of the Northern range under the control of the British. Even after coming of these districts under the British administration, their jurisdiction did not undergo any major changes.

At the time of transfer of these districts to the British, the zamindars wielded considerable influence owing to their military and financial strength.[72] There were a number of zamindars in the districts of the Northern range; most of whom were from the descendants of the ancient Hindu rulers while some were agents of the Muslim rulers. Some of them lived in the hills whereas others resided in the plains of the Northern range. These zamindars maintained retainers who helped them in the collection of the revenue, by paying a fixed sum to the British government. In the year 1832, due to eruption of conflicts with the Parlakimedi zamindari of Ganjam district, George Russel, first member of the Board of Revenue was sent as Special Commissioner to investigate the causes and suggest measures for suppression. To check future disturbances of these kind, Act XXIV of 1839 was passed and administered directly by the collector with extraordinary powers as an agent to the governor. The British government kept large reserves of men for conquest and defence of their territories and the people were left to make their own arrangements for domestic policing. There were *palegars* as military chiefs[73] who performed the functions of collecting revenue and maintaining law and order by a battalion of troops and they were vested with judicial powers also. The Palegars and gangs of robbers prevailed largely in the districts of the Northern range.[74] To mitigate this, the *darogha* and *thanadar* system was introduced, and the management and administration of the police was placed in the hands of the magistrates. This system, however, suffered from some defects. With the Regulation XI of 1816, the Collectors and their revenue subordinates, viz. *tahsildars*, village heads, etc. became the magistracy and the duties of the police were vested in them. This system of policing was discontinued after 1857. The Revolt of 1857 did not have any significant impact on the Northern range.

Though some stray incidents took place in the districts of the Northern range at Parlakimidi of Ganjam district and Yerragudem in Godavari agency under the leadership of Sheik Peer Saheb, Dundasena and Korakonda Subba Reddy. Subba Reddy of Yerragudem gathered a group of *koyas* tribals under the revolt who killed the village magistrate of Buttayagudem. He also joined hands with Nana Saheb who was rebelling in North India and wanted to enlist support from West Godavari district but he was captured and hanged along with six others and this revolt was put down by the British government.[75] With the revolt of 1857, the rule of East India Company was replaced by direct rule of the British crown. The British government had enacted the Madras Police Act of 1859, and the police of the Madras Presidency was organised under this Act. In the year 1860, Central Police Commission was set up, on the recommendations of which, the Indian Police Act of 1861 was framed based on the model of Irish constabulary. It was introduced in the Madras Presidency[76] and the police administration in the presidency was re-organised under this Act.

Under the British rule, the people were dissatisfied with various policies of the government and they had started expressing their grievances through violent and non-violent methods under the guidance of national leaders. The partition of Bengal in the year 1905 had provided impetus for national awareness and this reflected in the districts of the Northern range too. The people of the range responded spontaneously and organised a swadeshi campaign. The Home Rule Movement started by Annie Beasant and her English Daily 'New India' was a source of inspiration to the intellectuals of this range. The Northern range figures quite prominently in the contribution it made towards liberating our country from the British rule. The people had responded enthusiastically to Gandhi's call for satyagraha in the year 1919, and to this end, many towns of the districts like Vizagapatam, Rajahmundry, Narasapur, Eluru, Bezawada, Guntur, and Nellore of the Northern range observed a day of prayer and fasting on 6th April, 1919.[77] The British government was more concerned about the political outbreak in the districts of Guntur, Kistna, and Godavari. Nationalist agitation had first occurred in forcible manner in these areas.[78] The All India Congress Committee meetings had inspired the people, and the visits of Gandhi to the coastal districts of the Northern range, had spread the message of nationalism, amongst many leaders from this range motivating them to fight selflessly against the British rule.[79] The people of this range had responded enthusiastically to the cause of national struggle prompting them to give up their lucrative jobs and plunge into the national movement. Many local Panchayat courts were set up in the districts of the Northern range in order to boycott British courts and these bodies disposed of many property cases apart from propagating production and use *khadi*. The All India Congress Committee was held at Cocanada in the East Godavari district in the year 1924. It called upon the people to continue with the programme of constructive work and prepare for adoption of civil disobedience.[80] Many women of the districts of the Northern range were inspired by the Congress session and took active part in the freedom struggle. Vedantam Kamala Devi, Durgabai, Duvvuri Subbamma, Maganti Annapurnadevi, Goparaju Hanumayamma, Tanguturi Hanumayamma, are the names of few such women who participated in this struggle. This session had laid a strong foundation for further political awakening of the people of the Northern range.[81] Alluri Seetarama Raju, a leader of *Rampa* rebellion, strongly opposed the British in the Rampa sub-division of the Godavari and Vizagapatam agency. The British with assistance of Armed reserves, the Malabar Special Police, the Assam Rifles, and the East Coast Special Police contributed greatly in the suppression of Rampa rebellion.[82]

Gandhi visited the districts of the Northern range several times for the cause of Independence and this was a notable feature of the Northern range where the people were inspired to take part in the freedom struggle. The people of this range had actively participated in the freedom struggle and the Eluru municipality was the first to pass a resolution in favour of boycotting the visit of Simon Commission in the year 1928 with people holding demonstrations by carrying black flags. During the Dandi march in the year 1930, the salt law was broken in some districts of the Northern range, but it did not last long after the arrest of C. Rajagopalachari.[83] Many people, along with their leaders such as, Maganti Bapineedu, Bharati Devi Ranga, Vallabhaneni Sitamaha Lakshamma, Dandu Naryanaraju, Mulpuri Rangaiah, etc. and such women leaders as Annapurnadevi, Mulpuri Chukkamma, Sattiraju Syamalamba, Mudubi Venkatamma, etc., had actively participated from this range. A notable feature of the salt satyagraha was that large number of women participated actively in it and were imprisoned in the process; for instance, Khammampati Manikyanba was jailed with her six months old baby alongwith.[84] Many students were also inspired and stridently participated in the freedom struggle.

When the call was given for Civil Disobedience Movement at the national level in the year 1932, the people had promptly responded to the boycott and almost all the shops in the districts of this range were closed. Gandhi again visited the districts in the range for the cause of Harijan uplift and threw open many temples for entry of this community. Three Congress candidates were elected from the districts of the range to the Provincial Legislative Assembly thus manifesting it prominent role in the national struggle. Again in the year 1933, Gandhi visited different places of this range for the cause of Harijan uplift.[85] During the Quit India Movement in the year1942, people played significant part to bolster it. During the course of this movement, many acts of violence broke out in different towns and in one such incident, nine persons were killed when the police opened fire; the firing took place at Guntur on 13th August and Bhimavaram on 17th August, 1942.[86] Normalcy returned when the administrative power was finally transferred by the British to the Indians and India became independent in the year 1947.

Historical Background of the Police Administration

Maintenance of law and order in the society or a state is the primary function of the rulers regardless of the form of government structure that exists there. In the primitive societies, however, where might is right, the question of law and order in society hardly arises. With the progress of the civilisation, the State emerged as a potential organisation in different forms of regulatory authorities. The police play an important role in the field of administration being an executive arm of the government to perform endowed with the duty of maintaining law and order. The police force has been in existence in India in one form or the other from the very ancient times. The policing system in India is as old as its civilisation itself, but there was no unified code of law before the arrival of the British. *Mrichhakatikam*, a Sanskrit drama by Sudarka, and *Shakuntalam* by Kalidasa give a view of certain amount of policing in those times. The police administration is well-described in Kautilya's *Arthashastra* which provides the basic structure, organisation, and administrative set-up of police investigation processes, punishment, detection, and prevention. The Sangam text Thirukkural, a work by Thiruvalluvar, also gives description of the police administration. In ancient India, the chief police officer in the city was known as *Nagarpala*, and sometimes, Katapala were appointed in each district to keep record of local occurrences, arrivals, departures and other happenings. The police organisation in the ancient period was based on the traditional system of local responsibility and mutual co-operation in the rural areas while in towns, regular and salaried police personnel were employed.[87] During the rule of Delhi Sultanate, a slight change in the police system was noticed. In the Mughal reign, the administration of law and order was under the charge of officials like Kotwalas, Subedars, and Fauzdars assisted by Thanedars who were in charge of police administration. This system was, however, different from the earlier one. The policeman called *Sipahi* was official of the lowest rank in the police constabulary of the Mughals. The detective branch of the police assisted the police in criminal investigations. With the decline of Mughal power, the system of police administration fell into great disorder as a result of which petty chiefs and zamindars became powerful.[88] The system of police that was prevalent in the Southern India when the English first occupied it was the ancient hereditary Cauvalry system.[89] Under this system, certain predatory tribes undertook to protect the property of the village as a regulated village watch-and-ward system. As a part of this system, the *Talayaris, Kavalgars, Palegars*, and *Zamindars* performed the police functions.[90]

During the British regime, the aforesaid officials were divested of from police functions and were used for collection of land revenue. The Sibbandi crops — the customary constabulary of the Zamindars — were amalgamated with the police and they were kept as Armed Reserve.[91] These reserve forces were equipped with Sniders rifles and were under the charge of a European Inspector.[92] The companies of sibbandis were maintained to keep order in certain tracts, notably Golgonda.[93] The districts were divided into several Thanas and each was placed under a *Daroga*.[94] When this system failed to deliver, they reverted to the old system of village watchmen.[95] This reversion to the old system also did not prove successful. By the Madras Regulation XI of 1816, the village police was placed under the head of the village who was an agent of the Magistrate in the police administration.

The Torture Commission of 1855 was appointed which recommended for the separation of revenue and police functions and to place the police establishments under European officers. The Commission also recommended for discontinuance of the *Muffasil* police which existed before the advent of Europeans. A separate magisterial department was formed in the year 1857.[96] The Madras District Police Act XXIV of 1859 was embodied with the recommendation of the Commission and William Robinson, the first Chief Commissioner of Police, was made the first Inspector General of Police in the British India.[97] With enactment of this Act, the Madras Presidency police administration was organised as an instrument for prevention and detection of crime.[98] The Indian Police Act of 1861 was framed on the model of British constabulary and it was introduced throughout the Northern range as it was part of the Madras Presidency.[99] After the reorganisation of the police force in the Northern range, a part of Jeypore district became a separate police district in the year 1865. On the principle of metropolitan police, the town police was deputed in the three towns of Vizagapatam, Bimilipatam, and Vizaianagram. With the enactment of the Town Improvement Act of 1865, nearly 75 per cent of the municipal funds were allocated for the maintenance of the police.[100]

The First Law Commission presided over by Macaulay prepared a draft of the Indian Penal Code and the work carried out by the Second Law Commission led to the passing of the Indian Code of Civil Procedure and the first Limitation Act of India. In the year 1860, the Indian Penal code and in the year 1861, the Code of Criminal Procedure were passed. Before 1860, the English Criminal Law modified by several Acts was administered in the Presidency Towns of Madras.[101] The appointment of the Third Law Commission in 1861, led to the enactment of a general Law of Succession, codification of the Law of Contract and Evidence Act in 1872, and finally in 1877, to the enactment of a Law of Specific Relief. The commissions and the codes compiled by the British incorporated the principles of English laws with some variations to accommodate the Indian conditions. Sir Fredrick Pollock described the process of the introducing of English law into India in 1895 as "it was not too much to say that a modified English law is thus becoming the general law of British India. The Indian Penal Code, which was English Criminal law simplified and set in order, had worked for more than a generation, among people of every degree of civilisation, but with little occasion for amendment. In matters of business and commerce, English law had not only established itself but has been ratified by deliberate legislation, subject to the reform of some few anomalies."[102] The British government codified and passed a number of enactments like Indian Penal Code 1860, Police Commission Act 1861, Criminal Procedures Code 1862, and Indian Evidence Act 1872 which led to the evolution of the Indian police.[103] The police force was orderly arranged under Madras government as one battalion and its administration was extended to the Northern range.

The Criminal Tribes Act XXVII of 1871 was enacted by the British government for the registration, surveillance and control of certain criminal tribes. Under Section 20 of this Act, it was extended to whole of British India which included Northern range. [104] The main objective of the Criminal Tribes Act was to safeguard the rights of society against anti-social influence and its secondary aim was the reformation of the Criminal Tribes.[105] With the view to reduce organised crime and to bring the various castes habitually addicted to crime under control was the main provision in this Act.[106] A revised version of the Act was applied to the Madras Presidency in year 1911 replacing the earlier Act as the vast agency tracts of the Northern range were inhabited by tribes. Initially, the focus was on the nomadic tribes, especially the Yerukulas, and Yenadis, but later, many other tribes were notified as habitual criminal tribes under this Act in the year I913. These tribes earned their livelihood by committing crimes; actually, they were itinerant traders in the districts of the Northern range.[107] The British had introduced many trading policies to raise their revenue and this made many traditional petty traders, especially the tribal community unemployed, and for their livelihood, they had taken to crime which later became habitual. A number of crimes were committed by these tribes in the Northern range. The British government enacted special legislative measures for the settlement of the criminal tribal communities to make them sedentary. In the year 1924, the final amendment of the Act was passed and many such tribes were registered under this Act for the prevention and control of crimes in the Northern range.

Police Commission 1902-03

Police administrative reforms became priority for the British government with the territorial expansion and increased responsibilities, particularly with regard to the collection of revenue, to combat crime and to maintain law and order. Under Lord Curzon, the then Governor General, Police Commission was constituted in the year 1902 to enquire into the state of police system.[108] This commission consisted of seven members headed by Sir Andrew Fraser H.L., Chief Commissioner of the Central Provinces. This seven members commission consisted of two Indians Diwan Bahadur Srinivasa Raghavaivangar, and Rameshwara Singh, the Maharaja of Darbhanga.[109]

The commission looked into the state of the police organisation and the report with the recommendatory measures was delivered. The most notable recommendation was the constitution of a non-European Service and a single unified police Act for the whole of India. It also recommended for the division of the presidencies into ranges, formation of new police branches such as Criminal Investigation Department, river police, wireless wing, etc. for introduction in the structure of the police system. The Police Commission of 1902-03 also stressed on the executive administration of the police, their lack of professional approach, corruption, and consequential police-public estrangement.[110] The commissioners also reported that the police Act No. XXIV of 1861 had failed due to interference with the police by the civilian authorities. With implementation of most of the recommendations of the Police Commission Report of 1902-03, the Madras Presidency police administration came to be reorganised.

Lee Commission 1924

Civil servants under the East India Company were concerned with the administration of its commercial affairs. They were selected and recruited by its court of directors in England. The recruitment was made on the basis of patronage, rudimentary knowledge of Eastern trade and commercial accounts was considered to be a qualification for the candidates along with the physical fitness, but this system of nomination led to corrupt practices in the recruitment of the services. It was in the year 1833, that Lord Granville advocated the practice of recruitment of candidates through competition instead of nominations. The Government of India Act 1853, provided for young men to compete for entry to colleges, irrespective of their religion, place of birth, colour, or race. Until the year 1855, the appointments to the civil services were made by nomination, but later the system of nomination was abandoned. The recruitment of the European services was conducted by competitive examinations held in England and probationary training was also imparted in England.[111] In the year 1870, a qualifying open competitive examination was organised. With the recommendations of the Play Fair Commission 1876, the civil services were divided into higher and lower division. The higher services were the Superior Police Services consisting of an Inspector General, Deputy Inspectors General, District Superintendents, and Assistant District Superintendents.[112] The lower services were the Subordinate Police Services consisting of Inspectors, Sub-Inspectors, Head Constables, and Constables. The higher cadres were mainly Europeans or Eurasians.

Recruitment had hitherto been partly by open competition in England, partly by examination after nomination in India and partly by promotion of subordinate officers, but it was decided in 1905 that appointments in India should henceforth be made only with the special sanction of Government of India.[113] All the key posts in the police administration were occupied by Europeans and their rate of pay was higher than that of the Indians. The policy of Montagu Chelmsford reforms of 1919 emphasised on the Indianisation of the higher services.[114] Royal Commission was appointed in the year 1924 under the chairmanship of Lord Lee to inquire into the organisation and general conditions of services and also on the methods of recruitment for Europeans as well-Indians.[115] It had recommended the setting up of a Central Public Service Commission in India. The Commission recommended for the division of the All India Services into two, one at the central and the other at the provincial level, and their recruitment was vested in the provincial governments. With the enforcement of the recommendations of the report, partial induction of natives to the superior posts was started. Public Service Commission in India owed their origin to the recommendations of the Royal Commission.

The Northern range was one of the police ranges of the Madras Presidency and it consisted of the districts of Ganjam, Jeypore, Vizagapatam, Godavari, Kistna, Guntur, and Nellore. Each district of the Northern range was further divided into sub-divisions and again into police circles. In the year 1925, the old Godavari district was bifurcated into two districts, West and East Godavari. The transfer of the Ganjam and Jeypore police districts and parts of old Vizagapatam police districts to Orissa Province on 1st April, 1936 necessitated the redistribution of the remaining districts among the other ranges. On 1st May, 1936, the Nellore district was transferred from the Central range to the Northern range. Vizagapatnam police jurisdiction was divided into North and South Vizagapatnam in the year 1946.

The formation of each district, their area and headquarters, their importance, administrative alterations and sub-divisions along with the geographical features of the districts of the Northern range have been described to give an understanding about the important role played by the topography and ecological factors in moulding the economy and police administrative system. This which was a vast range with large tracts of fertile lands that contributed richly to its economy, coupled with the factor of dense population, made it administratively demanding. The historical background of the Northern range also explains the acquisition of its districts by the British. The history of police organisation has been traced from its origin in a system of village and local police and their joint responsibility through the changes introduced by the early British administrators and the various steps taken by them to this end by means of various reforms.

The British had enacted a number of administrative policies which made the people dissatisfied with their rule and they started agitating against their rule. The police, besides controlling the general crime, had to also deal with the political unrest. The Cauvalry system of policing was replaced by the village police administration under a Magistrate. As a sequel to a few commissions on the subject, finally the Madras District Police Act of 1859 was passed in the Madras Presidency, and in the year 1861, Police Act of 1861 was framed on the model of British constabulary with which the police came to be re-organised. This Northern range has a vast agency area with certain classes of the population who were nomadic tribes and habitual criminals. They earned their livelihood mainly by committing crimes and other such illegal activities. Under the Criminal Tribes Amendment Act of 1924, these nomadic criminal tribes were registered to render them sedentary by restricting their movement and detention in settlements. The British government had designed and organised the police administration and it had used the police force as an instrument to enforce law and restore peace. The police administration formed an important part of the judicial administration. It was an executive arm of the government for controling crime and performing the duty of maintaining law and order. The main functions of the police in any society are preservation of stability and ensuring protection against disorder. The police are a body of civil servants whose duties are preservation of order, prevention and detection of crime, enforcement of laws, and protecting the government, life and property of the people. The police force in India under the British rule was recruited, trained, promoted and posted lacking proper merit and was paid poor salaries which led to corruption during the British rule.

The concept of police was well-established during the ancient and medieval periods. During the modern era, the East India Company of England maintained the police force not only for the collection of land revenue, but also for enforcement of law. Throughout the British regime, various measures were taken to modernise and reorganise the police administration and reconstruct it on the debris of the old police system. Several commissions were set up to reform the police administration before it took the real shape. The period 1924-47 under the British rule saw rapid changes in the law and order system. The people of the Northern range had actively taken part in the freedom struggle along with the other parts of our country. Besides general crimes, the political offences committed as a result of the ongoing freedom struggle were also dealt by the police. These efforts were largely through legislative measures, implementation of recommendations of commissions and implementation of new administrative rules. The administrative system developed during this period had far-reaching impact on the police administration in India as the earlier system had remained largely unchanged. Although, policing system did exist before the advent of the British, but a unified system of police administration was first organised by them.

Importance of the Study

To administer the large acquired territories in this country and its diverse population, the British designed a police administrative system which played a key role in maintaining their dominance and hegemony. The police organisation, largely composed of native Indians, furthered the goals of colonial dominance through its functions of order, maintenance, crime control, and surveillance. This work analyses the important role that the police played in maintaining British rule in the Northern range. It is also useful in analysing the structure of the British colonial system and its characteristics of use of both force and consent. It provides a mechanism for understanding the disciplining and control of both the police administration and the public.

The organisational structure of the police was laid out in the Madras Police Act of 1859, which provides information on the formal functional relationships in the police organisation. The working of the colonial police in the pre-Independence Madras Presidency was also examined. The police administrative set-up in the Northern range was conceived and constituted by the British. The police administration of the range from the level of Deputy Inspector General of police to that of constable and from the district police headquarters to the police station form a unit. This study examines the police administration at various levels of the range and includes the organisational structure, police functions, crimes, special police forces and police-public relationship with reference to selection, recruitment, training, discipline, dismissals, promotions, rewards, grave crimes and other offences in the Northern range within the overall framework of the Madras Presidency. The study also identifies the role of the police as protector of life and property of the people, and at the same time, of the British rule. The British organised unified police administration which was an important wing of the public and judicial administration and it continues to be more or less the same even after Independence.

The scope of the study is confined mainly to the police administration in the Northern range of the Madras Presidency. The significance of the police system introduced in India by the British has not been fully covered by historians. A study of the police administration as a branch of the British government brings forth the impact of the British rule. The present work deals with the police administration in Northern range between the years 1924 to 1947.

Review of Literature

An attempt has been made to review a few important studies on police administration in India and their contributions to the subject. Mehartaj Begum,[116] in her work, *"District police administration"*, explained the police administration of the Kurnool district. It included the organisational structure of the police administration and police personnel management with reference to recruitment, training, promotion, and morale. David Arnold in his book, *"The Armed Police and Colonial Rule in South India"*, dealt with armed police forces that were primarily used for suppressing the disturbances and enforcing imperial authority in the context of the Madras Presidency in South India. Ramaswamy PN,[118] in his work on *"Development of criminal law in India"*, looked into the historical and sociological aspects and the importance of the police system in India. A work by Sumiti Kumar Chatterjee,[119] *"Indian Police"*, on the occasion of the centenary celebrations of the Indian police journal, 1859-1961, detailed the police from the advent of the British. Another work by the same authoress *"The police in ancient India"*, exhibits how the present administrative system has been inherited from the ancient system. Misra K K,[120] in his book, *"Police administration in ancient India"*, has offered a systematic account of all the aspects of police organisation and its functions in ancient India. Durbashin PR's [121] work, *"Police in Independent India"*, stressed on various administrative changes and the impact of science and technology on the police organisational structure after independence. *"The history of Andhra Pradesh police, 1861-1961"*,[122] is another book on this subject which highlighted the police history of the past century with particular emphasis on that of the Nizam and the British. It gives an overall picture of the evolution of the Andhra Pradesh Police with an account on different stages of its development. Chande MB,[123] in his book, *"The police in India"*, gives an analytical study of the attitude of the government, the political parties, the public, the press, and above all of the policemen themselves in their efforts to enforce efficiently the laws of the land. Giriraj Shah,[124] in *"Indian police -A Retrospect"*, has dealt with police in ancient India, medieval India and on rural and urban crime. Giriraj Shah,[125] in another such work, *"State Policing in India"*, has given a good account of the district police administration, centre-state police relations, state police organisation, and nucleus of a police station. Bhardwaj R K,[126] in his work, *"Indian Police Administration"*, expresses views of the common man in regard to police administration in India. Naranaswamy K,[127] in his work, "*Policing in India* — a case study of Andhra Pradesh", dealt with the historical background, personnel management, financial management, police-society relations and suggested the need for reforms. Devi Dayal Aggrawal's,[128] *"Central Bureau of Investigation and Policing in India"*, traces the history of intelligence and law enforcement. Another study on this topic, *"The History of the Madras Police, 1859-1959"*,[129] covers the development of the Madras police and the systems of police from the vedic times onwards. Though there are a number of studies on the police administration, yet these studies have only occasionally focussed on the different problems and issues relating to the police in general. There has been no systematic research study in particular on police administration in the Northern range. So, I have chosen to study, Police Administration under the British rule in the Northern range of the Madras Presidency 1924-47.

Areas and Period of the Study

The Northern range was a part of the erstwhile Madras Presidency and the districts of this range were under the British from 1759-47. Hence, the police administration during the period of the study 1924-47 comes under the British rule. This research work intends to study the "Police Administration under the British rule in the Northern range of the Madras Presidency 1924-47." The Northern range, one of the police ranges of the Madras Presidency, consisted of the districts of Ganjam, Jeypore, Vizagapatam, Godavari, Guntur, Kistna, and Nellore.

The year 1924 is significant for the appointment of the Royal Commission under the chairmanship of Lord Lee to inquire into the organisation and general conditions of police services and also the methods of recruitment for Europeans as well as Indians. This commission also referred in short as Lee Commission recommended the setting up of a Central Public Service Commission in India and also Provincial Public Service Commission. The Public Service Commission owed its origin to the recommendation of the Lee Commission. The year 1924 is significant as it is in this year that the partial induction of natives to the superior cadres was started under the recommendations of the Lee Commission, and also because in this year, the British government introduced the intelligence agencies. The police system developed during this period had far-reaching impact on the police administration in India as the system has continued unchanged following the end of British rule in 1947. This Northern range has a vast agency area inhabiting certain classes of population that were nomadic tribes and were habitual criminals. They earned their livelihood mainly by committing crimes. These nomadic tribes were enlisted as criminal tribe under the Criminal Tribes Act of 1871 which was introduced in the Madras Presidency in the year 1911. The Criminal Tribes Act was amended several times, with the latest in series being in the year 1924. The underlying principles for notification, registration, strict supervision, and restricted movement and detention in settlements were retained. The major alteration under this Act was that the local government was empowered to prescribe its own administrative rules. In the Northern range, besides the grave crimes of theft, robbery, house-breaking, murders, dacoity, etc., there were incidences of a number of riots, communal tension, labour and agrarian disputes, the activities of Communists and local factions in most parts due to the prevailing political unrest as a result of ongoing Freedom Movement.

The year 1947 proved eventful as India achieved Independence and with consequent transfer of power on 15th August 1947, the Indian government took over from the British who ruled the Indian sub-continent for over two centuries until 1947. The Indian police officers continued holding theire offices and continued providing direction and guidance to the police forces across the country.

Objectives of the Study

The main objective of the study is to find out as to what extent the police administration under the British rule in the Northern range of the Madras presidency had functioned during the period of study 1924 to 1947. The aim is also to understand the various dimensions of the police administration under the British rule and to evaluate the effectiveness in maintaining the law and order in the Northern range. I have followed historical method which essentially includes interpretation of data from primary and secondary source material. This work is descriptive and analytical in nature which is presented in a chronological order so as to study the impact of the British system of police in the Northern range as crime was inevitable here due to densely populated coastal districts wherein large areas are covered with agricultural lands and agency tracts inhabited by numerous criminal tribes. The purpose of this study is also to gain insight into various grave crimes of this range under the then prevailing socio-political, economic, and religious conditions and to assess how far the police administration was effective in this range bedevilled by the highest crime rate amongst other ranges.

Methodology and Source Material

The methodology chosen for this study entitled, "Police Administration under the British rule in the Northern range of the Madras Presidency, 1924-47" is essentially scientific which implies collection, classification, analysis of data and the method, to an extent, is descriptive. Much of the data on the police administration have been obtained from the Administrative Reports of the Inspector General of Police of Madras Province, Reports of the Home Department of Madras Province, Government Orders, Madras Presidency Administrative reports, records, letters, proceedings and dispatches, published in the period between the years 1924 to 47. These reports were obtained from various State Archives in India.

The primary source materials were collected from Andhra Pradesh State Archives, Hyderabad; Government of Andhra Pradesh Regional office of State Archives, Vishakhapatnam; Tamil Nadu State Archives, Chennai; Dr.V.S. Krishna Memorial Library, Vishakhapatnam, and also from Andhra University Law Department Library, Vishakhapatnam. The collected source material are Annual Administrative Reports of the Police Administration of the Madras Presidency for the years 1924-47, Criminal Investigation Department Reports of 1919, Government Orders of the Home Department, Police (Public), Law and Judicial Department, Government Letters, Collector's Standing Orders, Regulations, Minutes of consultations, Acts, District Gazetteers and Administrative Manuals, Statistical Atlas and contemporary Newspapers, Census Reports are important source materials used in my research work. The secondary source materials used in this study mainly consist of published books, articles, journals and unpublished works. These works helped in formulating the chronological, conceptual and theoretical framework employed in the study.

Chapterisation

The present study has been broadly divided into seven chapters including introduction and conclusion chapters. The first chapter is 'Introduction'; it describes the geographical and historical background of the districts in the Northern range, and traces various dynasties that ruled these districts at different periods of time. It also covers the police background, system of police, the organisation of provincial police forces and various related reforms. It also gives a brief description on the research area topic and its significance, a review of literature on police administration in India, the objective of the study and methodology.

The second chapter is 'Organisational structure of the police administration'. It details in the police administration, constitution of the police at various levels of the range, their selection through examinations, recruitment method and the rate of recruits, sanctioned strength and actual strength, and the strength of literates and illiterates among the recruited police. The training of these recruits in various Recruits Schools established in the Madras Presidency, the course of training, duration and methods of physical training and the facilities provided to the probationary trainees.

The third chapter 'Functions of the Police Department' delves upon the powers and functions of the various cadres of police at different levels of the administration of the range. The detailed methods of discipline are explained with statistics, the punishments meted to the police in their personal and official capacity, such as dismissals, black mark, reduction in scale and cadre, and rewards bestowed to them, like departmental promotion for their good performance and conferment of titles and medals for encouragement.

The fourth chapter 'Crimes and Offences' analyses the different types of grave crimes, such as murders, theft, dacoity, robbery, communal frenzy, labour unrest etc., along with few interesting cases and associated statistics, and lastly the offences, motives and punishments of the offenders, including criminal tribes in the Northern range.

The fifth chapter 'Special and Auxiliary Police Forces and their Services' pertains to various branches of police administration in the rural and urban regions, such as Criminal Investigation Department, Railway police, Traffic police, Port police, Village Vigilance Committees and Special police forces, like Armed Reserves, East Coast Special Police, Malabar Special Police, Civic Guards, and Presidency Emergency Police and the services rendered by them have been dealt in the study.

The sixth chapter 'Police-Public relations' explains the police role in preventive and punitive functions, public co-operation and rewards given to the members of the public in appreciation for their co-operation in crime control.

The seventh chapter is 'Conclusion', wherein inferences have been drawn on the contents comprising the preceding chapters of this study. In this chapter, the study has brought to light the important and positive role played by police administration in maintaining law and order and controlling crime in the Northern range, in its position as the largest range of the Madras Presidency, with ever-growing population and rapid urbanisation.

References

1. Mohd Abdul Waheed Khan, *A brief History of Andhra Pradesh*, State Archives, Government of Andhra Pradesh, Hyderabad, 1972, p. 112.
2. Maclean C.D., Manual of the Administration of Madras Presidency, Vol. I, Asian Educational Services, New Delhi, 1987, p.179.
3. Ramesan N, Andhra Pradesh District Gazetteers, East Godavari, printed by Director of printing and stationery at Government Secretary Press, Hyderabad, 1979, p. 159.
4. Mohd Abdul Waheed Khan, *Brief history of Andhra Pradesh*, State Archives, Hyderabad, 1972, p. 112.
5. Majumdar R.C., *The History and Culture of Indian People, British Paramountcy and Indian Renaissance*, Part-I, Bharatiya Vidya Bhavan, Bombay, 1963, p. 327.
6. G.O.No.168, Ms, Pub (police) dated 25th March 1931, Public (Police) Department, Government of Madras.
7. G.O.No.502, Revenue, dated 31st March 1925, Revenue Department, Government of Madras.
8. Report on the administration of the Police of the Madras Province for the year 1936, printed by Superintendent, Government Press, Madras, 1937, p. 2.
9. G.O.No.204, Home, dated 16th January 1937, Home Department, Government of Madras.
10. Report on the administration of the Madras Presidency for the year 1930, printed by Superintendent, Government Press, Madras, 1931, p. xxiii.

11. Report on the administration of the Police of the Madras Presidency for the year 1925, printed by Superintendent, Government Press, Madras, 1926, p. 1.
12. Administration Report of the Inspector General of police for the year 1925, printed by Superintendent, Government Press, Madras, 1926, p. 41.
13. Bandita Devi, *Some Aspects of British Administration in Orissa (1912-1936)*, Academic Foundations, Delhi, 1992, p. 18.
14. Maltby T.J., The Ganjam District Manual, Lawrence Asylum Press, Madras, 1918, pp. 76-77.
15. Ramesan N, Andhra Pradesh District Gazetteers, Srikakulam, printed by director of printing and stationery at Government Secretary Press, Hyderabad, 1979, p. 1.
16. Andhra Pradesh District Gazetteers, A Manual of the District of Vizagapatam in the Presidency of Madras, published by District Gazetteers, Madras,1994, p. 7.
17. Administration Report of the Inspector General of Police for the year 1925, printed by Superintendent, Government Press, Madras, 1926, p. 41.
18. Francis W, Visakhapatnam District Gazetteers, Asian Education Services, Madras, 1992, p. 1.
19. Report on the administration of the Police of the Madras Province for the year 1946, printed by Superintendent, Government Press, Madras, 1947, p. 2.
20. Francis W, Visakhapatnam District Gazetteers, Asian Education Services, Madras, 1992, p. 261.
21. Andhra Pradesh District Gazetteers, A Manual District of Vizagapatam in the Madras Presidency, published by District Gazetteers, Madras, 1994, p. 281.
22. G.O.No.204, Home, dated 16th January 1937, Home Department, Government of Madras.
23. Francis W, Frederick Nicholson, C.S. Middlemiss and C.A. Barber, Gazetteer of South India, Vol. I, Mittal Publications, New Delhi, 1988, p. 268.
24. G.O.No.502, Revenue, dated 31st March 1925, Revenue Department, Government of Madras.
25. Ayyar K.N.K., Madras District Gazetteers, Statistical appendix, together with a supplement to the District Gazetteers (1907 for Godavari District), printed by Superintendent, Government Press, Madras, 1935, p. 93.
26. Administration Report of the Inspector General of police for the year 1925, printed by Superintendent, Government Press, Madras, p. 41.

27. *Ibid.*, p. 91.
28. Ramesan N, Andhra Pradesh District Gazetteers, East Godavari, printed by Director of printing and stationery at Government Secretary Press, Hyderabad, 1979, p. 3.
29. Srinivasa Raghavaiyangar S, *Memorandum on the progress of the Madras Presidency during the last forty years of British administration*, Government Press, Madras, 1893, p. xii.
30. Dosagiri Rao, *Social change and political development in East Godavari District 1875-1925,* Satyakrishna Publishers, Kakinada, 2003, p. 3.
31. Madras District Gazetteers, West Godavari District, Vol. II, tables gathered for police, civil, criminal and jails statistics appendix for West Godavari District 1934, p. 1, and also see Administrative Report of Madras Presidency, 1925-1926, printed by Superintendent, Government Press, Madras,1927, p. 31.
32. Krishna Swamy Ayyar K.N, Madras District Gazetteers, statistical appendix, together with A Supplement to District Gazetteer (1907 for Godavari District), Madras, 1935, p. 341.
33. Madras District Gazetteers West Godavari District, Vol. II, tables gathered for police, civil, criminal and jails statistics appendix for West Godavari district, 1934, p. 1.
34. Administration Report of the Inspector General of police for the year 1925, printed by Superintendent, Government Press, Madras, p. 41.
35. Statistical Record of West Godavari, 1934, p. 45, also see Ramesan N, Andhra Pradesh District Gazetteers, West Godavari, printed by Director of printing and stationery at Government Secretary Press, Hyderabad, 1979, p. 1.
36. Chandra Sekhar, Census 1961, Andhra Pradesh District Census Handbook, West Godavari District, published by Government of Andhra Pradesh, 1967, p. i.
37. Hunter W.W., The Imperial Gazetteer of India, Oxford University, 1885, p. 309.
38. Administration Report of the Inspector General of police for the year 1925, printed by Superintendent, Government Press, Madras, p. 41.
39. Andhra Pradesh District Gazetteers, A manual of the Krishna district in the presidency of Madras, published by the state editor district gazetteers, Hyderabad, 1992, p. 1.
40. Gordon Mackenzie, A manual of the Kistna District in the presidency of Madras, compiled by the Government of Madras, printed by Lawbarg Press, Madras, 1885, p. 1.

41. Report on the administration of the Madras Presidency for the year 1925-26, printed by Superintendent, Government Press, Madras, 1927, p. 31.
42. Report on the administration of the Police of the Madras Presidency for the year 1925, printed by Superintendent, Government Press, Madras, 1926, p. 1.
43. Rajagopal M.V., Andhra Pradesh District Gazetteer, Guntur, Secretariat Press, Hyderabad, 1977, p. 1.
44. Administration Report of the Inspector General of police for the year 1925, printed by Superintendent, Government Press, Madras, p. 41.
45. A Statistical Atlas of the Madras Province, 1940-41, published by Economic Adviser to the Government of Madras, Madras, 1949, p. 193.
46. Ramesan N, Andhra Pradesh district Gazetteers, Krishna district Gazetteer, printed by Director of printing and stationery at Government Secretary Press, Hyderabad, 1977,pp. 1-2.
47. George Smith, *The Geography of British India, political and physical,* publisher John Murray, Oxford University, 1882, p. 373.
48. Rajagopal M.V., Andhra Pradesh District Gazetteers, Nellore District, printed by Andhra Pradesh at Government Central Press, (Revised Edition), Hyderabad, 1977, p. 1.
49. Administration Report of the Inspector General of police for the year 1925, printed by Superintendent, Government Press, Madras, p. 41.
50. Venkateswaran S, Census of India 1951, Vol. III, Madras and Coorg, Part-IIA, printed by Superintendent, Government Press, Madras, 1955, p. 2.
51. Rajagopal M.V., Andhra Pradesh Gazetteers, Nellore, Central Press, Hyderabad, 1977, p. 1.
52. Chandra Sekhar A, Census 1961, Andhra Pradesh District, Census Handbook, West Godavari District, published by Government of Andhra Pradesh,1967, p. ii.
53. Walch G.T., *The Engineering Works of Godavari Delta*, Vol. I, Madras, 1896, p. 1.
54. Chandra Sekhar A, Census 1961, Andhra Pradesh district, Census hand book, West Godavari district, published by Government of Andhra Pradesh, 1967, p. ii.
55. Francis W, Frederick Nicholson, C.S. Middlemiss and C.A. Barber, *Gazetteer of South India, Vol. I*, Mittal Publications, New Delhi, 1988, p. 299.

56. Maclean C.D., Manual of Administration of Madras Presidency, Vol. II, Asian Educational Services, New Delhi, 1989, p. 79.
57. Francis W, The Gazetteer of the Vizagapatam District, Asian Education Services, Madras, 1907, p. 5.
58. Rajagopal M.V., Andhra Pradesh District Gazetteers, Guntur District, Central Press, Hyderabad, 1977, p. 4.
59. Ramesan N, Andhra Pradesh District Gazetteers, Krishna District Gazetteer, printed by Director of printing and stationery at Government Secretary Press, Hyderabad, 1977, p. 3.
60. Rajagopal M.V., Andhra Pradesh Gazetteers, Nellore, Central Press, Hyderabad, 1977, p. 2.
61. Ramesan N, Andhra Pradesh District Gazetteers, East Godavari, printed by Director of printing and stationery at Government Secretary Press, Hyderabad, 1979, p. 3.
62. Ramesan N, Andhra Pradesh District Gazetteers, Srikakulam, printed by Director of printing and stationery at Government Secretary Press, Hyderabad, 1979, p. 2.
63. Challa Satya Murthy, *Water resources engineering: principles and practices*, New age International Publishers, New Delhi, 2006, p. 247.
64. Chandra Sekhar A, Census 1961, Andhra Pradesh District Census Handbook, West Godavari District, published by Government of Andhra Pradesh, 1967, p. iii.
65. Ramesan N, Andhra Pradesh District Gazetteers, West Godavari District, printed by Director of printing and stationery at Government Secretary Press, Hyderabad, 1979, p. 51.
66. Alam S.M., *Masulipatnam, A Metropolitan Port in the Seventeenth Century*, Islamic Culture, 1959, p. 169.
67. Chandra Sekhar A, Census 1961, Andhra Pradesh District census Handbook, West Godavari district, published by Government of Andhra Pradesh, Hyderabad, 1967, p. x.
68. Maclean C.D., Manual of Administration of Madras Presidency, Vol. II, Asian Educational Services, New Delhi, 1989, pp. 140-141.
69. Ramesan N, Andhra Pradesh District Gazetteers, Krishna District Gazetteer, printed by Director of printing and stationery at Government Secretary Press, Hyderabad, 1977, p. 49.
70. Francis W, Visakhapatnam District Gazetteers, Asian Education Services, Madras, 1992, p. 34.
71. Baden B.H. Powell, *The Land Systems of British India,* Vol. III, London, p. 67.

72. Sarada Raju A, *Economic Conditions in the Madras Presidency, 1800-1858*, Madras, 1948, p. 9.
73. Subodh Kapoor, *The Indian Encyclopaedia*, Cosmo Publications, New Delhi, 2002, p. 240.
74. Madras records, Military, Country Correspondence, Vol. XVL, p. 288.
75. Second Report on the Indian Penal Code, Military Orphan Press, Calcutta,1847, p. 35.
76. John Kelsall, Manual of the Bellary District, complied under the orders of Government, Lawrence Asylum Press, Madras,1872, p. 117.
77. John A.C. Boswell, Manual on the Nellore District in the Presidency of Madras, printed by Morhan H, Government Press, Madras, 1873, p. 588.
78. Ramesan N, Andhra Pradesh District Gazetteers, West Godavari District, printed by Director of printing and stationery at Government Secretary Press, Hyderabad, 1979, p. 45.
79. G.O.No.739, Home, dated 7th June 1861, Home Department, Madras Government.
80. Rao P.R., *History of Modern Andhra*, Sterling Publishers Ltd., Delhi, 1993, p. 105.
81. G.O. 232, Judl, 17th February I922, Judicial Department, Madras Government.
82. Venkatarangaiya M, *The Freedom Struggle in Andhra Pradesh*, Vol. III, The Andhra Pradesh state committee, Hyderabad, 1997, p. 79.
83. Ramesan N, Andhra Pradesh District Gazetteers, East Godavari District, printed by Director of printing and stationery at Government Secretary Press, Hyderabad, 1979, p. 44.
84. Dosagiri Rao I, *Social change and political development in East Godavari District 1875-1925*, Satyakrishna Publishers, Kakinada, 2003, p. 253.
85. *Ibid.*, p. 238.
86. Report on the Administration of the Madras Presidency for the year 1930, printed by Superintendent, Government Press, Madras, 1931, pp. xiii-xiv.
87. Rao P.R., *History of Modern Andhra*, Sterling Publishers Ltd., Delhi,1993, p. 119.
88. Rajagopal M.V., Andhra Pradesh Gazetteer, Nellore, Central Press, Hyderabad, 1977, p. 46.
89. Ramesan N, Andhra Pradesh District Gazetteers, Krishna

District Gazetteer, printed by Director of printing and stationery at Government Secretary Press, Hyderabad, 1977, p. 56.

90. Mishra K.K., *Police Administration*, Mittal Publications, Delhi, 1987, p. 64.

91. The Imperial Gazetteer of India, The Indian Empire, Vol. IV, Administrative, Clarendon Press, Oxford, 1907, p. 386.

92. Maclean C.D., Manual of the Administration of Madras Presidency, Vol. I, Asian Educational Services, New Delhi, 1987, p. 187.

93. John A.C. Boswell, Manual on the Nellore District in the Presidency of Madras, Government Press, 1973, Madras, p. 588.

94. Ramesan N, Andhra Pradesh District Gazetteers, East Godavari, printed by Director of printing and stationery at Government Secretary Press, Hyderabad, 1979, p. 159.

95. Ramesan N, Andhra Pradesh District Gazetteers, Srikakulam District Gazetteer, printed by Director of printing and stationery at Government Secretary Press, Hyderabad, 1979, p. 135.

96. Francis W, The Gazetteer of the Vizagapatam District, published in 1907, p. 206.

97. Fraser Tytler A, *Consideration on the present political state of India*, Vol. II, Kessinger Publishing {House}, London, 1816, p. 161.

98. Maclean C.D., Manual of the Administration of Madras Presidency, Vol. I, Asian Educational Services, New Delhi,1987, p. 283.

99. Ramesan N, Andhra Pradesh District Gazetteers, West Godavari District, printed by Director of printing and stationery at Government Secretary Press, Hyderabad, 1979, p. 160.

100. Devi Cayal Aggarwal, *CBI and Policing in India*, Kaveri Books, New Delhi, 2000, p. 86.

101. Government of Madras, Legal Department, The Madras District Police Act,1859, Act XXIV of 1859, printed by Superintendent, Government Press, Madras, 1937, p. 1.

102. G.O.No.739, Home, dated 7thJune 1861, Home Department, Madras Government.

103. Andhra Pradesh District Gazetteers, A Manual of the District of Vizagapatam in the Presidency of Madras, published by District Gazetteers, 1994, p. 281.

104. The Indian Penal Code Act 45of 1860, printed by Superintendent, Government Press, Madras, pp. 53-82.

105. Giriraj Shah, *Encyclopaedia of Crime, Police and Judicial System*, Volume-I, New Delhi, p. 1999, p. 1972.

106. Ranjit Sen Gupta, *Management of internal security, Freedom from fear*, Lancer Publication{s}, New Delhi, 1992, p. 7.
107. The Criminal Tribes Act XXVII of 1871, Office of the Superintendent of Government printing, Calcutta, 1897, p. 3.
108. Report of the Criminal Tribes Act Enquiry Committee, printed at the Government Press, Bombay, 1939.
109. Government of Bengal, Criminal Investigation Department, A Pamphlet on Gobinda Dom's gang of Hoogly-Burdwan declared under the Criminal Tribes Act VI of 1924, printed by Superintendent , Government printing, Bengal Government Press, Alipore , Bengal,1942, p. 346.
110. G.O.No.523, Home (Judl), dated 5th March 1917, Home Department, Government of Madras.
111. Ramesan N, Andhra Pradesh District Gazetteers, Krishna District Gazetteer, printed by Director of printing and stationery at Government Secretary Press, Hyderabad, 1977, p. 165.
112. Report of Indian Police Commission 1902-03, printed at Government Central printing office, Simla, 1904, p. 151.
113. Royal Commission on Public Service in India, Appendix to the Report of the Commissioners, Vol. XIII, Police Department, London, 1915, p. 172.
114. Report of Indian Police Commission 1902-03, printed at Government Central printing office, Simla, 1904, p. 142.
115. Government of Madras, Legal.

2

Organisational Structure of the Police Administration

The term 'Police' has been derived from the Greek word 'Polics'[1] which stands for the 'state or administration'. The police are a system of regulation for the preservation of order and the enforcement of law.[2] A policeman is a person paid to perform his duty according to the Acts or otherwise voluntarily.[3] The police are personnel empowered to enforce the law, protect life and property and mitigate public disorder. Police system is a body of civil servants and constitutes an important branch of the justice system with a specific responsibility of maintaining law and order, combating crime, preservation of order, prevention and detection of crime, and enforcement of laws. Police administration is a power of promoting public welfare, by restraining and regulating the use of property and liberty.

The police administration in the Northern range was organised by the British government, as an instrument for the prevention and detection of crime and to maintain law and order.[4] With the enactment of the Madras Police Act of 1859, Indian Police Act of 1861, Indian Penal Code of 1860, Criminal Procedure Code of 1898, Evidence Act of 1872 and the Regulation Acts, the British government organised the police administration in the Madras Presidency and for this purpose they recruited and trained the police force.

The police personnel were considered to be on duty and had power in every part of the General Police districts of Ganjam, Jeypore, Vizagapatam, Godavari, Kistna, Guntur and Nellore of the Northern range. They prevented all crimes, offences and public nuisances to preserve public peace, apprehended suspicious characters, detected and brought the offenders to the justice, collected and communicated the intelligence affecting the public peace, and last but not the least, obeyed and executed all orders and warrants lawfully issued to them.[5] Before the arrival of the British in the Madras Presidency, there was a different system of policing in prevalence wherein the police functions were performed by the *Talayaris*, *Kavalagrars*, Palegars, and Zamindars.[6] After the British established their rule, the Palegars and Zamindars were divested off their police functions and began to be used for the collection of land revenue only. The British divided the Madras Presidency into many district and these districts were further classified into several *Thanas* with each such institution placed under a *Daroga*. They performed police functions as well as revenue collection, but this system later failed as the *Darogas* turned corrupt and failed to restore order.[7] The Sibbandi Corps and the customary constabulary of the Zamindars were merged with the police force and kept as armed reserve.[8]

For a unified set-up, the British had developed the existing pattern of police system. In the year 1813, a special committee was appointed and the old system of village watchman was revived.[9] This system failed as the revenue collectors, who also had police responsibilities, committed many atrocities on the villagers. This led to the constitution of the Torture Commission in the year 1855.[10] This commission recommended the separation of revenue and police functions and placement of the police establishments under European officers. Thereafter, a separate magisterial department and a revenue department were constituted in the year 1857.[11] It also recommended for the setting up of proper organisation of an effective police force in the Madras Presidency. Accordingly, a separate department distinct from the revenue and magisterial departments was constituted in the year 1857. This new department consisted of a Chief Commissioner with 20 District Superintendents of Police and an equal number of Assistant Superintendents.[12] With the Revolt of 1857, the rule of East India Company came to an end and the British crown took over the initiation of organising police administration and they set up a Police Commission.[13] On the recommendations of the first Chief Commissioner of Police, William Robinson, the Madras Police Act XXIV of 1859 was passed and this was the beginning of the Madras police and it was introduced in the districts of the Northern range. Under Section 3(a) of this Act, the police force was established in the districts Ganjam and Vizagapatam of Godavari Agency.[14] Each district was placed under the European

Superintendent of Police who was assisted in his duties by Deputy European Superintendent of Police, Inspectors, head constables, sergeants and three grades of constables. A separate town police force for the three municipalities of Vizagapatam, Vizianagaram, and Bheemunipatnam was created and the municipalities borne 75 per cent of the cost of maintenance.

The Indian Police Act of 1861 was passed on the recommendations of the Central Police Commission of 1860.[15] A unified police administrative system was reorganised on the model of the British constabulary with European Superintendent for each district and European Assistant in large districts of the Northern range.[16] This Act had laid out certain provisions to contain public nuisance relating to controlling of traffic, prevention of cruelty to animals, health hazards, drunkenness, etc., were incorporated in the Act. Under Section 4 of this Act, the Inspector General of Police was the chief of the police administration in the Madras Presidency. A Provincial Force subordinate to the magistracy with Inspector General of Police as its head was constituted. Prevention and detection of crime and maintenance of public order were the main functions of the police under this Act. The police administration was extended to all the districts of the Northern range. It was in the year 1861 when the Indian Police Act V of 1861 was introduced with which the police came to be reorganised in the districts of Ganjam, Jeypore, Vizagapatam, Godavari, Kistna, Guntur, and Nellore of the Northern range.[17]

In the year 1902, a Police Commission was constituted by the orders of the Viceroy Curzon under the chairmanship of Fraser A.H.L to investigate into the state of police administration.[18] The important recommendations of the commission was the constitution of non-European services, a provincial service, an upper subordinate service, a lower subordinate service, the creation of ranges under the charge of European Deputy Inspector General of Police, the creation of the grade of Superintendents and the division of district into sub-divisions and circles, each under the charge of Inspector, and other important recommendations. The police administration of the Northern range was under the in-charge of Deputy Inspector General of Police.[19] The Royal Commission, also known as Lee Commission, was appointed in the year 1924 under the chairmanship of Lord Viscount Lee of Fareham to inquire into the organisation and general conditions of services and the methods of recruitment for Europeans as well as Indians. In the year 1926, with the recommendations of the Lee Commission, superior services in India were established with organisation of the Public Service Commission to this end.[20] The British Government also provided for the establishment of Public Service Commission in provinces besides the Federal Public Service Commission. In the year 1929, the Madras Public Service Commission was started, and in year 1937, the Public Service Commission was renamed as the Federal Public Service Commission.[21]

Principal Acts

The British government had codified and passed a number of enactments like Indian Penal Code of 1861, Criminal Procedure Code of 1862, Indian Evidence Act of 1872, Civil Procedure Code of 1859, which led to the evolution of the police administration.[22] Besides these principal Acts, there were other important Acts affecting the police administration in the Northern range, viz., Madras Act V of 1865, Scheduled District Act XIV of 1874, Police Act III of 1888, Madras Hereditary Village Act III of 1895, Madras Act XXI of 1936, India Act X of 1882 (for criminal procedure), India Act VIII of 1870 (which dealt with murder of female infants), India Act 1 of 1871 (dealt with prisoners), India Act V of 1861 (Sections 23, 25,30,31,33,41 of it dealt with police), Scheduled District Act of 1874, India Act XIX of 1852 (deals with the Abkary Act), India Act XVIII of 1853 (dealt with the sale of spirits in cantonments), India Act XXIV of 1859 (dealt with the regulation of the police within the territories of the Madras Presidency), India Act XIII of 1856 and XLVIII of 1860 (for better and effectual preservation of order), India Act 1 of 1871 (dealt with cattle trespass), India Act XI of 1878 (for Arms), India Act VIII of 1851 (for tolls on roads and bridges), India Act of 1858 (dealt with lunatic asylums), Indian Act I of 1859 (for Merchant seamen), India Act IV of 1875 (for merchant shipping), India Act 1 of 1876 (for telegraphs), India Act XII of 1882 (for salt), India Act VII of 1878 (for forests). All these Acts were implemented with few amendments in the Northern range during the period from 1924 to 1947 for administration of the police force.[23]

Besides the above Acts, the police administration also dealt in various other Acts. For instance, under the Arms Act, the police issued licences to import arms and military stores and under the Explosives Act, they dealt with the imports of explosives; with all the police officers except constables authorised under it to inspect for any arms and ammunition or explosive substances in any vehicle or building.[24] Under the Petroleum Act, the police issued licences for holding possession of carbide of calcium; under the Poisons Act, they issued licences for possession and sale of poisons; under the Immoral Traffic Act, they suppressed immoral traffic of women and children; under the Prohibition Act, they dealt with illicit transport or sale of intoxicating drugs.[25] Under Indian Cinematograph Act II of 1918, licences were issued to cinematograph theatres and the associated irregularities were curbed, which included, use of uncensored films. The offenders were sentenced to two months rigorous imprisonment and payment of a fine of Rs 200 in default.[26] Under the Motor Vehicles Act, vehicle registration, duplicate certificates of registration, driving licences, bus licences for plying or hire, permit for lorries were issued whilst the Hackney Carriage Act dealt with registration of rickshaws, issue of rickshaw driver's licence, etc.[27] Under the Indian Motor Vehicles Act, the District Superintendents of police maintained a record of the convictions secured against the holders of licences and permits.[28] Under the Abkary Act, the police officers except the constable could, without warrant, during any time of the day, enter, inspect and search the premises of a house or a shop in which sale or manufacture of liquor was suspected to be carried out and had powers to arrest such persons responsible and seize the product. The police of the Northern range dealt with various crimes under these Acts.

Police Administration

The police administration in the Northern range was organised with the enactment of the Madras Police Act XXIV of 1859. In the year 1861, it was reorganised on the lines of the Indian Police Act of 1861; the Irish form of constabulary system of police administration was established in the Madras Presidency which was a part of the Northern range and it continued unchanged even after gain of Independence.[29] During the period 1924-47, the Madras Presidency consisted of four ranges — Northern range, Central range, Eastern range and Southern range.[30] The Northern ranges consisted of Ganjam, Jeypore, Vizagapatam, Godavari, Kistna, Guntur, and Nellore districts. These districts were again divided into sub-divisions and each sub-division was further divided into a number of police circles which consisted of police stations and outposts.

The following were the police sub-divisions in the districts of the Northern range during the period 1924-47.

Name of the districts	*Name of the Sub-divisions*				
Ganjam[31]	Berhampur	Chatrapur	Bhanja-nagar		
Jeypore	Jeypore	Koraput	Malka-nagiri		
Vizaga-patam[32]	Vizaga-patam	Viziana-gram	Narasap-atnam	Parvati-puram	Srika-kulam
East Godavari[33]	Rajahm-undry	Peddap-urampet	Coconada	Bhadra-chalam	Pola-varam
West Godavari[34]	Bheem-avaram	Eluru	Kovvur	Narsapur	
Kistna[35]	Masulipatam	Bezawada	Gudiwada	Nuzvid	
Guntur[36]	Guntur	Narasa-rapet	Ongole	Tenali	
Nellore[37]	Gudur	Kandukur	Kavali,	Atmakur	Nellore

There were major administrative adjustments in the districts of the Northern range; in the year 1925, the Godavari district was bifurcated into East and West Godavari districts. In the year 1929, the Nellore district was transferred to the Central range.[38] The transfer of the whole of Ganjam and Jeypore police districts and parts of Vizagapatam police districts to Orissa province on 1st April 1936 necessitated the redistribution of the remaining districts among the other ranges. On 1st May 1936, the Nellore district was transferred from the Central range to the Northern range.[39] In the year 1946, the jurisdiction of Vizagapatam was bifurcated into Vizagapatam North and Vizagapatam South Police Districts. The jurisdiction of the former extended over the entire Srikakulam district and Vizianagaram taluk of Vizagapatam district with its headquarters at Vizianagaram.[40] There were other minor administrative change that took place in the districts of the Northern range besides these major alternations. The police force was organised at different levels in the Northern range and the following hierarchy existed in the police force in the Madras Presidency.

Inspector General of Police (Head of the Madras Presidency)

↓

Deputy Inspector General of Police (Head of the Northern range)

↓

Superintendents of Police (Head of the Districts)

↓

Deputy Superintendents of Police (Head of the Sub-divisions)

↓

Inspectors of Police (Head of the Police Circles)

↓

Sub-Inspectors (Head of the Police Stations)

↓

Head Constable

↓

Constable

Police Organisation at Range Level

Madras Presidency was divided into police ranges for effective and efficient administration. Under Section 4 of Act V of 1861, every 'General Police District' of the Madras Presidency fell within the charge of Inspector General of Police.[41] He was the head of the entire police administration of the Madras Presidency. For effective functioning of the police administration, the British government divided the Madras Presidency into ranges. The Northern range was one of its divisions and it consisted of districts of Ganjam, Jeypore, Vizagapatam, Godavari, Kistna, Guntur, and Nellore. This range was above the district and below the presidency level. The police administration in the Northern range was headed by a Deputy Inspector General of Police or Additional Commissioner of Police and the entire police administration was under his control.[42] An Additional Deputy Inspector General of Police was sanctioned during the year 1930 to take charge of the Criminal Investigation Department together with the two Railway Districts.[43]

Police Organisation at District Level

The districts were the important police administrative units of the Northern range. The police administration at this level played a major role. The police administration at the district level was under the in charge of District Superintendent of Police who was a member of Public Service Commission. Each district of the Northern range was headed by a District Superintendent of Police. The police administration at the district level was responsible for the maintenance of law and order and control of crime in the districts. In every district of the Northern range, there was a district police office at the district headquarters and the entire police in the districts was managed and controlled through the district office.[44]

All the laws and the rules passed by the police were transformed into action at this level. The police at the district level were responsible for effective maintenance of law and order and control of crime by proper maintenance of records and communicating the higher officials. At this level, the armed reserves, intelligence bureau, finger print bureau, etc., functioned as the auxiliary units to aid and assist the regular police. In case of any emergency, the special police reserves were deputed on the orders of the superior police officers. The district head office was under the immediate management of the Superintendent who was allowed an Inspector, titled Headquarter Inspector, and a number of police subordinates employed for office work.[45] The district headquarters police stations were established at the district headquarters of each district.

District Magistrate was the chief executive authority in the district, who was responsible to the government for the maintenance of law and order for which the police force was put under his control and direction and Superintendent of Police assisted him in these duties. Through Superintendent of Police, he exercised disciplinary control and technical supervision over Inspector General of Police and Deputy Inspector General of Police.[46]

Police Organisation at Sub-divisional Level

The districts were divided into a number of police sub-divisions for operational convenience. The administration at the sub-divisional level was the link between the circle level administration and district level administration. At this level, police work was co-ordinated and controlled and these police sub-divisions formed an intermediary link between the police circles, police stations and the district police offices. The main work of the authority at sub-divisional level was to carry out law and order, maintain discipline among the police force and other related matters like, preparation of reports, registration related to crime and offences, security, and other administrative aspects were maintained in the sub- divisional police offices. The police sub-divisions were under the charge of the Deputy Superintendent of Police, and sometimes when the workload was more, Additional Superintendent of Police were appointed. A new grade of Deputy Superintendent of Police with similar duties as that of an Assistant Superintendent of Police was created who were natives of India.[47]

Police Organisation at the Police Circles

The police sub-divisions of the Northern range were divided into police circles consisting of taluks[48], and they formed the link between police stations and the sub-divisions of the districts. The police circles were kept under the charge of Inspectors who were also known as the Circle Inspectors. In addition, there was one Inspector for every district of the Northern range for prosecution of cases, for the training schools and for the Criminal Investigation Department. These police circles consisted of police stations and outposts. The police stations in the Northern range were under the charge of Sub-Inspectors. Additional Sub-Inspectors were employed when the number of investigations exceeded 100 per annum.[49] For the prosecution of cases, a Sub-Inspector was placed at the headquarters of each sub-divisional magistrate. Sub-Inspectors were provided for the post of Reader for each Superintendent and also for the training schools and Criminal Investigation Department in each province. Officers of and above the Sub-Inspector level were only eligible to file charge sheets in the court. Head constables and constables constituted the lower level of the police organisation.

Organisation of the Police Stations and Outposts

The police stations were the basic unit in the police administration. The number of police stations in each police circle was determined on the basis of population, area, topography, crime, and such other factors. The police stations were established for a group of villages covering an area of 150 sq km. The police stations were the lowest level of police administration in the Northern range. They were mainly responsible for the maintenance of law and order, prevention and detection of crime, control of crime, collection of intelligence, prosecutions, traffic control, and protection of public life and property.

At each district headquarters of the Northern range, there was a police headquarter station under the charge of Station House Officer. He was under the immediate supervision of Superintendent, who was allowed an Inspector known as the Headquarter Inspector and he was assisted by a number of police subordinates employed for doing office work.[50] The police stations in the Northern range were under the in charge of Station House Officer and he was assisted in his duties by Assistant Sub-Inspectors, head constables, and constables. The headquarters police station was under the control of Superintendent of Police and he was assisted by Inspectors and other subordinate officials in the office work. The British government had sanctioned a separate cadre of prosecuting officers recruited from the bar designated as Assistant Public Prosecutors in the year

1941. The scheme was first tried in the districts of Guntur in the Northern range and later introduced in the district of East Godavari.[51] The subordinate police officers were both Europeans and natives.

The village officers assisted the police station-in-charge in police work. The police officer incharge of the police station carried out the functions within the limits and jurisdiction of the station.[52] The village headmen along with village watchmen kept a watch on crime and its perpetrators and reported to the police stations under his jurisdiction. The police stations formed the nucleus of the entire police administration and it was the lowest-tier of the executive hierarchy of the police organisation in the Northern range.

The police stations were the centre of police-public interface, a source of the police power and functions, and for registration of First Information Report under cognizable offences. The police stations provided security to public and property and petty quarrel cases were disposed off by them. The offenders were temporarily detained until they were produced in the court of law. Arms and ammunition were stored in police stations and they functioned day in and day out. They were the bedrock of police administration in the Northern range and functioned as crime, law and order, and traffic police stations andwere classified by the areas of jurisdiction. Some of the important records kept in the police stations were crime register, crime charts, remark book, distribution list of arms, station inspection report, and the like. All the police stations in the Northern range were inspected by Gazetted officers of the police department.[53] All the districts of Ganjam, Jeypore, Vizagapatam, Godavari, Kistna, Guntur, and Nellore belonging to the Northern range, comprised a number of police stations and outposts. In the faction-ridden areas of the districts of Vizagapatam, Guntur, and Kistna, additional temporary outposts were established. The following are the number of police stations and outposts in the Northern range during the years 1924-47.[54]

The number of police stations and outpostsare depicted graphically as follows:

Years	*No. of Police Stations*	*No. of Outposts*
1924	288	59
1925	287	59
1926	287	51
1927	289	41
1928	289	41
1929	244	31
1930	248	31
1931	248	21
1932	235	32
1933	235	32
1934	235	33
1935	235	32
1936	221	27
1937	221	25
1938	221	25
1939	221	25
1940	220	25
1941	220	25
1942	220	25
1943	230	25
1944	230	25
1945	235	27
1946	236	27
1947	237	23

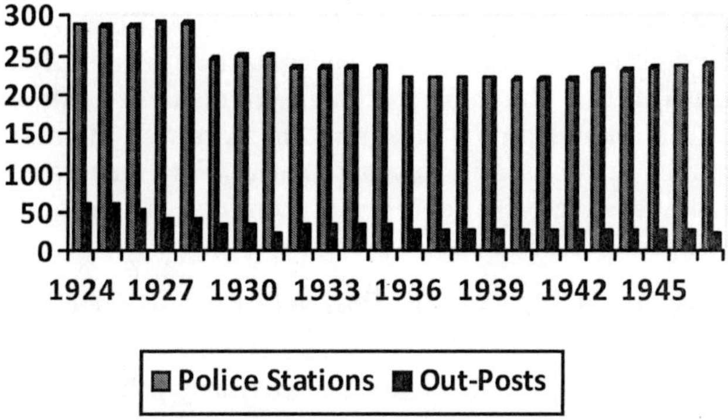

The above graph indicates that the number of police stations and police out-posts were more as the population of the Northern range was high during the initial years and the area of the range also consisted of vast agency tracts inhabited by criminal tribes. As the area of the range came to be reorganised and some portion of the range was transferred to the Orissa Province, the number of police stations and police outposts were reduced and remained almost steady, but, during the last few years of the British rule, due to the political agitation and public unrest, their numbers were slightly increased.

During the year 1926 in the Nellore district, there were 45 police stations and 10 outposts and there were nine Inspectors, 47 Sub-Inspectors, 96 Head Constables, 680 Constables and 26 police Talaiyaris.[55] In the Guntur district during the year 1931, there were 39 police stations and 12 outposts. The numbers of police stations in the East Godavari district during the year 1929 were 41 police stations and one outpost; however, the strength of police stations remained the same and that of the outposts was increased to three during the year 1933. In the West Godavari district during the year 1931, there were 19 police stations whereas there were no outposts.[56] In the district of Jeypore, there were 11 police stations established at Gunupur, Rayagada, Alamanda, and Narayanapatna and in the agency taluks of Parvatipur. Vizagapatam-II Town police station in the Vizagapatam district and Cocanada Taluk police station in the East Godavari district of the Northern range were under construction during the year 1945.[57] A temporary outpost was established at Kavali in the Nellore district in the year 1945.[58] In Bheemavaram division of the West Godavari district, there were three police stations — one each in Bheemavaram, Tadepalligudem, and Eluru. There were three police stations in Eluru. In Kovvur division, they were four police stations — one at Chintalapudi and three at Kovvur, while in Narsapur division, there were three police stations — one at Narsapur and two at Tanuku. The police station in Amudalavalsa, Chintapalli taluk, and Malkapuram in Vizagapatam were well-maintained.[59] These police stations and outpost in the Northern range had functioned satisfactorily in the maintenance of law and order throughout the period 1924-47.

Organisation of the Auxiliary Police Force and Special Police Forces

Along with the regular police, the auxiliary police forces were organised to assist the police in discharging their duties. The auxiliary police forces, such as Criminal Investigation Department, Railway Police, Traffic Police, Port Police, and others were organised for prevention and detection of crimes and preservation of public peace. Whenever any railway, canal or other public works were carried out in the Northern range, additional police force was sanctioned to maintain law and order by the Inspector General of Police. Besides this police force, there were Special reserve police forces which were deployed to quell any unlawful assembly, riots, disturbance to peace where ordinary police officers appointed for preservation of peace were considered insufficient for the purpose and for protection of the inhabitants and property.[60] The reserve police forces worked in tandem with the regular police force of the Northern range, such as the Provincial Armed Constabulary, East Coast Special Police, Armed Reserve Police, and Civil Guards who were put into service for activities and occasions, like crowd control, large unrest, organised crime, communal riots and disturbances, public meetings, fairs, festivals, elections, natural disasters and subversion against the British government. At the headquarters of the each district in the Northern range, the reserve police were maintained under the command of an Inspector.[61] The police force was arranged under the Madras government as one battalion and its administration was extended to all the districts of the Northern range. In many instances, the British government deployed these police forces in the Northern range during the period 1924-47. They were controlled by the orders of the Inspector General of Police and other higher level authorities. The armed reserve police came into contact with the general public only in the exigencies of maintaining law and order and to preserve peace. The British government could declare an area as disturbed in critical times and employed police forces in addition to the regular ones to meet such situations. The cost of the additional police force was borne by the inhabitants of the area and was apportioned amongst them by the District Magistrate.

Organisation of the Village Plice

The village was an important administrative unit of the Northern range and under the Regulation XI of 1816, the village police were placed under the heads of the villages whose police duties were defined and were vested with police powers.[62] The village headmen, *Karnam*, an accountant, watchmen, and *talayaris* were responsible for maintaining peace and tranquility in the village. With the recommendations of the report of the Police Commission 1902-03, the British government recognised the need and importance of the hereditary village police officials and co-operation of the village community. In the year 1935, as an auxiliary agency, the Village Vigilance Committees were formed[63] in the districts of the Northern range. These committees constituted a liaison between the authorities and the village populations in the control of crime and detection of offences. The members of these committees were chosen and selected personally by Gazetted officers.

Constitution of the Police Department

The constitution of the police department in the Northern range was same as in the other ranges which were according to the Police Acts and the recommendations of the Police Commission 1902-03. The police officers comprised Inspector General of Police and supervising staff, Deputy Inspector General, Assistant Inspector General, Superintendents, Assistant Superintendents, Inspectors, Sub-Inspectors and Constabulary of all ranks. Station writers and readers of the Superintendent, Assistant Superintendent and Deputy Superintendents were also enrolled in the police force under the Police Act.[64] The appointment of the Personal Assistants to the District Superintendents of Police was abolished in the year 1925.[65] The superior police officers consisted of Inspector General of Police, Deputy Inspector General of Police, Assistant Inspector General of Police, Superintendents of Police, Deputy Superintendents of Police, Assistant Superintendents of Police and the subordinate police officers were Inspectors and officers below this rank.[66] All these officers performed police functions according to the Police Act in the General Police Districts of the Northern range.

Inspector General of Police and Deputy Inspector General of Police

The police administration of the Madras Presidency was under the charge of Inspector General of Police and the Northern range was under his control and command. The head of the police administration in the Northern range was Deputy Inspector General of Police, who controlled all the police districts of the Northern range. The post of Assistant Inspector General of Police, crime branch was abolished in the year 1930.[67]

District Superintendent of Police

The District Superintendent of Police was the head of the district. In the Northern range, there was a District Superintendent of Police for each district of Ganjam, Vizagapatam, Jeypore, West Godavari, East Godavari, Kistna, Guntur, and Nellore. Some Deputy Superintendents were recruited from the subordinate native officers and they were in charge of the police sub-divisions in the districts. The police administration at the district level was carried out by Superintendent of Police and he was under the control of Magistrate. The Magistrate was responsible for preventive aspect and the

Superintendent and his subordinates were responsible for control of crime and maintenance of law and order.[68]

Inspectors

The sub-divisions of the districts in the Northern range were further divided into police circles under the charge of Inspector. They were also known as Circle Inspector. Additional Inspector was recruited for the prosecution of cases, for the training schools and for the Criminal Investigation Department. These police circles consisted of police stations and outposts.[69]

Sub-Inspectors

The police stations were under the charge of Sub-Inspector. When the number of investigations exceeded 100 per year, an additional Sub-Inspector was appointed to assist in the extra work. For the prosecution of police cases, a Sub-Inspector was placed at the headquarters of each sub-divisional magistrate. The Sub-Inspectors were provided for the post of Reader for each Superintendent and also for the training schools and for the Criminal Investigation Department in the Madras Presidency and they belonged to the probationary grade.[70]

Head Constables and Constables

The head constables and constables of different grade were recruited to carry out the police work in the police stations and outposts. At every police station in the Northern range, there was one head constable as the station writer and the ratio of head constables to constables was one is to ten. The number of constables required at a police station was determined by their fixed duties of escorts, guards, patrols and these duties varied from station to station. The highest rank of constables was the head constable. The head constables and constables were divided into three grades of pay and the head constable also performed duties of a station writer. Many times, the constables were employed on more responsible duties of the police under the direct orders of their superior officer.

Village Officers

The village headman and one or more watchmen were the village officers of the villages in the districts of the Northern range. The headman was the revenue and police head of the village. The village headman was responsible for communicating directly to the magistrate and the police of information concerning certain offences and offenders. He was a representative of the government in the village.[71] The village watchman was also the village servant and was subordinate to the village headman. The duties of the watchman were to keep watch at night, find out all arrivals and departures, observe strangers and report to the headman. He also maintained a record of each person in the village and if any crime occurred in his village jurisdiction, his business was to detect the culprit. These village officers were liable for punishments for neglect of duty and they were also rewarded for their good work.[72] The village officers cooperated with the regular police but they were not subordinate to the regular police.[73] The supervision and control of the village headmen was entrusted with the District Magistrate of the Northern range. The responsibilities of the village headmen in the performance of the village police duties was recognised and enforced in the Northern range of the Madras Presidency. Number of police officers and policemen in the Northern range during the years 1924-47 was as follows:[74]

Years	*No. of Police Officers*			*No. of Policemen*	
	No. of District Superintendents	*No. of Inspectors*	*No. of Sub-Inspectors*	*Head Constables*	*Constables*
1924	7	80	421	911	6142
1925	8	80	414	892	5849
1926	8	80	401	832	5269
1927	8	79	393	759	5360
1928	8	79	393	764	5410
1929	7	69	331	671	4778
1930	7	71	332	680	4853
1931	7	63	328	673	2796
1932	7	60	314	582	4649
1933	7	60	318	601	4637
1934	7	60	319	601	4637
1935	7	60	320	600	4633
1936	6	53	306	585	4279
1937	6	53	306	587	4281
1938	6	53	306	588	4314
1939	6	52	302	588	4314
1940	6	52	303	590	4321
1941	6	52	302	572	4322
1942	6	52	303	581	4521
1943	6	52	303	583	5314
1944	6	48	306	612	5523
1945	6	48	307	687	5943
1946	6	48	307	799	6105
1947	6	48	306	797	6656

The above table shows the number of District Superintendents for the range in the year 1924 were seven. When the Godavari district was bifurcated into East and West Godavari districts in the year

1925, the strength of the Districts Superintendents was raised to 8. However, the same strength of Districts Superintendents was maintained till 1936, and as the area of the Northern range came to be reorganised and some portion of the range was transferred to the Orissa Province, the number of Districts Superintendents of Police was reduced to six and it remained the same till Independence. The police officers and policemen in the initial years were more as whenever the workload was more, additional officers were recruited. Also, in the initial years, the recruitment was made easy as the area under the range was vast with significant population. During the last few years, the strength was more as additional police were recruited to deal with disturbances due to ongoing freedom struggle. The constitution of the police in the Northern range is shown graphically by pie diagram as follows:

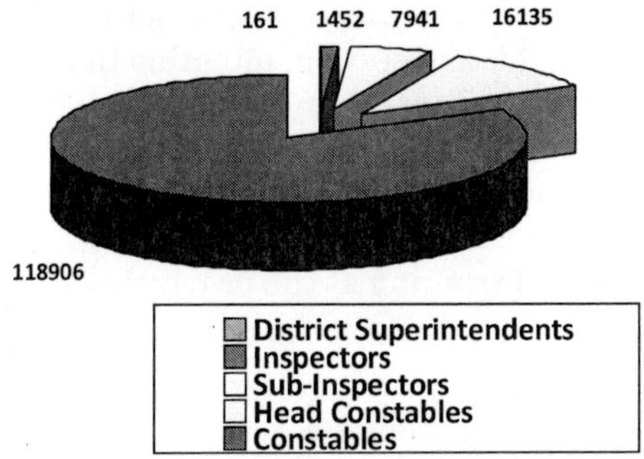

The above Pie diagram shows the constitution for the police department in the Northern range. It can be seen that, in the structure of the police strength, the majority numbers was the constables followed by the head constables, both of whom form the rank and file of the police force. Then there were Sub-Inspectors, Inspectors with the District Superintendents in that order and this proportion was same through out the range for the period 1924-47.

Selection and Recruitment of the Police Force

The main functions of police in the society are preservation of stability and to ensure security against disorder. The police in the Northern range were the body of civil servants whose duties were preservation of order, prevention and detection of crime, and enforcement of laws. They protected the government and also the life and property of the people. The police force in the Northern range was selected and recruited under the Police Regulation Act, Madras Police Act of 1859, and Indian Police Act of 1861. In the beginning of the British rule in India, the selection and recruitment to the higher grades of police was in the form of nomination.[75] They selected candidates from the families with high social status.[76] Few years later, the system of nomination was partly abolished and recruitment was made by open competition in England and by nomination and partly by promotion of subordinate officers in the Northern range. The British government, for the purpose of police constabulary, directly recruited men from good families with morale and integrity.[77] The constabulary was enlisted from the local population who had local knowledge of the region. Many of them belonged to the hill tribes who were illiterates but they were good trackers.[78]

Later, mostly those policemen were recruited who had good physique and a certain minimum educational qualification. When eligible men were not found, the ex-military personnel were recruited. The appointments were made with the special sanction of the government and this system of nominating the candidates, later, was abandoned completely and replaced by competition examinations.[79] Lord Macaulay introduced the system of recruitment of civil services through the competitive examination in the year 1853.[80] The selected candidates devoid of any police experience underwent a course of training at the provincial training school.

To induct Indians for the superior civil services, was one of the demands of the Indian political movement and the national leaders forced the British government for setting up of a Public Service Commission for recruitment to these services. On the recommendations of the Lee Commission of 1924, the first Public Service Commission was set up under the chairmanship of Sir Ross Barker on 1st October 1926 as recruiting agent which suggested for raising of the ratio of the Indians acting on the recommendations of the Lee Commission.[81] The police officers who were recruited in England formed the Imperial Services and the officers locally recruited formed the Provincial Services. The Madras Public Service Commission was set up in the year 1929 under the Madras Legislature Act of 1929, and the rules for the recruitment of police officers were framed by the Service Commission.[82] Madras Presidency was the first province in India to establish a Service Commission. Owing to the political situation, there was a shortage of British candidates. The Lee Commission recommended for filling up of 20 per cent of the superior posts by promotions from provincial civil services, and that of the 80 per cent future entrants, 40 per cent should be British and 40 per cent native Indians recruited directly. The Commission proposed to give substantial benefits to the European officers in the shape of various allowances. The Indians felt that the Commission's report was partial and liberal towards the European civil servants. The Indian legislature criticised the proposed increase in the emoluments of the European civil servants in the shape of overseas pay and other allowances. On the whole, the Indians were not satisfied with the rate of Indianisation of Indian Civil Services and other superior services. It had recommended for 50 per cent of the near 1000 civil service personnel to be Indians. The Public Service Commission was the final authority as far as recruitment to these services was concerned. During the year 1936, the Madras Public Service Commission Act of 1936 was brought into force and the previous Act of 1929 was repealed.[83] The superior police officers in the police force were recruited by competitive examination out of which most of them were Europeans.[84] They occupied key decision-making positions in the police department and were under the supervision of the British government. The recruitment process differed according to the level of the position and their existed element of direct entry. The recruitment methods were according to the Central Public Service Commission.[85] The educational requirements increased with the recruitments for higher posts. In the year 1937, the Public Service Commission was renamed as the Federal Public Service Commission.[86] Under it, the police were recruited in the Northern range and they were trained both physically and mentally to perform their police duties.

The general list of candidates was compiled by the Inspector General of Police of the Madras Presidency from the lists prepared by the Commissioners of divisions with the assistance of District Magistrates and Superintendents of Police of the Northern range. The persons eligible in the general list were the ones with good moral character, falling between the age range of 21 to 25 years, holding social position and possessing the necessary educational qualification of not lower than the University Matriculation or School Final examination, and were found physically fit for the police services by Zillah Surgeon.[87] The Superintendents of Police were recruited through a competitive exam and such successful police officers, later, underwent requisite training. The police officers, after their probation period, were posted in their respective districts for their practical training. The Assistant Superintendent, before being declared qualified for the service, was required to pass an examination to prove his colloquial familiarity with the vernacular of the district. They were required to pass an examination in criminal law and law of evidence. The Inspectors were not directly recruited and they were promoted from the cadre of Sub-Inspectors on the basis of seniority and good performance. They were promoted by the Superintendent of Police on instructions issued by the Inspector General of the Police. The selection of Inspectors was a departmental affair and the Inspector co-ordinated with the personnel of the police station and police circles. The Sub-Inspectors of police were directly recruited by the police department. They were in charge of the police stations and they had direct contact with the public. The Sub-Inspectors were recruited by the Deputy Inspector General of Police along with the approval of the Inspector General of Police. The Circle Inspectors, who rendered good services work, were promoted to Deputy Superintendent of Police. The recruitment of Inspectors was by an ordinary procedure of promoting the selected Sub-Inspectors. The Inspectors and the other police officers, except constables, were selected by the Inspector General of Police and the constables were recruited by the District and Assistant Superintendents of Police.[88] The constabulary was recruited from the same district from respected families with good character and antecedents, and in no case, members of criminal tribes were recruited. Recruitment was open during a part of the year and enlistments were made from the district and sometimes ex-military candidates were also recruited.[19] The head constables and constables in the Northern range were selected by the Deputy Inspector General of Police and they were promoted as Sub-Inspectors after passing certain departmental tests.

The Superintendents of Police of the districts were the recruiting agents and the selected constables were posted in their home districts in the Northern range. Sound elementary practical education for constables, along with physical training, was given to take necessary remedial action on occasion of riots, to warn the crowd before firing, fire-control, causalties, attending wounded, and the like. First-Aid training was given to the literate policemen. They were trained at the police stations and outposts — general impracticable beyond instruction — on orders issued from the headquarters, which was the duty of the Station House Officers.[89] They were recruited on the basis of their physique and education. Earlier, most of the constabulary were illiterates; however, through proper training, they were provided with required minimum education, and through enlistment system, the illiterates were gradually weeded out. Number of policemen in the Northern range who could and could not read and write during the years 1924-47 was as follows:[90]

Years	*Sanctioned strength of the policemen*	*No. of policemen who could read and write*	*No. of policemen who could not read and write*
1924	6921	5895	1026
1925	6741	5565	1176
1926	6253	5421	832
1927	6119	5536	583
1928	6174	5682	492
1929	5449	5105	344
1930	5533	5206	327
1931	5489	5099	390
1932	5231	5017	214
1933	5238	4990	248
1934	5238	4856	382
1935	5233	4859	374
1936	4864	4645	219
1937	4868	4639	229
1938	4902	4695	207
1939	4902	4701	201
1940	4911	4731	180
1941	4911	4753	158
1942	5211	5102	109
1943	5781	5641	140
1944	5812	5663	149
1945	6631	6521	110
1946	6904	6387	517
1947	7453	6514	939

The illiteracy in the police force is shown graphically as follows:

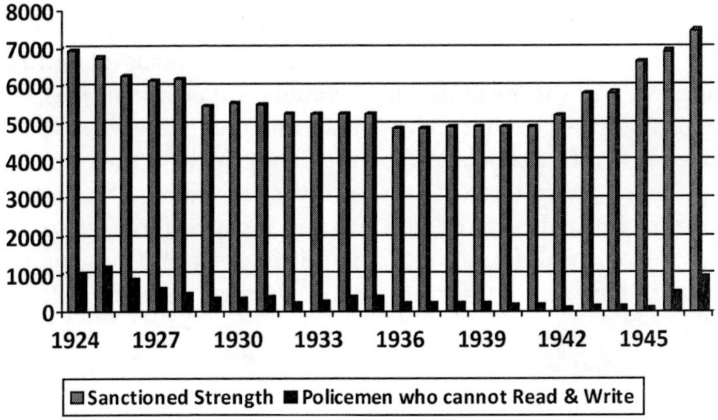

The above figures show that, in the initial years, the illiteracy amongst the policemen was high as many educated men were not easily available. During the middle years, the police were recruited from educated classes, and with proper training, prevalence of illiteracy was gradually reduced. This reflects the progress of literacy in this range which has been impressive in the context of the growing population. However, in the years 1946 and 1947, the literacy level in the policemen was less as those years were very turbulent both at national and district levels due to freedom struggle. The number of incidences of violence and mob attacks increased from the range during the course of freedom movement and additional recruitment was made to contain these disturbances. Also good number of policemen were sent out on war duties and this shortage was made up by recruiting men who were easily available from the uneducated classes.

The policemen were chosen from the local rural and agricultural classes who could read and write and met the standard measurement of five feet and five inches in height and 32 inches round the chest. Men from low castes were not chosen except in hill tracts of the Northern range. Every appointed police official received an enrollment certificate under the seal of the Inspector General of Police, and such certificates were seized, whenever such official was suspended or dismissed.[91]

The examinations for Inspectors were same as that of the Sub-Magistrates except for a departmental paper. The Assistant Superintendent, for qualifying, had to pass examinations in the vernacular of the district, and the subjects of criminal law and law of evidence. The recruits spent some time in the reserve for the purpose of familiarising themselves with their duties and they were trained in shooting and drill but not up to the standards of military efficiency.[92] For the lower and non-managerial positions, the police force were selected by the Madras government and they were trained at Police Recruits' Schools in the Presidency. Most of the recruits of the auxiliary police force were ex-military personnel. Some of the recruits of the police force and auxiliary police forces were also recruited from local Hindus and Christian converts.[93] The sanctioned strength of Police in the Northern range during the years 1924-47 is as follows:[94]

Years	*Total Strength*			
	Sanctioned		*Actual*	
	No. of Police officers	*No. of Policemen*	*No. of Police officers*	*No. of Policemen*
1924	531	6921	497	6235
1925	512	6741	473	6110
1926	503	6253	485	6101
1927	490	6119	511	6091
1928	490	6174	504	6138
1929	431	5449	455	5384
1930	421	5533	423	5501
1931	423	5489	430	5505
1932	405	5231	407	5285
1933	410	5238	395	5247
1934	410	5238	407	5234
1935	411	5233	416	5185
1936	388	4864	384	4854
1937	388	4868	384	4840
1938	388	4902	380	4887
1939	383	4902	370	4872
1940	384	4911	368	4902
1941	383	4911	368	4885
1942	379	5211	365	4921
1943	366	5781	351	5642
1944	381	5812	372	5549
1945	402	6631	394	6381
1946	413	6904	392	6487
1947	414	7453	401	6601

The above table illustrates the total strength of the police force, giving split-wise, their sanctioned and actual strength, in the Northern range. The sanctioned and actual strength of the police officers and policemen recruited for almost all the years was nearly equal. In some years, the actual strength was more than the sanctioned strength due to the re-organisation of the reserves and also due to the recruitment of additional staff for traffic control in the districts of Vizagapatam and East Godavari.

In the year 1924, the recruitments were made easily in all the districts of the Northern range and many constables were classed as illiterates.[95] The sanctioned strength of the permanent force in the year 1924 exclusive of the East Coast Special police was less than the sanctioned strength and this decline was owing to the abolition of the Rajahmundry Special Force. As a consequence of the abolition of the Agency Division, the police district of Jeypore was re-organised, and the Agency areas which formerly belonged to the districts of Ganjam, Vizagapatam and Godavari, were restored. As the police force in number of districts was below the sanctioned strength, recruitment was renewed, but it was stopped in between on the recommendation of the Police Retrenchment Committee. There was a slight increase in the number of departmental punishments awarded which constituted certain percentage of the actual strength of the force.[96] With effect from 1st February 1924, the appointments of Personal Assistants to District Superintendents of Police were abolished and 22 additional sub-divisions were formed.[97] In the year 1924, the freedom struggle movement in the Northern range necessitated an increase in the strength of the police.[98] Special constables and additional police force was employed under Section 17 of Police Act V of 1861 and the quartering of the additional police in the Northern range was under Section 15 of the same Act. They were employed as a preventive measure.[99] There were occurrence of a number of political agitations due to the continuing freedom struggle in most of the districts of the range during the years 1924-47.

The strength, during the year 1925, was kept low purposely with a view to meet the reduction anticipated on the reallocation of the force.[100] A good number of ex-military men from the Reserve police, holders of secondary school-leaving certificates and some who had studied up to third standard were recruited during the year 1925.[101] The recruitment was made mainly in the district of Jeypore of the Northern range and they were 67 during the year 1925.[102] The East Coast Special Police during the year 1925, apart from regular recruits, comprised of two subedars, eight jamadars, two havildar-majors, 10 halvidars, 12 Naiks and 187 constables.[103] During the year 1926, in the Nellore district of the Northern range, there were nine Inspectors, 47 Sub-Inspectors, 96 Head Constables, 680 Constables, and 26 police Talaiyaris.[104] This augmentation in the strength was so as to contain communal tensions which were of frequent occurrences mostly around the period of religious festivals.

In the year 1926, the number of vacancies in the police department was low and this reduction was due to the re-allocation of the districts.[105] Inspectors and Sub-Inspectors possessing high educational qualifications were recruited in the year 1927.[106] Total strength sanctioned for the year 1927 in respect of the police officers and men was 490 and 6,119 respectively, but the actual strength was 511 officers and 6,091 men.[107] The strength of the probationary police force for the year 1927 was 36 in Provincial Police Training School at Vellore which included one District Superintendent, eight Inspectors, 12 Head Constables and 13 Constables. The number of police personnel trained was three each in the Central Recruits

School, Vellore; Central Recruits School, Vizagapatam; Central Recruits School, Coimbatore; and Central Recruits School, Anantapur. Only Sub-Inspectors and Sergeants were trained in the four Central Recruits School and the strength of the temporary additional police force, who received training during this year, was 368.[108] In the years 1928-29, for recruitment, the preference was given to English-knowing men and members of the depressed classes. Such men, who had awareness of the the English language were recruited because of their utility as station writers and were made traffic head constables whereever the application of knowledge of English was required.[109] The type of ex-military men who applied for enlistment were generally unsuitable.[110] In many districts, it was found difficult to enlist men of required intelligence and physique, and when suitable men could not be found, they recruited ex-military men.[111]

During the year 1930, as a result of the Civil Disobedience movement in the Northern range, additional work was entrusted to the police and they were frequently called upon to maintain law and order. The activities related to the civil disobedience led to a series of riots in several places in the Northern range. Due to these political disturbances, many of the recruits who had secondary school-leaving certificates were enlisted as constables.[112] The standard of educational qualifications of the Sub-Inspectors, who were recruited during the year 1930 was high and many of them were graduates and the number of men in the force classified as illiterates showed a further decrease.[113] In order to maintain law and order more effectively, a new armed force with strength of 10 sergeants, 10 havildar-major, 50 head constables and 594 constables were recruited under the Presidency Armed Reserve during this year. This special police force consisted of ten detachments located in different districts of the Northern range.[114] In the years 1931-32, the recruitment process in almost every district of the Northern range was successful in enlisting services of the literate and additional recruitments were carried out in view of the political unrest.[115] In the Nellore district of the Northern range, the strength of the police force during the year 1936 was 10 Inspectors, { } Charge-Sergeants, four Sergeants, 64 Sub-Inspectors, two Havildar-major, 105 Head Constables, 788 Constables and four talayaries for meeting requirement of 45 police stations and 10 outposts.[116] In the years 1938-39, ex-military men were mostly recruited in the police department of the Northern range.[117] The strength of the permanent police force in the Northern range in the year 1938 increased due to reorganisation of the armed reserve and recruitment of additional staff for traffic control in the districts of Vizagapatam and East Godavari.[118]

The temporary additional staff of retention of two constables was sanctioned for the year 1939 in Vizianagaram Railway police station.[119] In Vizagapatam district, temporary police staff was sanctioned in the Vizagapatam harbour in the year 1939.[120] In the same district of the Northern range, a temporary Sub-Inspector was re-employed to investigate a fraud case of Bharatamata Commonwealth Insurance Bank for the year 1939.[121] The strength of the permanent police force in the year 1939-40 increased due to maintenance of temporary establishments, such as Coastal Special Police Force and recruits from the Central Recruits School in Vizianagaram, in connection with the world war.[122] Recruitment to the police force was difficult and suitable literate young men were not available during the years 1939-40. It became necessary to increase the maximum strength in the recruit schools in order to train the large number of recruits enlisted in place of policemen deflected for duties connected with the war and political unrest in the Northern range; it is another matter that slowly illiterate constables were eliminated from the force.[123]

A scheme for the enlistment of Indians and Anglo-Indians as Sergeants was sanctioned for the year 1940 and the first batch under this scheme was trained with the Malabar Special Police in 1941.[124] In view of the anticipated political unrest and towards the peak period of freedom movement, the recruitment was high and the recruits were trained efficiently. With the looming fear of airborne Japanese invasion, the government enlarged the district reserves in the year 1942 and brought new auxiliary forces into being.[125] The expenditure incurred by these police forces in suppressing the freedom struggle was borne by the Central government.[126] To lessen the workload on the Deputy Sub-Inspectors, personal assistants were sanctioned at the districts of Vizagapatam, East Godavari, and Kistna. To solve the problem of recruitment, temporary appointments were made against vacancies by lowering the standards of recruitment. In view of the temporary increase in the sanctioned strength of the Sub-Inspectors and Sergeants for duties connected with the war, and owing to the appointment of a few Sub-Inspectors as Sergeants, a number of permanent Sub-Inspectors were deflected from their regular duties. This necessitated the promotion of a large number of Head Constables as Sub-Inspectors as in charge of stations. All the armed reserves were mobilised and the detachments of the presidency general reserves were strengthened by additional platoons. There were instances of looting in some districts. The outbreak of war necessitated the employment of additional police staff for security purposes and other duties connected with internal security at many places and enlistment of a large number of recruits at the end of the year. In the year 1947, the reorganised armed reserves' strength was maintained well and most of them were mobilised during the year 1947. Owing to the labour unrest and communal and agrarian troubles, heavy strain was imposed on the armed reserves but they discharged their duties efficiently.[127]

Sports were given much importance; veteran sportsmen got themselves easily recruited and were given promotions for outstanding performances. They were also given a lot of appreciation and encouragement for their achievements in crime detection and functions assigned to them. Such Constables were promoted to the post of Head Constables as performance appraisal plays a key role in progression in the police force.[128] To keep up the morale of the police force, the government rewarded for their good work by way of conferring titles and certificates. The recruitments increased with the spurt in crimes, population, urbanisation, and unemployment in the districts of the Northern range. The primary reason for the gradual Indianisation of the police was the prevailing political conditions, to influence the public that the police were not an entirely alien force, and also to meet the demand of the Indian politicians for larger involvement of the Indians in the services. The Lee Commission examined the conditions in the All India and Provincial Services and recommended for 50:50 Indian-European ratio in the Indian Civil Services by the year 1939.[129] However, the superior positions in the Madras Presidency police remained in the European hands until Independence.

Training Schools

Training is an effort to improve and increase knowledge, skill, and aptitude, and the main objective of this pursuit is to ensure better performance in course of one's duties. All the recruited police officers and policemen of the Northern range were trained in the Recruit Schools of the Madras Presidency. There was a Provincial Police Training School at Vellore in the Madras Presidency for the training of the police officers and there were Central Recruitment Schools at Vellore, Anantapur, Coimbatore, and Vizianagaram for the training of the constabulary. The Central Recruits School at Vellore, which had remained closed for the past sometime, was reopened in the year 1925. The Central Recruits School at Coimbatore and the Central Recruits School at Anantapur which, too had remained closed, were reopened in the same year and the Central Recruitment School at Vizianagaram was reopened in the year 1929.

The course of instruction in these schools, *inter alia*, included criminal law and law of evidence, police procedure and practice, the habits and customs of the criminal gangs.[130] A revised curriculum of training was designed for Sub-Inspectors on practical and scientific investigation of crime on modern lines. Instruction in precis writing was introduced during the year1928 and it continued thereafter.[131] Instruction in riding was also given and a police band was maintained.[132]

The Inspector General of Police, Sayers F, in the year 1938 had recommended for a new curriculum of training on modern lines for efficient functioning.[133] The illiterates among the Head Constables and Constables were gradually eliminated. The health of the force was good as government quarters were provided to Sergeants, Sub-Inspectors, Head Constables, and Constables.[134] Physical training was also given in these schools. The recruited members of the police forces were regularly drilled in manual and platoon exercises along with baton exercises and lining streets to clear crowds during contingencies. The physical fitness of the police recruits was certified by the Zillah Surgeon. There were hostels attached to these schools.[135] These schools worked efficiently and produced good results[136] throughout the period 1924 to 1947.

In the provincial police training school at Vellore, officers belonging to the ranks of Deputy Superintendents of Police, Assistant Superintendents of Police, Inspectors, and Sub-Inspectors were trained for a year and then posted to districts for practical training. The Head Constables and the Constables were trained for a period of six months. The Constables were not promoted also Head Constables unless they passed specific tests.[137] The village police did not undergo any police training.[138] The training of the auxiliary police forces was imparted by the educated classes, learned professions, and urban units.[139] The training was conducted in these schools for the recruits from all the ranges of the Madras Presidency. The police recruits spent some time in the reserves for practical training. For the constabulary, the training schools existed in the Northern range and elementary practical education was given to them besides drill, physical training, musketry and the use of arms. They were trained to take action during riots, such as warning the crowd before firing, fire control, casuality, and other similar activities.[140] At the headquarters of each district, there was a school supervised by a specially selected Inspector or Head Constable, who all recruits had to come across before being sent to police sub-divisions of the districts of the Northern range.

The Station House Officers underwent the examination prescribed for their rank. Every member of the constabulary was enlisted on the condition of serving and residing wherever he was posted and they were retained within their own districts. The policemen enlisted were in the age group 18 to 25 barring exceptions that needed prior sanction of the Inspector General of Police. The schools for training of Constables were established for a group of districts and each school was under a Deputy or Assistant Superintendent who was assisted by Inspectors and Sub-Inspectors and the course was for a period of six months that ran throughout the year. They were given instructions in drill, discipline, elementary law and police procedure, etc.[141] One Head Constable from each district of the Northern range was sent to Intelligence Bureau for specialist training in fingerprints, footprints, and photography for investigating offences relating to coinage, forged currency notes, postal fraud, forgery, and other intricate cases. In handling difficult cases, like forgery slips and identification of unknown persons, they were assisted by the Fingerprint Bureau. The Sub-Inspectors were trained in fingerprint course who also visited jails to give instructions on taking and dealing with fingerprints to the Sub-Inspectors and other selected officers of the headquarters. These police officers after attending these courses, inturn, instructed others in the districts of the Northern range. This was an innovation and these courses tend to minimise the number of fingerprint slips.

During 1932, the usual training in the Provincial Police Training School was supplemented by some useful innovations. The Sub-Inspectors were taught practically how to take footprints, they studied and learned to apply the Facial Index System, special lessons in observation, and fingerprints expert gave lectures on the recording and classification of fingerprints. The Deputy Inspector General of Police attached to the Criminal Investigation Department and the Railways lectured on crime and maintenance of history-sheets. Few, selected habitual local criminals of different classes addressed the students on their *modus operandi* and experiences in their criminal careers. The Inspector General of Police and Deputy Inspector General of Police periodically inspected the Recruit Schools to the check their functioning. Training for the auxiliary special police forces was also given who mostly comprised Europeans and Anglo-Indians from educated classes, learned professionals, and urban units.[142] In the year 1925, the Inspector General of Police, F. Armitage, had inspected the provincial police training schools twice and the Central Recruits School at Vellore and Anantapur once. The Inspector General of Police had appreciated Assistant Superintendent, Keatinge, for his control and training of the East Coast Special Police during the year 1925.[143] The East Coast Special Police force was taken for demonstration purpose to Kalyana, Singapore in the Parvatipur Agency in March 1925 for a period of nineteen days and this occasion was useful for instructional purpose. The training of this force had attracted attention and its periodical inspection by a military officer had begun during this year.[144]

The selected Station House Officers organised games in each district of the ranges. This created an opportunity for the police officers to meet among themselves and discuss important matters and to maintain good physical fitness.[145] The Presidency Police Sports and the annual conference of police officers were held. In the year 1928, ex-military men were employed as instructors in schools as an experiment and it proved a success. [146] In the year 1930, the chemical examiner from Madras delivered a series of lectures to certain Inspectors and Sub-Inspectors on the technical aspects of investigation of crime and on preservation and dispatch of exhibits for chemical examination. These officers were instructed to teach other officers in their districts. From the year 1930 onwards, probationary Sub-Inspectors and superior officers were given instructions in these subjects in the police training schools,[147] which improved the training imparted there.

The annual sports were held for upkeep of general fitness and the district sports were held mostly in the district headquarters. The Presidency Police Week was held every year with inter-district sports and musketry competitions as its main items. The armed reserves had showed much enthusiasm for field sports.[148] The scheme, under which games were conducted in the selected rural centres by non-official committees under the guidance of the police, was extended to each district of the Northern range. The government approved a proposal for the police to instruct elementary and secondary school teachers on 'safety first' measures.[149] The training for the probationary police officers was opened throughout the year, and after training, these officers were posted to their respective districts. The Officers Conference used to be held and these gatherings were helpful as they discussed on important subjects and problems which brought efficiency in the police force. The health of the probationers was maintained by holding regular medical check-ups. Educated natives competed for the post of Inspectors as their salaries were increased from time to time, but the pay for the lower ranks was insufficient and did not attract them. Assistant

Superintendents and Inspectors were appointed on probation and they were required to attend the Police Training School at Vellore for a specified period. A new system was introduced in the year 1930 and two sessions were held for the training of sergeants.[150] Vincent H.L., Sub-Inspector, Vizagapatam district completed his probationary training and was posted back to his respective district in the year 1938.[151] The first batches of probationary Sub-Inspectors were trained under the revised curriculum at the police training schools in the year 1939. Scientific and modern methods of training were implemented for better crime control and to maintain law and order. Towards beginning of the year 1947, additional police force were trained to handle the political unrest. After the completion of training, the recruits were sent back to their respective districts for the practical training.

Central Recruits School at Vizianagram

The Central Recruitment School at Vizianagaram in the Northern range was closed in the year 1921 and was reopened in the year 1929. During the year of reopening, the strength was 419; after training, 229 were sent out; there were 42 casualties, and by the end of the year, 148 were enrolled.[152] In the year 1932, the number of recruits trained at Vizianagaram Central Recruitment School was 177 at the beginning of the year, 149 recruits were admitted during the year, and 303 numbers were sent out successfully to the districts after training. Number of casualties were 23; however, these were none at the end of the year. This school was remained closed and reopened on 15th November, 1939. The maximum number of recruits in each of the recruits schools was raised temporarily to impart training to the men due to the outbreak of war.[153] Large number of recruits were enlisted against the police staff as they had been sent for duties connected with the war and so it became necessary for the government to increase the maximum laid-down strength of recruits. For this purpose, the Central Recruits School of Vizianagram was reopened.[154]

The number of admissions at the beginning of the year were 265, all of whom passed and were sent to their districts for practical training.[155] This school was closed in the year 1940.[156] The police forces of the Northern range were given probationary training in the other recruits schools after which they were posted back to their respective districts, and most of the probationers trained were graduates.[157] The Central Recruits School at Vizianagaram was opened on 1st October, 1947 to train recruits required for prohibition duties. Many of the Head Constables who were declared fit for Sub-Inspector's job were given training in the training school for a period of six months from 1st July, 1947. The following tables show the names of the Central Recruits Schools of Madras Presidency during the year 1928, and the detailed statistics of the probationer police officers. This table does not include information on the Central Recruits School of Vizianagaram as it was closed till 1928.[158]

Name of school	*Number of recruits*	*Number, who received training*	*Number of recruits sent out after training*	*Number of casualties*
Central Recruits School, Vellore	177	477	235	156
Central Recruits School, Ananthapur	218	526	369	96
Central Recruits School, Coimbatore	141	508	337	56

The following table shows the names of the Central Recruits Schools of Madras Presidency during the year 1929 and the detailed statistics of the probationary police officers.[159].

Name of school	*Number of recruits*	*Number,who received training*	*Number of recruits sent out after training*	*Number of casualties*
Central Recruits School, Vellore	262	579	437	137
Central Recruits School, Ananthapur	256	586	498	85
Central Recruits School, Coimbatore	278	447	447	53
Central Recruits School,Vizianagaram	-	419	229	42

The above statement gives particulars regarding the admission and training of recruits in central recruit schools. During the year 1929, there were four probationary Assistant District Superintendent of Police and one Deputy Superintendent of Police under training in the Provincial Police Training School, Vellore. One probationary Assistant District Superintendent of Police and one Deputy Superintendent of Police, who were under training at the beginning of the year, were posted in the districts for practical training. About six probationary Sub-Inspectors and seventy-four probationary Sub-Inspectors passed out after the final examination. Also, 90 probationary Sub-Inspectors and two probationary Inspectors joined the school during the year 1929. The standard of education of the probationary Inspectors and Sub-Inspectors was higher than that of the previous years and many of the probationers were graduates. During the year 1930, there were four probationary Assistant District Superintendent of Police and one Deputy Superintendent of Police under training in the Provincial Police Training School. One probationary Assistant District Superintendent of Police and two probationary Deputy Superintendent of Police were recruited and underwent training at the beginning of the year following which they were posted to the respective districts. Two probationary Inspectors and 90 probationary Sub-Inspectors were in the school at the beginning and three more probationary Inspectors and 93 probationary Sub-Inspectors joined later. During the year 1930, in the Central Recruits School, Vizianagaram, 177 police officers were recruited while the casualties were 23 in number. In the training of the subordinate officers, there was high percentage of failures reported during the year 1936 and special steps were taken to train them in drills, riding and other outdoor works. All district sports were usually held at the district headquarters.[160] In the year 1945, the selected police recruits of the Nellore district were sent to the Central Recruits School, Vizianagaram for training. The standards of educational qualifications of the Sub-Inspectors recruited was high; many of them were graduates, and the number of men in the force classified as illiterates showed a further decline. The following table gives the names of the Central Recruits Schools and the number of recruits enlisted during the year 1939, who after training were sent out for duties connected with the war.[161]

In the Central Recruits School of Ananthapur, 31 recruits were from Banganapalle state. This shows that the recruits from the other provinces were also trained in these schools. The standard of the recruits was generally good, the schools were efficiently run, and the discipline and the conduct of the recruits was well-maintained. The management of the hostels was also attached to these schools. To perform police duties, the officials have to be constantly drilled in the methods relevant to their duties as better training, improved efficiency, and qualified police officers will result in greater prevention of crime and detection of criminals.

Name of school	*Number of recruits*	*Number, who received training*	*Number of recruits sent out after training*	*Number of casualties*
Central Recruits School, Vellore	287	512	481	29
Central Recruits School, Ananthapur	302	550	417	24
Central Recruits School, Coimbatore	189	472	349	11
Central Recruits School,Vizianagaram	-	265	265	-

Arms and Amenities

The Inspector General of Police was responsible for all matters related to training, discipline, promotions, dismissals, internal economy, and equipments.[162] The reserves and a portion of the regular police force were armed with smoothbores, guns, and carbines to encounter armed resistance from dacoits and other law-breakers. The police, depending upon the nature of assignment, carried weapons to suppress any unrest. All the arms and armoury were stored in the police station for ensuring public safety in times of riots and disturbances. The arms were stored in the police station under the charge of Inspector, who also maintained the list of the arms and ammunition. Number of armaments held by the police force in the Northern range during the years 1924-47 was as follows.[163]

The below table indicates that the number of weapons were more in the initial years as the strength of the special police forces was more, whereas for the later years, it remained almost even. From the year 1942, due to Quit India Movement, there was a sudden increase in the number of weapons as the British government took severe repressive measures and also recruited additional police force to suppress the freedom struggle. All the recruited police officers and policemen underwent training in the handling of weapons such as rifles, revolvers, smoothbores, lathis, and tear gas by military instructors in the recruits school. The police officers of the rank of Sub-Inspectors and above carried revolvers while the constabularies were equipped with rifles and smoothbores. Most of the police were armed with smoothbores and rifles; these weapons were kept in police stations and were not carried by policemen on ordinary duty. The armed reserves stationed in the district headquarters and in the agency areas, were armed with long snider rifles. The special police forces were mostly armed to deal with the emergencies. The general peace was secured by provisions of the Indian Arms Act which restricted the procession of fire arms and other weapons.

Years	*Rifles*	*Smoothbores*	*Revolvers*
1924	1013	2053	191
1925	1042	2184	182
1926	911	2114	213
1927	887	2051	220
1928	726	2009	231
1929	748	1655	223
1930	778	1839	223
1931	778	1839	257
1932	778	2197	259
1933	778	2128	257
1934	778	1780	261
1935	778	1784	286
1936	440	1720	284
1937	440	1732	311
1938	439	1731	314
1939	439	1729	324
1940	439	2081	335
1941	435	2099	332
1942	1431	2147	349
1943	1328	2401	426
1944	1501	2379	489
1945	1612	2692	493
1946	1657	2801	503
1947	1638	2632	512

Tear Gas

Tear smoke squads existed in the district headquarters of the districts in the Northern range and they were used to disperse the riotous crowd, unruly mobs and they were also used to overcome prisoners and dangerous lunatics. The government sanctioned the formation of tear smoke squads in Guntur and Vizagapatam and necessary equipments were supplied to them.[164] The special police forces had used tear gas to control the rioters which was earlier rejected on grounds of additional expense. An all India police conference which was held in Delhi in the year 1929, reported against the use of tear gas as it would have caused suffocation to the ordinary public and the police themselves[165]. Until the year 1940, tear gas was known as tear smoke.[166] Tear gas was used on many occasions, like political unrest, agrarian strike, and communal disturbances in the Northern range.

Wireless Grid

The police wireless grid was introduced in the year 1946 and a special staff was sanctioned for its formation. Capt. D.R. Clamp was appointed as police wireless officer on contract for one year from 18th June, 1946. A temporary post of Technical Assistant to the Police Wireless Officer was created during the year and Lt. A.D. Sylva held the temporary post. One Special Branch Inspector was trained in wireless operation and 19 partly trained operators were available at the time of commencement. The training of more operators was undertaken with the help of the Army Signal School in Madras and the Malabar Special Police Training School. The men underwent training in these places for three months and were given a further two months training in the wireless office in Madras and another two months operating practice within the district stations of the Northern range. A small training class for the operators with necessary apparatus was also established.[167]

The police wireless system was established in the Northern range for their communication to various police sub-divisions in the Northern range and they conveyed and received messages related to their department. There was a Superintendent of Police for wireless communications and he was under the control of the Deputy Inspector General of Police.

The economic and political unrest in the districts of the Northern range was due to Communist activities, labour troubles, and railway and postal strikes which caused heavy strain on these wireless stations. There was no major disruption of any part of the service since its inception. In the year 1946, need was felt for proper staff, better accommodation for the station, office workshop, training school and proper equipment for the efficient working of this scheme.[168] Wireless communication was maintained satisfactorily during the years 1946 and 1947. The refresher course for signalling instructors of the District Armed Reserves was held in the year 1947. The annual classification of the signallers was carried out by an Assistant Commandant and all the 74 individuals put up for the classification had passed. A few ex-Army wireless operators enlisted as police constables in districts were given two to three months practical training at Madras in handling the type of sets in use in the provincial wireless grid. There was considerable expansion of the provincial wireless network during the year. At the end of the year, 16 districts headquarters in addition to Bezawada were linked up with Madras, and a second control station was opened at Madras, to cope with the increase in the number of out stations. There were seven transportable stations, three in Kistna district and one attached to the Madras headquarters for the use of the touring officers of the Department. The set-up of static and transportable stations in all districts of the Northern range was linked with the headquarters at Madras.[169] It was of invaluable help in the disturbed state of the range. C.K. Vijayaraghavan, Inspector General of Police had recommended the government for reorganisation, increase in staff, equipment and accommodation to stop breakdown.[170] The police wireless system did good work under most difficult conditions since its establishment till Independence.

Health of the Police

The British government had taken care about the health of the police force by establishing the police hospitals and by conducting yearly medical check-ups.[171] Free medical facilities were provided whenever they fell sick, they were supplied with mosquito nets and repellents. The general health of the police force during the period 1924-47 was good in most of the districts of the Northern range as the percentage of admissions into hospital had declined. Malaria and venereal diseases were prevalent. Neosalvarsan injections were supplied free. There were a good many dysentery cases probably during the monsoons.[172] Malaria was the worst enemy to the health of the police force especially in the agency tracts of the Northern range.[173]

The Head Constables and Constables employed in certain stations of the Nellore district were also supplied mosquito repellents free of cost as anti-malarial measures.[174] Officially, the police force was sent to hospitals for their medical treatments when they were sick and the expenses were borne by the government.[175] The general health of the force was examined once in a year. Anti-malaria measures were taken by the government and dangerous diseases, such as tuberculosis were detected in the early stages amongst some of the police personnel in course of regular medical check-ups[176]. Those found unfit were weeded out and this proved advantageous to the government and also the police.

The Deputy Assistant Director of Hygiene had inspected the barrack accommodations and suggested that, with limited members and good water supply, it could prove beneficial in maintaining good health of the police.[177] For several years, malaria proved to be as the worst enemy to the health of the Police Force, especially in the Agency tracts and in the district of Ganjam, Vizagapatnam, and Nellore. Under a scheme for free supply of mosquito curtains to the men in the Agency tracts, some men in the Vizagapatam district Agency made purchases. This scheme was sanctioned by the government under which the cost of the curtains was recovered in six monthly instalments. There was prevalence of malaria due to bad seasonal conditions in the districts of West Godavari, Kistna, and Nellore in the year 1938. The annual medical examinations of members of the subordinate services serving in the *muffsil* was carried out in order to remove unfit men and to detect dangerous diseases vide government orders issued in the year 1940.[178] The health of the police in the districts of the Northern range was maintained in good condition by the supply of medical facilities through establishments of separate police hospitals.

Co-operative Societies

Co-operative societies were organised for the benefit of the police in the Northern range.[179] For financial aid, co-operative societies offered long- and short- term loans with minimum interest rates to the police. The saving of money by recurring deposits in the co-operative societies attracted all ranks of the force.[180]

In the year 1927, co-operative societies were newly-formed in the districts of East Godavari district and Nellore.[181] These co-operative societies worked satisfactorily throughout the period of study.

Accommodations

The provision of government quarters existed for the police, though only 50 per cent of the workforce could be provided with these while the rest had to manage with rented houses. For official discharge of duties, the constables were housed in government quarters mostly in faction-ridden districts of the Northern range. The government recommended for the construction quarters for all members of the police force in order to ensure efficiency, discipline, and contentment.[182] Due to restricted grants for buildings, progress in providing quarters was slow and only 50 per cent of the police officers below the rank of Inspectors were provided with quarters.[183] For the efficient discharge of police duties, the constabulary was housed in government quarters, especially in faction-ridden districts. There were instances where the policemen of a station were compelled to rent huts from either side of a faction. In the year 1929, the District Superintendent inspected the conditions of the accommodation and reported the government about the existence of damp and unhealthy mud floors, mostly in the low-lying areas. By the end of the year, the government improved the flooring in many huts so as to improve the health of the policemen.[184] The British government had taken care of the police during this period and organised transportation for the police force. For the speedy discharge of their duties, the police force maintained their own transport system; during emergencies the police were carried to the areas of unrest through lorries, vans, and buses and they were provided with temporary accommodations.

The British government had provided a number of facilities for the police to improve their working conditions by way of grant of pensions after service, provision of better quarters, supply of clothing and equipment, supply of mosquito nets for proper health, better hospital accommodation, railway passes and other facilities.[185] All these had attracted more recruits from the districts to serve in the police force. The principal arm of the British government for the preservation of order in the society was police.[186] The history of the police organisation has been traced from its foundations in the system of village and local police and their joint responsibility. With enactment of the Madras Police Act XXIV of 1859, the police administration was organised in the Northern range. It was reorganised after coming into force of the Indian Police Act of 1861 on the model of the Irish form of constabulary system. With the recommendations of the Police Commission 1902-03, the Northern range was placed under the charge of Deputy Inspector General of Police. The organisational structure of police department was designed to create an efficient means to prevent crime and maintain law and order. The head of police was responsible for administering and managing the British police department.

The Inspector General of Police was the chief of the Madras Presidency police administration. The Deputy Inspector General of Police was the head of the Northern range. The districts of the Northern range were placed under the charge of Superintendents of Police and the head of the district police office. The sub-divisions were under the Deputy Superintendents of Police, and the head of the sub-division police office. The police circles of the sub-division were under the charge of Inspectors who were the head of circle office. In each circle, there were number of police stations and outposts; the management of police stations was under Sub-Inspectors who costituted as their head and they were generally called as Station House Officers. They were assisted in their duties by Assistant Sub-Inspectors, Head Constables and Constables. The selection and recruitment of the police force was under the Indian Police Act of 1861 and the Police Regulation Act. Through competitive examination, the superior police officers such as Deputy Inspector General of Police, District Superintendents of Police, Assistant Superintendents of Police and Deputy Superintendents of Police were recruited. The Head Constables and Constables were enlisted by the Deputy Inspector General of Police from the local population of the districts of the Northern range. On the recommendation of the Lee Commission 1924, the Provincial Public Service Commission was started in the Madras Presidency in the year 1929. The police forces were paid their salaries with very marginal increments.[187] There was a difference in the scale of payment for the European and Indian police and their salaries were increased from time to time.[188] In the Northern range, the recruitment of the police force was less due to lower scale of payment which obviously did not attract many eligible men. For maintaining the British rule, the police became an important tool.[189] The strength of the police force was up to the sanctioned strength and additional police staff were sanctioned whenever any major unrest was anticipated.

The Recruits Training Schools existed in the Madras Presidency for the training of the recruits. There was a Central Recruits School in the Vizainagaram in the Northern range which was closed for some years and was reopened in the year 1929. The recruits were well-trained in these schools on modern and scientific curriculum; both physical and theoretical training was given; and for the practical training, they were posted back to their respective districts. The annual sports, district sports and other competitions provided opportunity for discussion on relevant subjects and problems which increased the efficiency of the force, in general. The money spent on this police gathering was, though very little, but it was duly spent and produced good results.[190] The police system in the Northern range had a long history, though in its present form it came into existence during the British rule. The police administration at the range level, down from the Deputy Inspector General of Police to the Constable and from the police headquarters to the police station, was an organic unit. The administrative set-up in a range was conceived and constituted by the British and continues to be more or less the same even after Independence. The police had an important role to play. Its functions were many and varied ranging from maintenance of law and order to maintaining public peace at all times

It was considered as an instrument for prevention and detection of crime and for security of property and life. The British organised the police at various levels for better control and function and for this purpose they had selected, recruited and trained them to protect the government, and the life and property of the people.

References

1. Giriraj Shah, *Encyclopedia of Crime, Police and Judicial System*, Vol. I, Anmol Publications, New Delhi, 1999, p. 2.
2. Mishra K.K., *Police Administration in Ancient India*, Mittal Publications, Delhi, 1987, p. 1.
3. Report of the Royal Commission on the Police Powers and Procedure, dated16th March, 1929, Lee of Fareham Viscount H.M., Stationery Office, London, 1929.
4. Government of Madras, Legal Department, The Madras District Police Act of 1859, printed by Superintendent, Government Press, Madras, 1937, p. 1.
5. *Ibid.*, p. 7.
6. Chande M.B., *The Police in India*, published by Atlantic Publishers and Distributors, New Delhi, 1997, p. 65.
7. Maclean C.D., Manual of the Administration of Madras Presidency, Vol. I, Asian Educational Services, New Delhi, 1987, p. 283.
8. Ramesan N, Andhra Pradesh District Gazetteers, East Godavari, printed by Director of printing and stationery at Government Secretary Press, Hyderabad, 1979, p. 158.
9. Report of the Indian Police Commission 1902-03, Government Central Printing Office, Simla, 1904, p. 7.
10. History of Police Organisation in India and Indian Village Police, published by the University of Calcutta with the permission of Government of India, University Press, Calcutta, 1913, p. 14.
11. Maclean C.D., Manual of the Administration of Madras Presidency, Vol. I, Asian Educational Services, New Delhi, 1987, p. 188.
12. Ramesan N, Andhra Pradesh District Gazetteers, Krishna District Gazetteer, printed by Director of printing and stationery at Government Secretary Press, Hyderabad, 1977, p. 164.
13. Devi Cayal Aggarwal, *CBI and Policing in India*, Kaveri Books, New Delhi, 2000, p. 107.
14. *Ibid.* p. 2.

15. James Vadackumchery, *National Police Commission*, Alph Publications, New Delhi, 1998, p. xvii.
16. Devi Cayal Aggarwal, *CBI and Policing in India*, Kaveri books, New Delhi, 2000, p. 87.
17. Government of Madras, Legal Department, The Madras District Police Act of 1859, Printed by Superintendent, Government Press, 1937, pp. 2-3.
18. Chande M.B., *The Police in India*, published by Atlantic Publishers and Distributors, New Delhi, 1997, p. 84.
19. Report on the Administration of the Madras Presidency for the year 1930, printed by Superintendent, Government Press, Madras, 1931, p. xxiii.
20. Ann Ewing, *The Indian Civil Service 1919-1924: Service discontent and the response in London and in Delhi*, printed in Great Britain, Modern Asian Studies, University of Cambridge, 1984.
21. Proceedings of the Indian Round Table Conference, dated 12th November, 1930 - 19th January, 1931.
22. Ranjit Sen Gupta, *Management of Internal Security, Freedom from Fear,* Lancer Publication, New Delhi, 1992, p. 7.
23. Maclean C.D., Manual of the Administration of Madras Presidency, Vol. I, Asian Educational Services, New Delhi,1987, p. 187.
24. The Defence of India Act of 1939, published by Manager of Publications, Government Press, Delhi, 1940, p. 72.
25. Report on the Administration of Police in the Madras Province for the year 1941, printed by Superintendent, Government Press, Madras, 1942, p. 23.
26. Report on the Administration of the Police of the Madras Presidency, 1925, printed by Superintendent, Government Press, Madras, 1926, p. 24.
27. Report on the Administration of the Police of the Madras Province,1939, printed by Superintendent, Government Press, Madras, 1940, p. 61.
28. M.R.Ry.Rai Bahadur, Collector's Standing Orders of Nellore District, printed by Superintendent, Government Press, Madras, 1931, p. 147.
29. Government of Madras, Legal Department, Madras District Police Act XXIV of 1859, printed by Superintendent, Government Press, Madras, 1937, p. 3.
30. G.O.No.168, Ms, Public (Police) dated 25th March, 1931, Public (Police) Department, Government of Madras.
31. Maltby T. J., The Ganjam District Manual, Lawrence Asylum Press, Madras, 1918, p. 2.

32. Francis W, The Gazetteer of the Vizagapatam District, Asian Education Services, Madras, 1907, p. 2.
33. Ramesan N., Andhra Pradesh District Gazetteers, East Godavari, printed by Director of printing and stationery at Government Secretary Press, Hyderabad,1979, p. 1.
34. Andhra Pradesh District Gazetteers, A Manual of the West Godavari District in the Presidency of Madras, Hyderabad, 1992, p. 2.
35. Ramesan N, Andhra Pradesh District Gazetteers, Krishna District, printed by Director of printing and stationery at Government Secretary Press, Hyderabad,1979, p. 2.
36. A Statistical Atlas of the Madras Province, 1940-41, published by Economic Adviser to the Government of Madras, Madras, 1949, p. 193.
37. Madras District Gazetteers, Statistical Appendix for Nellore District, Madras, 1929, p. 70.
38. Report on the Administration of the Police of the Madras Province for the year 1936, printed by Superintendent, Government Press, Madras, 1937, p. 2.
39. Report on the Administration of the Police of the Madras Province, 1936, printed by Superintendent, Government Press, Madras, 1937, p. 1.
40. Ramesan N, Andhra Pradesh District Gazetteers, Srikakulam, printed by Director of printing and stationery at Government Secretary Press, Hyderabad, 1979, p. 136.
41. Report of the Indian Police Commission 1902-03, Government Central Printing Office, Simla, 1904, p. 189.
42. Hirday Nath Kunzru, *The Public Services in India, Public Servants of India Society*, Allahabad, 1917, p. 108.
43. Report on the Administration of the Madras Presidency for the year 1930, printed by Superintendent, Government Press, Madras, 1931, pp. xxii-xxiii.
44. Abdul Waheed Khan, A *Brief History of Andhra Pradesh*, State Archives, Hyderabad, 1972, p. 112.
45. The Unrepealed General Act VII of 1895, 1887, 1897, Vol. III, Government of India Central Publication Branch, Calcutta, 1929, p. 302.
46. Handbook of Information on the Administration of the province of Madras, printed by the Superintendent, Government press, Madras, 1947, p. 24.
47. The Imperial Gazetteer of India, The Indian Empire, Vol. IV, Clarendon Press, Oxford, 1907, p. 389.

48. Handbook of Information on the Administration of the Province of Madras, printed by Superintendent, Government Press, Madras, 1947, p. 30.
49. Report of Indian Police Commission 1902-03, printed at Government Central Printing Office, Simla, 1904, p. 135.
50. The Unrepeated General Act VII of 1895, 1887, 1897, Vol. III, Government of India Central Publication Branch, Calcutta, 1929, p. 302.
51. G.O.No.2614, Home, dated 3rd June, 1941, Home Department, Madras Government.
52. The Unrevealed General Act V, 1909, Act X of 1882, Government of India, Central Publication Branch, Calcutta, 1909, p. 80.
53. Administration Report of the Inspector General of Police for the year 1924, printed by Superintendent, Government Press, Madras, 1925, p. 25.
54. Report on the Administration of the Police of the Madras Presidency for the years 1924 to 1947, printed by Superintendent, Government Press, Madras.
55. Madras District Gazetteers, Statistical Appendix for Nellore District, Madras, 1929, printed by Superintendent, Government Press, Madras,1932, p. 70.
56. Statistical Record of West Godavari, 1934, printed by Superintendent, Government Press, Madras,1935, pp. 176,45.
57. G.O.No.784, Home (Ms), dated 10th March, 1945, Home Department, Madras Government.
58. G.O.No.3470 Home (Ms) dated, 29th September,1945, Home Department, Madras Government.
59. G.O.No.1830, Home (Ms), dated 9th June, 1945, Home Department, Madras Government.
60. Government of Madras, Legal Department, The Madras District Police Act XXIV of 1859, printed by Superintendent, Government Press, Madras,1937, p. 5.
61. The Imperial Gazetteer of India, The Indian Empire, Vol. IV, Clarendon Press, Oxford, 1907, p. 389.
62. Village Officers Manual, Vol. I, prepared under the order of Government, printed by Superintendent, Government Press, Madras, 1893, pp. 5-15.
63. Report on the Administration of Police of the Madras Presidency for the year 1935, printed by Superintendent, Government Press, Madras, 1936, p. 8.
64. Report of Indian Police Commission 1902-03, printed at Government Central Printing Office, Simla, 1904, p. 132.

65. Report on the Administration of the Madras Presidency for the years 1925-26, printed by Superintendent, Government Press, Madras, 1927, p. 31.
66. Government of Madras, Legal Department, The Madras District Police Act XXIV of 1859, printed by Superintendent, Government Press, Madras, 1937, p. 2.
67. G.O.No.168, Ms, Pub (Police) dated 25th March, 1931, Department of Public (Police), Madras Government.
68. Handbook of Information on the Administration of the Province of Madras, printed by Superintendent, Government Press, Madras, 1947, p. 29.
69. *Ibid.*, p. 30.
70. Report on the Administration of Police of the Madras Presidency for the year 1925, printed by Superintendent, Government Press, Madras, 1926, p. 43.
71. Handbook of Information on the Administration of the Province of Madras, printed by Superintendent, Government Press, Madras, 1947, p. 27.
72. History of Police Organisation in India and Indian Village Police, published by the University of Calcutta with the permission of Government of India, University Press, Calcutta, 1913, p. 5.
73. *Ibid.*, p. 38.
74. Report on the Administration of the Police of the Madras Presidency for the years 1924 to 1947, printed by Superintendent, Government Press, Madras.
75. Hirday Nath Kunzru, *Political Pamphlets-II, The Public Services in India*, Servants of India Society, Allahabad, 1917, p. 108.
76. History of Police Organisation in India and Indian Village Police, published by the University of Calcutta with the permission of Government of India, University Press, Calcutta, 1913, p. 18.
77. Rushbrook Williams L.F., *India in 1923-24*, Central Publication Branch, Calcutta, 1924, p. 73.
78. John A.C. Boswell Mes, Manual on the Nellore District in the Presidency of the Madras, Government Press, Madras, 1973, p. 590.
79. The Imperial Gazetteer of India, The Indian Empire, Vol. IV, Clarendon Press, Oxford, 1907, p. 388.
80. Basudev Panda, *Indian Bureaucracy*, Uppal Publications, New Delhi, 1978, p. 6.
81. Proceedings of the Indian Round Table Conference, 12th November, 1930 - 19th January, 1931.

82. Handbook of Information on the Administration of the Province of Madras, printed by Superintendent, Government Press, Madras, 1947, p. 97.
83. Report of the Madras Public Service Commission for the year 1936-37, printed by Superintendent, Government Press, Madras, 1938, p. i.
84. The Imperial Gazetteer of India, The Indian Empire, Vol. IV, Clarendon Press, Oxford, 1907, p. 388.
85. Minutes of Evidence related to the Indian and Provincial Civil Services, printed in India, 1914, p. 279.
86. Ann Ewin, *The Indian Civil Service 1919-1924; service discontent and the response in London and in Delhi*, Modern Asian Studies, Great Britain,1984, pp. 33-53.
87. Maclean C.D., Manual of the Administration of Madras Presidency, Vol. I, Asian Educational Services, New Delhi, 1987, p. 190.
88. Francis W, Frederick Nicholson, C.S. Middlemiss and C.A. Barber, Gazetteer of South India, Vol. I, Mittal Publications, New Delhi, 1988, p. 115.
89. Letter No.F-78-28, Police dated 15th June 1926, from the Government of India to all local Governments and Administrations.
90. Report on the Administration of the Police of the Madras Presidency for the years 1924 to 1947, printed by Superintendent, Government Press, Madras.
91. Government of Madras, Legal Department, The Madras District Police Act XXIV of 1859, printed by Superintendent, Government Press, Madras, 1937, p. 4.
92. The Imperial Gazetteer of India, The Indian Empire, Vol. IV, Clarendon Press, Oxford, 1907, p. 389.
93. Madras Police Department Circular No.310-S, dated 3rd September, 1921.
94. Report on the Administration of the Police of the Madras Presidency for the years 1924 to 1947, printed by Superintendent, Government Press, Madras.
95. Administration Report of the Madras Presidency Police for the year 1924, Part-I, printed by Superintendent, Government Press, Madras, 1925, p. 30.
96. Report on the Administration of the Police of the Madras Presidency for the year 1924, Statistical Abstract for the British India-police, Madras, 1925.
97. Report on the Administration of the Madras Presidency for the

year 1925-26, printed by Superintendent, Government Press, Madras, 1927, p. 31.

98. G.O.No.171, Judl., dated 1st April, 1924, Judicial Department, Madras Government.

99. History of Police Organisation in India and Indian Village Police, published by the University of Calcutta, 1913, p. 52.

100. Report on the Administration of the Police of the Madras Presidency for the years 1925, printed by Superintendent, Government Press, Madras, 1926, p. 2.

101. Administration Report of the Madras Presidency Police for the year 1925, Part-I printed by Superintendent, Government Press, Madras, 1926, p. 45.

102. Report on the Administration of the Madras Presidency for the year 1925-26, printed by the Superintendent, Government Press, Madras, 1927, p. 32.

103. Police Administrative Report of the Madras Presidency for the year 1925, printed by Superintendent, Government Press, Madras, 1926, p. 7.

104. Madras District Gazetteers, Statistical Appendix for Nellore District, Madras, 1929, printed by Superintendent, Government Press, Madras, p. 70.

105. Inspector General of Police Report for the year 1926, printed by Superintendent, Government Press, Madras, 1927.

106. G.O.No.467, Home, dated 25th September, 1928, Home Department, Madras Government.

107. Administration Report of the Inspector General of Police for the year 1928, printed by Superintendent, Government Press, Madras, 1929, p. 4.

108. Administration Report of the Inspector General of Police for the year 1927, printed by Superintendent, Government Press, Madras, 1928, p. 3.

109. Administration Report of the Madras Presidency Police for the year 1925, Part-I, printed by the Superintendent, Government Press, Madras, 1926, p. 45.

110. Report on the Administration of the Madras Presidency for the year 1928-29, printed by Superintendent, Government Press, Madras, 1930, p. 29.

111. Report on the Administration of the Police of the Madras Presidency for the year 1928, printed by Superintendent, Government Press, Madras, 1929, p. 2.

112. Report on the Administration of the Police of the Madras Presidency for the year 1930 printed by the Superintendent, Government Press, Madras, 1931, p. 34.

113. *Ibid.*, p. 35.

114. *Ibid.*, p. xxiii.

115. Administrative Report of the Police of the Madras Presidency for the year 1932, printed by Superintendent, Government Press, Madras, 1933, p. 27.

116. Gazetteer of the Nellore District-1938, A-Volume, printed by Superintendent, Government Press, Madras, 1942, p. 278.

117. G.O.No.649 (Ms) dated 8th Feburary, 1939, Home Department, Madras Government.

118. Report on the Administration of the Madras Presidency for the year 1938, printed by Superintendent, Government Press, Madras,1939, p. 46.

119. G.O.No.6249, Home (Ms), dated 5th December, 1939, Home Department, Madras Government.

120. G.O.No.638, Home (Ms), dated 8th February, 1939, Home Department, Madras Government.

121. G.O.No.717, Home (Ms), dated 10th February, 1939, Home Department, Madras Government.

122. Report on the Administration of the Madras Presidency for the year 1939-40, printed by Superintendent, Government Press, Madras, 1941, p. 46.

123. *Ibid.*

124. Madras in 1940, Outline of the Administration, printed by Superintendent, Government Press, Madras, 1941, p. 13.

125. G.O.No.1407, Home, dated 1st April, 1942, Home Department, Madras Government.

126. G.O.No.44, Public (Police)(Confdl.), dated 28th January, 1942, Public (Police) Department, Madras Government.

127. G.O.No.3701, Home, dated 6th October, 1948, Home Department, Madras Government.

128. James Vadackumchery, *National Police Commission*, Alph Publications, New Delhi ,1998, p. 14.

129. Government of India, Report of the Royal Commission on the Superior Civil Services in India, Government of India Press, Simla, 1924.

130. Report of Indian Police Commission 1902-03, printed at Government Central Printing Office, Simla, 1904, p. 143.

131. Police Administrative Report of the Madras Presidency for the year 1928, printed by Superintendent, Government Press, Madras, 1929, p. 2.

132. *Ibid.*, p. 3.

133. Report on the Administration of the Police of the Madras Province, 1939, printed by Superintendent, Government Press, Madras, 1940, p. 3.

134. Report on the Administration of the Madras Presidency for the year 1938-39, printed by Superintendent, Government Press, Madras, 1940, p. 47.

135. Report on the Administration of the Police of the Madras Province, 1939, printed by Superintendent, Government Press, Madras, 1940, p. 4.

136. Report on the Administration of the Madras Presidency for the year, 1938, printed by Superintendent, Government Press, Madras, 1939, p. 47.

137. Report on the Administration of the Police of the Madras Presidency, 1927, printed by Superintendent, Government Press, Madras, 1928, p. 2.

138. Francis W, Frederick Nicholson, C.S. Middlemiss and C.A. Barber, Gazetteer of South India, Vol. I, Mittal Publications, New Delhi, 1988, p. 115.

139. Report of the Auxiliary and Territorial Forces Committee, dated 23rd January, 1925, Vol. I, p. 8.

140. Letter No.F-78-28, Police, dated 15th June, 1926, from the Government of India to all local governments and Administrations, p. 11.

141. Report of the Indian Police Commission 1902-03, printed at Government Central Printing Office, Simla, 1904, p. 143.

142. Report of the Auxiliary and Territorial Forces Committee, Vol. I, dated 23rd January, 1925, pp. 8, 13.

143. Report on the Administration of the Madras Presidency for the year 1925, printed by Superintendent, Government Press, Madras, 1926, p. 25.

144. Police Administrative Report of the Madras Presidency, 1925, printed by Superintendent, Government Press, Madras, 1926, p. 7.

145. *Ibid.*, p. 24.

146. Police Administrative Report of the Madras Presidency for the year 1928, printed by Superintendent, Government Press, Madras, 1929, p. 3.

147. Report on the Administration of the Madras Presidency for the year 1930 printed by Superintendent, Government Press, Madras, 1931, pp. xxii-xxiv.

148. Report on the Administration of the Police of the Madras Province, 1939, printed by Superintendent, Government Press, Madras, 1940, p. 3.

149. Madras in 1939, Outline of the Administration, printed by Superintendent, Government Press, Madras, 1940, p. 18.

150. Report on the Administration of the Madras Presidency for the year 1931-32, printed by Superintendent, Government Press, Madras, 1933, p. 28.

151. G.O.No.6238, Home (Ms), dated 4th December, 1938, Home Department, Madras Government.

152. Report on the Administration of the Madras Presidency for the years 1929-30, printed by Superintendent, Government Press, Madras,1931, p. 35.

153. Madras in 1939, Outline of the Administration, printed by Superintendent, Government Press, Madras, 1940, p. 18.

154. Report on the Administration of the Police of the Madras Province for the years 1939, printed by Superintendent, Government Press, Madras, 1940, p. 28.

155. *Ibid.*, p. 3.

156. Madras in 1940, printed by Superintendent, Government Press, Madras, 1941, p. 14.

157. Report on the Administration of the Madras Presidency for the years 1928-29, printed by Superintendent, Government Press, Madras, 1930, p. 30.

158. Report on the Administration of the Police of the Madras Province, 1928, printed by Superintendent, Government Press, Madras, 1929, p. 6.

159. Report on the Administration of the Madras Presidency for the year 1929-30, printed by Superintendent, Government Press, Madras, 1931, p. 35.

160. Report on the Administration of the Police of the Madras Province, 1936, printed by Superintendent, Government Press, Madras, 1937, p. 1.

161. Report on the Administration of the Police of the Madras Province,1939, printed by Superintendent, Government Press, Madras, 1940, p. 3.

162. Ram Reddy G, and Seshadri K, *Developing Society and Police*, Osmania University, Hyderabad, 1972, p. 112.

163. Report on the Administration of the Police of the Madras Presidency for the years 1924 to 1947.

164. Report on the Administration of the Police of the Madras Province, 1946, printed by Superintendent, Government Press, Madras, 1947, p. 5.

165. G.O.No.206, Judicial (Conf.), dated 16th April, 1929, Judicial Department, Government of Madras.

166. G.O.No. 339I, Home (Conf.), dated14th August I940, Home Department, Government of Madras.

167. Report on the Administration of the Police of the Madras Province, 1946, printed by Superintendent, Government Press, Madras, 1947, pp.5,6.

168. *Ibid.*, p. 6

169. Report on the Administration of the police of the Madras Province, 1947, printed by Superintendent Government press, Madras,1948, p. 6.

170. Report on the Administration of the Madras Presidency for the year 1946, printed by Superintendent, Government Press, Madras, 1947, p. 14.

171. Letter No.1614-H, dated 24th July, 1935, from Major General Connor F.P., Surgeon General with Government of Madras to the Joint Secretary to Government, Local Self Government, Public Health Department.

172. G.O.No.467, Judicial, dated 25th September, 1928, Judicial Department, Government of Madras.

173. Report on the Administration of the Madras Presidency for the year 1931-1932, printed by Superintendent, Government Press, Madras, 1933, p. 27.

174. G.O.No.4044, Home (Ms), dated 27th November,1945, Home Department, Government of Madras.

175. G.O.No 4366, Home (Ms), dated 5th December 1945, Home Department, Government of Madras.

176. Report on the Administration of the Police of the Madras Province,1930, printed by Superintendent, Government Press, Madras, 1931, p. 2.

177. Report on the Administration of the Police of the Madras Province,1925, printed by Superintendent, Government Press, Madras, 1926, p. 6.

178. G.O.No.889, Home (Ms), dated 22nd February, 1940, Home Department, Government of Madras.

179. Report on the Administration of the Police of the Madras Province,1925, printed by Superintendent, Government Press, Madras, 1926, p. 6.

180. G.O.No.467, Judl., dated 25th September, 1928, Judicial Department, Government of Madras.

181. Report on the Administration of the Police of the Madras Presidency,1927, printed by Superintendent, Government Press, Madras, 1928, p. 6.

182. G.O.No. 567, Judl., dated 28th August, 1926, Judicial Department, Government of Madras.

183. Report on the Administration of the Police of the Madras Province,1925, printed by Superintendent, Government Press, Madras, 1926, p. 5.
184. Report on the Administration of the Police of the Madras Presidency for the years 1929, printed by Superintendent, Government Press, Madras, 1930, p. 6.
185. Government of India letter No.E-78-26, Police, dated 7th January, 1927 to all Local Governments, p. 13.
186. Rushbrook Williams L.F., *India in 1923-24*, Central Publication Branch, Calcutta, 1924, p. 73.
187. The Madras District Police Act XXIV of 1859 (As modified up to the 1st June 1937), p. 3.
188. Francis W, Frederick Nicholson, C.S. Middlemiss and C.A. Barber, Gazetteer of South India, Vol. I, Mittal Publications, New Delhi, 1988, p. 115.
189. G.O.No. 485, Public (Police), dated 12th September, 1931, Public (Police) Department, Government of Madras.
190. Report on the Administration of the Police of the Madras Province,1939, printed by Superintendent, Government Press, Madras, 1940, p. 3.

3

Functions of the Police Department

The police department was an important administrative unit under the British rule as it was an instrument for the prevention and detection of crime.[1] During the British rule in the Northern range of the Madras Presidency, the main function of the police department was to maintain law and order. According to the Police Acts, the functions of the police force were to prevent commission of offences and public nuisances, bring the offenders to justice, collect information affecting public peace and to keep order in all public places. The police performed both the preventive and punitive functions. The police force was the principal arm of the British government for the enforcement of law and preservation of order.[2]

The Madras District Police Act 24 of 1859 (Section 21) and the Indian Police Act V of 1861 had the provisions of law about the powers and functions of the police force in the Madras Presidency. Under these Acts, every police officer in the Northern range had police powers in every part of the General Police District. The Inspector General of Police had the power to control and command the entire police force of the Madras Presidency. Every police officer after enrollment into the police service received a certificate under the seal of the Inspector General of Police in which the powers, functions and the privileges of the police officer were mentioned. The Auxiliary and the Special Police Forces had the same powers, privileges and protection. They were also liable to all duties and penalties and were subordinate to the same authorities as the regular police officers.[3]

The duties undertaken by the police were preservation of peace, prevention of crimes and offences, detection and apprehension of offenders and also discovery of stolen property. Their other duties were, like collection of evidence against persons accused of grave crimes and bringing them before the magistracy and courts. The regular police were assisted by the auxiliary police in crime control and for maintenance of law and order. The apprehending and watching of vagabonds, suspicious characters, patrol of the countryside and public roads, prevention of nuisances, laying information before the magistracy regarding any offences committed against the law, inspection and verification of weights and measures, management of public ponds, service and execution of summons, warrants and other lawful orders issued by the magistracy and the courts in any criminal matter, safe custody of prisoners under trial, escorts and guarding of treasure and convicts were some of the important functions of the police force.[4] Besides these ordinary duties, the police were also entrusted with the guarding of railway tracks, bridges, canals, roads, protection of the forest, traffic policing, prevention of smuggling, guarding of distilleries under the Excise Act, cantonment and contagious diseases Acts. During emergencies, the Special Police Forces were sanctioned to quell the unrest to restore order. The police were given special powers and functions under special ordinance during the political unrest in the Northern range especially during the Civil Disobedience Movement and Quit India Movement. The police officer had the power to arrest, without orders from a magistrate and without a warrant, any person who had committed offence against the law, such as murder, theft, robbery, dacoity, destruction of any private or government property, viz. police stations, forest products, railway lines, etc., under the Indian Penal Code.[5] Under Part V of the Indian Penal Code, the powers of the police to investigate into cognizable cases by registration of First Information Report were described.[6] The police in the Northern range dealt with the crime under the prescribed rules and regulations laid-down by the law.

The Indian Penal Code was drafted in 1860 under the chairmanship of Lord Macaulay, with the First Law Commission coming into force in the year 1862.[7] There was no particular definition of crime in the Indian Penal Code, but it made a distinction by two types, cognizable offence and non-cognizable offence. Under cognizable crime, the police could make inquiry into the case when the same was reported or came to notice without the reference of magisterial authority. The non-cognizable crime could be investigated by the police only after receiving orders from the magistracy.[8] The police in the Northern range had prevented the crimes, offences, public nuisances, apprehended suspicious characters, detected and brought offenders to justice to preserve the order. They collected and communicated the intelligence which affected the public peace and executed all orders and warrants lawfully issued to them by the competent authority. The police had played an important role as an agent of the law and British government. They functioned under various laws enacted by the government and also under their direction.

In grave cases, where the general police failed to obtain clues, officers of superior rank were engaged to work on them. The Special Reserve Police Forces and Auxiliary Police Forces were organised to assist the general police, such as, Criminal Investigating Department, Railway Police, Traffic Police, River Police, etc., and Special Police Forces, like Armed Reserves, East Coast Special Police, Presidency Special Police, Civic Guards, etc. The Special Reserve Police were deployed especially during the emergencies, such as political unrest, agrarian strikes, communal disturbances and natural calamities. The services of these police forces in the Northern range proved quite beneficial in crime control and in maintenance of law and order.

The Police Commission of 1860 was responsible for the formation of India's Provincial Police Forces and the Armed Reserves in the Madras Presidency, of which the Northern range formed a part. These police reserves were not military in nature but they were armed to control riots and to perform guard and escort duties.[9] In the Northern range, the primary police duties were performed by general police force assigned to each district in the range; besides this force, Special Police Forces were stationed at the district headquarters to deal with the riots, communal disturbances, labour troubles and any breaches of public peace. The duties of the Armed Reserves were to provide guards, escorts, and orderlies.[10]

The Presidency General Reserve and the Special Emergency Forces which were stationed at Vizianagaram and St. Thomas Mount had been amalgamated and came to be known as Range Armed Reserves. These were the local strategic police forces placed at the disposal of the concerned Deputy Inspector General of Police. The Railway Police Armed Reserves were deputed for railway protection duty and were at the disposal of the concerned Superintendent of Railway Police. The Railway Police was organised for the preservation of law and order within the railway limits. The Criminal Investigation Department was constituted to deal with crimes of special nature, non-local criminal organisations and for the surveillance of the criminal tribes. To recognise old offenders, the fingerprints of all convicts were taken and sent to the Fingerprint Bureau. The Traffic Police were organised mostly in the town areas of the Northern range for regulation of traffic under the Traffic Act. The Village Police were under the control of the district magistrates and their function was to assist the police in investigation and detection of crime. In special localities, *Ghat talayaris* were appointed to protect the highways from robberies conducted there and for guarding roads.[11] The River Police and the Port Police were established to regulate the traffic and for protection from crimes. The Port Police at Coconada port, Machillipatam port, and Vizagapatam port had functioned efficiently in the crime control.

These police forces were enlisted and controlled by the police department of the Northern range under the control of Deputy Inspector General of Police, Inspector General of Police and British government. These were employed to supplement the police force for emergency purpose. The British government had the power to declare an area to be disturbed or of dangerous state and employ these police forces in addition to the fixed complement of police force. The cost of the additional police force was borne by the inhabitants of the area and was apportioned among them by the district magistrate. The government, sometimes, exempted any person or class or section of the inhabitants from liability to bear a portion of the cost of maintenance of the Special Police Force.[12] Under special ordinances, the British government had sanctioned Special Police Forces with extra powers to deal with the political situation during the freedom struggle.[13] In the Northern range, the Inspector General of Police had commanded the police force to take action where necessary by use of lathi-charge and also open fire against rioters and nationalist agitators. The police had invoked military assistance during the years 1930-33 to maintain peace in the districts of the Northern range.[14] During the Civil Disobedience Movement in the year 1932, the police were given special powers and orders to open fire or use tear gas to preserve law and order. The numerous strikes in the Northern range during the years entailed continuous demands on the police reserves.[15] During the years 1939 to 1945, the police force of the Northern range went under great strain due to work related to outbreak of the World War II and also various political agitation activities undertaken by the Indian Congress. During this period, some trained signalmen were sent from the Ganjam armed police to take part in the war. A number of such emergencies occurred in the Northern range during this period where the Special Police Forces were used for restoring law and order.

Police Department

The main function of the Police Department was maintenance of law and order. In the Northern range, the primary police duties were performed by the police force assigned to each district. The police performed detective duties, court duties, preventive duties, etc., by maintaining a register of habitual offenders, suspected characters and released convicts.[16] The armed reserves were stationed in the district to deal with emergencies, such as occurrence of riots, communal disturbances, labour troubles and breaches of public peace which demand presence of a better armed and disciplined force than the regular force. The British government sanctioned special armed police force to quell the disturbances in addition to the ordinary fixed complement and they were quartered in the specified area with their cost borne by the inhabitants of the area. In many instances, the government employed these forces during the period 1924-47. They were sub-divided into one or more platoons of three to four sections each, each section inturn consisting of one Head Constable, one Naik, one Lance Naik and twelve Constables. Besides this, the other special police force, namely the Railway Police was employed for the preservation of law and order within the railway limits. The Criminal Investigation Department was constituted to deal with crime of a special character and criminal organisations of more than local importance. To enable old offenders to be recognised, the fingerprints of all convicts were taken and sent to the Fingerprint Bureau at Vellore in the Madras Presidency. The Village Police was under the control of the District Magistrates and it assisted the regular police in the investigation and detection of crime. In special localities, *Ghat Talayaris*, enlisted and controlled by the police department, were employed to supplement the police in guarding roads. The British government had the power to declare an area as disturbed or in danger and accordingly deploy any police force in addition to the ordinary fixed complement to be quartered in the specified area; the cost of the additional police force was borne by the inhabitants of the area and was apportioned among them by the District Magistrate, but the government sometimes exempted persons or class or section of the inhabitants from liability to bear a portion of the cost.[17]

The most common activities of the police force in the districts of the Northern range were uniformed patrol, criminal investigation and identification, and prevention and detection of crime.

Powers and Functions of the Police Department

The Provincial police force in the Madras Presidency was organised under the Police Act of 1861 and the Inspector General of Police was the chief head of the police department of the Madras Presidency who was assisted by the Deputy Inspector Generals and other subordinate police officers.[18] The following are some of the important powers and functions of the ranks in police force.

Inspector General of Police

Inspector General of Police was incharge of the police department in the Madras Presidency. He was the link between the British government and the police force in the Northern range. He was the executive head of entire police force of the Northern range and was assisted by the Deputy Inspector Generals and sometimes Additional Inspector Generals of Police.[19] He advised the government on all police matters, both administrative and operational. He had the power to frame orders and regulations during emergencies on the advice of the British government. He also had the powers to frame orders and regulations related to the prevention and detection of crime, promotion, preservation and maintenance of law and order, and public safety and security. His orther powers extended to the general management, utilisation and deployment of the police force, inspection and description of arms, and management and regulation of the police funds and manuals.

He was responsible to the government for the internal management, economy, equipment, training, discipline and efficient discharge of duties by the police force. He was responsible for making the police organisation efficient at all levels for prevention and detection of crime, and maintenance of law and order. He kept the government informed about the state of crime and other political, communal, rebellious and terrorist movements. The Inspector General of Police had the power to reallocate the strength within the police units according to the need of the administration. The strength of the police force and various ranks was fixed by the government and any increase or reduction was done with the approval of government. The Inspector General of Police had the powers of a District Magistrate and his powers were exercised according to the provisions of the Code of Criminal Procedure.

His main functions were planning, policy framing, and decision-making with consent of the government, and improving and making the entire police force an effective law enforcement agency. He was also responsible for the police management, training, and supervision in the police department. He exercised all disciplinary and financial powers of the police department with the government approval. His other important functions and responsibilities included the enforcement of code of conduct among the police officers of all ranks, police welfare, housing, and a proper mechanism for redressal of grievances. In the discharge of these functions, the Inspector General of Police had full authority to allot and assign any of the functions to the officers subordinate to him as permissible under rules and regulations.

Deputy Inspector General of Police

The Deputy Inspector General of Police was the head of the Northern range.[20] He assisted the Inspector General of Police in the supervision and management of the police department and in maintaining discipline, morale and training at all levels. He had a large measure of administrative control within his range in the matters of appointment, postings, leave, rewards and punishments. He maintained efficiency and discipline, ensured uniformity of procedure and practice and secured co-operation between the police forces of districts under his jurisdiction as well as harmonious working between the police and the magistracy. Organisation and implementation of preventive measures, particularly police beat system, patrols and surveillance, personal direction of measures necessary for maintenance of peace, public order, law and order, security and assistance to Inspector General of Police in operations were his some other important functions. He maintained co-ordination and co-operation within the police force and also with other branches of the police department such as Criminal Investigation Department and provided assistance in the matters of investigation in cases relating to apprehension of offenders, searches, seizures and preservation of scene. He was responsible for the preparation of schemes and contingency plans for maintenance of peace and order in connection with elections, festivals, fairs, and agitations implemented both at the range and district levels by the concerned police officers. He visited the areas where serious breaches of law took place and directed the operations to control the situation.

He carried out annual inspection of the Northern range and supervised the functions performed by the police department in the districts. He inspected the district headquarters police stations and other police stations and reported in this regard to the Inspector General of Police. He maintained discipline, uniformity of procedure and practice, and secured co-operation between the police and the magistracy. He controlled, instructed and advised the district superintendents. His duty was also to exercise a constant scrutiny over the course of investigation and ensures that superior officers take correct action. He also had a large measure of administrative control within the districts of the Northern range in the matters of appointments, postings, leave, rewards, and punishments.

He was also in charge of the Criminal Investigation Department and the Railway Police districts and also as regards to the work relating to the reclamation of criminal tribes. He was responsible for efficient functioning of investigation, coordination and supervision of all investigation of the Criminal Investigation Department cases. He supervised and controlled the Criminal Investigation Department and Fingerprint Bureau, and maintained mutual co-operation and liaison with other provinces. In capacity of the head of the Railway police, he supervised its functioning and communicated with the Inspector General of Police of the Madras Presidency. He paid visits alongwith the District Superintendents of Police to the districts, railways police stations and the crime branches in the Northern range and inspected the work records. He also visited the Fingerprint Bureau to check the work and was responsible for the publication of Gazettes. He had the power to dismiss, declare unfit, suspend or reduce to a lower post the subordinate police officer who neglected in discharging his duties.[21] He kept a watch on the crimes situation pertaining to grave offences, like dacoity, robbery, murder, etc., and he also exercised control over the police funds. His other functions included personnel management, budgetary control, and coordination within the range.

District Superintendent of Police

He was the police head of the district and was the in charge of the internal administration of the police department in the district. They were stationed at the headquarters of each district of the Northern range. The Superintendents were accountable to the chief of the range police, i.e., Deputy Inspector General of Police. The Superintendent, as head of the district police force, was in charge of the internal management of the district police department in performing the preventive and executive duties of the police force. He maintained discipline, promotions and dismissals in the department at the district level. The District Superintendents of Police were stationed at each district headquarters of the Northern range and there were Assistant Superintendents and Deputy Superintendents to assist them in their duties.[22] The District Superintendents were subordinates to the District Magistrates and they kept the District Magistrates informed on all matters concerning to peace of the district and the state of crime. The Magistrate was responsible for preventive aspects and the Superintendent and his subordinate officers were responsible for control of crime and maintenance of law and order. He took adequate arrangements during fairs and festivals and also during elections, riots, and agitations. He had responsibility to supply arms, vehicles, uniforms and was also responsible for training, promotion, and discipline. The District Superintendents also supervised the investigation of serious crimes, such as dacoity, highway robbery, and murder.

Deputy Superintendent of Police

The districts in the Northern range were divided into sub-divisions and each sub-division was placed under the charge of Deputy District Superintendents of Police. They functioned under the District Superintendents of Police and they kept him informed on all matters related to police administration of the sub-division and took his advice, wherever necessary. Their duties were similar to those of the District Superintendents but their jurisdiction extended only upto their sub-division. They also investigated cases of grave crime in the Northern range. The main function of the Deputy Superintendent of Police was to maintain law and order, crime control, collection and communication of the intelligence to the superior police officers, submission of periodical reports and to maintain cordial relations with the Superintendents and subordinate officers. Deputy Superintendent of Police exercised control over the matters of appointments, postings, leave, rewards, and punishments in his jurisdiction.[23]

Inspectors of Police

The sub-divisions were made up of police circles and were under the command of Inspectors of police often referred to as Circle Inspectors. Their main functions were investigation of important cases in their jurisdiction circles besides supervision of police work of the police circle, maintaining discipline among the subordinates and keeping the Superintendent of Police informed of the administrative matters of circle from time to time. The Inspectors of the Northern range used to inspect police stations falling in their circle and give necessary instructions. He inspected each of his stations once in three months throughout his circle and made enquiries about bad characters, the state of crime, and the general work of the police department. He worked together with the Village Vigilance Committees in his circle to improve co-operation between the general public and the police.[24] He supervised the work of the

Sub-Inspectors on prosecution of cases. During his visits to the police stations, he scrutinised station crime records and examined known depredators, checked register and duty roster maintained in respect of proper performance of beat duty to control crime. He visited villages once in a year to watch the progress of village police.

The Inspectors were in charge of investigation in all grave crimes, responsible from the initial stages to finalisation and prosecution of the case. Sometimes, he personally investigated cases of importance on the orders of the Superintendent of Police. He maintained case diaries of the investigations in his circles. On the occurrence of a crime, the Inspector proceeded to the spot to supervise and guided the investigation. Whenever any serious breach of peace was anticipated, the Inspector proceeded to the spot and took proper measures for its prevention and suppression. He supervised police arrangements on the occasions of public assemblies, elections and during fairs and festivals.

All cognisable cases under the Indian Penal Code and cases under special and local laws were entered in the Inspectors crime register and communicated to the immediate superior police. The Inspector compiled the annual review of crime and investigation of each station. The Station Inspection report was duly maintained and the Circle Inspector recorded his remarks on inspection of a station by him in the Inspectors visiting book and forward it to his immediate superior. The Station and Circle records of the districts were sent to the district headquarters police office by the Inspector once in a year.

Sergeants Major or Charge Sergeants

These special police officers had the same powers and privileges of the regular police.[25] During the period 1924 to 1947, these officers were mostly Europeans and were attached to the Armed Reserves of which they were in immediate charge. They had no functions of investigation but they were stationed in cantonments, ports, railway stations and other places where the police had to deal with the Europeans.[26]

Sergeants in Armed Reserves

They were in charge of platoons and were placed under the charge of Sergeant Major and were responsible for the training, discipline and general control of the platoons. Other Sergeants were employed in towns and at important railway stations in the Northern range. Their departmental status was at par with that of Sub-Inspectors. They were mainly to teach drill, check beats and assisted in keeping order and regulating traffic. They worked under the instructions from the Inspectors.[27]

The Sergeants were employed in certain towns and at important railway stations.

Sub-Inspectors

Under the Police Circles, there were police stations which fill under the control of a Sub-Inspector who was also known as Station House Officer.[28] The Sub-Inspector was assisted by Assistant Sub-Inspector, Head Constables, and Constables. The number of these officers varied from station to station depending upon the population and the volume of crime. Sub-Inspector was also assisted by the village officers in the discharge of his duty and the latter worked under his supervision. The Sub-Inspectors and officers above this level had the power to file a charge sheet in the court. The Sub-Inspector was in charge of a portion of a *taluk* and was directly responsible for investigation of crimes and police administration falling under his charge.

Head Constable

The Head Constables were employed for general duty in police stations, as station writer, as officer in charge of outpost and also in armed reserves. He acted as Station House Officer in the absence of Sub-Inspector and Assistant Sub-Inspector. He was authorised to hold inquests and made investigations when asked by the Sub-Inspector. He attended to court work under the orders of Station House Officer and investigated cases. He conducted enquiries into petty complaints and took care of arrested persons kept in the police station. He took the approval of Sub-Inspector before leaving the station on routine duty and also took steps for registration and investigation of cases reported under his charge. He also allocated duties to the constables and was in charge of station property, including arms and ammunition and carried out routine work of the station.

The Head Constables formed the main strength of the investigating team. They assisted in the investigation of cases, especially in preservation and collection of clues, like fingerprints, footprints, materials, photographs and also in collection of information, pursuit of clues, arrest of accused and recovery of property, and assisted in searches and seizures. Surveillance of specially marked persons, like known depredators, criminal tribes, and habitual criminals were too a part of their duties.

Constables

The Constable formed the lower ranks of the police force. The Constable was one who had utmost interface with public and he was the most accessible person for the public. Some of the important roles assigned to him were prevention and detection of crime and maintenance of law and order. Their main duties were to perform duties in beats and patrols, surveillance over habitual criminals and other potential criminals, collection of information and intelligence related to crimes and criminals, of rebellious, anti-political agitations, which they promptly communicated to their superior police officers. They maintained relations with local Village Vigilance Committees and of households in the beat area and conveyed information relating to persons and events that acted as potential cause for law and order situation or wide spread disturbances. They also assisted the investigating officers in the matter of arrests, recoveries, searches, identification and securing of witnesses and verification of information, execute warrants and serve summons, escort prisoners and arrested persons, and guard prisoners in custody and the station property. They also performed allotted duties in fairs, festivals, agitations, riots, public assemblies, elections, *bandobust*, and security duties. Enrollment certificate under the seal of the Inspector General of Police was issued to the personnel at the time of recruitment by which he was vested with powers, functions and privileges of a police officer.[29]

Village Officers

The administrative system of village headman and watchman prevailed throughout the Northern range during the British rule. The prevention of crime was among the important duties of the village headman, and he was expected to follow the instructions laid-down under Section 5, Chapter III of the Village Manual.[30] The village headman was responsible to keep watch on crime and collected information about the criminal tribes, which they reported to the police stations.[31] He was representative of the government in the village and had petty magisterial powers. He was responsible for the collection of all the revenue due to government from the village and had to perform a number of miscellaneous administrative duties. The village servants, three in numbers, were under his control — out of three, one was a village policeman, other was a messenger and the third attended to the distribution of water for irrigation.[32] Under the Criminal Tribes Act of 1924, the members of the criminal tribes were registered and were kept in the reformatory settlements of the Northern range and whoever escaped from the settlements was arrested without warrant by any of the police force or village watchman and was produced before the Magistrate. The duty of the village watchman in the Northern range was to watch the movements of criminal tribes and to inform the police stations.[33] Most reports of crime at the police stations were received from village magistrates through *talayaris* than the beat police constables in the Northern range. The main object of the village police system was to secure the co-operation of the public for better performance of police work and for crime control.[34] The village police cooperated with the regular police and also with the village officers to perform the functions efficiently. They also secured the aid of the village community.

The village responsibility was enforced through the village headman, who was assisted by one or more village watchmen. The headman was both the revenue and police head of the village.[35] The village headman was responsible for passing the communication directly to the magistrate and the police in giving information regarding offences and offenders. The other duties of the watchman was to keep watch at night, observe strangers and report to the headman. He also maintained a record of each person in the village and if crime occurred in his village jurisdiction, his business was to detect the culprit. These village officers were liable for punishments for neglecting their duties and, at the same time, they were also rewarded for their good work. [36] The village police officers were regarded as village servants and were subordinate to the headman. They were jointly responsible for the discharge of police duties according to the law.[37]

These village officers were not subordinate to the regular police.[38] The Village Vigilance Committees rendered notable public service. They constituted as a liaison between the authorities and the village populations which contributed in crime control and detection of offences together with rendering better understanding. This was an organisation of voluntary trained social workers who assisted the police during important local festivals religious occasions requiring crowd control and the maintenance of order. There was again an advance in the extent of co-operation of village officers with the police in the prevention and detection of crime in the year 1936.[39]

These statistics have been complied from the information reported by District Superintendent of Police and the growth of this new non-official agency of co-operation with the police, its magnitude and the volume of effective public service which this agency had rendered can be gauged from the below table.

Name of the district	*Number of property cases*	*Number of cattle-thefts*	*Number of offenders arrested*	*Number of gambling cases*
Ganjam	-	-	-	-
Vizagapatam	558	30	37	330
Jeypore	-	-	-	-
East Godavari	1008	41	44	11
West Godavari	413	36	50	55
Kistna	809	39	42	63
Guntur	863	31	14	-
Nellore	352	29	15	-

Functions of the Police Stations

The police station formed the lowest tier of the police executive wing in the hierarchy of the organisational structure. It was a place for the *de facto* exercise of police power and function. The complaints of the public against any crime, and First Information Report were recorded here and petty quarrel cases were disposed off, although in severe cases, temporary detention was ordered. In the police stations, the police force stored arms and ammunitions. The police stations were the foundation of police administration. There were many police stations in the Northern range and each police station was under a Sub-Inspector who was assisted by Head Constables and Constables. The number of police stations in each police circle was determined on the basis of crime, population, area, topography, etc. Each circle had three to 10 police stations. Several records and registries were maintained in the police station which included communication register, case diary, circle information book, annual review of crimes, crime charts, graphs, criminal intelligence files, etc.[40] The police station crime maps were useful for the circle and superior officers to see at a glance the areas in which crime was rife. Gang registers were also maintained where the history of the organised gangs existed; their depredation and organisation were mentioned in them for sake of crime-control data at the headquarters police station.

The police stations were the lowest level in the police organisation where the actual work of the police was undertaken. As the basic and the primary level, they were responsible for maintenance of law and order, prevention and control of crime, and protection of life and property of the Northern range. The police stations were established for a group of villages and were located in *taluk* or in the head quarters or in the important villages in the area of its jurisdiction. The police stations were headed by Station House Officer, who inturn, was assisted by Assistant Sub-Inspector, Head Constables and Constables. The strength of the police force varied from station to station depending upon population and volume of crimes. Village Officers helped the police force in discharging their duties and the Station House Officer worked under the supervision of the Circle Inspector. The police force consisting of Head Constables, Constables and the such other staff was deployed depending upon the beat duties and the crime rate within the station limits.[41] The district headquarters police stations were divided according to the nature of the alloted functions, viz., crime, law and order, and traffic and were classified according to the jurisdiction into I town, town and II town categories.[42] The police stations had an important administrative function to perform and people approached police stations to solve their problems. All the cognizable and non-cognizable crimes were dealt by the police. An offence was placed before the Magistrate by a person directly through a complaint or by the police or by the Magistrate's own knowledge.

The auxiliary police units, such as Criminal Investigation Department, Railway Police, Traffic Police, Port Police, Armed Reserves, Fire services, and the Civic Guards assisted the police department in discharging their duties. The main function of the Criminal Intelligence Department was to deal with the investigation of grave crimes. This department had Fingerprint Bureau and Shorthand Bureau which used scientific methods in criminal investigation. The functions of the Railway Police were to deal with crimes within the railway districts and there was presence of railway police stations and outposts. The Railway Police functions directly under the control of the Deputy Inspector General of Police. The civic guards functioned for ensuring security arrangements during festivals and strikes and also towards traffic control and smooth conduct of political meetings.

Preventive and Punitive Police Functions

Prevention of crime was an important function amongst all the functions performed by the police.[43] Prevention of crime was important for maintaining law and order by overawing the native population. There are some offences where the police has very little preventive powers, especially in case of murder. In the Northern range, large measures of preventive methods were taken by the police force through various legislative Acts.[44]

The subject of prevention of crime would be incomplete without referring to the important branch of it which relates to reform of the criminals.

Regular and efficient patrolling and direct or indirect surveillance over bad characters and habitual offenders were some of the preventive functions of the police administration. Road patrols were enforced through the appointment of *ghat* police force, who patrolled the country roads day and night. Travelling by night was common in the Northern range and road dacoities were frequent offences. To provide safety to the public, road *talariyaris* were appointed on important roads, outposts were established to prevent crimes, roads were made secure, and the police on patrol duties were armed. The police performed the beat duties in the villages and towns for the security of the public as a preventive measure. The method of surveillance consisted of paying a visit to the suspect's house and ascertaining by a personal interview, secret watching, etc.[45] The lightning of the streets greatly improved the prevention of crimes as well-lit streets provided security of person and property.

The police department in the Northern range had taken many preventive methods to control crime. One of the well-recognised methods of preventing offences against property was to take vigorous action against the receivers of stolen property. Whoever persons involved in the matter of stolen property were brought to book. Under the Penal Code, the preventive action by the police force was in relation to an unlawful assembly which cause disturbance of peace. Under such circumstances, the officer in charge of the police station ordered an assembly to disperse, if necessary, by force. With the detection of crimes and offenders, the police prevented occurrence of crime. The people were made aware of civic sense and also about traffic offences. Pamphlets were distributed and stuck on the walls motivating people to report occurrences of crimes and related details for which they were awarded.

Criminal Tribes Act of 1924

Another important preventive measure taken by the police in prevention of crimes committed by the criminal tribes in the Northern range was under the provisions of the Criminal Tribes Act of 1924. The Criminal Tribes Act XXVII of 1871 was introduced in the Madras Presidency which was enacted for registration, surveillance and control of certain criminal tribes and eunuchs. A number of nomadic habitual tribes existed in the districts of the Northern range. Under Section 20 of the Criminal Tribes Act, it was extended to the districts of the Northern range.[46] The main objective of the Criminal Tribes Act was to safeguard the rights of society against anti-social influence and its secondary aim was reformation of the criminal tribes.[47] With the view to reduce organised crimes, and to bring the various castes habitually addicted to crime under control, was the main provision in this Act.[48] Under the Sections 24-26 of this Act, the names and residences of all eunuchs were also registered, as they were reasonably suspected of kidnapping and for committing offences under the Indian Penal Code (Section 377).[49] The Act was amended several times and the final amendments were made in the year 1924.

Under this Act, the government had registered the habitual criminals as criminal tribes and took their fingerprints; such registered members had to report themselves at fixed intervals to a police officers. The purpose was to restrict their movements to a particular area.[50] The criminal tribes in the districts of the Northern range were classified into two types, settled and wandering. The settled earned their livelihood by agriculture labour and were involved in petty theft cases. The wandering tribes moved in gangs and earned their livelihood by hunting and by such crimes as theft, burglary, dacoity, and various forms of cheating.[51]

They had committed many non-bailable offences and so were systematically registered by the police. As they were described as habitual criminals, there was restriction on their movements and the registered members were forced to report on regular basis to the local police stations in the districts of the Northern range.[52] The introduction of this Act has resulted in a considerable decrease in crimes. Whosoever registered member guilty of violating the rules under this Act were punished with rigorous imprisonment for a term of one year for first conviction and with imprisonment of two years for the second one. If they were convicted for more than three times, they were liable for the punishment of whipping. Under the Indian Penal Code, if the registered member committed any crime, he was convicted with rigorous imprisonment not less than seven years. If he was convicted for the third time, he was punished with transportation for life.[53] Their movements were restricted to a particular area under Section 12 and {also subject them to discipline}.[54] The government had instructed the police stations and the headmen of the villages for proper surveillance with the purpose of identifying the criminal communities who were addicted to commission of non-bailable offences. Registration of such members was done by a First Class Magistrate or by a District Magistrate.

In the Northern range, certain tribes were declared as criminals under Section 3 of the Criminal Tribes Act, and the provisions under Section 10 (1) (a) and (b) were applied to the tribes of Donga Lambadis and Donga Yanadis.[55] Under Sections 11 and 16 of the Criminal Tribes Act, specified members of the criminal tribes were restricted in their movement. The working of this Act had resulted in a large reduction of organised crime and crime by habitual offenders in the Northern range. It also enabled villagers, who were afraid of retaliation, to free themselves from the tyranny exercised over them by the criminal communities by way of burglaries and thefts.[56] The Criminal Tribes Act applied to the bad characters and especially to the wandering tribes of the Northern range.[57] The most troublesome criminal tribes were the Donga Lambadis, Donga Yanadis,[58] Donga Dasaries, Donga Yerukalas, Dommaras, Donga Woddars, Jogulas, Donga Yanadis, etc., and they came to be registered under this Act.[59]

The Yanadis were a criminal tribe declared under the Criminal Tribes Act during the years 1913, 1915, 1917, and 1929 as members of the tribes residing in most of the villages in the plains and committing offences. There were 222 males and two females on the criminal tribes registers of the district of Godavari excluding those who were once registered and removed.[60] Donga Yanadis were expert house-breakers, robbers, and dacoits but their gangs were small, unstable and wandering and the villagers dreaded and detested them. They were a bunch of determined characters who were prepared to resist arrest and retaliate by committing fresh crime with increased ferocity when any of their friends were put into jail.[61] Donga Lambadis tribe were mostly seen in the areas of Guntur, Nellore, and Kistna districts of the Northern range. They had committed a number of organised crimes in the Northern range. The Dandasis tribes were declared as criminal tribes by the government notification under Section 3 of the Criminal Tribes Act. Some of the registered members of Dandasis tribes resided in the old Vizagapatnam district, in the areas of Chicacole and Tekkali circles of the old Ganjam district, and Paderu, Rogalu and Gangaraju Madgole stations of the Jeypore police district. On the formation of the new Orissa province, some of these tribal areas came under it.[62] In the year 1937, Dandasis and other tribes of Vizagapatam district were transferred from Ganjam and Jeypore police district under the Sections 3 and 10 of the Criminal Tribes Act.[63]

Under Section 3 of the Criminal Tribes Act, The Oriya Domas and Audiniya Dombsin of the Agency portions of the old Padwa taluk were registered. The Ghasi Dombs, Dandasis, and Donga Yanadies in the plain portions of Chicacole and Tekkali police circles, Mundapottas in Tekkali police circle, and the tribes in parts of Vizagapatam district were specified as criminal tribes.[64] The tribe Nakkalas of the Northern range, registered in the year 1913, had committed a number of house-breaking thefts. The tribes Telaga Pamulas, registered during the year 1917, were professional thieves, burglars, dacoits and jewel snatchers.[65]

The Anipe-malas in Kottapeta station limits, known for burglary and a number of convictions recorded against them, were too registered under the Act. The tribe Dommaras were spread all over the Northern range and they wandered in groups who were by profession acrobats, snake-charmers, ropes and pole-dancers. The men depended more on crime to maintain themselves and they committed dacoity, robbery, burglary, and theft. This range was subjected to incursions by gangs of Dommaras from the Hyderabad state. There were number of registered members in Rajanagaram and Polavaram and some of the tribal members lived by working as agricultural labourers, by rear and sale of pigs and by making mats, etc. The tribes Reddikis, who belonged to a sub-sect of Kapus of the Vizagapatam district of the Northern range, were also declared as criminal tribe. They had acquired a bad name for their rowdyism and riotous behaviour in Cocanada and for their disregard of law and order. Many of them were convicted for various crimes, including robbery, dacoity, house-breaking, and theft in the Northern range.[66]

Yerukalas were also registered under this Act and they were often convicted for minor crimes of house-breaking in the Northern range.[67] The introduction of this Act had resulted in a considerable delcine in crimes against property as will be seen from the following figures: In the year 1924, the crimes against property numbered 1530, and after nearly ten years, in the year 1932, the number of crimes was 1371.[68] The police in the Northern range maintained records of these criminal tribes and their movements were watched. Better registration and surveillance of these tribes by the police had resulted in crime control.

The Madras Registration of Habitual Offenders Act XXX of 1943 was enacted for habitual criminals. The Agency areas of the Northern range were inhabited by these tribes and there were many recorded minor incidents of petty crimes and criminal activities. Fresh registrations under the act numbered 3027, while 3516 numbers were removed from the registers on account of good conduct or on other counts. The provisions of the act were worked with great consideration so as to avoid undue hardship to the members. The restriction under Section 10 (1) (a) of the Act were imposed in suitable cases and to the extent necessary so as to curb the criminal propensity of the active members. Those who conducted themselves properly and proved worthy of the concession, temporary exemption was granted to them and sometimes, they were recommended for entire removal from the registers. The Audiniya Dombs of Jeypore district and Yanadis of Nellore district were registered under Sections 3 and 10 of the Criminal Tribal Act and under Section 11, the movements of Telaga Pamulas were restricted to the plains of Ganjam, Vizagapatam, and East Godavari districts thus preventing them from entering the Agency tracts.[69] The Jogulas and Annaboyinapally Malas were noted for cattle-lifting.[70] The criminal tribes who were convicted were transferred to settlements for the unexpired periods of their sentences for good conduct.[71] Their movements and entry was watched by the village police and reported to the police stations. In cases of good behaviour, registration of certain members were cancelled. Some of the criminal tribes who were not declared in the Ganjam and Jeypore districts under Section 3 of this Act were Dandasis,[72] Donga Yenetis,[73] Munda Pottas, Oriya Dombs[74] of Ganjam district and Dombs commonly known as Audiniya Dombs[75] and Ghasis[76] of Jeypore district.[77] In case of the registered members who led a honest live or were too old or too weak to commit crime, the restrictions imposed under Section 10(1) (a) were relaxed.[78]

Criminal Tribes Settlements and Reclamation

To prevent and reduce the crimes committed by the habitual criminal tribes, settlement and reformatory measures were undertaken by the British government. The preventive and punitive side has always been the concern of the police. This co-ordination and central control was accomplished by creation of a special branch in the Criminal Investigation Department. The Department had administered by a set of common standards and forms for notification, registration and restriction of criminal tribes. Initially, the reformatory settlements were under the missionaries and some private organisations, but later the British government took over. The provision of funds for settling and reclaims of these tribal gangs were met by the local government.[79] The Madras government established and maintained reformatory settlements for the members of the criminal tribes.[80] There were Superintendents to supervise the law and order of these settlements.[81] The reformation movement had made good progress and an Inspector of Police was appointed to establish communal panchayats among the members of the tribes. The communal panchayat system is reported to be working well in most of the settlements, especially among the Dandasis and Panoes of Ganjam district.[82]

There were many pre-existing criminal tribes settlements in the Northern range[83] which continued satisfactorily under the administration of the Commissioner of Labour. There was Stuartpuram settlement and Sitanagaram settlement in Guntur district, and Bitragunta settlement, Bitragunta reformatory and Chintaladevi settlement in Nellore. A criminal settlement at Kalichedu and Kavali were opened in the year 1913 which was later extended to Allur and Bitragunta. In the year 1918, the Kalichedu settlement was abolished and the strength was revised. In the year 1936, the total strength compised of 10 Inspectors, one Charge Sergeant, four Sergeants, 64 Sub-Inspectors, two Havildars Majors, 105 Head Constables, 788 Constables and four *talayaries* for 45 stations and outposts.[84] Under welfare measures, houses were built and land for cultivation and opportunities for alternative livelihood were provided to many of these settlers. Others made a livelihood out of charcoal burning and marketing of their produce. These settlers were reported to be settling down happily after being reclaimed from criminal lives.[85] The administration of the criminal tribes settlements and the reclamation centres was under the charge of the Deputy Inspector General of Police. Agriculture was the main occupation of the settlers in the Sitanagaram settlements and Yanadi colonies. These settlers showed greater interest in agriculture; seeds were supplied free and money advances were given by the Agriculture Department. The industries, like chapli-making, weaving, stone quarrying and manufacture of matches, etc., were carried on in these settlements and the Yanadis took to charcoal making which was remunerative. The health of these settlers was taken care by the rural medical officers and anti-malaria measures were undertaken.[86] Certain members of the following tribes were for the first time brought under Section 3 of the Act and subjected to the provisions of Section 10 (1) (a) and (b) of the Act.[87]

Name of the Tribe	*Area to which restricted*
Donga Woddars	Sitanagaram settlement.
Donga Dasaris	Siddhapuram, Aziznagar and Sitanagaram settlements.
Donga Yerukalas	Siddhapuram, Stuartpuram and Sitanagaram settlements.
Nattam Korachas	Sitanagaram settlements.
Donga Yanadis	Sitanagaram settlements.

The system of "Holding in Abeyance" vide orders issued under rule 10 relative to Section 10 (1) (a) was introduced in the year 1931 in districts of the Northern range. The principles of the system and the manner in which it should work were impressed on the district officers by the Deputy Inspector General of Police during their regular inspections.[88] The criminal tribe members were made to realise that when they showed a tendency to reform, they were encouraged by being given freedom from reporting. The application of the "Abeyance" system of control of criminal tribe members was adequate, and in addition to this, the practice of enforcing joint responsibility among them continued to yield beneficial results.[89] Details regarding the strengths of these settlements and the number of inmates for the year 1927 are furnished below[90]:

Name of the Settlements	*Strength*		
	Men	*Women*	*Children*
Stuartpuram, Guntur	662	588	731
Sitanagaram, Guntur	325	298	372
Bitragunta, Nellore	304	264	521
Kavali, Nellore	189	138	107

The removal of surveillance over wandering gangs during the year 1946 had no perceptible effect on the control of such gangs or on the state of crime and in view of the contemplated repeal of the Criminal Tribes Act, the present practice was continued.[91] There was a marked increase in crime in the year 1947 due to unemployment and abrogation of the Criminal Tribes Act.[92] In the year 1947, the government decided to repeal the Criminal Tribes Act and fresh registrations under this Act and proceedings of registration of individuals under the Habitual Offenders Act was not undertaken. The restrictions imposed on members of the tribes were also considerably relaxed.[93] The Criminal Tribes Act and the Madras Restriction of Habitual Offenders Act were introduced to prevent habitual crimes. With the passing of the Madras Act X of 1947, the application of the provision of the Criminal Tribes Act to the Madras Presidency was suspended, except for the purpose of Section three of the Madras Restriction of Habitual Offenders Act.[94]

Preventive Functions of the Village Officials

The prevention of crime was an important duty of the village headmen in pursuance of which he followed the instruction given in Section 5 of chapter II of the village officers manual. They prevented crime within their jurisdiction and in the neighbourhood by alerts and intelligent watching of the arrivals of the strangers of suspicious character, movements of the members of criminal tribes, known as depredators, and notorious suspects residing in their villages.[95] In each village, there was a village headman to attend to the general administration of the village. The village headman was the representative of the government in the village and exercised petty magisterial powers. The duty of the village headman and watchmen was to give prompt information at the nearest police station about the arrival and departure of members registered as criminal tribes or about those who resided in their village under the Criminal Tribes Act.[96] The village headman was the lowest rung officer vested with criminal justice powers to try ordinary theft cases and was assisted by the village panchayat to dispose of simple civil suits of trivial nature. The village headman was also called as village *munsif*, who under Regulation Act of XI, 1816 was empowered to take cognisance of petty offences. He was empowered to punish the offenders by imprisonment in the village choultry for twelve hours and to the lower castes offenders, by putting them in the stocks for not more than six hours. The supervision and control of the village headmen were entrusted with the Collector or Deputy Commissioner of the range.

The cattle thefts were very common in the districts of the Northern range which caused loss to the community dependent on agriculture. Trackers were appointed by the police on good wages to detect and prevent the cattle theft. As a preventive measure, certificates were issued to the owners of the cattle to prevent the thefts.[97]

Petty civil offences, like property disputes were solved in the villages by the village headmen who had magisterial powers. The Madras Village Lands Disputes Regulation 1816, as amended by the Madras Survey and Boundaries Act 1897, was implemented in the Northern range in case of disputes relating to occupying, cultivating and irrigating of land which arose between the proprietors, renters and their ryots. In the areas of the districts of the range where land revenue was fixed, either permanently or for a term of years, {people who had claims and these} were extended to the Collector of the district in which the lands were situated. With these preventive measures, the police of the Northern range controlled crime in large scale. The District Magistrates and the District Superintendents of Police issued circulars to village officers regarding the proper discharge of their police duties.[98] Madras Act I of 1889, Regulation V

1816, Madras Act VIII of 1840, and Regulation XII of 1816 are some of the main Acts which describe the civil powers of the village heads. To improve the condition of the village police, the Madras Hereditary Village Officers Act, 1895[99] repealed.

Borstal Schools

The main function performed by the police was prevention and detection of crime and punitive work. The Borstal schools were set up for the juvenile delinquents; they were educated and trained in some craft or industrial skills[100] which were beneficial for them on leaving these schools to find suitable employment and lead honest lives. Under Section 562 of the Criminal Procedure Code, the court released certain offenders on the security of good conduct. The term 'Juvenile' has been defined in clause (h) of Section 2, General Clause Act of 1897, as per which, a boy who has not attained the age of 16 or a girl who has not attained the age of 18 were punishable under law for offence under this clause.[101] Under the Juvenile Offenders Act, juvenile offenders were not imprisoned in jails, but instead were sent to the Borstal Schools for reformation. In the year 1940, Juveniles were responsible for many thefts in the districts of Kistna and Guntur. The police had traced all and sent them to Certified Schools for correction. Another case of interest which was recorded in the year 1941 was that of a Kepmari juvenile of the Trichinopoly district, who committed a daring money theft of an amount of Rs. 5000 near the Imperial Bank of India at Bezwada in Kistna district. He was arrested and a major portion of the property was recovered by the police and the accused was sent to Borstal School at Tanjore.[102]

Functions of the Auxiliary Police

The executive functions of the police force were many and it covered every branch of the civil administration.[103] The other important functions of the police force was uniformed patrol, criminal investigation, traffic regulation, taking special measures for controlling commercialisation of liquor, prostitution, and gambling and measures towards juvenile delinquents, etc.[104] The Vigilance Committees in the districts of the Northern range worked as an auxiliary agency to assist the regular police.[105] These committees constituted a liaison between the authorities and the village populations and this helped in the control of crime and detection of offences. The police officers during their tours stressed the village police for their co-operation and the latter were suitably rewarded for their good work. A considerable number of criminal cases were reported by Village Vigilance Committees in almost all districts and the village police and the public also helped the police in decreasing the crime figures.

The special and other auxiliary police had rendered their services in prevention of crime in the Northern range. The special police forces including the Civic Guards, a volunteer police force had rendered their services during political unrest, festivals, traffic control and assisted the regular police. The additional duties of the police had increased enormously with the progress of war and freedom struggle. Control over foreigners, vigilance over lines of communications, anti-British activities and the maintenance of internal security were the extra tasks of the police during 1940s. The threat of invasion by the Japanese forces created new problem of internal security and harbours and naval areas of the Northern range were provided protection. The police had provided valuable services during Quit India Moment of 1942 when they were entrusted with responsibility of guarding telegraph and railway lines; however, these Civic Guards were disbanded in the year 1944.[106] The auxiliary police forces, like Railway Police, Port Police, Criminal Investigation Department had prevented occurrences of offences in the districts of the Northern range.

Several changes were introduced in the police from 1924 to 1947, like formation of an Intelligence Bureau, armed reserves and district reserve units, wireless and motor transport unit and a motor vehicle taxation branch which functioned towards control of crime and maintenance of law and order. An order of the government was passed in the year 1928 for abolishing the grant of money rewards in case of police officials except Constables and Head Constables.[107] This had a significant increase, both in the total number of private individuals rewarded and the amount expended. However, good work by police officers was recognised by grant of good service entries and accelerated promotion, and in case of private individuals, by issue of letters of appreciation or parchment certificates; all these resulted in better prevention and control of crime.

Inspection by the Police Officers

Inspections were an integral part of police duty. The Inspector General of Police and Deputy Inspector General of Police inspected the district police offices in the districts of Ganjam, Jeypore, Vizagapatam, East Godavari, West Godavari, Guntur, Kistna, and Nellore of the Northern range.[108] They also inspected the Criminal

Investigation Department, the Recruits Schools and the headquarters police stations of the Northern range. The Gazetted officers also inspected the police stations of the range. When the general elections were held in the year 1926, there were incidences of disturbances in spite of police *bandobast* but the police handled the situation with firm and tact and restored order.[109]

The work of the Deputy Inspector General of Police during the year 1927 was of a high standard and received the greatest assistance from the subordinate police officers. The work of majority of District Superintendents of Police was satisfactory. F.A. Hamilton was the Inspector General of Police, who visited the districts of Vizagapatam twice. The Deputy Inspector General of Police of the Northern range was in camp for 88 days during the year 1928. He inspected the districts of Nellore and Kistna and parts of Jeypore. He made a long tour in Guntur district and the rest of the districts he could not tour due to railway strikes, viceroy's visit and the activities of the Indian National Congress.[110]

In the year 1928, the Deputy Inspector General of Police made special mention of the Superintendents of Police in the Northern range — they were Martin in Vizagapatam, Sweney in Kistna, Kearns in Nellore, and Beckett for the assistance which they rendered as Assistant Inspector General of Police and Mullaly for his work as Personal Assistant to the Deputy Inspector General of Police of the Criminal investigation Department.[111] Public peace was well-maintained by the police during the period due to better supervision and execution of work by the police force in the Northern range. Crime was well-reported and promptly investigated with several habitual and dangerous criminals arrested by policemen on night rounds and convicted in burglary cases. During the year 1947, the superior officers visited the districts and also inspected the Police Training School, Central Recruits Schools and the Fingerprint Bureau. The year 1947 was eventful as the police had to undertake many difficult and arduous duties, handled all situations with tact, vigour and firmness and its morale continued to be high.[112] The police had dealt with various crimes in the Northern range during the period 1924-47, and their efficiency can be gauged by the cases they had dealt, especially those related to property lost and recovered. The percentage of property recovered by the police in the Northern range during the years 1924-47 is as follows:[113]

Years	*Percentage of stolen property recovered by police*
1924	19
1925	21
1926	24
1927	24
1928	27
1929	24
1930	21
1931	22
1932	32
1933	26
1934	28
1935	29
1936	30
1937	40
1938	24
1939	24
1940	35
1941	33
1942	31
1943	34
1944	35
1945	35
1946	33
1947	33
Average	29

The percentage of stolen property recovered are shown graphically as follows:

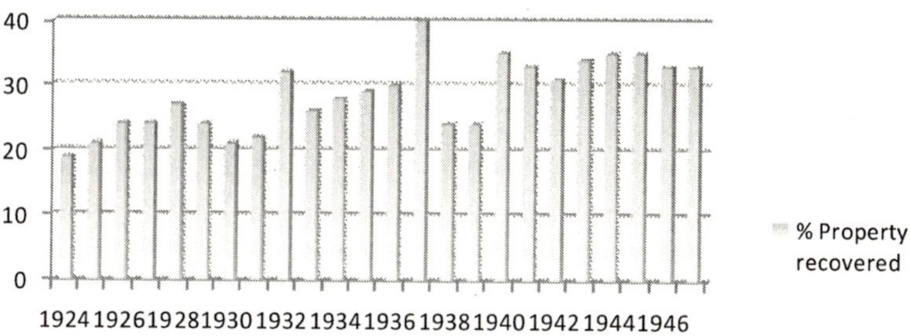

The above graph shows the percentage of recovery of stolen property by the police in the Northern range during this period. The average percentage of recovery of the stolen property was nearly 30 per cent which reflects the good work of the police considering the huge population of the range which was inhabited by large number of nomadic criminal tribes. The value of the property stolen by acts of robbery, burglary and theft are considerable and percentage of recovery varies from district to district in the Northern range. In majority of the cases, the police were unable to recover the stolen goods due to the time which lapsed between discovery of the loss and its reporting to the police station. In most of the districts of this range, the regular criminals melted down the stolen gold and silver jewellery objects soon after theft, and if the loss was not reported immediately, the chances of identifying the stolen property were remote. The police force was overstrained and overworked, abused in the Press and by the public but still performed their duty well, faithfully, loyally and with their morale unshaken.[114]

Discipline and Dismissal

With the enactment of the Indian Penal Code, the Criminal Procedure Code, the Evidence Act and Police regulations, every policeman was bound by these set of codes of conduct, also known as the law of the book, which none could violate. It was in statutory form and published for public use and was enforced by the courts. By the year 1862, these Acts were introduced and with these Acts, the police force was brought under discipline and regulated lines. The discipline of the police force was dealt by the officers of the police department. The entire police force of the Northern range followed all rules which were stated in the Madras Police Act and these rules were from time to time changed in the regulation for good order of their service. The Special Police Forces were also liable to all penalties as the ordinary police officers.[115] The Inspector General of Police was responsible for all matters, viz., training, discipline, promotions, dismissals, internal economy, equipment, etc., related to the administration of the police force in the Madras Presidency. He had the power to frame orders and regulations on the advice of the British government.[116]

The Inspector General of Police, Deputy Inspector General of Police and the District Superintendent of Police had the powers to dismiss, suspend or reduce to a lower post or time scale any subordinate police who was found negligent in discharge of his duties or found unfit or guilty of breach of orders. The certificate of enrollment issued to the police during the recruitment was seized whenever they were not in service due to the aforesaid reasons.[117] {Every police officer was guilty of any violation of duty, willful breach or negligence.}[118] No police officer was allowed to take part in any trade or calling unless permitted and they were not allowed to have money transaction with any other police officer. Any member of the police force was liable to imprisonment for receiving bribes.[119] They were not permitted directly or indirectly to take or receive any present, gratuity or fee without the permission of the District

Superintendent. For such offences, they were liable to a penalty not exceededing six months pay or to imprisonment, with or without hard labour not exceeding six months, or both.[120]

The police were directed not to extort, exact, seek or obtain any bribe or unauthorised reward or consideration by any illegal threat or pretence or by with holding or dealing in any information rendering him guilty for which he was liable for conviction on production before magistrate. They were fined not more than 12 months of pay or to imprisonment with or without hard labour not exceeding 12 months, or both.[121] The police were directed never to prosecute on the basis of a confession alone, but they were allowed, based on the admissions of the accused, to follow up the clue.[122] They were not permitted to use threat or promise.[123]

The constabulary in the Northern range was enlisted on condition of serving and residing wherever it was required, but for practical purposes, the general body was broken into 22 district corps and they worked as separate bodies within the district. The policemen were generally retained within the same district they hailed from. The lower ranks, Head Constables and Constables, were required to reside in lines or hut together in the vicinity of the station house. This arrangement was made for proper discipline and supervision and in order that men were at hand to meet emergency and ordinary duty. The constabularies were granted occasional casual or sick leave by the Superintendent.

The superior police officers of the police department dealt the discipline of the police force. The punishments meted to the police were by conviction before the Magistrates under the Indian Penal Code or else by departmental notice. The police officers who were convicted by a criminal court for any offence were sentenced to imprisonment and they were not readmitted into the service without the special order of the Inspector General of Police. If the police officer was acquitted, he was liable to be discharged from the service on the ground that there was evidence of his being guilty. The departmental punishments were made by assigning black marks in service documents, imposition of fine, reduction in rank and dismissal from service. The enrollment certificates under the seal of the Inspector General of Police were ceased whenever the person stood suspended or dismissed.[124]A suitable uniform was prescribed for all grades of policemen of the Northern range and they were dressed in the uniform at all times. The cost of the uniform to all officers below the rank of Inspector was defrayed at the cost of the government. The articles that were supplied by the government at the time of joining, if were improperly used or damaged by any policeman, the cost of the same were deducted from his pay. From the number borne on his uniform, the Constable could be distinguished from the district force personnel and the division he served, could be identified. They could temporarily remove their uniforms on special orders or for performing special duty.[125] The Head Constable and Constable were supplied with two suits of white drill every year and a woolen coat every third year. In the Northern range, the District Superintendent, Inspectors and their assistants had their own uniforms according to the approved pattern[126]. The different grades of police below Sub-Inspectors were distinguished by the badges they wore on their uniforms. The Head Constables of Crime Branch of the Criminal Investigation Department were supplied with khaki drill shorts and *khaki twill shirts*.[127] At the time of appointment, uniform and other articles were supplied to the police officers at public cost and when anyone left the police force, or was dismissed or suspended, he had to return all the articles and uniforms he had received. When the police dealt with juvenile delinquents, they wore plain clothes and did not use handcuffs.[128] The retired police officers were allowed to wear uniforms on ceremonial occasions.[129] In the year 1945, the government abolished the police forage caps to the uniformed Europeans and the Anglo-Indian Inspectors.[130]

Judicial punishments were awarded to the police for the offences committed in official and private capacity.[131] The members of the police were dismissed for corruption, drunkenness, disorderly behaviour, insubordination, suspicious conduct, for bringing false charges and also for persistence absence without leave. The police for the above offences were punished with deferred black marks, fines, suspensions, censures, depromotions, removals, and dismissals.[132]

The punishments meted to the police force were by conviction before magistrates under the Police Act XXIV of 1859 and the Indian Penal Code or else by departmental notice. No police officer convicted by a criminal court for any offence and sentenced to imprisonment was readmitted to the service without the special order of the Inspector General of Police.[133] All the punishments awarded to the policemen were entered the defaulters book. The police officers below the rank of Superintendent had no power to inflict any punishment except extra drill and confinement to quarters. The police officers who were found to be inefficient were punished with reduction in their pensions or gratuities. In the year 1924, a number of policemen were dismissed due to absence for a long time without prior notice.

In the year 1925, an Inspector was removed from the service for systematic misuse of railway warrants and other irregularities. A Sub-Inspector was dismissed in the Ganjam district of the Northern range for dereliction of duty in a case of murder. The District Superintendent of Police while touring Jeypore district of the Northern range dismissed on charges of corruption two Sub-Inspectors, three Head Constables and fourteen Constables. One of the Sub-Inspectors had been subsequently reinstated by government.[134] The black marks were awarded to many Constables during this year, viz., 1925. The Indian Police Commission had stated in their report that malaise of dishonesty existed in the police.[135] It was observed that this may because the constabulary had more interface with people. The living conditions and poor pay scales were responsible for prevalence of corruption in the police forces. In case of grave offences committed by the police officers, they were judicially punished. They were convicted for offences committed either in their official capacity or in their private capacity. Here is a citation in which the rules were violated. In the year 1925, in the West Godavari district, a Yanadi fellow who belonged to an identified criminal tribe was made forcefully to accept a theft which occurred in a Sub-Inspector's house and later this was proved wrong. For this, the Sub-Inspector was punished with six months rigorous imprisonment and other Constables who worked with the Sub-Inspector were also sentenced to four months of rigorous imprisonment. In the same year, a Constable of Guntur district was fined with Rs. 50 for extorting bribes from bullock cart puller. In Ganjam district, a man suspected to have committed a murder was roughly handled by the police in their attempt to make him confess his crime, during course of which he died. The station police reported the occurrence as a case of suicide; they were subjected to trial in the Sessions Court where they got acquitted. In the Jeypore district, a Constable with a Sub-Inspector on investigation duty, tied up and beat badly a Domb tribal to make him confess and deliver the property. A case was filed on the police in a Sessions Court.[136] In the year 1926, few police officers were convicted in criminal courts of the Northern range in which they were punished along with others who were guilty of bribery.[137]

This shows that the police had not scrupulously followed the police rules at all times.

In the East Godavari district of the Northern range, a Sub-Inspector was dismissed for receiving illegal gratification in the year 1927.[138] The police were not permitted to accept any fees without the permission of their superiors. Another case of dismissal was recorded in the year 1928 in the district of Ganjam where an Inspector was dismissed for misconduct and for inefficient investigation. In the same district, a Sub-Inspector was dismissed for misappropriation of government money.[139] The police were supposed to investigate on the facts and they had to follow the exact clues for investigation.

A Head Constable and a Constable in collusion with the complainant in a buffalo theft case had wrongly confined some Khonds in Nolaghat station of Ganjam district in order to extort confessions. These policemen, charged under Sections 303, 348, and 109 of the Indian Penal Code, were convicted and sentenced to various terms of imprisonment.[140] In the Northern range, cattle thefts were committed mostly by the tribes for the extracting hides and for food consumption.

On 7th September, 1927, Peterson, the Assistant Armourer of the East Coast Special Police ran amok and killed the Havildar-Armourer and the Commandant of the police and later shot himself.[141] The government ordered a joint enquiry by the District Magistrate, Vizagapatam, and the Inspector General of Police. When the facts were disclosed, the government disbanded the East Coast Special Police for lack of discipline.

The British government had given powers to the police force to suppress the freedom movement. The police had taken advantage of this situation during the Civil Disobedience Movement 1932. For instance, Katragadda Rama Sithamma of Megalrajapuram was arrested for celebrating Independence Day and she was fined Rs 400, a hefty sum in those days. Besides this, the Circle Inspectors had forcibly taken away her own gold bangles, six pairs of gold bangles of her daughter-in-law and her son's moveable property. During the same year, Kodali Sriamulu of Marriwada, a freedom fighter was fined Rs 1,000. To realise the fine, the police took away large heaps of paddy and other movable property belonging of his family. In these above cases, the police force had acted against the law.[142] by misusing their powers by unduly extorting the public.

Conditions in jails were very bad as these were over crowded during the period of political struggle. In the year 1932, the police had represented to the Joint Magistrate, Bezwada, to recommend mixed diet to P. Viraraghava Gupta, Nanduri Venkateswararao and Bommidi Narasimham who were convicted and sentenced to one year rigorous imprisonment as a measure of punishment. In the year 1933, a Head Constable of the Guntur district was convicted for causing hurt to a woman with a view to compel to restore the stolen property. For this offence, the Head Constable was dismissed.[143]

In the year 1939, four constables of the Nellore district were fined under Section 342, Indian Penal Code for wrongful confinement of a person concerned in a nuisance case. They were departmentally reduced by a rank for one year.[144] The following are the number of police officers and policemen dismissed in the Northern range during the years 1924-47:[145]

Years	*No. of police officers dismissed*	*No. of policemen dismissed*
1924	5	51
1925	4	43
1926	3	39
1927	3	38
1928	7	74
1929	2	29
1930	1	27
1931	5	21
1932	2	20
1933	1	21
1934	-	19
1935	-	22
1936	-	9
1937	-	11
1938	-	6
1939	1	17
1940	-	15
1941	-	23
1942	2	48
1943	-	36
1944	-	42
1945	-	33
1946	-	29
1947	-	27

The number of police officers and policemen dismissed are shown graphically below:

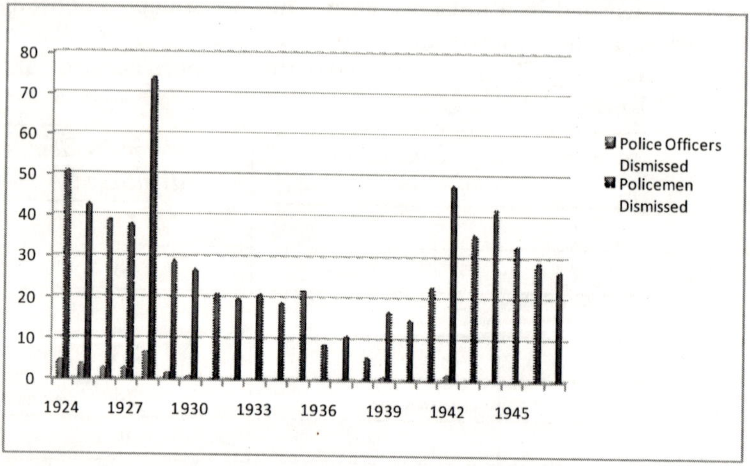

The above figures indicate that the dismissal of policemen in the Northern range was very high in the initial years which gradually declined over the years. The increase in dismissals in the beginning was due to absence without leave. During the following years, instructions were issued to the district officers to use discretion in the matter of granting casual leave. In the year 1925, the number of policemen dismissed departmentally from the Northern range was high and their number gradually decreased towards the end of the year 1947, which was due to improvement in the discipline of the police force.[146] During the year 1925, there was prevalence of laxity in discipline to curb which measures were taken by the Inspector General of Police as a result of which punishment figures fell considerably. Discipline was also well-maintained in the auxiliary police forces and in the East Coast Special Police, during the year 1925, 14 men were fined for absence from duty.[147] In the year 1938 and 1939, there was an increase in the percentage of subordinate officers and many personnel were punished departmentally chiefly due to tightening up of discipline.[148] Inspector General of Police had financial powers under which he issued sanctions to purchase motor vans during the year 1939.[149] In the same year, orders were passed for officers above the grade of Sub-Inspectors for acceptance of money rewards offered by the Customs Department.[150] The Constables central schools for training were established for a group of districts, each school being under a Deputy or Assistant Superintendent who was assisted by a staff of Inspectors and Sub-Inspectors. The training course was for a period of six months and it remained opened throughout the year. They were given instructions in drill, discipline, elementary law, police procedure, etc.[151] To provide healthy diversions in rural areas, games were organised in each district by selected Station House Officers. The practice of granting money rewards to police officers for good work was abolished except to Head Constables and Constables.[152]

The percentage of policemen punished departmentally, which included absence without leave figures, was most frequent. The dismissals and suspensions increased and many were judicially punished for offences committed in their official capacity or for extortion of a very grave character.[153] In one such case, in the year 1930, a Constable of Rajahmundry town station was sentenced to six months rigorous imprisonment for theft of government cash from the station for which he was dismissed.[154]

In the year I932, the British government admitted that excessive violence had been used by individual policemen against Congress demonstrators and picketers, but seldom were officers responsible appropriately punished as that would have been damaging to the morale of the rest of the force. [155] In the year 1939, only one police officer was dismissed in the Vizagapatam and in the same year, one police officer in Guntur district and another in Nellore district were punished similarly. During this period, the discipline in the police force was well-maintained and the dismissal of personnel gradually decreased.

Promotions and Rewards

The direct recruitment to the Indian police was made both in England and in India on the basis of a competitive examination. With establishment of the provincial public services on the recommendation of the Lee Commission of 1924, the Madras Public Service Commission was constituted in the year 1929.[156]

In addition to this direct recruitment, appointments were made to the superior posts in the Indian Police by promotion from the Madras Police Service. The promotions of the police officers were made after departmental examinations, which entailed consultation by the District Magistrate and conveyance of his opinion to the Inspector General of Police through the Deputy Inspector General of Police. The British government organised sports and veteran sportsmen could get easily recruited and conferred promotions whenever they won medals. They were also given recognition and encouragement for their achievements in crime detection and performance of their police functions. Good work done by the police officers was recognised by way of good service entries and accelerated promotions in rare cases.

Constables were promoted to the post of Head Constables as and when due and performance appraisals played a key role in the promotions of the service personnel.[157] To keep up the morale of the police force, the government rewarded with titles and certificates to meritorious Constables and officers for outstanding work performed.[158] To the police officers, only in rare cases, promotion was given in recognition of good work. The British government granted periodical increments to Sub-Inspectors and Constables taking merit and good service into account.[159] The village officers were specially appreciated and handsomely rewarded for their good work.[160] A six months course of training was given in the police training school to the Head Constables selected for promotion as Sub-Inspectors with a view to improve their standard of work and the training provided so proved useful.[161]

Titles, honours, and money rewards were conferred on the police force for their good work. Medals were bestowed on police officers for capturing notorious criminals and for their conduct in dealing with the riots. The titles that were bestowed on police officers were Order of British Empire, Member of British Empire, Rao Bahadur, Khan Sahib and Rao Sahib. The King's Police Medal for gallantry and also for meritorious service, Bar to the King's Police Medal for gallantry, Indian Police Medal for gallantry and for meritorious service, Bar to the Indian Police Medal for gallantry and the Kendall Humanity Medal were medals awarded to members of the force for exemplary valour.[162] The Kendall Humanity Medal was offered by the Executive Committee of the Bombay Humanitarian League.[163] The Indian Police Medal was first time awarded in the year 1932.[164]

The other titles given to police officers and policemen were Kings Police Medal and the Indian Police Medal which were given for gallantry and meritorious services. The British government and some private individuals also gave rewards to police officers, private individuals and members of the criminal tribes for valuable cooperation. At the time of giving these rewards, the necessity of mutual co-operation between the police and the public was impressed upon the awardees. The British government gave rewards to keep up the police morale high and this also protected them from public criticism by emphasising discipline and generating government counter-propaganda in their defence. The good work done by the police officers recognised by way of good service entries and cash rewards was stopped in the year 1938 to all police officers except for Head Constables and Constables.[165]

To private individuals, letters of appreciation and parchment certificates were issued in recognition of their valuable services and for rewards, they were given the choice between kind and cash. The rewards were given to private individuals for increasing public interest in cooperating with the police for crime control. The government, Magistrates, Zamindars, private individuals and other government departments[166] also rewarded the police and public for their good work during the period 1924-47. However, the rewards granted by the District Magistrates were decreased.[167] These rewards were considered as a mark of respect and also encouraged the common people to react against crimes in society. By means of rewards, members of public were spurred for eliciting their cooperation.[168] The following are some of cases of interest from the Northern range during the period 1924-47.

A sum of Rs 100 was offered by the villagers of Koyyalagudem in the East Godavari district during the year 1924 to the Sub-Inspector of that station for tracing and arresting a gang of members who had escaped from criminal settlements and were a source of annoyance to the villagers.[169] The Zamindar of Katravulapalli in East Godavari district presented a silver cup for award to the Head Constable who had performed detective work in the district since the holding up of district sports of November, 1924. In the year 1925, a sum of Rs 100 was offered by the villagers of Koyyalagudem in East Godavari district to the Sub-Inspector of the station for tracing and arresting a gang member who had escaped from the tribal settlement. The police and private individuals were rewarded Rs 650 by the government in connection with a case relating to counterfeit currency notes in the Kistna district in the year 1925 and expressed their appreciation to the temporary Deputy Superintendent of Police, M.R. Ry. Rao Sahib K. Brahmayya Pantulu. In the same year, a reward of Rs 250 was granted by the District Magistrate of Guntur to the villages of Isukatripuravaram for attacking the gang headed by the notorious Yerakala dacoit Kondigadu and killing him and two other members of the gang. A reward of Rs 500 was offered by Zamindar of Udaiyarpalaiyam in the year 1925 for apprehension of Kodukkur Arumugam, which was distributed among one Inspector, six Sub-Inspectors, one Head Constable, four Constables, one Karnam and three private individuals. The Zamindar of Katravulapalli in East Godavari district presented a silver cup for award to the Constable who had performed the smartest piece of detective work in the district.[170]

A reward of Rs100 was granted by the Chamber of Commerce to the Sub-Inspector of the Port Police of Cocanada port in the East Godavari district in recognition of good work done towards prevention of cargo thefts.[171]

A villager and a Yanadi from the Nellore district were rewarded for giving information to the Village Vigilance Committee members about the culprits in case of housebreak and theft.[172] In East Godavari district, a woman was rewarded for her presence of mind in arresting a thief who entered her house.[173]

The Chamber of Commerce, Cocanada, offered Rs 150 to the Port Police for their good work in the year 1928.[174] In the East Godavari district, M.R. Ry. D. Sitaramaswami offered a silver cup to a police officer for good detective work and the Maharajah of Pithapuram paid Rs 100 to a Sub-Inspector for recovering a valuable emerald. In the West Godavari district, parchment certificates were given to 10 persons in recognition of their assistance to the police in the year 1929.[175] In the West Godavari district of the Northern range, a village magistrate personally helped a Sub-Inspector in chasing and arresting criminal tribe members, who had escaped from settlements notwithstanding the fact that his own house had been attacked by burglars on account of his zeal in assisting the police.[176] The village magistrate of Doddipatla in West Godavari district along with his followers jumped into the canal at the risk of their own lives and captured a known depredator and for this, the village magistrate and his followers were suitably rewarded.[177]

Three school students in West Godavari district while returning from school arrested four suspected culprits and handed them over to the police. For this smart work, each boy was gifted with a fountain pen.[178] A woman in the West Godavari district was presented with a golden bangle for her courageous act in holding up a burglar, till the neighbours came, who was escaping after committing burglary. The burglar was arrested by the police with the stolen money.[179]

A reward of Rs 830 was sanctioned to the police officers of Guntur district and the Criminal Investigation Department and Rs 250 to private individuals for rounding up a gang of Erukala absconders from the Sitanagram Settlement, who were responsible for many burglaries in the districts of Guntur, Kistna and West Godavari.[180] A widow of a Constable in the East Godavari district was awarded Rs 3 per mensem for similar act of bravery.[181] One civic guard in the East Godavari district was granted Rs 100 for the arrest of an armed communist.[182] In the West Godavari district, a private individual was awarded Rs 100 for arresting C.N. Lakshmikantham, who had earlier escaped from police custody.[183] In Jeypore district, a group of villagers were rewarded for detection of a case of house-breaking.[184]

An Order of Government was passed in the year 1938 for abolishing the grant of money rewards in case of police officials except Constables and Head Constables.[185] This increased both the quantum of private individuals rewarded and the amount expended therefor. The good work by police officers was recognised by the grant of good service entries and by promotions, while in case of private individuals, this was done by issue of letters of appreciation or parchment certificates. The following are the number of promotions and rewards recorded in the Northern range during the years 1924-47:[186]

Years	*Promotions*	*Rewards*
1924	-	834
1925	-	991
1926	-	1052
1927	-	1151
1928	-	1697
1929	-	1343
1930	-	1869
1931	-	1834
1932	2	1617
1933	-	1069
1934	-	1205
1935	1	1363
1936	-	1576
1937	-	1916
1938	-	1793
1939	3	1084
1940	-	1345
1941	1	1745
1942	-	1921
1943	-	2385
1944	-	2812
1945	-	3149
1946	1	3416
1947	-	3254

The above figures of number of rewards are shown graphically as follows:

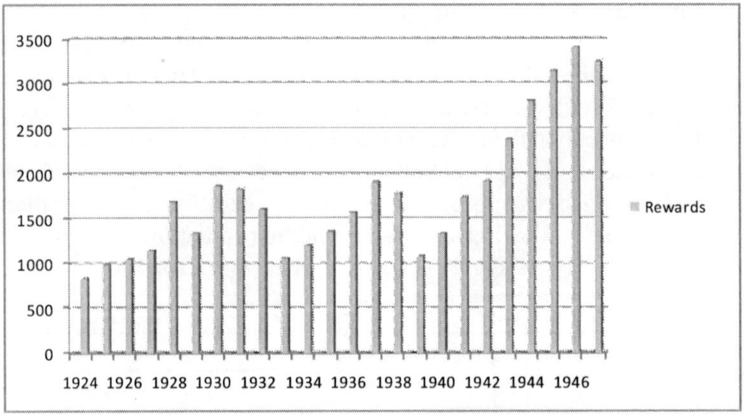

These figures indicate that the rewards were freely granted to the police and private individuals to impress on the public the necessity of mutual co-operation between the police and the public. Due to the liberal and steadily increasing grants from the government, it had become more and more possible to reward deserving policemen and show appreciation of the help rendered by the public. From the graph it can be seen that, the trend in rewards shows a gradual increase, which reflects that the government, private individuals, zamindars, and other public departments had been able to encourage both the public and police for co-operation in crime control. This rewarding system improved the public-police relationship and played an important role in the prevention and detection of crimes in the Northern range.

As for promotions between the years 1924 to 1947, only on five occasions promotions were given, two in the year 1932 in the Vizagapatam district, one in the year 1935 in the West Godavari district, two in the year 1939 in the Vizagapatam district and one in the Guntur district, one in the year 1941 in the East Godavari district, and one in the year 1946 in the Nellore district.

In the year 1927, police force were rewarded by promotion; they were none in respect of the Northern range, although cash rewards were given to 127 policemen in Ganjam, 48 in Vizagapatam district, 45 in Jeypore district, 222 in East Godavari district, 91 in West Godavari district, 183 in Kistna district, 188 in Guntur district and 247 in Nellore district with a total 1,151 policemen receiving these cash rewards.[187]

The rewards were given by the British Government to private persons who assisted the police by providing information. In the West Godavari district, 10 parchment certificates were given to respectable persons in recognition of their assistance to the police in the year 1929.[188] Mostly, rewards given to private persons were distributed in form of some useful articles. The Customs Department had offered monetary rewards to the police officers for their good work and cooperation. The orders of acceptance were passed during the year 1939.[189]

The police department functioned as an important administrative unit under the British rule. The police force in the Northern range helped in checking offences, brought the offenders to justice, collected information affecting public peace, and maintained order in all public places. The police force was the principal arm and an instrument for prevention and detection of crime.

For effective police functioning, the auxiliary police forces and special police forces, such as the Criminal Investigation Department, Railway Police, Traffic Police, Port Police, village officers, village vigilance committees, Armed Reserve Police, East Coast Special Police, and Malabar Special Police had assisted the regular police. The police officers of different cadres had powers and functions to protect the life and property of the people and maintained law and order at different levels at the police divisions of the Northern range. The superior officer toured the districts for better performance of the police administration and these inspections also acted as a restraint on the acts and behaviour of the subordinate officers.

The reclamation and rehabilitation of criminals and criminal communities was one of the functions of police administration. The police took the census of the criminal gangs and communities and attempted to make them settle in particular areas for better surveillance. To control criminal activities of the criminal tribes, reformatories and settlements were established. There were six settlements of which one was managed by the Salvation Army and the rest by the government. Agriculture was the main occupation in most of the settlements. Rural dispensaries were opened in four settlements. Education was made compulsory for school-going children of all settlers. Free mid-day meals were provided by the government in the schools managed by them. Under the preventive functions, the Criminal Tribes Act was passed in the Northern range and a number of habitual criminal tribes of the Northern range were registered under this Act. Their movements were restricted to prevent them from committing crimes. They were confined to the settlements under police surveillance. The British government had maintained criminal settlements and reformatories at various places in the Northern range for the prevention of crimes committed by the criminal tribes. The Deputy Inspector General of Police of the Northern range and the Criminal Investigation Department was entrusted with the supervision and control of all the settlements.

The predominance of natives in the ranks of the police force called for a need to discipline and control the recruited natives to serve the administration. The Inspector General of Police, Deputy Inspector General of Police and the District Superintendents of Police had the powers to dismiss, suspend, reduce to a lower post or time-scale any subordinate police official in case of showing negligence in discharge of duties, on being unfit and found guilty of breach of orders. The superior police officers of the police department dealt with the discipline of the police force and punishments awarded were by conviction before the Magistrates under the Indian Penal Code and by departmental proceedings. The police officers convicted by a criminal court for any offence were not readmitted into the service.

Judicial punishments were awarded to the police personnel for offences committed in their official and private capacity. The members of the police force were dismissed for corruption, drunkenness, disorderly behaviour and insubordination, suspicious conduct, for bringing false charges and also for persistent absence without leave. The police, for these offences, were punished with deferred black marks, fines, suspensions, censures, depromotions, removals and dismissals. The promotions of the police officers were made after departmental examinations after due consultation with the District Magistrate and conveyance of his opinion to the Inspector General of Police through the Deputy Inspector General of Police. The British government organised sports events and veteran sportsmen could get easily recruited and promoted for outstanding achievements. Good work done by the police officers was recognised by way of good service entries and accelerated promotions. The performance appraisals played a key role in the promotions of the police force. The government rewarded meritorious policemen with title, certificates, and promotions in recognition of good work on their part. Titles, honours, medals, and cash rewards were conferred on the police force for their good work and to keep the police morale high. The cash rewards were stopped in the year 1938 to all police officers except for Head Constables and Constables. Village officers were specially appreciated for work of excellence, and in suitable cases, were handsomely rewarded for their commendable work.

Maintenance of law and order imposed a heavy strain on the police with the number of cases of rioting or unlawful assembly rising phenomenally during the period 1925-47. The increase was the result of communal tension, industrial and agrarian labour unrest, and the activities of the communists besides the general crime prevalent.

References

1. Government of Madras, Legal Department, The Madras District Police Act XXIV of 1859, printed by Superintendent, Government Press, Madras, 1937, p. 1.
2. Rushbrook Williams L.F., *India in 1923-24*, Central Publication Branch, Calcutta, 1924, p.73.
3. Government of Madras, Legal Department, The Madras District Police Act XXIV of 1859, printed by Superintendent, Government press, Madras, 1937, pp. 4, 6.
4. *Ibid.*, pp.3, 4.
5. Government of Madras, Legal Department, Act No.XVI of 1927, printed by Superintendent, Government Press, Madras, 1928, p. 20.
6. Gigiraj Shah, *Encyclopaedia of Crime, Police and Judicial System, Vol. I, History and Origin of Indian Police,* Anmol Publications, New Delhi, 1999, p.1961.
7. The Indian Penal Code, 1860, Act No. 45 of 1860, dated 6th October, 1860, pp. 53, 82.
8. Giriraj Shah, *Encyclopedia of Crime, Police and Judicial System*, Vol. I, Anmol Publications, New Delhi, 1999, pp. 1960, 1961.
9. Madras Legislative Council Proceedings, Vol. VII, dated 22nd March, 1922.
10. Report on the Administration of the Madras Presidency for the years 1938-39, printed by Superintendent, Government Press, Madras 1940, p. 28.
11. Handbook of Information on the Administration of the Province of Madras, 1945-46, printed by Superintendent, Government Press, Madras, p. 28, 29.
12. *Ibid.*, p. 30.
13. Chief Secretary, Madras to Secretary, Home Department, Government of India, dated 13th June, 1918.
14. G.O.No. 275, A (S-I)Public (Police) (Confdl.) dated 12th May,1930, Public Department, Government of Madras.
15. Report on the Administration of the Madras Presidency for the years 1938-39, printed by Superintendent, Government Press, Madras, 1940, p. 31.
16. The Imperial Gazetteer of India, The Indian Empire, Vol. IV, Administrative, Clarendon Press, Oxford, 1907, pp. 392, 393.

17. Handbook of Information on the Administration of the Province of Madras, printed by Superintendent, Government Press, Madras, 1947, pp. 28, 29.
18. Government of Madras, Legal Department, The Madras District Police Act XXIV of 1859, printed by Superintendent, Government Press, Madras, 1937, p. 3.
19. Ram Reddy G, and Seshadri K, *Developing Society and Police*, Osmania University, Hyderabad, 1972, p. 112.
20. Abdul Waheed Khan, A *Brief History of Andhra Pradesh*, State Archives, Hyderabad, 1972, p. 112.
21. The Madras District Police Act XXIV of 1859 (as modified up to the 1st June, 1937), p. 4.
22. Abdul Waheed Khan, A *Brief History of Andhra Pradesh*, State Archives, Hyderabad, 1972, p. 112.
23. Handbook of Information on the Administration of the Province of Madras, printed by Superintendent, Government Press, Madras, 1947, p. 30.
24. *Ibid.*, p. 29.
25. Government of Madras, Legal Department, The Madras District Police Act XXIV of 1859, printed by Superintendent, Government Press, Madras, 1937, p. 5.
26. Report of Indian Police Commission 1902-03, printed at Government Central Printing Office, Simla, 1904, p. 140.
27. Handbook of Information on the Administration of the Province of Madras, 1945-46, printed by Superintendent, Government Press, Madras, 1947, p. 33.
28. *Ibid.*, p. 30.
29. Government of Madras, Legal Department, The Madras District Police Act XXIV of 1859, printed by Superintendent, Government Press, Madras, 1937, p. 4.
30. M.R. Ry. Rai Bahadur N Gopalaswami Ayyangar, Collector's Standing Orders of Nellore District, printed by Superintendent, Government Press, Madras, 1931, p. 139.
31. Mishra K.K., *Police Administration*, Mittal Publications, Delhi, 1987, p. 66.
32. Handbook of Information on the Administration of the Province of Madras, printed by Superintendent, Government Press, Madras, 1947, p. 27.
33. The Criminal tribes Act of 1871, Act No. XXVII of 1871, Office of the Superintendent, Government Printing, Calcutta, 1897, p. 12.
34. History of Police Organisation in India and Indian Village Police, published by the University of Calcutta with the permission of the Government of India, University Press, Calcutta, 1913, p. 36.

35. Village Officers Manual, Vol. I, prepared under the Order of Government, printed by Superintendent, Government Press, Madras, 1893, p. 29.
36. *Ibid.*, p. 5.
37. *Ibid.*, p. 40.
38. *Ibid.*, p. 38.
39. Administrative Report of the Madras Presidency for the years 1936, printed by Superintendent, Government Press, Madras, 1937, p. 8.
40. Home Department Resolution No.1112-1120, dated 8th November, 1905, Madras, p. 7.
41. Government of Madras, Legal Department, The Madras District Police Act XXIV of 1859, printed by Superintendent, Government Press, Madras, 1937.
42. Mehartaj Begum, *District Police Administration*, Anmol Publications, New Delhi, 1996, p. 101.
43. History of Police Organisation in India and Indian Village Police, Being select chapters of the Report of the Indian Police Commission for 1902-03, published by the University of Calcutta, Calcutta, 1913, p. 47.
44. The Imperial Gazetteer of India, The Indian Empire,Vol. IV, Administrative, Clarendon Press, Oxford, 1907, p. 393.
45. History of Police Organisation in India and Indian Village Police published by the University of Calcutta, with the permission of the Government of India, University Press, Calcutta, 1913, p. 47.
46. G.O.No.523, Home (Judl.), dated 5th March, 1917, Home (Judicial) Department, Government of Madras.
47. Report of the Criminal Tribes Act enquiry committee, printed at the Government Press, Bombay, 1939, p. 12.
48. Government of Bengal, Criminal Investigation Department, A pamphlet on Gobinda Dom's gang of Hoogly-Burdwan declared under the Criminal Tribes Act VI of 1924, printed by Superintendent, Government Printing, Bengal Government Press, Bengal, 1942, p. 346.
49. The Criminal Tribes Act XXVII of 1871, Office of the Superintendent Printing, 1897, Calcutta, p. 13.
50. The Criminal Tribes Act, 1911, Government of India, a collection of the Acts passed by the governor-general of India in council in the year 1911, Calcutta, 1912, p. 34.
51. Administrative Report of the Madras Presidency for the year 1928, printed by the Superintendent, Government Press, Madras, 1929, p. 5.
52. The Rishi of Bangladesh: A History of Christian Dialogues, Cosimo Zene, published by Routledge Curzon, 2002, New York, p. 169.
53. The Criminal Tribes Act XXVII of 1871, Office of the Superintendent Printing, 1897, Calcutta, pp. 10, 11.
54. The Criminal Tribes Act, 1911, Government of India, a collection of the Acts passed by the governor-general of India in council in the year 1911, Calcutta, 1912, p. 9.

55. Report on the Administration of Police of the Madras Presidency,1932, printed by Superintendent, Government Press, Madras, 1933, p. 22.
56. Administration Report of the Inspector General of Police for the year 1937, printed by Superintendent, Government Press, Madras, 1938, p. 11.
57. G.O.No. 2764, Judl., 23rd November, 1916, Judicial Department, Government of Madras.
58. Administrative Report of the Madras Presidency for the year 1928, printed by Superintendent, Government Press, Madras, 1929, p. 5.
59. Gazetteer of the Nellore district-1938,Vol. A, printed by Superintendent, Government Press, 1942, p. 271.
60. Krishna Swamy Ayyar K.N., Madras District Gazetteers, Statistical Appendix, together with A Supplement to District Gazetteer (1907 for Godavari District) Madras, 1935, p. 344.
61. G.O. No. 2412, Home, dated 9th May, 1928, Home Department, Government of Madras.
62. Letter from E.C. Wood, District Magistrate, Vizagapatam, to the Secretary to Government, Home Department, dated 24th June, 1936, R.C.No.409/36 C-2.
63. G.O.No. 204, Home, dated 16th January, 1937, Home Department, Government of Madras.
64. Fort St George Gazette, dated 12th January, 1937, Part-I, Madras, 1937, pp. 33, 34.
65. Krishna Swamy Ayyar K.N., Madras District Gazetteers, Statistical Appendix, together with A Supplement to District Gazetteer (1907 for Godavari District) Madras, 1935, p. 343.
66. *Ibid.*, p. 344.
67. Gazetteer of the Nellore District-1938, Vol. A, printed by Superintendent, Government Press, 1942, p. 271.
68. Krishna Swamy Ayyar K.N., Madras District Gazetteers, Statistical Appendix, together with A Supplement to District Gazetteer (1907 for Godavari District) Madras, 1935, p. 345.
69. Report on the Administration of the Police of the Madras Presidency, 1927, printed by the Superintendent, Government Press, Madras, 1928, p. 18.
70. Gazetteer of the Nellore District-1938,Vol. A, printed by Superintendent, Government Press, Madras, 1942, p. 271.
71. G.O.No. 290, Home, dated 1st February, 1945, Home Department, Government of Madras.
72. G.O.No.116, Judl.(Police) dated 13th March, 1923, Judicial Department, Government of Madras.
73. G.O.No.28, Judl., dated 15th March, 1926, Judicial Department, Government of Madras.

74. G.O.No. 439, Home (Judicial), dated 16th February, 1920, Home Department, Government of Madras.
75. G.O.No. 1386, L, dated 27 th June, 1927, Law Department, Government of Madras.
76. G.O.No. 2169, L, dated 25th July, 1930, Law Department, Government of Madras.
77. G.O.No. 294, Home, dated 9th January, 1937, Home Department, Government of Madras.
78. Report on the Administration of the Police of the Madras Presidency, 1927, printed by Superintendent, Government Press, Madras, 1928, p. 18.
79. Home Department Resolution No.1112-1120, dated 8th November, 1905, p. 8.
80. G.O.No.2764, Home (Judl.), dated 23rdNovember, 1916, Home (Judicial) Department, Government of Madras.
81. The Criminal Tribes Act XXVII of 1871, Office of the Superintendent Printing, 1897, Calcutta, p. 8.
82. Report on the Administration of the Madras Presidency for the years 1925-26, printed by Superintendent, Government Press, Madras, 1927, p. 31.
83. John Marriott and Bhaskar Mukhopadhyay, *Britain in India, 1765-1905, Justice, Police, Law and Order,* Vol. 1, Pickering and Chatto, London, 2006, p. 227.
84. Gazetteer of the Nellore District, 1938, Vol. A, printed by Superintendent, Government Press, 1942, p. 278.
85. Administrative Report of the Madras Presidency for the years 1936, printed by Superintendent, Government Press, Madras, 1937, p. 28.
86. Administrative Report of the Madras Presidency for the years 1947, printed by Superintendent, Government Press, Madras, 1948, p. 28.
87. Report on the Administration of the Police of the Madras Presidency, 1938, printed by Superintendent, Government Press, Madras, 1939, p. 24.
88. Report on Administration of the Police of the Madras Presidency for the year 1932, printed by the Superintendent Government press, Madras, 1933, p. 22.
89. Report on the Administration of the Police of the Madras Presidency, 1938, printed by Superintendent, Government Press, Madras, 1939, p. 24.
90. Report on the Administration of the Police of the Madras Presidency, 1927, printed by Superintendent, Government Press, Madras, 1928, p. 18.
91. Report on the Administration of the Police of the Madras Presidency for the years 1946, printed by Superintendent, Government Press, Madras, 1947, p. 14.

92. Administrative Report of the Madras Presidency for the years 1946, printed by Superintendent, Government Press, Madras, 1947, p. 22.

93. Administrative Report of the Madras Presidency for the years 1947, printed by Superintendent, Government Press, Madras, 1948, p. 22

94. Report on the Administration of the Police of the Madras Presidency for the years 1947, printed by the Superintendent, Government Press, Madras, 1948, p. 13.

95. Collectors Standing Orders of Anantapur District by M.R. Ry.Rai Bahadur, printed by Superintendent, Government Press, Madras, 1931, p. 139.

96. John Marriott and Bhaskar Mukhopadhyay, *Britain in India, 1765-1905, Justice, Police, Law and Order,* Vol. 1, Pickering and Chatto, London, 2006, p. 354.

97. History of Police Organisation in India and Indian Village Police, published by the University of Calcutta with the permission of Government of India, University Press, Calcutta, 1913, pp. 50,51.

98. Report of Indian Police Commission, 1902-03, printed at Central Print Office Simla, 1904, pp. 143,146.

99. Government of Madras, Legal Department, The Madras District Police Act XXIV of 1859, printed by Superintendent, Government Press, Madras, 1937, p. 1.

100. History of Police Organisation in India and Indian Village Police, published by the University of Calcutta with permission of the Government of India, University Press, Calcutta, 1913, pp. 52,53.

101. The Madras Prison and Reformatory Manual, printed by Superintendent, Government Press, Madras, 1939, p. 1.

102. Report on the Administration of the Police in the Madras Province for the year 1941, printed by Superintendent, Government Press, Madras, 1942, p. 14.

103. Mishra K.K., *Police Administration in Ancient India*, Mittal Publications, Delhi, India, 1987, p. 6.

104. Ram Reddy G, and Seshadri K, *Developing Society and Police*, Osmania University, Hyderabad, 1972, p. 111.

105. Report on the Administration of the Police of the Madras Presidency, 1935, printed by Superintendent, Government Press, Madras, 1936, p. 8.

106. Ramesan N, Andhra Pradesh District Gazetteers, West Godavari, printed by Director of Printing and Stationery at Government Secretary Press, Hyderabad, 1979, p. 161.

107. G.O. No. 2412, Home, dated 9th May, 1928, Home Department, Government of Madras.

108. Report on the Administration of the Police of the Madras Presidency, 1925, printed by Superintendent, Government Press, Madras, 1926, p. 24.

109. The History of the Andhra Pradesh Police 1861-1961, published by Inspector General of Police, Hyderabad, 1961, p. 222.

110. Report of the InspectorGeneral of Police F.A. Hamilton, Madras, dated14th July, 1928.

111. Report on the Police Administration of the Madras Presidency, 1927, printed by Superintendent, Government Press, Madras, 1928, p. 25.

112. Administration Report of the Police in the Madras Presidency for the year 1947, printed by Superintendent, Government Press, Madras, 1948, p. 14.

113. Report on the Administration of the Police of the Madras Presidency for the years 1924-47, printed by Superintendent, Government Press, Madras.

114. G.O.No.485, Public (Police), dated 12th September, 1931, Public (Police) Department, Government of Madras.

115. Government of Madras, Legal Department, The Madras District Police Act XXIV of 1859, printed by Superintendent, Government Press, Madras,1937, p. 7.

116. Ram Reddy G and Seshadri K, *Developing Society and Police*, Osmania University, Hyderabad, 1972, p. 112.

117. Government of Madras, Legal Department, The Madras District Police Act XXIV of 1859, printed by Superintendent, Government Press, Madras, 1937, p. 5.

118. Government of Madras, Legal Department, Madras District Police (Amendment) Act XXI of 1936, printed by Superintendent, Government Press, Madras, 1937, p. 4.

119. Second Report of the Indian Penal Code, W. Ridsdale Military Orphan Press, Calcutta, 1847, p. 35.

120. Government of Madras, Legal Department, The Madras District Police Act XXIV of 1859, printed by Superintendent, Government Press, Madras, 1937, p. 7.

121. *Ibid.*, p. 8.

122. Section 27 of the Evidence Act, 1882, printed by Superintendent, Government Press, Madras.

123. G.O.No.275, A (s-1) Public (Police), Confdl., 4th May, 1930, Public (Police), Department, Government of Madras.

124. Government of Madras, Legal Department, The Madras District Police Act XXIV of 1859, printed by Superintendent, Government Press, Madras, 1937, p. 4.

125. *Ibid.*, p. 6.

126. Royal Commission on Public Service in India, Appendix to the Report of the Commissioners, Vol. XIII, Police Department, London, 1915, p. 172.

127. G.O.No.3024, Home (Ms), dated 19th October,1945. Home Department, Government of Madras.

128. G.O.No 2041, 28th April, 1941. Home Department, Government of Madras.
129. G.O.No.4225, Home (Ms), dated 7th August1939. Home Department, Government of Madras.
130. G.O.No.2665, Home (Ms), dated 6th August, 1945. Home Department, Government of Madras.
131. Report on the Administration ofthe Police ofthe Madras Province,1939, printed by Superintendent, Government Press, Madras, 1940, p. 4.
132. Report on the Administration of the Police in the Madras Province for the year 1941, printed by Superintendent, Government Press, Madras, 1942, p. 51.
133. Maclean C.D., Manual of the Administration inMadras Presidency, Vol. I, Asian Educational Services, New Delhi, 1987, p. 189.
134. Report on the Administration of the Police in the Madras Presidency, 1925, printed by Superintendent, Government Press, Madras, p. 3.
135. Report of the Indian Police Commission, 1902-03, Government Central Printing Office, Simla, 1904, p. 21.
136. Police Administrative Report of the Madras Presidency, 1926, printed by Superintendent, Government Press, Madras, 1927, p. 4.
137. G.O.No.567, Home, 28th August, 1926, Home Department, Government of Madras.
138. Report on the Administration of the Police in the Madras Presidency, 1927, printed by Superintendent, Government Press, Madras, 1928, p. 3.
139. Report on the Administration of the Police inthe Madras Presidency, 1928, printed by Superintendent, Government Press, Madras, 1929, p. 4.
140. Report on the Administration of the Police in the Madras Presidency, 1927, printed by Superintendent, Government Press, Madras, 1928, p. 4.
141. G.O.No.467, Judicial, dated 25th September,1928, Home Department, Government of Madras.
142. Venkatarangaiya M, *The Freedom Struggle in Andhra Pradesh (Andhra)*, Vol. IV, The Andhra Pradesh state committee, Hyderabad, 1974, p. 335
143. Report on the Administration of the Police in the Madras Province, 1933, printed by Superintendent, Government Press, Madras, 1934, p. 4.
144. Report on the Administration of the Police in the Madras Province,1939, printed by Superintendent, Government Press, Madras, 1940, p. 4.
145. Report on the Administration of the Police in the Madras Presidency for the years 1924-47, printed by Superintendent, Government Press, Madras.

146. Police Administrative Report of The Madras Presidency 1940, printed by Superintendent, Government Press, Madras, p. 48.
147. Report on the Administration of the Police of the Madras Presidency, 1925, printed by Superintendent, Government Press, Madras, 1926, pp. 3,7.
148. Administrative Report of Madras Presidency 1940, printed by Superintendent, Government Press, Madras, 1941, p. 12.
149. G.O.No.2427, Home (Ms), dated 2nd May, 1939, Home Department, Government of Madras.
150. G.O.No.2617, Home (Ms), dated 11th May, 1939, Home Department, Government of Madras.
151. Report of Indian Police Commission 1902-03, printed at Government Central Printing Office, Simla, 1904, p. 143.
152. Madras in 1938, printed by Superintendent, Government Press, Madras, 1939, p. 18.
153. Report on the Administration of the Police of the Madras Province, 1924, printed by Superintendent, Government Press, Madras, 1925, p. 6.
154. Report on the Administration of the Police of the Madras Province, 1930, printed by Superintendent, Government Press, Madras, 1931, p. 4.
155. G.O.No. 600, Public (Police), 7th November, 1932, Home Department, Government of Madras
156. Handbook of Information on the Administration of the Province of Madras, 1945-46, printed by Superintendent, Government Press, Madras, 1947, p. 97.
157. James Vadackumchery, *National Police Commission*, Alph Publications, New Delhi, 1998, p. 14.
158. G.O.No .765, Public Police, dated 1st July, 1932, Home Department, Government of Madras.
159. Report on the Administration of the Police of the Madras Province, 1936, printed by Superintendent, Government Press, Madras, 1937, p. 1.
160. Collectors standing orders of Nellore District by M.R. Ry.Rai Bahadur, printed by Superintendent, Government Press, Madras, 1931, p. 140.
161. Report on the Administration of the Police of the Madras Province,1946, printed by Superintendent, Government Press, Madras, 1947, p. 14.
162. Report on the Administration of the Police of the Madras Province,1939, printed by Superintendent, Government Press, Madras, 1940, p. 4.
163. G.O.Ms.No.5214, Home, dated 30th September, 1939, Home Department, Government of Madras.
164. Report on the Administration of the Police in the Madras Presidency for the year 1932, printed by Superintendent, Government Press, Madras, 1933, p. 28.

165. G.O No.2412, Home, dated 9th May, 1938, Home Department, Government of Madras.
166. Report on the Administration of the Police of the Madras Presidency, 1925, printed by Superintendent, Government Press, Madras, 1926, p. 46.
167. *Ibid.*, p. 7.
168. Report on the Administration of the Police of the Madras Presidency, 1928, printed by Superintendent, Government Press, Madras, 1929, p. 5.
169. Report on the Administration of the Police of the Madras Province, 1925, printed by Superintendent, Government Press, Madras, 1926, p. 2.
170. *Ibid.*, p. 5.
171. Report on the Administration of the Police of the Madras Province, 1924, printed by Superintendent, Government Press, Madras, 1925, p. 24.
172. Report on the Administration of the Police of the Madras Province, 1938, printed by Superintendent, Government Press, Madras, 1939, p. 5.
173. Report on the Administration of the Police of the Madras Province, 1927, printed by Superintendent, Government Press, Madras, 1928, p. 5.
174. Report on the Administration of the Police of the Madras Province, 1928, printed by Superintendent, Government Press, Madras, 1929, p. 6.
175. Administrative Report of the Madras Presidency, 1929 printed by Superintendent, Government Press, Madras, 1930, p. 6.
176. Police Administrative Report of the Madras Presidency, 1925, printed by Superintendent, Government Press, Madras, 1926, p. 7.
177. Administrative Report of the Madras Presidency, 1928, printed by Superintendent, Government Press, Madras, 1930, p. 5.
178. Administrative Report of the Madras Presidency for the year 1928, printed by Superintendent Government Press, Madras, 1929, p. 5.
179. *Ibid.*, p. 7.
180. Report on the Administration of the Police of the Madras Province, 1933, printed by Superintendent, Government Press, Madras, 1934, p. 5.
181. Report on the Administration of the Police of the Madras Province,1939, printed by Superintendent, Government Press, Madras, 1940, p. 5.
182. Report on the Administration of the Police of the Madras Province, 1941, printed by Superintendent, Government Press, Madras, 1942, p. 4.
183. Report on the Administration of the Police of the Madras Province, 1933, printed by Superintendent, Government Press, Madras, 1934, p. 47.

184. Report on the Administration of the Police of the Madras Province, 1927, printed by Superintendent, Government Press, Madras, 1928, p. 5.
185. G.O. No. 2412, Home, dated 9th May, 1938, Home Department, Government of Madras.
186. Report on the Administration of the Police of the Madras Presidency for the years 1924-47, printed by Superintendent, Government Press, Madras.
187. Inspector General of Police Report for the year 1927, printed by Superintendent, Government Press, Madras, 1928.
188. Administrative Report of the Madras Presidency for the year 1929, printed by Superintendent, Government Press, Madras, 1930, p. 6.
189. G.O.No.2617, Home (Ms), dated 11th May, 1939, Home Department, Government of Madras.

4

Crimes and Offences

The word crime has been derived from Latin word meaning 'to accuse'. The Sanskrit root verb of crime is 'Kri' which means 'to act'.[1] The concept of crime has been different at different places and at different times. The subject of crime has varied interpretations, but at the bottom of it, crime is nothing but a failure to live up to the recognised standards of the society. Social life is maintained by the preservation and maintenance of law and when these laws are jeopardised, the society refers them as commitment of crimes.[2] So, violation of law is failure to live up to the recognised standards of the community and it becomes a crime. When offence is committed, a punishment is awarded to eliminate the wrongdoers from the society. In general, the term crime is defined as an act punishable by law. The punishments for offences in India included fines, imprisonment, transportation of life, and death sentences, among others.[3]

The Indian Penal Code was drafted in the year 1860, and came into force in the year 1862 in the Northern range of the Madras Presidency. Lord Macaulay was the chairman of the drafting committee of the Indian Penal Code that was based on the laws of England. There was no particular definition of crime in the Indian Penal Code. The distinction is made by classifying the crimes into two types, cognizable and non-cognizable offences. Under cognizable crimes, the police made inquiries into a case when reported or it came to their notice and the crime was investigated by the police without reference to magisterial authority. Non-cognizable crimes were investigated by the police only after receiving orders from the magistracy. There were some cases of crimes under the Indian Penal

Code where prosecution could not be launched unless a complaint was made by the aggrieved party. In case of serious crimes, the government takes initiative to punish the wrong doer by initiation of criminal proceedings. The punishments are awarded to the wrongdoers through the rules of Indian Penal Code.[4]

The main functions of law in the society are to preserve stability and ensure security against disorder.[5] The police functions according to the rule of law for maintaining law and order.

The crime can be classified into professional, organised, spontaneous, and instantaneous.[6] The common crimes in the Northern range were murder, dacoity, robbery, theft and other case like cheating, forgery, counterfeit of currency, infanticide, culpable homicide, rapes, etc. The motives for these crimes were socio-economic reasons, communal causes, factional fights, family disputes, sexual jealousy, etc. The police in the Northern range dealt with a variety of crimes related to political, socio-economical and religious offences, such as factional riots, labour troubles, agrarian strikes, communal tensions, and other offences. The police force was an important arm of the British government for preservation of order and enforcement of law.[7] The crime was checked in two ways, by preventive means and by exemplary punishment.[8] Police was a sub-system in criminal justice system. [9] In the Northern range, during the period 1924 to 1947, along with the general crimes, the police also dealt with the political unrest caused by the Freedom Movement.

Mode of Collecting Crime Statistics

To have a better centralised control of the districts, the British government had introduced the practice of collection and collation of crime statistics. The statistical crime data on all offences were collected from the districts of the Northern range. The compilation of statistics had begun in the early part of the nineteenth century, but detailed statistical compilation was not done until the latter half of the century. This period, 1924-47, also saw filing of regular returns of crime statistics by the Madras police. The crime statistics were used as a tool of management to understand the cause of crime and as an index of efficiency of the police organisation. The crime data collected from the districts indicated action taken under various Sections of the Indian Penal Code and the Criminal Procedure Code. The crime and organisational statistics gave the District Superintendent of Police and higher police officers a clear idea on the state of law and order throughout the districts of the Northern range. The reports and crime figures gave the British police supervisory officers at the district headquarters a clear picture of the developments in the range. To overcome the outbreaks of the crime, the beat and patrol system were altered and special parties of police were organised in the Northern range under the Madras Police Act of 1859. A system of classification of crime and criminals was based on the lines of the *mofussil* system and it was modified to suit the city conditions restricting itself only to house-breaking and house-thefts. This system was introduced by Inspector General of Police, Hamilton, to maintain a regular record of professional crimes and criminals and to assist investigating officers in the prevention and detection of crime.[10]

The police stations maintained all the records related to crimes and criminals in their concerned jurisdictions.

The crime records containing criminal history of individuals and localities were maintained for each village for effective control of crimes in the villages.[11] For statistics under the crime and offences, the government relied on the police department. Crimes were first reported to the police station, either by the magistrate or by the beat constable, or by the complainant. Thereafter, First Information Report was prepared which was the first step taken by the police before investigation. The occurrences was first entered in the station house register and the police station house officer reported it to the police headquarters and the divisional Inspector. The crime reports were checked daily in the district office and arranged according to the divisions and the classes of offences. The crime charts, registration of known depredators and other habitual criminals were recorded and preserved. Each division Inspector kept a crime register and entered all the crimes reported daily to the station house. On the first of each month, the Inspector prepared an extract from his crime register. The crime extracts received from the Inspectors were compared in the headquarters office with the crime reports already filed. The objections and differences were noted from the extracts and reports, and then the crimes were ledgered. A revised curriculum of training for Sub-Inspectors, designed to concentrate attention upon the practical and scientific investigation of crime on modern lines, was introduced in the year 1939.[12] To systematically deal with spurt in the crime rate, the beat and patrol systems were altered and special parties of police were organised, which resulted in important captures.

Types of Offences

The word 'offence' is denoted as an act which was made punishable under the Indian Penal Code. An offence committed by a person was liable to punishment under this Code. An act done by a person, whether intended or unintended, which caused death or grievous hurt or any damage or lost of property without permission of the owner, was said to be an offence under this Code. The things done in the exercise of the right of private defense was not an offence.[13] The punishments to the offenders under the provisions of the Indian Penal Code were fine, death sentence, imprisonment, and transportation of life, among others. The punishments were rigorous with sentence for hard labour while the other one was simple imprisonment. The fines were of two types, individual and collective. The usual offences in the Northern range were murder, dacoity, robbery, housebreaking, cattle-theft, political, social, economical and communal, etc.[14]

Under various Sections, such as 238, 302, 303, 392 to 399, 402, 449 to 452, 454, 455, 457 to 460 of the Indian Penal Code, different offences were dealt. The offences, like murder was dealt under Sections 302, and 303, dacoity under Sections 395, 396, 399, and 402, robbery under Sections 392, 393, 394, 397,and 398, house-breaking under Sections 449 to 452, 454, 455, and 457 to 460, of the Indian Penal Code.[15] Under the Madras Children Act of 1920, the juvenile and adolescent offenders were sent for detention to the Borstal schools where they were provided proper custody, education, and training.[16] The police of the Northern range also dealt crimes under the Arms Act, Gambling Act, Excise Act, Prohibition Act, Explosives Act, Immoral Traffic Act, Indian Railway Act, Indian Passport Act, Forest Act and others Acts.

The motives for crimes were social, economical, political and religious. Most of the murders in this range were related to family disputes and sexual jealousies,[17] whereas dacoity, housebreaking, and cattle theft were mainly for economic reasons. In the Northern range, the people responded greatly to the freedom struggle through agitations and participated in the national movement for the Indian independence which resulted in political unrest in the range. Communal riots and disturbances between the religious groups also contributed to crimes in the Northern range. Crime is always committed in one form or another and the type and magnitude of crime varies from place to place. The Northern range was no exemption to crime as this range was vast, highly populated, economically rich, and most of the range was Agency area.

The government had ordered the police for surveillance of dangerous criminals[18] throughout India and in the year 1911, the Criminal Tribes Act XXVII of 1871 was introduced in the Madras

Presidency. Under this Act, some of the wandering tribes who committed various types of crime, both intra- and inter-range, were notified as habitual criminals. In the year 1913, the nomadic tribes, viz., the Yerukulas, Yenadis and others tribes of the Northern range were brought under this Act.[19] The Criminal Tribes Act final amendment was made in the year 1924 under the British government order for improving the surveillance over these tribes.[20] The reasons for these tribes to commit crimes were lack of property, vagrancy, wanderlust, lack of stability and general purpose in life, restlessness, and aimlessness. The classification of crime and restriction on the movements of habitual criminals had controlled the crime in the Northern range.[21]

Major portion of the Northern range was covered with agency tracts and the forest offences, such as theft and smuggling of the forest products were common as forest produce was the property of the government.[22]

Theft or destruction of the government property, such as public buildings, telegraphic lines, railways, roads were regarded as an offence and these were protected by the police force. The offences related to the railways were thefts in running passenger trains, passenger sheds, goods shed and yards, mail and luggage vans and railway materials and these offences were dealt by the Railway police.[23] To deal with these offences, several railway police stations and outposts were established in the Northern range. In the harbour areas of Coconada, Machillipatam, and Vizagapatam, the offences were house thefts, cycle thefts and stealing scrap iron and brass material which were dealt by the Port Police. Special Police Forces were organised in the Northern range for guarding and for protection other property, like such as telegraphic lines, bridges, roads and highways.

Under the Madras Children Act 1920, nothing was an offence committed by a child less than twelve years of age.[24] The girl juvenile delinquent, when arrested or remanded or committed for trial, were not detained under police custody. The magistrate decided the place of custody for the girl juvenile delinquent; he would put such child under the custody of any person, who in his opinion, would produce her at the time of hearing. In exercising police powers under such cases, the police officers wore plain cloths and they did not use handcuffs.[25] A majority of crimes committed by an adult had a background of some delinquent behaviour in their childhood or young age.[26]

The main functions of the police administration were preventive, detective and punitive in nature.[27] Punishments for crimes and offences were dealt under the Indian Penal Code, Criminal Procedure Code, Civil Procedure Code, Evidence Act and other Acts. The police officer without orders from a magistrate and without a warrant, could arrest any person against whom suspicion existed of his having been associated with any offence punishable with imprisonment. The following are the different types of crimes in Northern range which had occurred during the period 1924-47.

Theft

This is an offence related to property: whoever, intending to take dishonestly any moveable property out of possession of any person without that person's consent was said to commit theft. The punishment awarded to the culprit for theft was imprisonment for a term of three years or fine or both.[28]

Sometimes, the culprit was punished with imprisonment for a term of seven years and was also liable to fine depending upon the intensity of the theft. In the Northern range, most theft cases were those relating to jewellery, lifting cycle, pick-pocketing and thefts of telegraph and telephonic lines.

Cattle were valuable property of the people, especially to the agricultural classes in the Northern range and cattle thefts were very common in this range. Cattle theft caused very serious loss, both direct and indirectly, to the community mainly dependent upon agriculture. Cattle were stolen for their hide, out of personal jealousies, for consumption and extortion purposes.[29] Sometimes the cattle were poisoned due to personal jealousies. These offences were mostly committed by the wandering tribes in the Northern range. Such offenders were punished under Section 215 of the Indian Penal Code.[30] Most of the cattle thefts in this range were committed by members of the criminal tribes. The tribes Dombus of Jeypore district were famous for commiting cattle thefts with intention of skin extraction. The system of branding with distinctive letters and numbers on the skins of cattle which had died a natural death, or had been honestly killed, and the possession by the tribals, skin merchants or others of unbranded skins, was considered as suspicious and such people were arrested by the police.[31] The Lambadis in the districts of East Godavari, Kistna, and Guntur was accounted for cattle thefts during the year 1933.[32] The introduction of this system had resulted in the decrease of incidences of cattle theft in most of the districts of the Northern range.

The annual numbers of thefts were large in this Northern range as this range contained many nomadic castes and tribes whose hereditary occupation was crime. Vast illiterate population with low standard of living, less earning abilities and opportunities, unemployment, and high prices of foodgrains were also a motive for the theft. Cattle theft was widely prevalent form of crime in the Northern range as it contained vast agency tracts along with many habitual criminal tribes whose main occupation was crime. Number of cases of thefts and cattle-thefts in the Northern range during the years 1924 to 1947 are shown in the table below:[33]

Years	*Thefts*	*Cattle-thefts*
1924	5322	578
1925	5119	494
1926	4999	595
1927	5146	699
1928	4914	605
1929	5054	575
1930	4919	594
1931	4893	567
1932	4401	450
1933	4271	446
1934	4276	414
1935	4228	499
1936	3442	479
1937	3699	537
1938	3738	548
1939	3698	568
1940	3995	575
1941	3825	539
1942	3983	596
1943	4022	569
1944	4113	510
1945	4127	507
1946	4932	546
1947	5573	599

The number of theft and cattle-theft cases are shown graphically as follows:

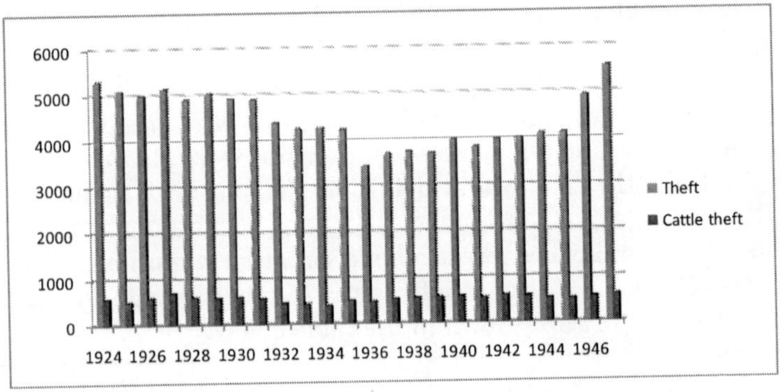

The above graph illustrates the cases of thefts, which were high in numbers for the decade 1924 to 1934; thereafter, these cases show a sharp decrease while during the later years, there was a steep increase in these cases. During the years of war, there was a huge demand for hides and this effected in the increase of cattle thefts. The high increase in the initial years was due to economic stress, agrarian disputes, famine conditions, and unfavourable seasonal conditions. Some increment was also due to the rise in the prices of foodgrains. With better reporting and registration of crimes and due to the measures taken by the police, the number of cases decreased in the middle years. In the tail years, the increase in cases was due to political unrest caused as a result of the freedom struggle.

The graph also shows the number of cases of cattle thefts remained steady throughout the period. These cattle thefts were mostly due to occurrence of famine conditions and were committed by criminal tribes. The reason for the cases of cattle thefts being less in number was because the government issued orders to the District Magistrates in the Northern range to give deterrent sentences to these offenders. The criminal tribes of the Northern range were organised criminals who committed a number of crimes in the range. The following are some of cases of interest regarding theft in the Northern range during the period 1924-47.

Here is a theft case which shows how the police were able to find the culprit after a year of committing the offence. In the year 1935, theft occurred in the Nurses' quarters at Mission Hospital in the Nellore district in which the property stolen was a ring. No evidence was found and the case remained undetected for some time. In the year 1936, the owner of the ring noticed her property being sold in a shop in Nellore town, as such, she informed the police who seized the ring. The police with the aid of the Fingerprints Bureau were able to catch the offender who was a servant in the hospital and he was convicted.[34]

A peculiar case was recorded in the year 1933: A Kabuli trader in the Jeypore district, unable to recover money from a local merchant, beat the latter and his wife and took away the merchant's two young sons and sold them to a *Muttadar* of that place for Rs 200. The *Muttadar* was convicted under Section 370, Indian Penal Code and the Kabuli under Sections 394, 342 and 323[35] as possession of any stolen property was considered as an offence under the Indian Penal Code.

The criminal tribes of the Northern range had committed many offences, both organised and unorganised. In the Vizagapatnam district, a gang of prisoners belonging to Telaga Pamula tribe acting in concert, suddenly attacked their escort and thirteen of them escaped after stealing a police carbine and injuring the Constables.[36] Later, they were caught and convicted.

Under the Juvenile Offenders Act, the juvenile offenders were not imprisoned in the jails, but were instead sent to the Borstal Schools for reformation. In the year 1940, juveniles were responsible for many thefts in the districts of Kistna and Guntur. The police traced all of them and sent them to Certified Schools for correction. Another case of interest which was recorded in the year 1941 was a Kepmari juvenile of the Trichinopoly district who committed a daring monetary theft of Rs 5000 near Imperial Bank of India at Bezwada in Kistna district. He was arrested and a major portion of the property was recovered by the police and the accused was sent to Borstal School at Tanjore.[37]

Robbery

In the offence of robbery, it could be either a case of theft or extortion. A person who commits robbery is one who in presence of a person, by putting him in fear of death or hurt then and there, carries away things by force. Punishment laid down for committing robbery was rigorous imprisonment for a term of ten years, with or without fine. In the Northern range, cases of robbery were highway robberies, field robberies, house robberies, and mail robberies. In case of robbery committed on highway between sunset and sunrise, the imprisonment was extended to fourteen years.[38] The distinct rise in the number of reported robbery cases vis a vis dacoity was due to economic conditions, activities of the criminal tribes, failure of crops, floods, and unemployment in almost all the districts of the

Northern range. Number of cases of robbery in the Northern range during the years 1924 to 1947 are shown in table given below:

Years	*Robbery*
1924	242
1925	161
1926	146
1927	163
1928	126
1929	117
1930	144
1931	120
1932	139
1933	135
1934	89
1935	99
1936	80
1937	65
1938	92
1939	64
1940	71
1941	64
1942	64
1943	89
1944	69
1945	50
1946	48
1947	76

The number of robbery cases are shown graphically as follows:

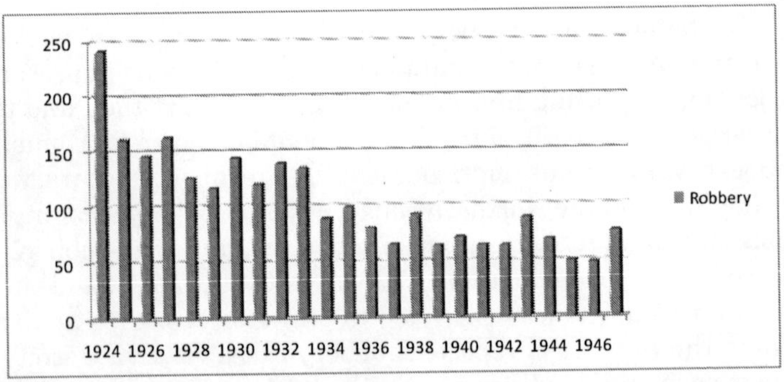

The above graph explains the cases of robbery and it can be seen therefrom that the number of cases were more in the initial years, but over the period, these cases gradually decreased. The increase in robbery cases in the initial years was due to the activities of the criminal tribes. The most notorious among them were responsible for many highway robberies. With strict enforcement of the Criminal Tribes Act and better reporting by the public, the crime figures showed a decline. The police organised day and night patrols in lookout for suspicious loafers at public places, such as parks, markets, cinemas, bus-stands, and railway stations. At times, a Constable from the central crime station was deputed to watch these public places and due to these organised measures, the cases of robbery decreased over the years. The following are some of the cases of robbery of interest in the Northern range during the period 1924 to 1947.

In the year 1932, a large gang of twenty people had attacked the house of a banker with arms in Garagaparu village of the West Godavari district in the Northern range and looted six lakh rupees. All the twenty offenders were arrested by the police and an amount of five lakh rupees was recovered.[39] Another case occurred in the year 1936 at Pittapur in the East Godavari district in which robbers broke into the house of a middle-aged woman, slit her tongue, inflicted serious wounds on her and stole all her jewellery. In the same year, three local Yenadis tribals had committed a mail-robbery in the district of Nellore; later, the police had arrested all of them and the culprits were convicted in the court.[40] Another case of mail-robbery in the Guntur district of the Northern range was recorded in the year 1941 where a mail-runner carrying mails from Santhamanagar Railway station was attacked and was robbed cash worth Rs 100.[41]

In the year 1939, a case was recorded where a female coffee hotel keeper in the Nellore district robbed an eight years old girl of her jewels worth Rs 101. She had locked the girl in a room in the hotel. A *komati* boy heard the cries and rescued the girl. The woman was arrested and sentenced for transportation for life.[42] The above are some of the cases of interest recorded in the districts of the Northern range during the period 1924-47.

Dacoity

Dacoity was the legal term used by the British in India for commitment of robbery by gangs and it was derived from the word '*daka parna*' meaning 'to plunder'.[43] The dacoits were robbers by profession and dacoity was used to mean any robbery carried out by a gang of not less than five persons with a common cause. Dacoity was common in all the districts of the Northern range during the period of the study. The crime, dacoity was said to be committed when five or more persons conjointly commited or attempted to commit a robbery, with every member of the gang said to have committed dacoity. Sometimes, dacoity was committed along with murder; in such cases, every member of the gang were punished with death or imprisonment for life or rigorous imprisonment for a term of ten years and they were also liable to fine.[44] Dacoity or robbery, when commited with attempt to cause death or grievous hurt, when armed with deadly weapon, the offenders were punished by imprisonment of not be less than seven years.

The dacoity committed by wandering or habitual criminals was punished with rigorous imprisonment for a term of seven years with liability to pay fine.[45] In the Northern range, types of dacoities were highway dacoities, field dacoities, and house dacoities. The travelling by night was common in the Northern range and road dacoities were frequect occurrences. To provide safety to the public and prevent such crimes, road *talariyaris* were appointed on important roads and outposts were established. With regular system of patrol, roads were made quite secured and the police on patrol duties were armed.[46] The following are the number of dacoity cases recorded in the Northern range during the year 1924 to 1947.[47]

Years	*Dacoities*
1924	117
1925	53
1926	103
1927	41
1928	25
1929	26
1930	31
1931	50
1932	35
1933	25
1934	42
1935	29
1936	16
1937	11
1938	21
1939	21
1940	16
1941	11
1942	20
1943	17
1944	19
1945	19
1946	6
1947	27

The number of dacoity cases are shown graphically as below:

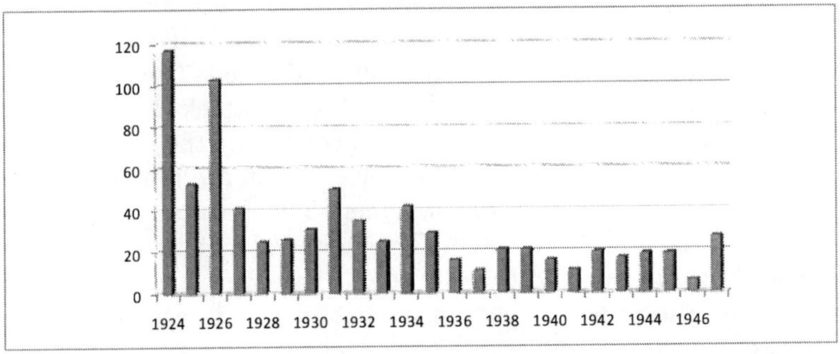

The above graph shows the cases of dacoity which were high in number in the initial years and over the period of time, the quantum of cases gradually reduced. The increase in the dacoity cases pertained mostly to looting and in the initial years, the increase was due to the bad seasonal conditions and high prices of staple foodgrains. These dacoities were mostly committed by local organisations of bad characters and by the members of the criminal tribes.

The decrease in the cases over the years was due to special measures taken by the police administration by constructing dedicated settlements for the notified criminal tribes. These tribes were settled in these villages under police guards and the police ensured that no registered member of the tribe was absent without notice. The separation of large agency areas of Ganjam and Jeypore contribute to the decrease in the cases of dacoity. The increase in population, proper street lighting and the concentration of the police in certain areas had reduced dacoities in the Northern range during the years 1924 to 1947. The following are some of the cases of dacoity of interest in the Northern range during the period 1924-47.

In the year 1925, a house dacoity was committed in Vizagapatam by unusually large gangs of 47 bad characters from the villages in the Vizagapatam and Ganjam districts in which 20 persons were arrested by the police and convicted.[48] In the year 1936, in Kurupam of the Vizagapatam district, a debtor engineered a 'torchlight dacoity' in the houses of two of his creditors with the object of retrieving jewels which were mortgaged with them. The dacoits managed to get away with the jewellery worth Rs 3000 but they were caught by the police. A major portion of the property was recovered.[49] Another case of torchlight dacoity by an unknown gang was recorded in the Nellore district, was detected in which the 24 accused were caught. For this, the investigating police and several private individuals shared money reward of Rs 499.[50]

In the year 1939, higher number of ten dacoity cases were recorded in the East Godavari district which were highest in the range. These cases of looting were due to rise in food prices on account of the World War II.[51] A gang of 16 dacoits from a number of villages in the East Godavari district border attacked the house of a wealthy fisherman in the Vizagapatam district in the year 1941. In course of the commission of the offence, one of the inmates of the house speared a dacoit in his abdomen. The dacoits removed the wounded man and left the scene. The wounded man had died in the hospital at Pittapur and three of the dacoits were arrested.[52] The police and the public played an important role in controlling the crime of dacoity.

House-breaking

House-breaking was an offence under the Indian Penal Code. Illicit entry into a house or a building for the purposes of committing theft was said to be house-breaking. Property possessed by the culprit in this manner is called as stolen property, if such property is criminally misappropriated or the person who possessed such stolen property was punishable under the code.[53] The offenders were punished with imprisonment for a term of three months or with fine up to five hundred rupees, or with both. Persons habitually dealing in stolen property or receiving it knowingly were also punished with imprisonment for life or with imprisonment of either description for a term of ten years apart from liability to pay fine.[54]

The offence of house-breaking was classified according to the method used.[55] In the Northern range, house-breaking was committed habitually by ex-convicts, criminal gangs, and temple burglars.[56] The following are the number of house-breaking cases recorded in the Northern range during the period 1924-47.[57]

Years	*House-breaking cases*
1924	2920
1925	2508
1926	2318
1927	2295
1928	1980
1929	2117
1930	2196
1931	2323
1932	2003
1933	1734

Contd...

Years	*House-breaking cases*
1934	1661
1935	1566
1936	1242
1937	1441
1938	1705
1939	1301
1940	1643
1941	1531
1942	1329
1943	1531
1944	1551
1945	1676
1946	1877
1947	2515

The number of house-breaking cases are shown graphically as follows:

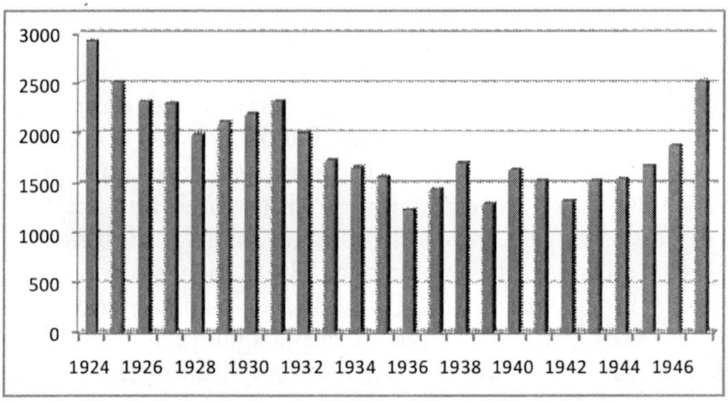

The above graph illustrates the cases of house-breaking which were high in number in the initial years and over the period, these cases had reduced, although they increased during later years. The high increase in the initial years was due to agrarian disputes, famine conditions and unfavourable seasonal conditions and also due to rise in food prices after the declaration of world war.

The decrease over the period was due to the effective measures taken by the police to put an end to the activities of the local criminal organisations and bad characters. Vigilance over criminal organisations, assistance by Village Vigilance Committees and co-operation between the Criminal Investigation Department and the District Intelligence Bureau in the detection and prevention of crime, had reduced the number of house-breaking crimes. The following are some of the cases of house-breaking of inertest in the Northern range during the period 1924 to 1947.

In the year 1926, in the district of East Godavari of the Northern range, a woman complainant showed an unusual presence of mind when her house was broken into by a thief. Immediately after the thief entered the house, she slipped out and fastened the door and informed the police. The thief was arrested by the police and was convicted.[58] During the year 1933, a single gang of Yerukala absconders, who were members of the criminal tribes from the Sitanagaram Criminal Tribes settlement, committed about 112 burglaries.[59]

In the year 1936, a *vakil* in Vizianagaram of the Vizagapatam district caught a burglar after a terrible fight in his house with the help of the neighbours. The police with the help of the Fingerprint Bureau established that the culprit had seven previous convictions and was wanted for escaping from the Jubbulpore jail. The same convict in the year 1926, managed to evade capture after his escape from Vizagapatam jail. The police had searched his house in Puri and found Rs 6000 worth of stolen property which was concerned with the cases of the Ganjam district.[60]

In the year 1939, a grave burglary was recorded in the district of Jeypore; a person by name Ramalinga Pandaram who was a notorious bad character of Travancore had committed an offence of house-breaking from the Jeypore palace during which he took away Rs 10,000. The police, with the help of finger prints, found as a clue on one of the suitcases in the palace. The police had arrested the offender.[61] In the same year, a gang of four Bouriah criminal tribe members of the United Provinces committed burglary in the palace of the Zamindar of Kasimkota in the Vizagapatnam district and stole property worth Rs 15,000. They were arrested due to the smart act of Head Constable of Anakapalle police station in Vizagapatnam district and the railway police at Vizianagram.[62] A man, with eight previous convictions, acting as an agent of a cloth merchant from Bombay, was arrested in Tenali in the Guntur district and he was found with house-breaking implements. This case was recorded in the year 1939.[63] Since the introduction of the classification of the house-breaking offence, the attention of the police was directed more closely to the discovery of professional criminals and criminal organisations in the Northern range.

Murders

The murder is death caused intentionally by an act of a person. Punishment for murderers was death or imprisonment for life and the culprit was also liable to fine. Punishments were given according to the severity of the offence committed. For such crime, the offender was punished with imprisonment for life or with life conviction along with imposition of fine or punished with death.[64] In the Northern range, the motives for murder were sexual matters, family disputes, factionalism, robbery and other causes.[65]

The only class of murder in which the police could take preventive steps was factionalism. In the Northern range, large measures of protection against murder were taken by the Madras government through various legislative Acts.[66] As per an old Indian saying, the three causes for trouble and unhappiness in daily life are zar, zoru, and *zamin* which mean gold, woman, and land respectively.[67] This is true of the crime of murder as majority of the cases were directly related to sexual jealousy, land disputes, village factionalism, and plunder for gain. The following are the number of murder cases recorded in the Northern range 1924-47.[68]

Years	*Murders*
1924	162
1925	166
1926	143
1927	153
1928	153
1929	152
1930	181
1931	193
1932	163
1933	176
1934	207
1935	175
1936	161
1937	192
1938	207
1939	224
1940	214
1941	209
1942	215
1943	218
1944	216
1945	214
1946	238
1947	248

The number of murder cases are shown graphically as follows:

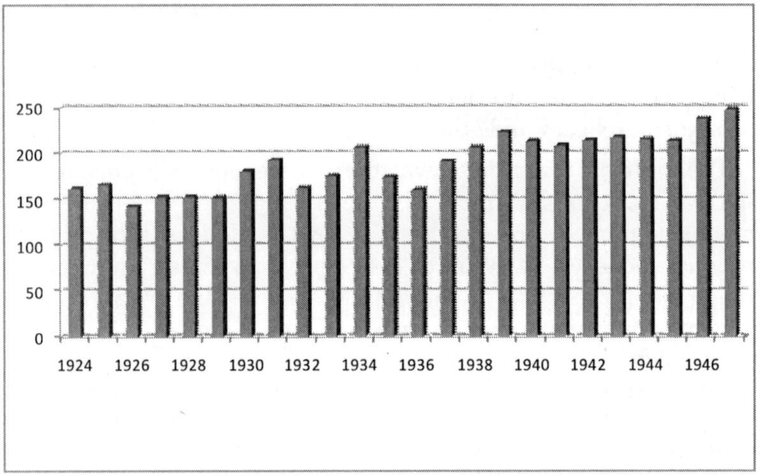

The above graph explains the cases of murders from which it can be seen that the cases had increased over the period. The increase is attributed not to the occurrence of more crime, but to the fact that the crime was better reported and registered. The rise in figures arose mostly due to family disputes and petty quarrels, drunken brawls, and due to existence of large number of people without employment owing to demobilisation. The other factors that have also contributed to the increase was acute economic conditions, scarcity of food grains, high cost of living, and prevalence of communal and labour troubles throughout this range. In the tail years, the increase in murder cases was due to rapid urbanisation of the districts and increase in the population. The following are some of cases of interest relating to murder in the Northern range during the years 1924 to 1947.

On 7th September, 1927, an incident of murder was recorded wherein an Assistant Armourer of the East Coast Special Police took a bayonet and stabbed to death the Havildar Armourer due to grievance over his promotion. Then he ran to the office with a rifle carrying bayonet and shot the Commandant of the force, Peterson, and then shot himself. [69] The government ordered for an enquire committee to investigate the matter.

In the year 1928, in Berhampur taluk of Ganjam district, a Kalinga suspected the chastity of his brother's wife. He waited during the night at the door of the house with a knife and allowed the women to meet her paramour and then killed both of them. He was punished with transportation for life.[70] In the year 1933, there was a revolutionary commotion in the Northern range in which one of the leader was Bhankarachari. He committed a murder and absconded; the police traced and arrested him and at the time of his arrest, he had three revolvers in his possession. [71]

In the West Godavari district, an Excise Inspector was found lying in his kitchen unconscious with multiple injuries, who later died in the hospital. His Brahman cook was chargesheeted for the murder but was acquitted.[72] A Sub-Inspector of Bapatla police station in the Guntur district was fatally murdered in the year 1935 by an old offender whose house he was about to be search for stolen property.[73] A case in the agency tracts of Vizagapatam district was recorded in which a youth murdered a young boy for sake of earrings which were of trivial value; the accused was hanged for this act.

In West Godavari district in the year 1935, a mentally deranged Kapu slashed his enemy with a knife. On the arrival of the local Sub-Inspector, he stabbed the village magistrate and another man. He came back to village two days later and stabbed people at random killing a woman. When he was caught, he jumped into a well and drowned. Another case of interest was recorded in the same year, where an old offender killed the Sub-Inspector of Bapatla police station, Guntur district whose house the Sub-Inspector was about to search for stolen property.[74]

An ex-convict in the Nellore district in the year 1936 had intimacy with his neighbour's wife who also helped him financially. This had enraged her husband and he went with along with several others to the ex-convict's house and hacked him to death. The parts of his body were burnt and the rest was buried but the left hand of the deceased was found. The police, with the help of the Fingerprint Bureau, were able to establish the identity of the deceased by comparison with the fingerprints already on record in the Bureau. The husband and two others were sentenced to five year rigorous imprisonment. In the same year, a kamma in Kistna district, alleged to have lost a fortune in unsuccessful speculation in a film company. To make up for the loss, he conspired and murdered his uncle for inheriting his property.[75] Another case in the agency tracts of the Vizagapatam district was that of a youth who murdered a young boy for sake of earrings carrying trivial value; the accused was hanged.[76] Another young man in East Godavari district killed a four year old cousin for her gold bangles; he was arrested by the police and sentenced to death.[77] The areas prone to murders, according to the police records, were confined to the Cocanada and Ramachandrapuram police circles of East Godavari district.[78]

In the year 1937, a government *talaiyari*, who was taking Kist collection of over Rs 400 to the Sankaranainar koyil sub-treasury, was knocked off his bicycle and murdered and all the money was stolen. A local Village Vigilance Committee member organised a search party and the offender was arrested. The entire money was recovered and death sentence was imposed on the culprit. In the same year, another case of interest happened in the East Godavari district in which the Session Judge appreciated the police for investigating a case in which a woman from Peddapur was murdered in Cocanada and her body was thrown under a culvert. The identity of the woman was not established until three months and there was no clue for the police to proceed. Once the identity was known, vigorous action was taken and a man and a woman, who proved to be culprits in the matter were hanged.[79]

At Setarampuram in Nellore district in the year 1938, a man had murdered his wife's lover and faked the incident as a suicide. A *ryot* of the village had given information to the police authorities and the body was exhumed thus bringing the crime to light. The husband and his associate connected in the murder were convicted.[80] In another such case in the Vizagapatnam district, a dispute between the village *munsif* and three others led to the murder of the *munsif*. The accused was arrested and sentenced to death. In the same district, a husband killed his wife and her uncle in case of a domestic trouble that ensued for which he was sent to gallows. In Cocanada, a vagabond of Bezwada, a known depredator of Madras and a student of Coimbatore Agricultural College conspired and entered the house of bank clerk armed with a dagger, a sword and a revolver and killed him. All three of them were sentenced to transportation for life.[81]

In a village in the Guntur district, there was factious enmity between four brothers and the village *munisf*, the *karanam* and the villagers. The brothers were notorious rowdies and had threatened the village officers with death. One of them was a member of local forest panchayat board and was exacting illegal collection from the villagers. On 7th May, 1941, the village *munisf* and the *karanam*, along with a large number of villagers, attacked the four brothers in their house and murdered them and attempted to dispose off the bodies by burning them. The Sub-Inspector of police arrived in time to prevent this and 25 persons including two village officers were charged in this case.[82]

In the year 1946, a receiver of a stolen property and his sister murdered a notorious Donga Yenadi of the notified criminal tribe when he demanded the return of the stolen property. The accused were sentenced to transportation for life. In the same year, a Kamma landlord of West Godavari district was brutally murdered in cold blood while asleep at the instigation of some of his relatives who were later traced by the police and booked.[83]

The caste Hindus of a village in the Vizagapatam North district wanted to seize the land enjoyed by a Harijan and made all attempts to drive him away. When they failed in their endeavours, he was brutally attacked and killed[84]; all the offenders were arrested. In the factious areas, especially in the Godavari, Vizagapatam, Guntur, and Nellore districts of the Northern range, the government had taken measures under the Criminal Procedure Code to prevent the offences.[85] Murders are the only crime where the police cannot take preventive course, but faction murders can be prevented.

Counterfeiting Coins and Currency Notes

The manufacture of counterfeit rupees and coins of different values was a constant offence throughout the presidency and the Northern range. These offences were mostly carried out by criminal tribes and professional gangs. The police were successful in seizing the collections of false coins, moulds, and apparatus used for making them and also arresting the false coiners and forgers of currency notes. Counterfeiting currency notes or bank notes or any associated with this process was punished with imprisonment for life or with imprisonment of either description for a term which extended to ten years along with liability to pay fine.[86] The Criminal Investigation Department had solved a number of such cases and prevented the crimes in the Northern range, although offences of this nature were usually dealt by the regular police force. The crime branch of the Criminal Investigation Department investigated several important cases covering smuggling, misappropriation, fraud, cheating, and murder by poisoning in the Northern range during this period.[87]

The following are some of interesting cases relating to counterfeiting of coin and currency notes in the Northern range during the years 1924 to 1947.

A case of forgery of currency notes was recorded by the police wherein some rich and influential men of the Guntur district were involved; they were caught by the police force and convicted during the year 1925.[88] A gang of forgers of currency notes from the district of Nellore and Guntur conspired at Madras and got a block made for counterfeiting one hundred rupee currency notes. The police arrested three of them at the Madras Central Station on their way to Kalahasti and two more at Kalahasti. Two persons were convicted in this case by the Sessions court in Madras.[89] In the year 1926, a currency notes case was recorded in the Guntur district of the Northern range where parliamentary members, 'Mallala Brothers' were involved.[90]

In the year 1928, currency notes forged in Burma found their way to the Madras Presidency through steamships. The seizure of such notes in Cocanada led to the captures in Rangoon and averted their wider circulation. Two of the accused concerned in the Cocanada cases were convicted.[91] Another case of interest during the same year 1928 was that of two railways carriage Inspectors of goods in East Godavari district, who with some of their associates, carried on the currency note duplicating tricks. They used to select a rich young man and convince him that they, by means of photography, were able to duplicate hundred rupee currency notes. All the offenders in the case were convicted.[92]

Three Mohammedans, while using counterfeit rupee coins in the bazaar in Guntur town were noticed by the police. When the latter investigated the coins, these were found to be counterfeited by two of the brothers who were goldsmiths. One was arrested at Narasaraopet, Guntur district and the other at Mogalrajapuram, Kistna district. The counterfeit notes of Rs 100 of T.E.87 series were already in circulation in the districts of Kistna and West Godavari and had later spread all over the Madras Presidency, of which the Northern range was a part. Most of these counterfeit notes were found in race course. The Criminal Branch of the police enquired about the origin of this series and took action to stop further circulation.[93]

In the year 1930, a gang consisting of two goldsmiths and two others was formed in the East Godavari district for counterfeiting rupees. A well-to-do man of Annavaram was approached to finance this scheme but he, instead, gave information to the Sub-Inspector of police, Annavaram. A raid was arranged and the head of the gang was caught while in the act of striking counterfeiting rupees and they were convicted. In the year 1933, a case of counterfeiting of rupees in a secluded cave in the Veligunda hills of Nellore was detected. A considerable influx of forged ten rupees notes from Burma was also investigated by the Criminal Investigation Department.[94]

At Mendapata in East Godavari district in the year 1936, a gang of 10 rupee notes forger was busted from which 35 counterfeit notes were seized, all the culprits were convicted and charge sheeted.[95] Two men from Northern India were discovered in Nellore district in the guise of pilgrims passing off counterfeit coins. When the police searched them, materials for manufacturing the coins were discovered; both the men were sentenced to four years rigorous imprisonment.[96] There was a large cache of counterfeit rupees at the Krishnapatam salt factory in Nellore district. The Criminal Investigation Department assisted the local police and led to the capture of a notorious gang of counterfeiters and seizure of materials used by them; all the accused were sentenced to rigorous imprisonment. In the Nellore district, one, Kondala Rao Chowdry obtained money from the villagers in Cuddaph district with the promise of teaching them the art of minting and manufacturing currency notes. When he and his associate appeared with some negatives of five rupees currency notes at Chakrayapet, they were arrested.[97]

Cheating

Cheating was an offence during the British period. Whoever, by deceiving any person, fraudulently or dishonestly induced the person for any property to such an act, or omission of the same, caused damage or harm to that person in body, mind, reputation or property, was said to 'cheat'. Punishment for cheating was imprisonment for a term of one year or with fine or with both.[98] The crime branch of the Criminal Investigation Department did useful work and it investigated all the important cases, which included smuggling, misappropriation, fraud, cheating and murder by poisoning. [99] The following are some of the cases of interest where the Criminal Investigation Department, along with it branches, had assisted the police in crime detection and prevention.

A notorious cheat and inter-provincial criminal named Ramanujam alias Sundarsanam, after making good his escape from the Cochin jail, operated in the Madras city. He issued bogus demand drafts and induced the Bombay motor company to deliver cash. Styling himself as Dr Desiken, proprietor of Desikan Company, Engineers, he attempted to cheat the Fiat Motor Agency and P&O bank of Rs 5,400 and Rs 41,000 respectively. He was arrested with great difficulty and was convicted and sentenced to undergo two years rigorous imprisonment. He escaped from the custody of the Vizagapatam district police while being escorted from the district jail, Vizagapatam to the presidency jail, Alipore, to stand his trial in a series of cases in Calcutta, Simla, Lahore and other places. The intelligence department suspected him to be operating in Bombay, and finally a Sub-Inspector identified him in Cuddapah, and he was arrested.[100]

In the Vizagapatam district, a banking concern known as the Barathamatha Commonwealth Insurance Bank had made fraudulent transactions and cheated many people. The bank had a number of branches in various parts of India, Burma, and Ceylon. This case was investigated by the Criminal Investigation Department [101] and the culprits were convicted.

In the year 1931, a person by name Sri Haridoss disguised as a social reformer with divine powers created unrest among the hill tribes of Vizagapatam agency tracks. He was arrested on the 25th September and interned in Bellary but he managed to escape; he again reappeared in the year 1932 in a village of the Vizagapatam agency with his followers. The police arrested him and four of his followers; they were prosecuted and sentenced to long terms of imprisonment. He again escaped but was recaptured by the police in the year 1933.[102]

In the Ganjam district, the village magistrates in certain cases connived in the cheating of the Venus Life Assurance Company by furnishing false death reports regarding insured persons and colluded with the claimants in their bogus claims against the Insurance Company.[103] A cheat operating at inter-district level posing himself as a *sanyasi* gained the confidence of a government servant in the Nellore district and persuaded him to adorn an idol with Rs 2000 worth of jewels for a special puja. While the puja was in progress, the cheat absconded with the jewels. Another case of interest was that of a young man of the Guntur district who posed himself as a Lieutenant of the Royal Indian Naval Reserve and was found travelling in a first class compartment from Madras to Waltair. He used railway warrants for his journeys and was arrested on suspicion by the railway police. Several forged documents were seized from him and he was sentenced to two years imprisonment.[104] A notorious cheat working at inter-provincial level, namely, Santhilal Jainabhai Shah, cheated about 30 medicos in Vizagapatam town, posing himself as an agent of a firm in Bombay. He was convicted and sentenced to rigorous imprisonment.[105]

Justifiable Homicide

Justifiable homicide means death caused by doing an act with the intention of causing death or injury that is likely to cause death; such offence was also called as culpable homicide..[106] The deaths treated as justifiable homicide were caused by private parties in exercise of their right of private defense and by the police in execution of their duties. In many cases of culpable homicide, the Criminal Investigation Department and the Fingerprint Bureau proved useful in meting out due punishments to the culprits. The Chemical

Examiner's Department also helped the police in the detection of crimes in the Northern range. The Department had examined various articles for poison in humans and in cattle-poisoning cases, for blood in homicidal, and hurt cases, blood and semen in rape cases, and other unnatural crimes.[107] The following are some of the cases of justifiable homicide worth mentioning which had occurred in the Northern range during the years 1924 to 1947.

In the year 1925, the police had raided the Kondapalli forest in Kistna district of the Northern range and opened fire on a gang of Yerakala absconders of whom one was wounded and died subsequently of his wounds.[108] In the year 1927, in Bapatla station of the Guntur district, a man killed a sadhu in his private defense as the sahdu was attempting human sacrifice on him.[109]

During the year 1928, a householder in Jeypore district heard some noise at the back of his house. He went around armed with a spear and found two burglars. One of them escaped and the other also attempted to escape, but the householder thrust a spear and killed him; the next morning, the police arrested the householder.[110] In the year 1929, a trap container with a loaded country gun was laid by a resident of the Jeypore district against wild animals. His niece, who came to his house, stamped against the string accidentally and the gun went off injuring her badly; she died later and the man committed suicide.[111] A steam tug, which belonged to the Public Works Department, was too close to the anicut by the forbidden route of the Dowlaishwaram anicut and sank with 14 persons on board and except for two persons, the rest swam to the bank. This incident had happened in the year 1930.[112]

During the year 1937, in Rajahmundry in the East Godavari district of the Northern range, an iron cylinder that was used for rockets at a marriage celebration exploded causing injuries to some people and killing nine.[113] In the Kistna district, an escaped Yanadi prisoner was rounded up by a party of police and villagers and was shot dead by a Constable as he was making a murderous attack with a knife on the police.[114] In another case, person who tried to rape his daughter was beaten to death by his son in the East Godavari district of the Northern range.[115] Three cases of justifiable homicide were reported to the police in the year 1938 in Chirala which had occurred as a result of labour trouble in the Guntur district.[116] In all these crimes, the police had successfully detected the culprits and legal action was taken.

Riots and Disturbances

Unlawful assembly was considered an offence against the public tranquility in the British period. An assembly of three or more persons was designated as an unlawful assembly who had the common object of disturbing the law and order, and such assembly, was punished[117] with imprisonment of either description for a term which extended to six months, or with fine, or with both. Joining unlawful assembly, armed with deadly weapons, was also punished with imprisonment for two years or with fine or with both.

Rioting referred to the use of force or violence used by an unlawful assembly, with every member of such assembly cosidered guilty of the offence punishable either by a term of two years or with fine or with both. Rioting, armed with deadly weapon, that was likely to cause death, was punishable with imprisonment for three years or with fine or with both. Harbouring offender who had escaped from custody or whose apprehension had been ordered, was punishable with imprisonment for life.[118] Rioting and unlawful assembly were frequent occurrences during this period in the Northern range and this was due to agrarian disputes, labour disputes and the fundamental sectarian hostility existing between the Hindus and the Muslims.

Voluntarily causing disturbance to any assembly which was lawfully engaged in the performance of religious worship or religious ceremonies, were punished with imprisonment for a term of one year or with fine or with both. A number of cases were recorded in the Northern range relating to mass political agitations, especially during the national struggle for freedom, agrarian strikes, and communal unrests which forced the British government to sanction special and additional police to maintain the law and order. There was a wave of labour unrest in some of the districts of the Northern range which resulted in a series of strikes. The relations between landlords and tenants grew worse and there was widespread agrarian unrest in the deltas areas. It was indeed noteworthy that the police, who were subjected to an unusually heavy strain in dealing with diverse complicated situations as detailed above, showed remarkable efficiency and maintained law and order very satisfactorily.[119] The factional fights were also common in most of the districts of the Northern range and to contain these, the government had established outposts. The following are some of the cases of interest where the police of the Northern range had tactfully controlled riotous conditions. Sometimes, the reserve police were also used to suppress the unruly mobs.

Local board elections in West Godavari and Kistna districts led to riots and outrages in which several people were killed and many injured during the year 1933. Another case was in Musupudi of the Kistna district wherein a Head Constable, while engaged in investigating a theft case, was set upon by the villagers, beaten, and confined in a house. Thirteen of the offenders were charge-sheeted and convicted in this case.[120] An incident of rioting with deadly weapons occurred in the Pattupur village of the Ganjam district between the followers of Raja of Sanmokimidi and the ex-Rani. The police had proceeded against the leaders under Section 107 of the Criminal Procedure Code. In the same district, there was a border dispute in the Parlakimedi agency between the villagers of Sandiriguda and Asriguda; the police proceeded against them under Section 107 of the Criminal Procedure Code.[121] In another case, damage caused by pigs belonging to the tribes Pamulas of Tadikonda of the Guntur district enraged the local Kammas who fired upon the huts of the Pamulas[122], the police convicted the culprits. On the 25th August, 1937, about 200 Malas and Madigas looted paddy granaries at Bommalur in the Kistna district; 34 perpetrators were charged in this case. [123]

A customs Sub-Inspector and his staff in the East Godavari district detected a case of smuggling by a gang from Yenam. This gang lodged a false complaint of theft against them to the French police and the Sub-Inspector was detained. When he was indentified the next day and released, the smugglers were chargesheeted for rioting.[124] In the year 1941, while the police were engaged in the apprehension of the absconders in cases of dacoity in the West Godavari district, the relatives of the offenders attacked the police party. The attack soon developed into a serious riot and the police were compelled to open fire on the rioters to restore order and the rioters were booked under law.[125]

In four cases of rioting at East and West Godavari, Kistna, and Guntur districts, firing was resorted to when the mob tried to rescue the gamblers who were arrested for cock-fighting. In a village of the Nellore district, a merchant who refused to sell rice at controlled price, enraged the villagers, who then attacked him and attempted to loot his house.[126] In the year 1947, there was a land dispute between the Koyas and the Zamindar of Nadigudem in the West Godavari district. The Sub-Divisional Magistrate prevented both the parties from entering the lands, but the Koyas, backed up by the communist party, violated the order and committed theft of paddy attacking the police party with their bows and arrows and injuring three police officers. The police opened fire which resulted in five deaths and injuries four persons. In another incident, the communists instigated the villagers of Gazullanka in the Kistna district and cut the nanal grass during night time from the disputed land. The Armed Reserves stationed in the village for *bandobast* tried to prevent but the villagers surrounded the force and attacked. The police party opened fire in self-defence killing four, including a woman.[127] In the village of Kalikova in the Kistna district, fire was opened upon by the police on a riotous mob who tried to attack the police with lethal weapons, two men died and others were injured in the melee.[128] The communist programme of intentionally fomenting industrial unrest led to various violent clashes, necessitating the police to open fire on the rioters.

Political Disturbances

Besides the general crimes, the period 1924 to 1947 was a peak time for the freedom struggle and the British issued new ordinances to control the political situation, and under this, all activities like holiding assemblies, foisting Indian flags, singing national song, making public speeches, and working of All India Congress Committees were also declared unlawful.[129] To suppress these anti-British movements in the districts of the Northern range, additional police force was sanctioned and it was equipped with more powers. The British government resorted to severe policy of repression during the Non-co-operation Movement, Civil Disobedience Movement, Quit India Movement and all such mass campaigns till the Independence.

The Rampa fituri of 1924 was led by Allur Seetarama Raju in the Rampa hills of the Godavari region[130]. He mobilised the hill tribes against the British and had organised guerrilla action. The group attacked many police stations for arms and ammunition. The British government had sanctioned special armed police reserves, Malabar Special Police Force, and two companies of Assam Riffles to suppress the rebellion and under the Special Commissioner Rutherford, the whole operation of suppression took place.[131]

The police captured Allur Seetarama Raju in the year 1924 along with several of the rebels and the resistance was crushed.[132]

During the Dandi March in the year 1930, the salt law was broken in the Guntur and Kistna districts and this later extended to Nellore, East Godavari and West Godavari districts of the Northern range. This Movement did not last long and after the arrest of C. Rajagopalachari, it came to a standstill. The economic impact of the violation of salt-making law was negligible, though it bred a spirit of lawlessness in most of the districts.[133] The police found difficult to check the movement, especially so in the areas, where it had the participation of villagers but it was eventually brought under control by a series of prosecutions. Picketing of liquor and foreign cloth shops was another important activity of this movement which witnessed some violent incidents, especially at Ellore and Bezwada. In many situations, the police were compelled to open fire. There were also many other such disturbances, though of minor importance. During this year 1930, the crime rate increased in the Kistna district and recorded highest in the Madras Presidency. This was due to the spirit of defiance to law and authority created by the Civil Disobedience Movement.[134]

In connection with the Civil Disobedience Movement in the year 1932, two serious confrontations occurred, one at Gudivada and the other at Eluru between the police and riotous mobs. At Gudivada, a mob attacked a party of Reserve Police under W.F.A. Hamilton, Assistant Superintendent of Police. In this incident, the police opened fire and the mob was dispersed and later, one hundred and eighteen persons were arrested, charged and convicted. In Eluru, a mob of about 3000 labourers and others who were armed with sticks attacked upon the Reserve Police under the District Superintendent of Police, Mr Sanjeevi Pillai. The police opened fire in which 25 men were injured and one was killed; eighteen rioters were convicted and sentenced to imprisonment in this case. A serious riot occurred on the 30th March, 1931 at Vadapalli of the East Godavari district which compelled the police to open fire in self-defence injuring 17 of the rioters in the process.[135]

In the Nellore district, there occurred a serious clash when the depressed classes were denied entry into a temple on the opening day when Gandhi toured the province in the months of December, 1933 to March, 1934 collecting funds for Harijan cause.[136] In the year 1938-39, during picketing at Chirala in the Guntur district, the police opened fire to restore order. A judicial enquiry into the firing was held and the action taken by the police was justified.[137] During the freedom struggle, the students played a great role, as a part of which they boycotted schools and colleges. In Narasapur taluk of the West Godavari district, two young men were fined rupees 20 for the charge of picketing at the municipal high school.[138]

Many great leaders, like Srimathis Duggirala, Kamalamba Dasari Krishnavenamma, Dasari Lakshmibayamma, B.Viyyanna, D. Anjayya, K.L. Narasimha Rao, M. Guru Raju, G. Ramabrahmam and several others were convicted and imprisoned during the freedom struggle. In the year 1942, in the West Godavari district, a violent mob set fire to the Revenue Development Office at Bheemavaram, attacked the building in Taluk office compound and attempted to break open the sub-jail. In the Tenali railway station of the Guntur district, some of the carriages of passenger train were set on fire.[139]

Many police stations, railway stations and government properties were destroyed by the mob during the freedom movement. During Quit India Movement of 1942, at Attili, a village in West Godavari district, a bunk near the Attili railway station was set on fire under the leadership of Maganti Chakrapani and the followers attacked the railway station and destroyed the records and other things. He was soon arrested, convicted and sentenced to one year imprisonment by the Joint Magistrate of Narasapur. Large amount of railway property estimated at Rs 2,735, was destroyed in this incident and a collective fine of Rs 5,000 was imposed on the communities of Relangi; however, Attili was exempted.

During the freedon struggle in the year 1942, freedom fighters like B.Viyyanna, K.L. Narasimha Rao, M.Guru Raju, Ramabrahmam and several others were arrested at Gudivada and sentenced to rigorous imprisonment under Sections 145 and 188 of the Indian Penal Code. Help or support given to the political agitators was considered as an offence in such cases. In the year 1942, in Bheemavaram taluk of the Northern range, two women were arrested and convicted on the charge of providing medical aid to the wounded agitators; they were sentenced to rigorous imprisonment for two years.[140] The echoes of the freedom movement at the centre were heard in the districts of the Northern range which manifested in people of this range participating with great enthusiasm. Many great leaders with their followers showed their anger by destroying the public and government properties, for instance, by burning many police stations and railway stations. The Vendra railway station incident is noteworthy in this context; this station was about five kilometres away from Bheemavaram and was next to the railway track running between Nidadavolu and Bheemavaram. Under the leadership of Bhupathi Raju, Subba Raju with his followers, attacked the railway station and set it on fire. The Railway Sub-Inspector of police, Bheemavaram, received the message and arranged guards at the railway junction. The case was referred to the Sessions Judge by I.V. Seshagiri Rao, the Sub-Divisional Magistrate and the prosecution was conducted by R.V. Rama Rao, Public Prosecutor. Later, the judgment was finally delivered in the year 1943 by Syed

Kadir Muhammad, Session Judge of the West Godavari division at Eluru which sentenced all the convicts.

The Quit India Movement had a great impact on the people of Northern range. In this connection, the police opened fire on the farmers who were involved in the riots and killed seven farmers.[141] In Guntur, there was a similar demonstration supported by several thousands of farmers. In the taluk of Bhimavaram in West Godavari district, the police had opened fire to control the crowd in which several people were injured.[142] The police were given special powers by the British government through special ordinances during the freedom movement to suppress the political unrest and were also well-trained for this purpose. In many instances, the police had to open fire and resort to lathicharge on the crowd to restore law and order.

Agrarian Disputes

In the Northern range, the zamindars had the powers for revenue collection and policing powers. These zamindars used harsh methods for collecting the revenues and this had strained their relationship with the *ryots*. The relations between landlords and tenants grew worse with passing time and there were widespread agrarian unrests and anti-zamindari agitations in several places in the deltas areas of the Northern range. There were demonstrations by Andhra peasants in the Northern range which took place in the form of propaganda marches advocating the abolition of zamindari system. The Taluk Ryots Associations were also formed in the Godavari district. These agrarian troubles caused widespread public unrest and the police were occupied most of their time in quelling these riots. In most of the incidences, the District Superintendents visited and preserved for public order. Agrarian movements in various parts of the Northern range during the years 1924-47 gave cause for anxiety but the disputes were handled with tact and firmness by the police. There was a certain amount of agricultural labour unrest and the difficulties of the police were increased by the premature and injudicious use of strikes as weapon in some instances.

There was eruption of trouble in the Kalyanasingapur valley in the Visakhapatnam Agency. For some years, the tenants of the Maharaja of Jeypore in this part of the Agency renounced their allegiance to the Maharaja, refused payment of the estate dues and were united in their defiance of all authority. In the year 1931, a strong Armed Reserve Force under the District Superintendent of Police was sent to Kalyanasingapur to enforce their submission to law and this force was attacked by strong bodies of people with bows and arrows. The police returned the attack with rifle fire causing several deaths. The male inhabitants thereupon abandoned their homes and took to the hills. The valley was for long garrisoned by armed police. In the meantime, the death of late Maharaja in 1931 and the interregnum before anointment of his successor could be effected, created legal difficulties which prevented further strong executive action. It was feared that this would lead to a *fituri*, so, in January 1933, a strong force of the combined Armed Reserves of Visakhapatnam, Jeypore, East Godavari, and Ganjam marched into the Agency. By a series of rapid operations, day and night, the resistance was crushed by the government throughout the affected area. The Armed Reserves of Ganjam, Jeypore, Visakhapatnam, and East Godavari districts were sent on annual training tours to the Agency areas.[143] These tours had benefitted the government as well as the people of the Agencies as they were, thus, protected from the rebellions.

In the year 1933, the tribal group of Khond tenants of the Agency had renounced their allegiance to the Maharaja and refused payment of the estate dues and remained united in their defiance against the authority. A strong armed force of the combined Armed Reserve of Vizagapatnam, Jeypore, East Godavari and Ganjam districts marched into the Agency under the District Superintendent of Police and the situation was brought under control. In the same year, discontentment among the tenants of the southern villages of the Venkatagiri estate in the Nellore district continued and there were skirmishes between the tenants and the zamin officials. Similar trouble broke out in the Parlakemdi estate in the Ganjam district[144], but the police intervened and brought the situation under control.

The agrarian movement by the peasants in the Northern range had created public unrest. They were propaganda demonstrations throughout the villages advocating abolition of zamindari system. As a result, several peasant associations and taluk *ryot* associations were formed in the East and West Godavari districts of the Northern range. Under the leadership of Ranga N.G., the grievances of the *ryots* were represented to the British government.[145] The agrarian trouble in the Venkatagiri Samasthanam occurred at the end of the year 1937 when a dismissed *karanam* of this village along with other influential discontented *ryots* induced the zamindari *ryots*, who in the Podili division launched a no-tax campaign. The District Superintendent of Police immediately visited that area and averted a serious situation.[146]

The working classes in some villages of Amalapur taluk in the East Godavari district formed themselves into a union and struck down work during transplantation and harvesting season demanding higher wages. External labourers were employed by the *ryots* but the situation was under control and there occurred no serious incident.[147] There was vigorous propaganda against the zamindari system in the Kistna district and there was also some unrest in a part of the Vizagapatnam district.[148] In the Madgole area of the Vizagapatam district, an attempt was made by 10,000 hill folk to undermine the authority of the *muttadars* on the advice of two individuals for which they were warned. In the Kistna district, an intensive campaign of stayagraha and social boycott was instituted by the *ryots* of the Munagala zamindari against the zamindari system. These rebellious agrarian movements were brought under control by the police.[149]

With the constitution of the Estate Land Act Enquiry Committee, vigorous propaganda was commenced by agrarian leaders in several taluks in the Kistna district against the zamindari system. Action under Section 107 of the Criminal Procedure Code, was however, averted.

There was land dispute between Koyas and zamindars of Nandigudem in the West Godavari district. The Sub-Divisional Magistrate prevented both the parties from entering their lands, but the Koyas with the support of the Communist party, committed theft of paddy and attacked the police party with their bows and arrows injuring three police officers. The police opened fire resulting in five deaths and injury to four persons. Agrarian movements in various parts of the Northern range, particularly in the Kistna district, especially in the years 1938-39, disturbed the public peace but were handled with tact and firmness by the police force.[150] In the Venkatagiri zamindari, a dispute erupted about grasing rights claimed by the neighbouring villagers over the Kalavagunta forest, however, timely intervention of the police and the concerned authorities, led to an eventual compromise. In the agency tracts of the Vizagapatam, new ideas of liberty and self-government carved a spirit of unrest in the parts of Modgole zamindari in the Vizagapatam district, but under Section 110 of the Criminal Procedure Code, order was restored.[151] Throughout the period of study, agrarian unrest prevailed and there was vigorous propaganda against the zamindari system. The British government had sanctioned special police platoons to suppress the strikes. Public order was restored by systematic patrols and by establishment of temporary police stations.

The magisterial authority also played an important role in restoring law and order.

Labour Disputes

At the instigation of the communists, there were agricultural labour unrests in certain places of the Northern range whereunder the workers struck down work demanding enhanced wages. This led to industrial unrest and violent clashes all around, resulting in a number of strikes. In a few instances, the police had opened fire on the rioters to restore law and order. In the districts of the Northern range, very few disturbances occurred due to the prompt action of the police.[152] In the year 1938, in the Guntur district, the police were able to preserve peace in all the lightning strikes of the district except at Chirala town where they had to resort to firearms to restore order. A judicial enquiry into the firing was held which resulted in justification of the action taken by the police.[153] A labour dispute in the tobacco factory at Chirala in the Guntur district resulted in a riot to quell which the police opened fire on the mob as a result of which three men were killed.[154]

On 14th February, 1939, a riotous mob of 2,000 workers staged a stay-in strike in the Chittavalasa jute mill in the Vizagapatam district and refused to leave the mill. The police had to open fire to restore order, killing one and injuring several others, in the process. The mill was closed for several months during that year. The cases against the rioters were dropped under the orders of the government.[155] Actually, in this case, the labourers of mill had went on a strike for 18 days to protest the dismissal of a woman worker. Prompt action was taken against the leaders under the Defence of India Rules and adequate police *bandobast* was provided in the mill area.[156]

There was a wave of labour unrest during the period 1924-47 in most of the districts resulting in strikes and consequent dislocation of normal police work.

Social and Communal Tensions

In the districts of the Northern range, communal situation between the Hindus and the Muslims became very sensitive during religious festivals. These two communities use to clash on account of disputes over the issue of the Hindus holding procession in front of mosques and wearing of tiger disguises during *Dasara* festivals. The Muslims, on the other hand, were opposed to both processions and disguises. When both these communities clashed, the Hindus burnt the factories, shops, and properties owned by the Muslims, who in turn, looted Hindu shops and burnt their houses in retaliation. Also in this range, there were frequent clashes between high caste and low caste Hindus over caste superiority. The persistence of inter-communal bitterness and political restlessness account for increased number of public disturbances in the Northern range that continued to exist throughout the period 1924-47.[157] The social difference among the people also existed in the districts of the Northern range mostly between the lower and upper castes of Hindus.

In the year 1925, in some villages there was friction between communities which had caused minor disturbances, the most important being at Chennur in the Nellore district where resentment in people of other castes about self-assertion of Devangis resulted in some of the houses getting looted. A clash occurred between the Kammas and Malas at Kovvali in the West Godavari district in the year 1925. This necessitated maintenance of a police outpost at the village for most part of the year to prevent further breach of peace.

The Hindu-Muslim tensions in Nellore erupted in spite of orders issued under the Police Act as a result of a procession that was organised during Dasara festival without the notice of the authorities. The police and the magistrate interfered and averted as serious situation and this led to the arrest of three leaders and a firm action was taken on others under Section 144, Criminal Procedure Code.[158] In Jeypore district, a native of Kalahandi, Kripasindu Das, moved about naked in the disguise of digambara swami pretending to do miracles. At an opportune moment, the police arrested him and sent to Rajahmundry jail.[159] After the release, he was sent to Benares by the police of Vizagapatam, under the orders of the governor. Due to prompt action of the police, a serious communal situation was averted.

In the year 1933, the local board elections in the West Godavari and Kistna districts led to factious riots and outrages in which several people were killed and many injured.[160] The police had handled the situation with tact and preserved order. A political outrage was contemplated in Cocanada in the year 1933 when a bomb concealed in a boat, unwittingly struck by a boatman, exploded and caused injuries to nine persons. Investigations into this occurrence revealed the existence of a revolutionary association in the Andhra districts. Its leader was one Bhayankarachari, an undergraduate who was a notorious person. Among the immediate plans of this group, was the murder of Mustafa Ali Khan Sahib, Deputy Superintendent of Police of Coconada, who was responsible for suppression of the Civil

Disobedience Movement of 1930-32. Revolvers, daggers and a volume of incriminating correspondences were seized. The culprit absconded and took shelter in Hyderabad state where he was traced and arrested with three revolvers in his possession after a fierce struggle. Nine other conspirators were arrested and imprisoned for a term of 14 years.[161]

At Musupudi in the Kistna district, a Head Constable and a Constable, while investigating a theft case, were set upon by the villagers beaten and confined in a house, later 13 of the 18 assailants were charge-sheeted and convicted.[162] At Ramapuram in the Nellore district, disputes regarding their fishing rights in the Pulicat Lake led to a kind of guerrilla warfare between two parties of 600 fishermen which culminated in an attempted mass attack by them.[163]

In the Nellore district, there occurred serious clashes when the depressed classes were denied entry into a temple on the opening day. Gandhi toured the province in the months of December, 1933 to March, 1934 collecting funds for Harijan cause.[164] At Timmasamudram in the Guntur district, a dispute over caste superiority broke out between the Malas and Madigas and it resulted in rioting.

The Muharram and Sri Ramanavmi festivals synchronised in the year 1935; so, in the districts of West Godavari, Kistna, and Guntur, restrictions were imposed at public places and this was resented by the Muslims who abandoned their Muharram celebrations.[165] At Nimmakayala Kallapalle in the East Godavari district in the year 1936, a Sub-Inspector with a small police party stopped gambling at a cock fighting event for which he was assaulted. The Deputy Superintendent of Police on receiving the information proceeded to the scene with Armed Reserves and punished all the offenders.

In the year 1936, a man from village Punnuru in Nellore district was smoking at street drama in the neighbouring village of Leburu in the presence of the leading Reddies of that village. This was attributed to wilful disrespect and three days later, the men of Leburu, armed, attacked the Punnuru village and in the ensuing clash, one man was killed and many others injured.[166] The damage caused by the pigs belonging to the Pamulas of Tadikonda of Guntur district had enraged the local Kammas and they set fire to the huts belonging to the Pamulas.[167]

In the year 1938, in Koneripudi of the Guntur district, some Mohammedans and Kamma had a quarrell on some issue of cattle. The next morning two parties of Kammas and Mohammedans, numbering about 200 people, indulged in open fight with battle axes, spears and other weapons. Two Kammas and nine Mohammedans were sentenced to gallows while 20 others of both the parties were sentenced to various terms of imprisonment.[168]

In the year 1941, in the Nellore district, the police were obliged to fire on the rioters in an incident during festival of Dasara. In spite of police *bandobast*, the mob surrounded the police party and attempted to overpower it. The Sergeant in charge of the police party opened fire and dispersed the rioters. A girl was killed and an old lady was injured as a result of the firing. A huge crowd gathered at the mortuary demanding corpse of the girl and soon, the mob began to throw stones at the police; the police had somehow restored order. In these communal clashes, many people were murdered from both the parties. The government had ordered for quartering of an additional police force and Priestley, a police officer, enquired into the disturbances. The Presidency General Reserve from six districts were brought to Nellore to deal with various disturbances.

In another place of Nellore at Kaluvoy, the communal tensions intensified and the police had to disperse the rioters by resorting to lathi charge and they arrested 69 rioters. The feelings between the two communities continued to be strained which necessitated the government to station the Armed Reserves at these places.[169] In the Nellore district, the police were obliged to fire on the rioters in which three Muslims were killed during procession of Hindus near Anjaneya temple. The District Magistrate prohibited Hindu processions from playing music within fifty yards of any mosque. In the year 1925, on a revision petition against one such prohibitory order, a judge of a High Court observed that on serving notice before such possession, the police arrangements would be made. On 15th March, 1926, the Hindus took musical procession from Anjaneya temple. Additional police including a body of East Coast Special Police were dispatched to the district at a cost of Rs 4,432. In the year 1927, during Dasara, some Hindus secretly organised a procession with music and entered the market street. A magistrate controlled the procession and stopped them to play music. An order was passed under Section 144 of Criminal Procedure Code forbidding the Hindu processions form playing music in the streets where there were mosques, for two months. This government order was modified from time to time and this issue of conflict was debated between public interest and the private right. In the years 1935 and 1936, during the Sri Rama Navami festival, signs of conflicts appeared in some villages of Nellore and the police under the Section 30 of the Police

Act, took appropriate action to preserve peace. The Hindu-Muslim communal conflicts occurred now and then in different parts of the Northern range, but by the firm action of the police, the latter could preserve law and order.[170] There were many cases of riots and disturbances although most of them were of minor nature, but on few occasions, the police had to open fire to restore law and order. There were sporadic Hindu-Muslim clashes in the districts of Guntur and Nellore throughout the period 1924-47. Tear gas was used in a large measure successfully to disperse the unruly mob. It was also used to disperse the non-gazetted officers who defied orders under Section 144 of the Criminal Procedure Code in December, 1947. The smoke squads in Guntur and Vizagapatnam were provided with necessary arrangements for supply of requisite equipments to them.[171] Maintenance of law and order imposed a heavy strain on the police, with the number of cases or rioting or unlawful assembly rising from 1,315 in 1946 to 1,648 in 1947. The persistence of inter-communal bitterness, constitutional controversy and political restlessness account for increased number of public disturbances.

Escapes

The police had the power to arrest without warrant any person who was observed to be associated with the commission of a crime or when they had reason to believe that crime was committed by the suspected person. The police arrested and kept in custody the vagabonds, habitual offenders, persons with doubtful antecedents or those who were conditionally released from jail or prison for the sake of maintenance of law and order within their territorial jurisdiction. The police had the power to handcuff the under trial for escorting and preventing his escape. There were many incidents of prisoners escaping from jails and from custody while they were led to prisons or courts. Officers were convicted for offences committed in their official capacity. The concerned police officials were convicted under the Indian Police Act and the Indian Penal Code for negligently allowing prisoners to escape.

A very few isolated cases of escapes were recorded from this range. Some of the escapes were intra-mural (from interior of the jails) while some were extra mural (from exterior of the jails).[172] In almost all the cases, the absconders were captured and jail wardens who were responsible for it, were either prosecuted or departmentally punished. Many prisoners escaped from the police escorts from lock-ups and jails. Some of them were recaptured and the police officers who were responsible for this, were convicted for negligent act of allowing prisoners to escape by punishing them departmentally..[173]

In the year 1929, four prisoners escaped from the sub-jail at Bezawada by cutting the bars of the cells. One prisoner of Yerukala tribe was recaptured and the others were arrested few days later by the police of the West Godavari district.[174] An undertrial prisoner, who was an inpatient in the government headquarters hospital at Eluru in the West Godavari district, escaped during night by removing the chains fastened to the bed; he was, however, captured later and imprisoned.[175] In the Vizagapatam district in the year 1933, a gang of tribal prisoners acting in a concert suddenly attacked the police escort and 13 of them escaped with a police carbine after injuring the constables.[176] Fire was opened upon these prisoners in which one of them was wounded. Those who escaped were recaptured with the stolen carbine. In the year 1934, an incident occurred in the Bapatla taluk of the Guntur district, where the Sub-Inspector of police was stabbed by an old offender whose house he was about to search for stolen property. The officer attacked the offender bravely and shot him.[177] Old offenders, convicts, habitual criminals and the criminals tribesmen were kept under strict surveillance by maintaining criminal history records in respect of them, keeping their movements under watch by the village officers and ordering very serious offenders registered under the police sheet to show their attendance at frequent intervals in the police stations. The old offenders received enhanced punishment under Section 75 of the Indian Penal Code and they were ordered to notify residence under Section 565 of the Criminal Procedure Code. Those persons who failed to notify their residence were severely punished and convicted.[178]

Criminal Tribes

Once the Criminal Tribes Act was passed in the Northern range, a number of habitual criminal tribes of the Northern range were registered under this it. Their movements were restricted to prevent them from committing crimes. They were confined in the settlements under the police surveillance. The main objective of the Criminal Tribes Act was to safeguard the rights of the public against anti-social elements and also for reformation of the habitual criminal tribes.[179] The introduction of this Act had resulted in a considerable decrease in crimes against life and property. The criminal tribes were classified into two categories, settled and wandering. The settled tribes were agriculture labours and were involved in petty cases of crime. The wandering tribes moved in gangs and they earned their livelihood by hunting, snake charming, performing acrobatics, and by crimes, such as theft, burglary, dacoity and various forms of cheating. The reasons for these tribes to indulge in crimes were lack of property, vagrancy, lack of stability and general purpose in life, restlessness, and aimlessness. The classification of crimes and the restriction on the movements of the habitual criminals had controlled the crime in the Northern range to a large extent.[180] Some of the tribal communities, who committed many non-bailable offences, were systematically registered by the government under the Criminal Tribes Act of 1924. The registration of these gangs was done by the Criminal Investigation Department.[181] As they were described as habitually criminal, restriction was put on their movements and the registered members were forced to report to the local police station periodically.[182] The working of this Act had resulted in a large reduction of organised crimes along with those by the habitual offenders in the Northern range. The reformation movement made good progress in the Northern range and an Inspector of Police was appointed to establish communal panchayats among the members of these tribes. As the range had large tracts of agency areas which were inhabited by these tribes, there were many incidents of crimes and criminal activities committed by the tribes. In the year 1936, with the transfer of two districts of Ganjam and Jeypore to the Orissa Province, the criminal tribes of these districts came under the jurisdiction of the newly-formed province.[183]

Special settlements were constructed for the notified tribes and these tribes were settled in villages under the police guard.[184] The duty of the police was to ensure that no registered member of the tribe was absent without notice. These police guards, who kept a watch over these tribes, were provided with all facilities. The Head Constables and Constables in charge of these tribal settlement stations in the Northern range were supplied with uniforms.[185] On introduction of the reform schemes, the crime came to be better controlled as there was improvement in detection, the older generation of habitual criminals gradually passed away, and due to efficient working of the Criminal Tribes Act. The government granted rewards liberally for the acts of co-operation of the village officers, police, and the public, which proved beneficial in keeping the crime under check.

The criminal tribes of the Northern range had committed many offences, both organised and unorganised, during the period 1924-1947. A group of prisoners in the Vizagapatam district belonging to Telaga Pamula tribe, who were prisoners acting in concert, suddenly attacked their escort and thirteen of them escaped stealing a police carbine after injuring the constables.[186]

They were later caught and arrested. A gang of Yerukala absconders, who were members of the criminal tribes from the Sitanagaram Criminal Tribes Settlement of the Guntur district, committed about 112 burglaries during the year 1933.[187] This was the highest recorded figure in the Northern range and also in the Madras Presidency.

During the year 1936, three local Yenadi tribals had committed a mail-robbery in the district of Nellore; later, the police arrested all of them and the culprits were convicted in the court.[188] In the year 1939, a gang of four Bouriah criminal tribe members of the United Provinces committed burglary in the palace of the zamindar of Kasimkota in the Vizagapatam district and stole property worth Rs 15,000. They were arrested by the Head Constable of Anakapalle police station in Vizagapatam district and the railway police at Vizianagram.[189]

In the Kistna district, a fugitive Yanadi prisoner was rounded up by a police party and villagers and was shot dead by a Constable as he was attempting a murderous attack with a knife on the police.[190] A receiver of a stolen property and his sister murdered a notorious Donga Yenadi of the notified criminal tribe when he demanded the return of the stolen property.[191] The notorious Yerakala dacoits headed by Kondigadu were attacked by the villagers of Isukatripuravaram of the Guntur district during course of which he and two other members of the gang were killed. These criminal tribes also cooperated with the police and village officers in crime control by providing information about the culprits. In the year 1938, a Yanadi tribal fellow from the Nellore district, gave information to the Village Vigilance Committee members about the culprits in a case relating to house-breaking and theft.[192] The full extent of crimes in the Northern range was under control due to improvement in reporting of the crimes. This decrease in volume of crime was attributed to factors, viz., inter-district cooperation, coordination of work, vigilance in regard to presence of strangers, proper intelligence sharing with the villages, and to constant encouragement given to the circles and police stations. The application of the Abeyance System of criminal tribes control also contributed in the reduction of all forms of crime.

There were some other important cases which the police dealt during the period 1924-47 under various Acts. The public nuisance was an act of illegal omission which caused many common injuries, dangers, obstructions, and annoyance to the public. Negligent acts likely to spread infectious diseases dangerous to life were punished with imprisonment of either description for a term which extended to six months, or with fine, or with both.[193] To prevent such offences, special police arrangements were made during the fairs and festivals in the Northern range.[194] Medico-legal work in the Northern range was carefully done, no incorrect or improper certificates were issued by private medical practitioners and they also conducted post-mortem examinations in local fund dispensaries without any grouse. There were no adverse comments in judgements on wound certificates granted by such practitioners.[195]

Offence infanticide was also common and was committed mostly due to fear of social disgrace or on account of domestic discord. Due to superstitious beliefs and ignorance, this offence was committed. Gambling was common offence in the districts of the Northern range, especially during the festival seasons. Those persons who kept any office or place for the purpose of drawing any lottery, were punished with imprisonment of either description for a term which was extendable to six months, or with fine, or with both. The police during the period of study, with the assistance of the village officers, had registered a number of gambling cases. Kidnapping was an unlawful act which was punishable by the penal code.[196] There was scare of children-lifting in some parts of the East Godavari district of the range. Some children disappeared in the Sabhari valley of the East Godavari Agency, and a scare was mongered that the children were kidnapped for sacrifice. Two Koyas tribals were caught in the act of kidnapping, whose arrest put an end to the trouble. There was another case in the plains of the same district in which there were strong reasons to suspect that a little girl had been sacrificed, but actual proof against the two Brahmins, suspected in the matter, was not detected. The provisions of certain sections of the Suppression of Immoral Traffic Act were applied in the Northern range especially in Bezwada, Cocanada, Rajahmundry, Vizagapatam, Ellure, and Vizianagaram districts.[197] The police under these Acts had considerably kept the crimes and offences under control.

Offences Committed by the Police

The police also committed offences under their private and official capacity for which they were punished judicially and departmentally. All the police officers were supposed to follow the rules and they were not permitted to use threat or promise. Whoever policeman disobeyed the law or caused injury to any person was punished with simple imprisonment for a term extendable to one year, or with fine, or with both. Unlawfully engaging in trade or receiving any gratification was regarded as an offence that was punishable under the Indian Penal Code by imprisonment for a term two years, or with fine, or with both.[198] The police were convicted for offences committed in their official capacity, such as negligently allowing prisoners to escape from custody, accepting gifts, forceful convictions, etc. Escapes from the police custody, jails, and lock-ups were common offences for which the police officers so responsible, were punished departmentally or under Indian Penal Code or by Sessions Courts.[199]

Here is a case of interest where a police officer had murdered the Havildar-Armourer and the Commander, Peterson and then shot himself. The reason was jealousy over promotion. Another case of interest in which the rules were violated relates to the Godavari district in which a Yanadi fellow who belonged to an identified criminal tribe was made forcefully to accept a theft that occurred in a Sub-Inspector's house. But later, it was proved wrong. For this, the Sub-Inspector was punished with six months rigorous imprisonment and other Constables, who colluded with the Sub-Inspector, were also sentenced to four months rigorous imprisonment.[200] Another case of interest of such offence is: A constable in Jeypore district accompanied his Sub-Inspector on investigation duty, they both tied up a Dong tribal, and beat him with a stick to extract confession and make him deliver property. The police had no powers to beat someone to give false statements. This case was committed to the Sessions Court. In many cases, prosecutions by the police were declared false after trial or enquiry, but no case was declared false during the year 1924 in Jeypore and East Godavari districts.[201]

During the year 1925, some of the police cases were found false after trial in the districts of Jeypore and East Godavari. The system of setting apart special days exclusively for the trial of police cases had been in force in all districts except Jeypore and West Godavari.

Offences affecting public health, safety and convenience, spreading an infection of any disease dangerous to life, selling unwholesome food or provisions, and adulteration of food and drinks were also dealt by the police, the punishment for such crimes being imprisonment.[202] These offences come under Special and Local Laws and Nuisance Sections of the Indian Penal Code. These cases were put under control by vigorous police activity in municipal areas and on roads in interest of public safety and sanitation. The Boy Scout troop of Nellore town rendered assistance during festivals. The public were educated in queue formation, wherever necessary and possible.

Cognizable Offences

The Indian Penal Code made a distinction of crimes by dividing them into two types, cognizable and non-cognizable offences. Under cognizable crimes, the police made inquiry into the case when reported so or it came to their notice without the reference of magisterial authority. The police in the Northern range had dealt with different types of crimes and offences of socio-political, economic and religious nature. The magnitude of these crimes differed. The police was construed as an agency of oppression and suppression under the British rule, though their work demanded extraordinary skills, restraint and character. By the revised, modern, and scientific methods of investigation, the police was able to control the increasing volume of crime. The following table shows the cases of cognizable offences in the Northern range during the years 1924 to 1947.

Years	*No. of cognizable crimes*
1924	29257
1925	28344
1926	26212
1927	20801
1928	25812
1929	31180
1930	24068
1931	30234
1932	31368
1933	33892
1934	38801
1935	38258
1936	44993
1937	44631
1938	41269
1939	48782
1940	61593
1941	62514
1942	65441
1943	67342
1944	73251
1945	76583
1946	77082
1947	87557

The number of cognizable crimes are shown graphically as follows:

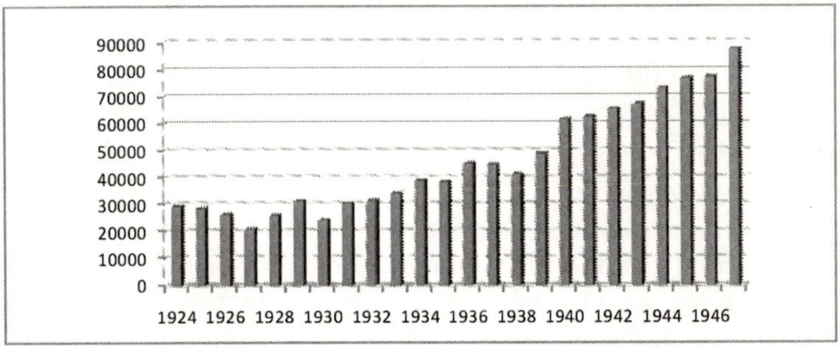

The above graph shows the increase in total number of cognizable crimes in true sense which were noticeable in all the districts of the Northern range. The true cases of cognizable crimes recorded in the years 1924, 1925, 1926 and 1927 shows a downfall and this was due to the improved methods of detection, good work done in handling of wandering gangs and close supervision of criminal tribes contributed which indicates the sound police administration in the Northern range. The proportion of offences against persons and property was highest in the districts of Jeypore and West Godavari among the other districts of Northern range[203] and also in the Madras Presidency.

In the years 1929, 1930 and 1931, the volume of crime was low as there was a notable decrease in ordinary thefts and railway thefts by nearly 50 per cent in the Northern range.[204] Better labour conditions and absorption of large number of the unemployed in various occupations created by the economic depression combined with the vigorous action taken under the security section accounted for this decrease. In the Kistna district, special steps were taken by the government by printing and pasting notice in all the villages to see that the crime was well-reported. The result was that there was an increase in the crime by 342 cases. The increase does not reflect that the crime was has high, but, it indicates that the crime was better reported with the experimentation. Theft cases were recorded highest in the Madras Presidency in the districts of Vizagapatam and East Godavari in the year 1929.[205] For five successive years, ending with 1936, the percentage of detection of total cognizable crimes increased to 45.3 per cent to which the West Godavari district contributed about 8.4 per cent. Attention was paid to habitual criminals, intelligent handling of the cases, more extended use of the Station Crime History system, prompt dissemination of information regarding crime and criminals, quick dispatch of crime cards and the grant of liberal rewards to the public, village officials and the police, all of which contributed in better control of crime.

In the year 1937, there was a very large increase in number of factious murders in the different places of the Northern range. The peculiar thing about factious murders was that the factions were well-known to the Police, the Magistracy and the public, but were extremely difficult to stop. In many districts of the Northern range, faction murders were a bane.[206]

In the year 1938, the Inspector General of Police had said, "I must again draw serious attention to the colossal number of murders due to faction. I am still of opinion that a great number of such crimes are preventable but not preventable by the police without some change on the or at least without some attempt to use the law as it stands at present in a more liberal manner. In my last year's report, I suggested remedies but the Government are of the opinion that the measures laid down in G.O. No. 1110, Public (General) dated 21st June, 1937 are sufficient to meet the case. The Government Order relates to the speedy application of the security sections of the Criminal Procedure Code and toe the disposal of such cases, as far as possible, in the villages themselves in the most summary manner allowable under the law. I regret to say that these measures, even when applied, have little effect. There is always the Court of Appeal which must, in the nature of things, pay more attention to the application of case law and legal theory to any set of circumstances than to the peace of an area and the preservation of lives. This is with regard to instances of long standing faction where it is just possible sometimes for the police to put a case before a court, but does not touch those more numerous instances where the faction is well known to the magistracy, the police and where the law cannot be applied unless there are overt acts to prove to the satisfaction of the legal mind that such faction holds the seeds of future death, arson and pillage. Such a state of affairs is surely a blot upon administration and the reputation of the country as a whole, and every means should be explored and attempted for its removal."[207]

The seasonal condition also had an effect on the crimes in the Northern range besides other factors; whenever there was an unfavourable season, the prices of the grains increased and the crimes were also much during the bad seasons. The unfavourable seasonal conditions of the year 1938 had an inevitable effect on the volume of crime which showed an increase. The percentage of detection of total cognizable crime was 43 which was slightly less than the previous year. The increase in crime in the Madras Presidency during the year 1938, recorded in the district of Vizagapatam, was 14.6 per cent and in East Godavari, it was 11.1 per cent. Better reporting and registration of crimes were marked features of the year 1938-39 and this accounted partly for the increase.

In the years 1938 and 1939, there was a rise in the volume of cognizable crimes along with that of true cases of this type excluding offences under the Special and Local Laws and the nuisance sections of the Indian Penal Code. The active co-operation by Village Vigilance Committees, adequate control by the police over looting gangs and bad characters, enforcement of the system of joint responsibility for the good conduct of criminal tribe members, and effective help rendered by the Central Crime Branch of the Criminal Investigation Department and District Intelligence Bureaus kept the professional crime under check.[208] The trend of total cognizable crimes and its relation to the prices of the two staple foodgrains rice and cholam, had steadily increased since 1940. In the years 1941-42, there was increase in the volume of crime and it was due to the general economic conditions of the years. During this year 1941, the murder cases in the districts of Vizagapatam and Guntur alone contributed highest number of cases in the Madras Presidency, recording 52 each. It recorded abnormal increase in the district of Nellore and was also high due to communal disturbances. The districts of East Godavari and Kistna were recorded low number of cases in this year. Distress was prevailing throughout Northern range as there was blackout restriction, panic and evacuation, movements of refugees from Burma and Malaya, and the congestion on the railways.[209] There was a increase in crime in all the districts of the Northern range in the years 1944 and 1945 and this was due to the extraordinary high prices prevailing and other adverse conditions created by the war.[210] The most noticeable increase was in the district of Nellore which recorded 24.0 per cent and while in the West Godavari distrtict, it was 20.2 per cent.[211]

The crime rate during the year 1946 had increased due to the increased prices of staple foodgrains and essential commodities that continued to remain at a very high level throughout the Northern range. The north-east monsoon set in late and caused heavy rains in the Guntur and Nellore districts. The unprecedented heavy rains in the month of December caused many rivers to flood and caused damage to the standing crops and irrigation works. There was a wave of labour unrest in most of the districts resulting in strikes and consequent dislocation of normal police work. Crime was almost high in the year 1947 in all the districts of the Northern range due to the high prices of staple food grains. The south-west monsoon was ill-distributed and arrived late in almost all districts of the range thereby delaying the cultivation of both the dry and the wet crops.[212] The north-east monsoon was a failure which resulted in serious damage to the crops. Unemployment followed the demobilisation of military personnel. There were widespread labour, communal, and agrarian unrests which diverted the police from their normal functions. In the year 1947, the Northern range was politically restive due to the ongoing freedom movement which manifested in increase in number of riots, communal tensions, and the activities of the communists and local factions in most of the districts of the Madras Presidency, especially the Nellore and Kistna districts. The police force was engaged most of times against political agitators and could not devote much time to general crimes, and on several occasions, they had to open fire in order to restore law and order.[213]

The number of cases of rioting and unlawful assembly increased with passing time, but the public peace on the whole was well-maintained by the police force through out the range. Many districts were free from serious cases of rioting; on ten occasions the police had opened fire either in self-defence or to restore order; in four cases in the district of East and West Godavari, Kistna, and Guntur, firing was opened when mobs attempted to rescue gamblers, but later, they were arrested. On one occasion, when a merchant in a village of Nellore district had refused to sell rice at a controlled rate, the villagers became so enraged that they attacked him and attempted to loot his house. There was a episode of communal tension in the Northern range during this year. Elaborate and effective police arrangements were made during festival seasons, especially during Muharram, Dasara and other important festivals wherever tension prevailed between Hindus and Muslims. There were few labour troubles, however, the culprits were successfully handled by the police force and law and order was maintained. With the consequent transfer of power on 15th August, 1947, the Indian government took over the reins of administration.[214] The police in the Northern range dealt with cognizable and non-cognizable offences; under the fomer, the police made inquiry into the case when reported, while in case of the latter type, the police investigated only after receiving orders from the magistracy.

The statistical crime data on all offences were collected from the districts of the Northern range. The crime statistics were used as a tool of management to understand the cause of crime and as an index of efficiency of the police organisation and the action taken under various Sections of the Indian Penal Code and the Criminal Procedure Code. The reports and crime figures gave the British police supervisory officers at the district headquarters a clear picture of the developments in the range. The First Information Report was prepared on reporting of a crime which was the first step taken by the police before investigation. The occurrences were first entered in the station house register and the police Station House Officer reported it to the police headquarters and the divisional Inspector. The crime reports were checked daily in the district office and arranged according to the divisions and the classes of offences. The efficiency of police functioning was measured either on the basis of number of arrests or the rate of conviction in respect of cases brought by the police to the courts.

The common crimes in the Northern range were murder, dacoity, robbery, theft and other cases like cheating, forgery, counterfeit of currency, infanticide, culpable homicide, rapes, etc. The motives for these crimes were socio-economic reasons, communal causes, factional fights, family disputes, and sexual jealousy. The police in the Northern range also dealt with crimes related to political, socio-economical, and religious offences such as, factional riots, labour troubles, agrarian strikes, and communal tensions. Crimes were first reported to the police station, either by the Magistrate or by the Constable, or by the complainant.

As the period 1924 to 1947 was a peak time of the freedom struggle, the people of the Northern range had actively participated in the Non-co-operation Movement, Civil Disobedience Movement, Quit India Movement and other campaigns till the achievement of Independence. The British in order to control the political situation, declared certain acts, such as assembling, delivering public speeches, holding Indian flags, and singing the national song as unlawful. To suppress these activities, the British government resorted to severe policy of repression in the Northern range. The Northern range had large tracts of agency areas and was inhabited by tribes some of whom were habitual criminals and were responsible for many offences in the range. These habitual criminal tribes were registered as the criminal tribes under the Criminal Tribes Act. The working of this Act and reformatory settlements resulted in a large reduction of organised crime by habitual offenders in the Northern range.

The abnormal rise in the prices of food stuffs, cloth and other necessities of life aggravated the prevailing general economic distress, which coupled with the failure of monsoon and the suspension of the Criminal Tribes Act, tended to swell the volume of crime. The trend of crimes in the Northern range was in relation to the poor rainfall, high prices of staple foodgrains, distress due to blackout restriction, panic and evacuation, and the movements of refugees from Burma and Malaya. The reasons for the increase in crimes were adverse conditions created by the pre- and post-war times. The other factors for the rise were labour strikes, political unrest, communal tensions, and the activities of communists and local factions in most of the districts of the Northern range. Crime is always committed in one form or the other and the type and the magnitude of crime changes from place to place. Though, owing to labour unrest, and communal and agrarian troubles, a heavy strain was imposed on the police, yet, they discharged their duties efficiently. The government also sanctioned for the formation of special police in order to ensure effective maintenance of law and order throughout the Northern range. The police wireless system did good work under most difficult conditions and it proved a great help in the then disturbed conditions in the range. The Northern range was no exemption to crime as this range was vast, highly populated, growing economy and most of the range was Agency area.

References

1. Ramaswami P.N., *Magisterial and Police Guide*, Vol. 1, The Madras Law Journal office, Madras, 1951, p. 2.
2. Orvill C. Snyder, *An Introduction to Criminal Justice,* Text and Cases, Little, Brown and Company, New York, 1953, p. 11.
3. Leitch Ritchie, *British World in the East*, A Guide, Vol. I and II, W.H. Allen and Co., London, 1847, p. 388.
4. Giriraj Shah, *Encyclopedia of Crime, Police and Judicial System*, Vol. I, Anmol Publications, New Delhi, 1999, p. 1960.
5. Munshi K.M. and Diwakar R.R., *Law and Culture,* Bharatiya Vidya Bhavan, Bombay, 1965, p. 13.
6. Mehartaj Begum, *District Police Administration,* Anmol Publications Pvt. Ltd., New Delhi, 1996, p. 100.
7. Rushbrook Williams L.F., *India in 1923-24*, Central Publication Branch, Calcutta, 1924, p. 73.
8. Fraser Tytler A, *Consideration on the present political state of India*, Vol. II, printed for Black, Parbury and Allen, London, 1816, p. 10.
9. James Vadackumchery, *National Police Commission*, Alph Publications, New Delhi, 1998, p. 198.
10. Report on the Administration of the Police of the Madras Presidency, 1925, printed by Superintendent, Government Press, Madras, 1926, p. 48.
11. Home Department Resolution No.1112-1120, dated 8th November, 1905, p. 1.

12. Report on the Administration of the Madras Presidency for the year 1938-39, printed by Superintendent, Madras, 1940, p. 47.
13. The Indian Penal Code, 1860, Act 45 of 1860, dated 6th October, 1860.
14. Report of the Indian Statutory Commission, Vol. II, Recommendations, Logos Press, New Delhi, 1930.
15. Report on Administration of the Police of the Madras Province for the year 1932, printed by Superintendent, Government Press, Madras, 1932, p. 12.
16. Collector's Standing Orders of Nellore District, M.R. Ry. Rai Bahadur, printed by Superintendent, Government Press, Madras, 1931, p. 145.
17. Report on the Administration of the Police of the Madras Presidency, 1925, printed by Superintendent, Government Press, 1926, Madras, p. 10.
18. Home Department Resolution No.1112-1120, dated 8th November, 1905, p. 1.
19. G.O.No.523, Home, (Judl.), dated 5th March, 1917, Home (Judicial) Department, Government of Madras.
20. G.O.No.2395, Home, dated 19th May, 1941, Home Department, Government of Madras.
21. Report of the Inspector General of Police, Madras, dated 30th June, 1929, printed by Superintendent, Government Press, 1930, Madras.
22. Government of India, Legislative Department, Act No.XVI of 1927, printed by Superintendent, Government Press, Madras, 1930, p. 20.
23. Administrative Report of the Inspector General of Police for the year 1929, printed by Superintendent, Government Press, 1930, Madras.
24. Bhardwaj K.K., *Indian Police Administration*, National Publications, Madras 1978, p. 89.
25. G.O.No.2041, Home, dated 28th April, 1941, Home Department, Government of Madras.
26. Bhardwaj K.K, *Indian Police Administration*, National Publications, Madras, 1978, p. 89.
27. Fraser Tytler A, *Considerations on the present political state of India*, Vol. II, London, 1816, p. 10.
28. The Indian Penal Code,1860, Act 45 of 1860, dated 6th October, 1860.
29. Report on the Administration of the Police of the Madras Presidency, 1929, printed by Superintendent, Government Press, 1930, Madras, p. 19.

30. History of Police Organisation in India and Indian Village Police published by the University of Calcutta with the permission of Government of India, University Press, Calcutta, 1913, pp. 50,51.
31. Francis W, The Gazetteer of the Vizagapatam District, Asian Education Services, Madras, 1907, p. 205.
32. Report on the Administration of the Police in the Madras Province for the year 1933, printed by Superintendent, Government Press, Madras, 1934, p. 16.
33. Report on the Administration of the Police in the Madras Province for the years 1924-47, printed by Superintendent, Government Press, Madras.
34. Report on the Administration of the Police in the Madras Province for the year 1936, printed by Superintendent, Government Press, Madras, 1937, pp. 18,19.
35. Report on the Administration of the Police in the Madras Province for the year 1933, printed by Superintendent, Government Press, Madras, 1934, p. 17.
36. *Ibid.*, p. 17.
37. Report on the Administration of Police in the Madras Province for the year 1941, printed by Superintendent, Government Press, Madras, 1942, p. 14.
38. The Indian Penal Code, 1860, Act 45 of 1860, dated 6th October, 1860.
39. Report on the Administration of the Madras Presidency for the year 1932, printed by Superintendent, Madras, 1933, p. 12.
40. Report on the Administration of Police in the Madras Province for the year 1936, printed by Superintendent, Government Press, Madras, 1937, p. 14.
41. Report on the Administration of the Police in the Madras Province for the year 1941, printed by Superintendent, Government Press, Madras, 1942, p. 14.
42. Report on the Administration of the Police in the Madras Province for the year 1939, printed by Superintendent, Government Press, Madras, 1940, p. 15.
43. Edwardes S.M., *Crime in India*, printed by Oxford University Press, Madras, 1924, p. 41.
44. Government of India, Legislative Department, The Prisoners Act of 1871, Office of the Superintendent of Government Printing, Calcutta, 1894, p. 9.
45. The Indian Penal Code, 1860, Act 45 of 1860, dated 6th October, 1860.

46. History of Police Organisation in India and Indian Village Police published by the University of Calcutta with the permission of Government of India, University Press, Calcutta, 1913,p. 47.
47. Report on the Administration of the Police in the Madras Presidency for the years 1924-47, printed by Superintendent, Government Press, Madras.
48. Report on the Administration of the Madras Presidency for the years 1925-26, printed by Superintendent, Government Press, Madras, 1927, p. 35 (also see Report on the Administration of Police of the Madras Presidency, 1925, p. 12).
49. Report on the Administration of the Police in the Madras Province for the year 1936, printed by Superintendent ,Government Press, Madras, 1937, p. 14.
50. Report of the Administration of the Police of the Madras Province, 1936, printed by Superintendent, Government Press, Madras, 1937, p. 5.
51. Report on the Administration of the Police of the Madras Province, 1939, printed by Superintendent, Government Press, Madras, 1940, p. 12.
52. Report on the Administration of the Police in the Madras Province for the year 1941, printed by Superintendent, Government Press, Madras, 1942, p. 13.
53. Government of Madras, Legal Department, The Madras Police Act V of 1861, printed by Superintendent, Government Press, Madras, pp. 3,4.
54. The Indian Penal Code, 1860, Act 45 of 1860, 6th October,1860.
55. Report on the Administration of the Police of the Madras Province,1925, printed by Superintendent, Government Press, Madras, 1926, p. 12.
56. Report on the Administration of the Police of the Madras Presidency, 1925, printed by Superintendent, Government Press, Madras, 1926, p. 12.
57. Report on the Administration of Police in the Madras Presidency for the years 1924 to 1947, printed by Superintendent, Government Press, Madras.
58. Report on the Administration of the Police in the Madras Province for the year 1926, printed by Superintendent, Government Press, Madras, 1927, p. 12.
59. Report on the Administration of Police in the Madras Province for the year 1933, printed by Superintendent, Government Press, Madras, 1934, p. 16.
60. Report on the Administration of the Police in the Madras Province for the year 1936, printed by Superintendent ,Government Press, Madras, 1937, p. 16.

61. Report on the Administration of the Police in the Madras Province for the year 1939, printed by Superintendent, Government Press, Madras, 1940, p. 54.
62. *Ibid.*, p. 16.
63. *Ibid.*, p. 17.
64. The Indian Penal Code, 1860, Act 45 of 1860, dated 6th October, 1860.
65. Report on the Administration of the Police of the Madras Presidency, 1928, printed by Superintendent, Government Press, Madras, 1929, p. 9.
66. History of Police Organisation in India and Indian Village Police, published by the University of Calcutta with the permission of Government of India, University Press, Calcutta, 1913, p. 47.
67. Edwardes S.M., *Crime in India*, printed by Oxford University Press, Madras, 1924, p. 18.
68. Report on the Administration of the Police in the Madras Presidency for the years 1924 to 1947, printed by Superintendent, Government Press, Madras.
69. G.O.No.467, Judicial, dated 25th September, 1928, Home Department, Government of Madras.
70. Report on the Administration of Police of the Madras Presidency, 1928, printed by Superintendent, Government Press, Madras, 1929, p. 9.
71. The History of the Andhra Pradesh Police 1861-1961, published by Inspector General of Police, Andhra Pradesh, Hyderabad, 1961, p. 230.
72. Report on the Administration of Police in the Madras Presidency for the year 1933, printed by Superintendent, Government Press, Madras, 1934, p. 12.
73. Report of the Administration of the Police of the Madras Province 1935, printed by Superintendent, Government Press, Madras, 1936, p. 5.
74. *Ibid.*, p. 14.
75. Report on the Administration of the Police in the Madras Province for the year 1936, printed by Superintendent, Government Press, Madras, 1937, p. 13.
76. *Ibid.*, p. 5.
77. Report on the Administration of the Police of the Madras Province 1937, printed by Superintendent, Government Press, Madras, 1938, p. 5.
78. Ramesan N, Andhra Pradesh District Gazetteers, East Godavari, printed by Director of printing and stationery at Government Secretary Press, Hyderabad, 1979, p. 158.

79. Report on the Administration of the Police in the Madras Province for the year 1937, printed by Superintendent, Government Press, Madras, 1938, p. 11.
80. Report on the Administration of the Police in the Madras Province for the year 1938, printed by Superintendent, Government Press, Madras, 1939, p. 6.
81. Report on the Administration of the Police in the Madras Province for the year 1939, printed by Superintendent, Government Press, Madras, 1940, p. 11.
82. Report on the Administration of Police in the Madras Province for the year 1941, Government Press, Madras, 1942, p. 11.
83. Report on the Administration of the Police in the Madras Province for the year 1946, printed by Superintendent, Government Press, Madras, 1947, p. 7.
84. Report on the Administration of the Police in the Madras Province for the year 1947, printed by Superintendent, Government Press, Madras, 1948, p. 8.
85. G.O No. 1110, Public (General), dated 21st June, 1937, Public (General) Department, Government of Madras.
86. Government of India, Legislative Department Act No.VI of 1943, Madras, p. 1.
87. Report on the Administration of the Police of the Madras Province, 1946, printed by Superintendent, Government Press, Madras, 1947, p. 14.
88. Report on the Administration of the Police of the Madras Province, 1925, printed by Superintendent, Government Press, Madras, 1926, p. 12.
89. Report on the Administration of the Madras Presidency for the year 1925, printed by Superintendent, Government Press, Madras, 1926, p. 12.
90 Andhra Patrika, dated 2nd December, 1926.
91 G.O No. 425, Public (Police), dated 6th August, 1929, Public (Police) Department, Government of Madras.
92. Report on the Administration of the Madras Presidency for the year 1928, printed by Superintendent, Government Press, Madras, 1929, p. 13.
93. Report on the Administration of the Police of the Madras Presidency, 1929, printed by the Superintendent, Government Press, 1930, Madras, p. 15.
94. Report on the Administration of the Police in the Madras Province for the year 1933, printed by Superintendent, Government Press, Madras, 1934, p. 16.

95. Report on the Administration of the Police in the Madras Province for the year 1938, printed by Superintendent, Government Press, Madras, 1939, pp. 18,19.

96. Report on the Administration of the Police in the Madras Province for the year 1937, printed by Superintendent, Government Press, Madras, 1938, p. 16.

97. Report on the Administration of the Police in the Madras Province for the year 1939, printed by Superintendent, Government Press, Madras, 1940, p. 17.

98. The Indian Penal Code, 1860, Act 45 of 1860, dated 6th October,1860.

99. Report on the Administration of the Police in the Madras Province for the year 1946, printed by Superintendent, Government Press, Madras, 1947, p. 14.

100. G.O.No.467, Judl., dated 25th September,1928, Judicial Department, Government of Madras.

101. Report on the Administration of the Police in the Madras Province for the year 1937, by the Superintendent, Government Press, Madras, 1938, p. 16.

102. The History of the Andhra Pradesh Police 1861-1961, published by Inspector General of Police, Andhra Pradesh, Hyderabad, 1961, p. 229.

103. Report on the Administration of the Police of the Madras Province,1933, printed by Superintendent, Government Press, Madras, 1934, p. 7.

104. Report on the Administration of the Police in the Madras Province for the year 1941, printed by Superintendent, Government Press, Madras, 1942, p. 15.

105. Report on the Administration of the Police in the Madras Province for the year 1939, printed by Superintendent, Government Press, Madras, 1940, p. 17.

106 The Indian Penal Code, 1860, Act 45 of 1860, dated 6th October,1860.

107. Madras in 1947, Outline of Administration, Part-1, printed by Superintendent, Government Press, Madras, 1926, p. 47.

108. Report on the Administration of the Police of the Madras Presidency,1925, printed by Superintendent, Government Press, Madras, 1926, p. 13.

109. Report on the Administration of the Police of the Madras Presidency, 1927, printed by Superintendent, Government Press, Madras, 1928, p. 13.

110. Report on the Administration of the Madras Presidency for the

year 1928, printed by Superintendent, Government Press, Madras, 1929, p. 13.

111. The Hindu, dated 15th February, 1929.

112. Report on the Administration of the Police of the Madras Presidency, 1929, printed by Superintendent, Government Press, Madras, 1930, p. 16.

113. Report on the Administration of the Police in the Madras Province for the year 1937, printed by Superintendent, Government Press, Madras, 1938, p. 17.

114. Report on the Administration of Police in the Madras Province for the year 1938, printed by Superintendent, Government Press, Madras, 1939, p. 20.

115. Report on the Administration of the Police in the Madras Province for the year 1946, printed by Superintendent, Government Press, Madras, 1947, p. 7.

116. Report on the Administration of the Police in the Madras Province for the year 1938, printed by Superintendent, Government Press, Madras, 1939, p. 20.

117. Second Report on the Indian Penal Code, Military Orphan Press, Calcutta, 1847, p. 14.

118. The Indian Penal Code, 1860, Act 45 of 1860, 6th October,1860.

119. Report on the Administration of the Madras Presidency for the year 1947, printed by Superintendent, Government Press, Madras, 1948, p. 22.

120. Report on the Administration of Police in the Madras Presidency for the year 1933, printed by Superintendent, Government Press, Madras, 1934, p. 13.

121. Report on the Administration of the Police of the Madras Province, 1935, printed by Superintendent, Government Press, Madras, 1936, p. 14.

122. Report of the Administration of the Police of the Madras Province, 1937, printed by Superintendent, Government Press, Madras, 1938, p .5.

123. *Ibid.*, pp. 13,14.

124. *Ibid.*, p. 15.

125. Report on the Administration of the Police in the Madras Province for the year 1941, printed by Superintendent, Government Press, Madras, 1942, p. 11.

126. Report of the Administration of the Madras Presidency for the year I944-45, printed by Superintendent, Government Press, Madras, 1946, p. 58.

127. Report on the Administration of the Police in the Madras Province for the year 1947, printed by the Superintendent, Government Press, Madras,1948, p. 11.

128. Report on the Administration of the Police in the Madras Province for the year 1947, printed by Superintendent, Government Press, Madras, 1948, p. 8.

129. The Hindu, dated 26th September, 1932.

130. G.O.No.3102, Home, (Ms), dated, 9th November, 1943, Home Department, Government of Madras.

131. Rao P.R., *History of Modern Andhra*, Sterling Publishers Ltd., Delhi, 1993, p. 116.

132. Report of the Administration of the Madras Presidency for the year 1921-22 printed by Superintendent, Government Press, Madras, 1923, pp. xiii-xiv (also see M. Venkatarangaiya, *The Freedom Movement in Andhra Pradesh*, Vol. II, 1921-1931, Hyderabad, 1965, pp. 79-93).

133. Report on the Administration of the Madras Presidency for the year 1930, printed by Superintendent, Government Press, Madras, 1931, pp. xiii-xiv.

134. *Ibid.*, pp. xxiv-xxv.

135 The History of the Andhra Pradesh Police 1861-1961, published by Inspector General of Police, Andhra Pradesh, Hyderabad, 1961, pp. 225,226.

136. Report on the Administration of the Police in the Madras Province for the year 1933, printed by Superintendent, Government Press, Madras, 1934, p. 15.

137. Report of the Administration of the Madras Presidency for the year 1938-39, printed by Superintendent, Government Press, Madras, 1940, p. 32.

138. G.O.No.1013, Public (General), dated 9th November, 1943, Public (General) Department, Government of Madras.

139. The History of the Andhra Pradesh Police 1861-1961, published by Inspector General of Police, Andhra Pradesh, Hyderabad, 1961, pp. 237, 238.

140 G.O.No.7434-2, Public (General) Department, dated 6th March, 1943, Public (General) Department, Government of Madras.

141. The Hindu, dated 12th August, 1942.

142. The Hindu, dated 17th August, 1942.

143. The History of the Andhra Pradesh Police 1861-1961, published by Inspector General of Police, Andhra Pradesh, Hyderabad, 1961, pp. 230-231.

144. Report on the Administration of the Police in the Madras Province for the year 1933, printed by Superintendent, Government Press, Madras, 1934, p. 14.

145. Andhra Pradesh Congress Committee Proceedings, 1937, p. 3756.

146. Report on the Administration of the Police in the Madras Province for the year 1937, Government Press, Madras, 1938, p. 13.

147. Report on the Administration of the Police in the Madras Province for the year 1938, printed by Superintendent, Government Press, Madras, 1939, p. 15.

148 Report of the Administration of the Madras Presidency for the year 1938-39 printed by Superintendent, Government Press, Madras, 1940, p. 49.

149. Report on the Administration of the Police in the Madras Province for the year 1939, Government Press, Madras, 1940, p. 13.

150. Report on the Administration of the Madras Presidency for the years 1938-39, Superintendent, Government Press, Madras, 1940, pp. 46,49.

151. Report on the administration ofthe Police in the Madras province for the year 1938, printed by the Superintendent Government press, Madras, 1939, p. 15.

152. Report on the Administration of the Police in the Madras Province for the year 1937, printed by Superintendent, Government Press, Madras, 1938, p. 13.

153. Report of the Administration of the Madras Presidency for the years 1938-39, Madras, Superintendent, Government Press, 1940, p. 48.

154. Madras in 1938, Outline of the Administration, printed by Superintendent of Government Press, Madras, 1939, p. 17.

155. Report on the Administration of the Police in the Madras Province for the year 1939, printed by Superintendent, Government Press, Madras, 1940, p. 14.

156. Report on the Administration of the Police in the Madras Province for the year 1941, printed by Superintendent, Government Press, Madras, 1942, p. 13.

157. Report on the Administration of the Police in the Madras Presidency for the year 1933, printed by Superintendent, Government Press, Madras, 1934, p. 12.

158. Report on the Administration of the Police of the Madras Province, 1925, printed by Superintendent, Government Press, Madras, 1926, p. 11.

159. Report on the Administration of the Police in the Madras Province for the year 1928, printed by Superintendent, Government Press, Madras, 1929, p. 11.
160. Report on the Administration of the Police in the Madras Presidency for the year 1933, printed by Superintendent, Government Press, Madras, 1934, p. 13.
161. G.O.No.488 (Ms), Public (General), dated 14th May, 1934,Public Department, Government of Madras.
162. Report on the Administration of the Police in the Madras Province for the year 1933, printed by Superintendent, Government Press, Madras, 1934, p. 13.
163. *Ibid.*, pp. 13,14.
164. *Ibid.*, p. 15.
165. Report on the Administration of the Police of the Madras Province for the year 1935, printed by Superintendent, Government Press, Madras, 1936, p. 15.
166. Report on the Administration of Police in the Madras Province for the year 1936, printed by Superintendent, Government Press, Madras,1937, p. 14.
167. Report on the Administration of the Police of the Madras Province for the year 1937, printed by Superintendent, Government Press, Madras, 1938, p. 12.
168. Report on the Administration of the Police in the Madras Province for the year 1938, printed by Superintendent, Government Press, Madras, 1939, pp. 13,14.
169. Report on the Administration of the Police in the Madras Province for the year 1941, printed by Superintendent, Government Press, Madras, 1942, p. 12.
170. Gazetteer of the Nellore district-1938, Vol. A, printed by Superintendent, Government Press, 1942, Madras, pp. 273,274.
171. Report on the Administration of the Madras Presidency for the year 1947, printed by Superintendent, Government Press, Madras, 1949, p. 15.
172 The Madras Prison and Reformatory Manual, Vol. II, printed by Superintendent, Government Press, Madras, 1939, p. 161.
173. Report on the Administration of the Police in the Madras Province for the year 1947, Government Press, Madras, 1948, p. 12.
174. Report on the Administration of the Police of the Madras Presidency for the year 1929, printed by Superintendent, Government Press, 1930, Madras, p. 19.

175. Report on the Administration of the Police in the Madras Province for the year 1947, Government Press, Madras, 1948, p. 13.

176 Report on the Administration of the Police of the Madras Province for the year 1933, printed by Superintendent, Government Press, Madras, 1934, p. 19.

177. *Ibid.*, p. 232.

178. Report on the Administration of the Police of the Madras Presidency, 1925, printed by Superintendent, Government Press, Madras, 1926, p. 16.

179. Report of the Criminal Tribes Act Enquiry Committee, printed at the Government Press, Bombay, 1939.

180. Administrative Report of the Madras Presidency for the year 1928, printed by Superintendent, Government Press, Madras, 1929, p. 5.

181. Report on the Administration of the Police of the Madras Presidency for the year 1911, Statistics of British India, Part-VI, Administrative and Judicial-Police, printed by Superintendent, Government Press, Madras, 1912, p. 132.

182. Cosimo Zene, *A History of Christian Dialogues*, published by Routledge Curzon, New York, 2002, p. 169.

183. G.O.No.204, Home, dated 16th January, 1937, Home Department, Government of Madras.

184. Rushbrook Williams L.F., *India in 1923-24*, Central Publication Branch, Calcutta, 1924, p. 219.

185. G.O.No.5407, Home (Ms), dated 14th October, 1939, Home Department, Government of Madras.

186. Report on the Administration of the Police in the Madras Province for the year 1933, printed by Superintendent, Government Press, Madras, 1934, p. 17.

187. *Ibid.*, p. 16.

188. Report on the Administration of the Police in the Madras Province for the year 1936, printed by Superintendent, Government Press, Madras,1937, p. 14.

189. Report on the Administration of the Police in the Madras Province for the year 1939, printed by Superintendent, Government Press, Madras, 1940, p. 16.

190. Report on the Administration of the Police in the Madras Province for the year 1938, printed by Superintendent, Government Press, Madras, 1939, p. 20.

191. Report on the Administration of the Police in the Madras Province for the year 1946, printed by Superintendent, Government Press, Madras, 1947, p. 7.

192. Report on Administration of the Police of the Madras Province for the year 1938, printed by Superintendent, Government Press, Madras, 1939, p. 5.

193. The Indian Penal Code, 1860, Act 45 of 1860, dated 6th October, 1860.

194. Annual Report of the Director of Public Health with the Government of Madras for the year 1936, printed by Superintendent, Government Press, Madras, 1937, p. 22.

195 Report on the Administration of the Madras Presidency for the year 1928, printed by Superintendent, Government Press, Madras, 1929, p. 24.

196 The Indian Penal Code, 1860, Act 45 of 1860, dated 6th October, 1860.

197 The History of the Andhra Pradesh Police 1861-1961, published by Inspector General of Police, Andhra Pradesh, Hyderabad, 1961, pp. 232,233.

198. The Indian Penal Code, 1860, Act 45 of 1860, dated 6th October,1860.

199. *Ibid.*, p. 16.

200. Report on Administration of the Police of the Madras Presidency for the year 1925, printed by Superintendent, Government Press, Madras, 1926, pp. 5,6.

201 Administrative Report of the Inspector General of Police for the year 1926, printed by Superintendent, Government Press, Madras, 1927, p. 11.

202. Second Report of the Indian Penal Code, W. Ridsdale Military Orphan Press, Calcutta, 1847, pp. 84 -85.

203. *Ibid.*, p. 23.

204. Report on the Administration of the Police of the Madras Presidency for the year 1931, statistical abstract for British India-Police, 1932, pp. 26,27.

205. Report on Administration of the Police of the Madras Presidency for the year 1929, printed by Superintendent, Government Press, Madras, 1930, p. 15.

206. The History of the Andhra Pradesh Police 1861-1961, published by Inspector General of Police, Andhra Pradesh, Hyderabad, 1961, p. 223.

207. Report on Administration of the Police of the Madras Presidency for the year 1938, printed by Superintendent, Government Press, Madras, 1939, p. 12.

208. Report on the Administration of the Madras Presidency for the years 1938-39, printed by Superintendent, Government Press, Madras, 1940, p. 43.

209. The History of the Andhra Pradesh Police 1861-1961, published by Inspector General of Police, Andhra Pradesh, Hyderabad, 1961, p. 235.
210. Report on the Administration of the Madras Presidency for the years 1944-45, printed by Superintendent, Government Press, Madras, 1946, p. 21.
211. Report on the Administration of the Madras Presidency for the year 1946, printed by Superintendent, Government Press, Madras, 1947, p. 6.
212. Report on the Administration of the Madras Presidency for the year 1947, printed by Superintendent, Government Press, Madras, 1948, p. 12.
213. *Ibid.*, p. 9.
214. G.O.No.3701, Home, 6th October, 1948, Home Department, Government of Madras.

5

Special and Auxiliary Police Forces and their Services

The special and auxiliary police forces were a unit of the regular police force organised to maintain law and order. They were established with the enactment of the Madras Police Act of 1959, and were reorganised under the Indian Police Act of 1861 to assist the regular police. They had the same powers equivalent to those of ordinary police. They generally performed the same duties as general police officers and were also liable to all duties, discipline and punishments.[1] In most jurisdictions, the auxiliary police officers were empowered to make arrests for crimes that occured in their presence. With the fear of airborne Japanese invasion, the British government in the year 1942, established new auxiliary forces.[2] The special police forces were kept as reserves and they functioned as a subsidiary to the regular police especially during emergences and the auxiliary police assisted the regular police in prevention and detection of crime and maintenance of law and order. The special police forces such as Provincial Armed Police, Presidency General Reserves, Malabar Special Police, East Coast Special Police, Emergency Police Forces, and Armed Reserve Police were kept as reserves at all the district headquarters to control any crowd unrest. The Criminal Investigation Department, Railway Police, Traffic Police, Port Police, Fire Services, *Ghat Tailyaris*, formed the auxiliary branches of the police to assist in various fields of police administration.

Services of the Special Police Forces

The special police forces were organised in the Northern range along with the regular police and they functioned as a subsidiary to the regular police especially during emergences. These paramilitary forces were established to quell any unrest and to serve as an aid in the maintenance of law and order and also in maintaining internal security. They functioned as an emergency force intended for special tasks. They provided essential services, such as guarding, escorting, and providing security. and were armed or unarmed depending on their duties. They were unpaid volunteers or paid members of the police service.

These Special Police forces helped in the maintenance of internal security and also helped the public in contingencies like natural calamites, fairs and festivals and in other situations of unrest. They also functioned as an emergency force intended for special responsibilities connected with guarding and escorting and provided essential services, such as motor transport, coast guard and fire service. Officers of superior rank and special abilities were sanctioned to work on the Special Police forces. The Special Police forces were established to deal with difficult cases to restore law and order during political unrest, agrarian strikes, industrial strikes, communal troubles and also during natural calamities. The Special Police were recruited mostly from the ex-military men and formed a unit within the regular police force as reserves. Most of these forces were organised as paramilitary force whose task was to serve as an auxiliary to the general police force.

Sergeants, Sergeants-Major also known as Charge Sergeants, Havildars, Havildar-Majors, Naik and constabulary formed the constitution. The forces were organised into companies, platoons or troops. They all functioned under the supreme command of the Inspector General of Police of the Madras Presidency. All the superior cadres were Europeans. By the year 1930, the European Sergeants were replaced with Indians due to efforts of Rajagopalachari.[3] They had no functions of investigation and were stationed at cantonments, ports, railway stations and other places where the police had to deal with the Europeans.[4] Sergeants were in charge of platoons and were under the Sergeant-Major and were responsible for the training, discipline and general control of the platoons. Other Sergeants were employed in towns and at important places in the Northern range. Their departmental status was equal to that of Sub-Inspectors and they worked under instructions from the Inspectors.[5] These forces were trained by military officers in physical training, arms, signalling etc., but not up to the standards of the military. They were also trained in bayonet fighting and this training was initiated in the year 1925.[6] They were generally activated only on orders from the higher level authorities. The special police usually did not came into contact with the general public unless they were assigned the duty of maintaining order during political unrest, fairs, festivals, elections, and natural calamities. They were sanctioned to quell outbreaks of any unrest, organised crime, to guard, and depending on the type of assignment, they carried lathis or lethal weapons. The Police Commission of 1860 was largely responsible for the formation of police forces in the Northern range. The following are the Special Police Forces that were stationed in the Northern range during the period 1924-47.

Services of the Malabar Special Police

The Malabar Special Police was a paramilitary unit of the regular police in the Northern range. They assisted the police in maintaining law and order during emergencies. They were equipped with arms to quell any unrest and were trained by the military officers. Since its inception, the Malabar Special Police had successfully overcome all limitations and established itself as an important part of police foreces. The origin of this force can be traced in the Nayar Sibbandy Corps raised under native chieftains. They were developed to overcome the Moplahs and they were made permanent in the year 1897 in the Madras Presidency. The force consisted of officers from Indian Civil Service and officers of the British army and they were experts in guerrilla warfare. An Inspector General of Police commented, "Their discipline and general behaviour were excellent, they marched admirably and in spite of frequent attacks of fever and the greatest hardships, there was never any grumbling." The Malabar Special Police were trained in wireless communications for operational purposes. They were rewarded for their good service by the British government and were also liable for punishments.

Colebrook was the Assistant Commandant of the Malabar Special Police in the year 1925 and the strength of this force consisted of 24 Indians officers, 30 Havildars, 34 Naiks, four Jamadars and 587 Constables. Military officers inspected the force twice and great attention was paid to the systematic training of the force to maintain its efficiency.[7] The Malabar Special Police was reorganised on 1st April, 1926 and they were given military training at St. Thomas' Mount.[8] The general health of this force was maintained by regular medical check-ups and they were provided with mosquito nets and repellants during their camps in the Agency tracts of the Godavari free of cost. Some policemen from the Reserves underwent refresher courses with the Malabar Special Police. During the period 1924-47, recruitments norms were relaxed because of the measures taken by the British government as they improved their working conditions with better salary payments and many were induced to join.[9]

Owing to the unpopularity of the *manasabdars*, disturbances broke out in the year 1858 and over the years, many rebellions were frequent in the Godavari Agencies which were suppressed by the police forces. Due to these frequent *fituris*, the British government had stationed Special Police Forces and they suppressed all rebellions. In the year 1879, the Scheduled District Act was extended to the Agency tracts of the Northern range and in the same year, a second rising called Rampa rebellion took place which led to the establishment of police troops.[10] In the year 1858, the British government had established military control in these Agency areas as the tribals demonstrated their insecurity in the form of *fituri* in Godavari district of the Northern range. The Malabar Special was stationed in the Godavari Agency on a special duty to suppress the Rampa Fituri. Alluri Seetharama Raju had rebelled against the British government for the cause of the tribal people of Rampa in the Godavari Agency. Seetharama Raju had mobilised the hill tribes and organised guerrilla action against the British in the Gudem limits of the Vizagapatam Agency. The rebels had attacked a number of police stations and outposts and stole many rifles and arms. The British government had set up a number of police outposts in these areas and around Chintapalli, Krishnadevipeta, and Rajavommangi.[11] The British government had further strengthened the Malabar Special Police to suppress the rebellion under the charge of Rutherford. Under Upendra Patnaik, the Malabar Special police attacked the rebels who opened fire and wounded a Constable. The police force had returned fire and killed two of the rebels and wounded several of them. They had captured one of the closest associate of Raju and recovered 303 rifles. The government had ordered for mobilising more police parties for further suppression.[12] The Malabar Special Police force was reorganised with effect from 1st April, 1926.[13] During the war years, this force was largely preoccupied in guarding vulnerable points. Large scale communist disturbances necessitated the movement of these companies to those disturbed areas and a company was deputed to Gannavaram of Kistna district in June, 1946, but was withdrawn due to clashes which took place between its personnel and some villagers.[14] All these various duties necessitated frequent movements of these force many of which had taken place at a very short notice.[15] During the period 1924-47, one of the four companies of the Malabar Special Police had continued to be on special duty throughout the year which was deputed to Bezwada for the maintenance of law and order.

The British government ordered for the formation of four Special Armed Police Units modelled on the Malabar Special Police Force which was to be stationed round about Guntakal and Bezwada.[16] The Deputy Inspector General of Police, Railways, and Criminal Investigation Department, Madras was appointed as a Special Officer in charge of information of these units. In consideration of the availability of accommodation, it was decided to raise one unit at Tadepallegudam in the West Godavari district of the Northern range in the year 1947. The recruitment to these units was made by District Superintendents of Police and the units were formed at these places.[17]

Services of the East Coast Special Police

The East Coast Special Police was organised on the lines of the Malabar Special Police and was employed for agency operations of the Northern range. Keatinge was in charge of the East Coast Special Police Force in the year 1925.[18] The permanent strength of the force was under the in charge of Assistant Superintendent of Police and was organised in two companies with seven Indian officers and 221 of other ranks. A temporary additional company was sanctioned for Agency operations.[19] They were also sanctioned due to political unrest in the districts of Guntur, Kistna, and Godavari of the Northern range.[20] This police battalion was formed for the use in any of the districts or the Agency division in the Northern range.[21] The hill tracts of the Vizagapatam and Godavari districts, known as Agencies, were inhabited largely by tribes and had been declared as 'Partially Excluded Areas' under Section 91(1) of the Government of India Act, 1935.[22] The government had set up outposts and armed police were stationed to maintain law and order.

The East Coast Special Police Force was well-trained and they were also liable to discipline and punishment. In the year 1924, 15 men from this force were fined for absence without notice. Keatinge was appreciated by the government for his abilities in training these forces. This force was taken for demonstration purpose to Kalyan Singapur in the Parvatipur Agency in the year 1925 and it was absent from the headquarters for a period of 19 days which was utilised for instructional purposes. The training of this force had attracted attention and its periodical inspection by a military officer had begun during the year 1925.[23]

The East Coast Special Police were deployed to suppress this rebellion in the Agency tracts which was cut off from the coastal plain by the Eastern Ghats.[24] The East Coast Special Police, which was stationed in the Agency, had played a considerable part in suppressing Rampa rebellion and in spite of its suppression, there was further sporadic unrest in the agencies. The *Fituri* of 1922-24 in the Northern range was located in the Rampa hills of the Godavari region led by Allur Seetarama Raju who had mobilised the hill tribes against the British policies and had organised sustained guerrilla action. The Rajahmundry Specials and the local reserves, like the Malappuram Special Police in Malabar, proved no match to these armed and organised guerrillas. As a result, the British government sanctioned Malabar Special Police Force. There was a fight between the police party and the rebels in course of which the police captured several rebels along with Aggiraju, a close follower of Seetarama Raju and the police recovered 303 rifles from them, in spite of all this, the rebellion continued. Then the government obtained the services of two detachments of the Assam Rifles from the Government of Assam which was made to station at Narsipatam. As the rebels moved on to Padwa taluk of Jeypore district, it became difficult for the forces to suppress their movements, and so, 200 more Assam Rifles were pressed into service. The *fituri* was finally suppressed with the help of these Special Police Forces.

This shows that the British had protected their rule with the help of the Special Police Forces and were also able to restore peace and order. As the East Coast Specials had little experience of combat, it was soon abolished.[25] In the year 1925, under Keatinge the strength of the East Coast Special Police was two Subedars, eight Jamadars, two Havildar-Majors, 10 Halvidars, 12 Naiks and 187 Constables.[26] Peterson took over the charge of this force and in the year 1927, a party under him went to Kalyan Singapur and to the surrounding villages in the Parvatipur Agency of the Ganjam district to arrest offenders on account of which they were absent from the headquarters for 33 days.[27] The Deputy Inspector General of Police, Northern range, took a party of one Subedar, five non-commissioned officers and 50 men to Nellore to suppress the trouble in that district.[28] In the Nellore district, during a Hindu festival procession, adequate police arrangement was made under the protection of 450 policemen, including half-a-company of the East Coast Special Police and men from the Armed Reserves.[29]

Here is a citation of a case of interest. On 7th September, 1927, due to grievance over his promotion, the Assistant Armourer of the

East Coast Special Police took a bayonet and stabbed to death the Havildar-Armourer. Then he ran to the office with a rifle with bayonet fixed over it and shot the Commandant of the force, Peterson and then shot himself.[30] This incident reflects the low morale and laxity of discipline in the force. Forbes held the charge of the East Coast Special Police force after the death of Peterson and at that time, the strength of the force was 1 Subedar Major, two Suberdars, eight Jamadars, four Havildar-Majors, nine Halvidars, 14 Naiks and 210 Constables. Desertion and resignations occurred chiefly amongst the men recruited and men were fined for absence, due to lack of discipline prevalent and men who were found unfit for service in the special force, were discharged. The recruitments to this force were kept in abeyance as the future of the force was uncertain.[31] During the year 1931, Inspector in charge of Armed Reserves were graded separately and designated as Sergeants-Major and Charge-Sergeants and they were declared eligible for free quarters as in the case of Sergeants. The British government ordered the Inspector General of Police to investigate into the matter and the report was submitted by the InspectorGeneral of Police. The Madras government had admitted that the constitution of the East Coast Special Police as a separate force was a failure. A District Superintendent of Police was sanctioned for the post of the Commandant, East Coast Special Police, but the force had been abolished and the District Superintendent of Police was attached to the Criminal Investigation Department.[32] After the abolition of the East Coast Special Police, the District Armed Reserves were strengthened in its place.[33]

Services of the Armed Reserves

At the headquarters of the districts, Reserve was maintained under the command of the Inspector. This reserve supplied men for escorts, guards and other miscellaneous duty and served to strengthen the police in any part of the district during disturbances or emergencies.[34] A separate full strength Armed Reserves were sanctioned and stationed in the Northern range to deal with emergencies.[35] These Special Police Forces were not intended to be military in nature and were highly armed to control the riots and to perform guard and escort duties.[36] A number of such situations arose in the Northern range during the period 1924-47, where the Special Police Force were successful in restoring law and order. The District Armed Reserves were already in existence before 1924 and greater attention was paid to discipline and training. They were maintained in an efficient state and kept up to the strength except in a few districts of the Northern range. The British government had proposed for the formation of police battalions drawn from the existing constabulary to supplement the regular army units in guard duties and internal security work. Due to emerging political unrest, these police battalions were established to deal with the political disturbances[37] and this reserve police force was projected for the districts of the Northern range.

In the year 1925, Armitage F, Inspector General of Police, proposed the establishment of the Special Police on a permanent basis and reorganisation of the District Armed Reserve Police to the British government.[38] The District Armed Reserves stationed at the Northern range were reorganised and strengthened in the Ganjam, Vizagapatam, Jeypore, and East Godavari districts by the British government in April, 1929 with the abolition of the East Coast Special Police.[39] The Emergency Force and provision for escort in these reserves were increased. In order to allow more time for intensive training, the Inspector in charge of these forces were relieved of store work by the appointment of Store Accountants.[40] With a view to attract the right type of ex-military men, the pay of the Sergeants was increased and their conditions of service improved. The Armed Reserves were recruited from the ex-military men as an experimental measure which proved to be successful. They were maintained in an efficient state and were mobilised for annual training. Numbers of inefficient men were weeded out and their places were replaced by ex-sepoys.[41] The Armed Reserves were sub-divided into one or more platoons and the latter into four sections, each consisting of one Head Constable, one Naik, one Lance Naik, and twelve Constables. All the Head Constables were trained in the Central Recruits School of Vellore and they were sent back to their reserves after the training.[42] All the reserves were mobilised once or twice in a year and bi-annual tours were conducted in the Agency areas of the Northern range. They were trained in bayonet fighting and in military policing but not up to the efficiency matching that of the military force and they were inspected by a military officer.

They were also trained for the first time in mob work in the year 1928.[43] In the Guntur district, arrangements were made with the District Medical Officer to train the reserves in first-aid.[44] The Inspector General of Police, Stokes, had arranged for reorganisation of these forces on the orders of the British government. The Armed Reserves which were not located at the district headquarters were abolished and they were the Parvatipuram Reserve and Rajahmundry detachment of the Coconada Reserve.[45] In the Armed Reserve at Coconada of East Godavari district, during the year 1926, there were two Sergeants and one Jamadar.[46]

The Armed Reserves were reorganised and strengthened in the year 1929 and were sanctioned by government in the districts of Ganjam, Vizagapatam, Jeypore and East Godavari of the Northern range.[47] In the year 1928, an additional Armed Reserve was newly formed at Rajahmundry.[48] They were stationed in the Northern range to deal with the emergencies, the occurrence of riots, communal disturbances, labour troubles and breaches of public peace.[49] Owing to communal disturbances in the district of Nellore, the Deputy Inspector General of Police of the Northern Range took with him a party of one Subedar, five non-commissioned officers and 50 men who were stationed at Nellore for eight days [50] to quell the riots to restore peace.

The government sanctioned the formation of Special Armed Police units at Tadepalligudem, Elluru, Bheemavaram, and Tanuku. The Armed Reserved force in Tanuku was later shifted to Palacole. These Armed Reserve forces were confined only to important towns and were deployed to disperse large crowds and processions. The Armed Reserve was maintained in efficient condition and instructions in bayonet fighting for them were initiated in the year 1925.[51] Proposals for reorganisation of the reserves were submitted to the government with reference to the order on Stoke's report. The bicycle sections of the District Armed Reserves were introduced on the recommendations of the Stoke's report.[52] Train guards were drawn from the reserve men on all passenger trains of the south Indian railways during the strikes. An additional Armed Reserve was newly-formed at Rajahmundry during the year 1929. Men who were old, were replaced by younger men and the percentage of natives at the headquarters of the Reserves were kept low and all the reserves were mobilised at least once during the year. Attention was paid to the systematic training of the force and its efficiency was increased by inspections by a military officer.[53] The duties of these Armed Reserves were to provide guards, escorts, and orderlies.[54] Special mobilisations were carried out on the occasions of the Mahamakham and Puskaram festivals at Kumbakonam in the Kistna district and during the visit of the Viceroy to the province. In order to allow more time for intensive training, the Inspectors in charge of the Reserves in these districts were relieved of their store work by the appointment of Store Accountants. The emergency forces and provision for escorts in these Reserves were increased and a scheme for an annual training camp for the officers and men of the Reserve was organised.

A combined force from these Reserves was sent in connection with anticipated disorders to Kalyan Singapur in the Vizagapatam district under the District Superintendent of Police, Vizagapatam towards the end of the year 1929. The force acquitted itself creditably and gained good practical experience. With a view to attract the right type of soldiers, the pay of Sergeants was increased and their conditions of service were improved.[55] A separate Armed Reserve was provided for the West Godavari district in the year 1930.[56] With the growth of the political unrest, vacancies were rapidly filled and due to the persistence by government, the police battalions were replaced by the army in dealing with political disturbances.[57] These striking forces were mooted and planned for operation in areas where unrest was most likely to occur.

In the year 1939, the Vizagapatam Reserve toured in the districts which proved to be beneficial; the East Godavari Reserve could not perform its tour owing to the pressure of local work in dealing with the labour and agrarian disputes.[58] The Rajahmundry Reserve Police in the East Godavari district was stationed in the year 1939 and the payment was sanctioned by the municipality.[59] For guarding of the Godavari railway bridge, additional Armed Reserve platoon were sanctioned to Rajahmundry.[60] They were sanctioned to maintain the internal security such as guarding of certain vulnerable points, like petrol dumps at Waltair, Vizagapatam and guarding railway bridges at Godavari, Kistna, East and West canals.[61] In the year 1939, there was a construction of roads between Peddapuram municipality and Samalkot panchayat in the East Godavari district for security purpose of which temporary staff of one police Constable was sanctioned.[62]

The Armed reserves platoons at Kistna district and East Godavari districts were retained at Bezwada and Rajahmundry.[63] To accommodate the Armed Reserves, temporary huts were constructed for them.[64] In the Vizagapatam district of the Northern range, the Armed Reserves police had training camp at Padwa during the year 1939 and it served as a joint training camp with the Koraput district of Orissa.[65] With the mounting congress agitation reaching its peak during the Quit India Movement of 1942 and with the fear of looming airborne Japanese invasion, the British government had enlarged the district reserves.[66] In the year 1945, there was temporary increase in strength and employment staff.[67] The Armed Reserve guards in East Godavari district were discontinued at the Burma-shell storage at Cocanada in the year 1945.[68] For the Krishna Pushkaram festival, police force were deputed for *bandobast* duty in the year 1945.[69] At the Bezawada Pushkaram festival, police officers and subordinates were on duty at festival centres.[70]

The Armed Reserve was mostly kept up to strength during the year 1946 and almost all of them were mobilised at least once during the year. The percentage of natives of the headquarters of the reserve was kept as low as possible to avoid communal and labour tensions. The railway strikes in the range during the period 1924-47 imposed a very heavy strain on these reserves, yet they discharged their duties well on all occasions. The Vizagapatnam South Armed Reserve performed the agency tour during the year, but the reserves of Vizagapatnam North and East Godavari were not able to perform the tour. A cumulative training programme covering individual, section, platoon, and company training was introduced and carried out successfully in the reserves for the year 1946. The introduction of this varied training programme in the place of monotonous parades eliminated the boredom which was one of the chief causes of unrest in the early part of the year.

The training cadres in all branches, including courses in small arms, physical training, and signalling for men deputed from the district Armed Reserves, were held. A refresher course for signal instruction of the district Armed Reserves was held during this year. The annual classification of the signallers was carried out by an Assistant Commandant and 77 of them, put up for classification, passed.[71] In the year 1947, the reorganised Armed Reserve was generally kept up to the strength and most of them were mobilised due to labour unrest, communal and agrarian troubles and the political riots put heavy strain on the Armed Reserves, but they discharged their duties efficiently.[72] Here is a citation where this force was used for guarding purpose. In the Kistna district, the communists instigated the villagers of Gazullanka and cut away grass in the night from a land which was under dispute. When the Armed Reserve attempted to prevent the dispute, the villagers surrounded the force and attempted to annihilate it. The police party had to open fire in self- defence, killing four in the process, including a woman and injuring an associate. A non-official committee with the Additional District Magistrate as its president enquired into the incident and submitted its report.[73] The government sanctioned the Special Armed Police units at Tadepalligudem to suppress the disturbances due to political unrest in the year 1947.[74] The bicycle section of the District Armed Reserves was introduced during the year 1926 on the recommendations of the report of Stokes.[75] The wireless installations, motor transport and the ambulance had worked satisfactorily and gave fairly good service during the period 1924-47. During the period of study, the demand for the armed reserve for *bandobast* increased and these reserves rendered their services well on all occasions, especially during strikes, 'Hindustan' visit and governor's visit to Vizagapatam.

Services of the Presidency General Reserve

Due to political unrest in the Northern range in the year 1930, the need for a new armed police force was felt as the political movement had become more severe and widespread in the districts of the Northern range. Cunningham C.B., the Inspector General of Police had reported to the government that the reinforcements sent to the Kistna and Godavari districts during the *satyagraha* movement had left several other districts dangerously short of armed reserves. He had asked for the creation of an emergency force of six hundred officers and men to deal with the trouble without reducing the local forces below the point of safety.[76]

This new force was the Presidency General Reserve Police Force which had recruited a number of young men and ex-military men into the force and had trained them with discipline; they were also equipped with muskets and smoothbores. They were organised as a temporary force, but later, they became permanent. By the year 1931, their numbers increased to 660 and the mobility was facilitated by motor transport, hired buses, and lorries.[77]

Both the Presidency General Reserve Police and District Armed Reserves of the Northern range worked successfully in suppressing the political agitations.[78] The Special Police Forces had used tear gas to control the rioters in the year 1930 which was earlier rejected on grounds of additional expense. An All India Police Conference which was held at Delhi in the year I929 which reported against the use of tear gas as it would cause suffocation to the ordinary public and also the police themselves.[79] Until the year 1940, tear gas was known as tear smoke.[80] During the year 1931, the Presidency General Reserve Police Force had a strength of 10 Sergeants, 10 Havildars-Major, 50 Head Constables and 594 Constables sanctioned for public safety as there was political unrest due to the Civil Disobedience Movement. The Presidency General Reserve Police consisted of 10 detachments located in districts with housing facilities. They were equipped with 410 muskets and 303 rifles.[81] In 1931, Presidency General Reserve was established under a permanent footing. Outdoor executive staffs were appointed during that year to enforce the Motor Vehicles Taxation Act.

The Civil Disobedience Movement was suppressed by these forces and they had used lathis and muskets to maintain law and order in the Northern range. The British government gave a lot of importance to maintaining of high morale of these forces and it was also successful in keeping mass agitations under control during the political struggle. The police force had performed their duty successfully and loyally with unshaken morale.[82] The British government had taken care to keep up the morale of the police force by way of rewards that were lavishly given to the Constables and officers. With the Government of India Act of I935, the Malabar Special Police, the Presidency General Reserve and the District Reserves were increased in their numbers and they were reorganised for improvement. The Presidency General Reserve and the District Reserves together totalled nearly 4,000 men in 1936. Their training included route marches, arms drill, signalling, house surrounding, skirmishing, and mob operations. It was a paramilitary force which was used to suppress the political movement and also other agitations.[83]

Few troops were made available for internal security and whenever there was unrest, they were used as repressive agent. In the year 1940, Special Emergency Force was organised with a thousand men whose most recruits were ex-sepoys and this force was under the charge of Inspector General of Police. The freedom movement had reached its peak in the year 1942 with the launch of Quit India Movement and the threat of airborne Japanese invasion of southern India seemed a near possibility.[84] The British government had enlarged the district reserves by nearly seven hundred men in 1942 and brought new auxiliary forces into operation in the Northern range.[85]

On the outbreak of the World War II, the Madras Special Police had been increased from four to sixteen companies. These were dispatched to the places of unrest in the presidency during the war and these special forces were well-trained.

The efficiency of the District Armed Reserves and the Presidency General Reserve improved as a result of better methods of training and the introduction of younger and more energetic men. The numerous strikes during the year entailed continuous demands on the Reserves. The emergency platoon was called out for duty in connection with a series of strikes as well as processions and demonstrations taking place against the introduction of Hindi in schools.[86] The communal tensions in the Northern range prevailed throughout the period 1924-47, especially in the districts, like Guntur and Nellore. In the year 1941, in the Nellore district, the police opened fire on the rioters in an incident during festival of Dasara. In spite of police *bandobast*, the mob surrounded the police party and attempted to overpower it. The Sergeant in charge of the police party opened fire and dispersed the rioters. A girl was killed and an old lady was injured as a result of the firing. In this connection, a huge crowd gathered and began to throw stones at the police, but somehow the police was able to restore order. In these communal clashes, many people were killed. Priestley, a police officer enquired into the disturbance under the orders of the government. To preserve peaces in these areas, an additional police force was stationed on the orders of the government. The Presidency General Reserve Police Force from six districts were brought to Nellore to deal with various disturbances. At Kaluvoy of Nellore district, the communal tensions grew intense to quell which, the police had to disperse the rioters by a lathi charge and arrested 69 rioters. The feelings between the two communities continued remained strained necessitating the government to station two Armed Reserves at these places.[87] This force had worked efficiently during the political unrest in the Northern range.

Services of the Civic Guards

The Civic Guards were formed in the Northern range in the year 1940 on voluntary basis to assist the regular police and they were well-trained and kept as reserves. They provided valuable services during the Quit India Movement of 1942. There was a mass destruction caused by political agitators to the government property and the Civil Guards were entrusted with the responsibility of guarding Telegraph and Railway lines. They had contributed successfully in the crime control during this period 1924-47 in the Northern range. Whenever any canals, railway, or other public works were operated in the range, the Inspector General of Police had the power to appoint an additional police force.[52] In the year 1945, Sergeants were attached to Godavari railway bridge for guarding purpose in the East Godavari district.[88]

The strength of these Civic Guards was revised from time to time and sometimes, Guard Commanders were recruited. All the recruits to the Civic Guards were trained in squad drills, lathi drills, and first aid. Some selected Guard Commanders and Civic Guards were also trained in the handling of arms and bayonet fighting. These Civic Guards were employed on routine duties, such as controlling of traffic at fairs, festivals, and shandies; process service; and checking of bad characters. They also assisted the regular police in night patrol in the detection of crime and the arrest of offenders and other duties in urban areas.[89]

In the initial stages, the organisation and training of the Civic Guards caused extra burden on the Inspectors and Sub-Inspectors. They were of little use in serious emergencies, such as riots, lootings, and during communal clashes. The quality of the Civic Guards varied from district to district in the Northern range; as they lacked discipline, they were disbanded in the year 1945.[90]

This force, like the other ones, was also liable to discipline and punishments. In the year 1941, one Civic Guard in the East Godavari district was granted a reward of Rs 100 for the arrest of an armed communist at great personal risk.[91] One group of Civic Guards were abolished at Rajanagaram in the East Godavari district of Northern range in the year July, 1945, 27 groups in November, 26 groups in the Kistna district in the month of April, five groups in the Vizagapatam district in November, and 23 groups in May.[92]

The Armed Reserves, the Presidency General Reserve, and Special Emergency Force were amalgamated and reorganised with effect from the 1st of May, 1946. Each Armed Reserve had a headquarter wing consisting entirely of specialist staff under the command of a Sergeant. In several districts, the reorganised Armed Reserves included a certain number of platoons for railway protection. The Reserves were generally kept up to strength and almost all of them were mobilised at least once in a year. The strain of duties imposed on them had continued to be severe throughout the period 1924-47. A police wireless grid with facilities for communication with district headquarters was established.[93] These special emergency police forces controlled the riots by lathi charges, opening fire and also used tear gas to disperse the unrestful crowd. During the freedom struggle, the Northern range was facing conditions of political unrest and there were many strikes and agitations propagating against the British rule. These reserve police forces had helped in the crime control during these emergencies.

Services of the Auxiliary Police Forces

Auxiliary branches of the police had officers of special abilities with specialisation. They aided and assisted the regular police in prevention and detection of crime. In the Northern range, the law and order was well-maintained with police administration throughout the period 1924-47. The following are the units of the police administration.

Services of the Criminal Investigation Department

Criminal Investigation Department was a unit of the police department which was organised to assist the regular police in prevention and detection of the crime. [94] The Criminal Investigation Department was popularly shortened as the C.I.D. It was set up for the purpose of collating and distributing information regarding organised crime and to assist in the investigation of crimes which were of special character. Criminal Investigation Department was organised in the year 1906 in the Madras Presidency.[95]

It was intended to supervise investigation work throughout the Madras Presidency, especially where specialised skills were involved in detection work; the police of several districts were also involved. Initially, it was intended to investigate usual crime, but later, it was involved in the matters related to political activity. With the growth of freedom movements, it dealt with the anti-British organisations and collected associated information and communicated it to the British government.[96] The CID. officers used to report the government about the political activities, such as meeting, seditious speeches, agitations, secret associations, and clubs. The Shorthand Bureau was established to get the exact information about the political speeches. By 1929, the department carved a Special Branch with in it, and in the year 1930, the district intelligence units were formed. With the increase of the professional and organised crimes, these units also dedicated their time in crime control. The Criminal Investigation Department was constituted to deal with crime of a special character and with criminal organisations of more than local importance.[97]

The main function of the Criminal Investigation Department was to assist in the investigation of specified crimes which were of special character entrusted by the police. They maintained crime report for tackling crime and criminal information and crime analysis was made to improve prevention, investigation, and prosecution of crime. Their duties were to investigate criminal cases, which spanned across multiple districts or even the Presidency. In the Northern range, they had investigated complicated cases, like communal riot cases, circulation of counterfeit currency and very complicated murder cases. The local police along with their normal duties found it tough to allot men to these complicated cases. They dealt with the cases when they were ordered either by a judicial court or by the Inspector General of Police or by the government.

The hierarchy of the Criminal Investigation Department had its own cadre. The head of the department was Deputy Inspector General of police who was also the administrative charge of the Railway Police of the province. The police officers and men generally added the prefix 'Detective' before their regular rank. These offices were transferred to the regular police or vice-versa. They had no prescribed uniform and generally they were in plain clothes to control crime relating to the local gangs, gamblers, prostitutes, petty thieves and other habitual offenders. The Criminal Investigation Department officers were specially trained to deal with complex and complicated cases. In addition to political work, the criminal offences investigated by them were false impersonation, bogus banking, cheating, fraud, and note forgery. The two Sub-Inspectors previously trained at the Bombay mint in testing counterfeit coins were also trained in the investigation of currency note forgery cases under Mr Stewart, Photographic Expert of the Madras Survey Department.[98]

The officers of the Criminal Investigation Department also dealt with the investigation of major crimes, such as rape, murder, fraud and other offences that require intricate detection. The Criminal Investigation Department also undertook the investigating of offences relating to coinage and forged currency and others cases for investigation over a wide field. They were responsible for acting upon intelligence received and then building a case from analysis of the initial incident till the arrest and prosecution of the suspects. The Criminal Investigation Department worked as central organisation for coordinating the work of the District Intelligence Bureaux in dealing with organised crimes. They maintained a record of habitual offenders, known depredators, criminal tribes and others suspicious characters with assistance of the police.

The Criminal Investigation Department was reorganised during the year 1929 and split up into two branches — Special and Crime.[99] They were placed under the direct control of the Inspector General of Police of the Madras Presidency. The Superintendents of Police, Crime and Special Branches were designated as Assistant Inspector General of Police, Crime and Special Branches respectively. The Criminal Investigation Department was again reorganised following the sanction of an additional post of a Deputy Inspector General. The Deputy Inspector General of Police, Criminal Investigation Department also exercised supervision over the two Railway Police districts. To keep in touch with and to maintain a continuous record of the movements of known inter-district criminals and suspects, a Central Crime Intelligence Bureau with headquarters at Madras and nine Branch Bureaux at selected district headquarters were established and they were called the District Crime Bureaux or the District Intelligence Bureaux. These bureaus published a weekly crime and information sheet for circulation to all police stations of the districts and concerned stations located outside the Northern range. These sheets kept the station police informed and vigilant and were of great value; substantial progress was made in the preparations of histories and photographs of active criminals and their classifications, of information files on crime, stolen property and connected matters. The Central Bureau reviewed the crime of the districts monthly, or as and when occasion required, and prepared and maintained histories, files and indices relating to inter-district criminals and their crimes. The District Bureaux were well-developed to respond helpfully to references form investigating officers.[100]

The gazette officers of the Crime Department watched and maintained the records of all the policemen in the crime detachments. The policemen who were found to lack keenness and interest or found unsuitable for crime work or showed no detective ability were removed from the Crime detachments. The Chemical Examiner, Madras, delivered a series of lectures to selected Inspectors and Sub-Inspectors on the technical aspects of the investigation of crime and on the preservation and dispatch of exhibits for chemical examination. These officers, in turn, trained other officers in the districts of the Northern range.[101] This way all the officers of the force were able to improve their investigating skills.

Services of the Fingerprint Bureau and Crime Branch

This department also included the Provincial Finger Print Bureau and Crime Branch. These two branches were under the control of a separate Deputy Inspector General of Police. These branches undertook the investigation of offences relating to coinage, forged currency notes, postal fraud, forgery and other intricate cases in which inter-state and inter-provincial swindlers were involved. In handling such intricate and difficult cases, like forgery slips and identification of unknown persons, they were all assisted by the Fingerprint Bureau. Sub-Inspectors trained in Finger Print course visited jails and gave instructions in taking and dealing with fingerprints to the Sub-Inspectors and other selected officers of the headquarters of the districts of the Northern range. The police officers attending these courses, in turn, instructed others in the districts of the range. This was an innovation and it was hoped that these courses would tend to minimise the number of fingerprint slips.

The fingerprint testing staff visited all the districts, jails and sub-jails and tested the fingerprint slips. The fingerprint bureau dealt with the identification of unknown persons and these testers visited the districts jails and tested the slips placed before them. These testers used to get expert fees for attending courts in private cases and for furnishing written opinions in civil courts. In the year 1925, the scheme of recording fingerprints of railway menials was stopped.[102] One Sub-Inspector and 23 Head Constables were trained in the method of preserving and identifying footprints. Footprints were made use of in 17 cases to track or identify the offenders. To enable old offenders to be recognised, the fingerprints of all convicts were taken and sent to the Fingerprint Bureau at Vellore[103]. The Chemical Examiner assisted by a Sub-Inspector to the Criminal Investigation Department gave valuable opinions and advice in all the cases. The Fingerprint Bureau had 2,80,505 slips on record at the end of the year. The number sent for search was 24,450 of which 17,503 related to cases in the Madras Presidency. About 4,802 cases were traced and expert fingerprint evidence was given on 302 occasions. There was a firearms index maintained in the department and the firearm expert use to give evidence in courts and delivered instructional lectures to the District Police on firearms and their identification at several places in the Northern range.

A separate branch called the 'X' branch was formed in the year 1947 in the Criminal Investigation Department to combat blackmarketing and corruption which had considerable success during this period in the Northern Range.[103] The Criminal Investigation Department functioned to prevent crimes and offences, detect and apprehend the offenders, and to discover stolen property. They also collected evidence against persons accused of grave crimes and brought them before the magistracy and courts. They apprehended and watched the movements of the vagabonds and suspicious characters.

Services of the Police Wireless Grid

A police wireless grid was facilitated for communication among the district headquarters in the Northern range. A special staff was sanctioned as Police Wireless officer on contract and one Special Branch Inspector and other operators were given three months training and a further one month training in the wireless offices in Madras and another two months operating practice in the district stations. The wireless operators were trained with the help of the Army Signal School in Madras and the Malabar Special Police training school. A few ex-army wireless operators enlisted as police Constables in districts were also given two to three months practical training at Madras in handling the type of sets in use in the Provincial Wireless Grid.

One Head Constable from the District Intelligence Bureau of each district of the Northern range was sent for specialist training in fingerprints, footprints and photography.[104] There was an office of Special Branch Inspector in Vizagapatam[105] and Hamilton W.F.A. was the Superintendent of Police Special Branch, Criminal Investigation Department. Many district headquarters of the range including Bezwada, were linked up with Madras and a second control station was opened at Madras. There were three transportable stations in the Kistna district. In addition, several wireless telegraph stations were installed owing to the border situation. The police wireless system did good work under difficult conditions and it proved as a great help in the disturbed conditions of the Northern range.[106]

As the work load increased, temporary additional staff was sanctioned for the Criminal Investigation Department.[107] In the year 1924, temporary staff comprising of a Inspector, a Sub-Inspector and three constables were sanctioned for the investigation cases of murder, forgery, false-coining, cheating, and postal fraud.[108] The intelligence department had heavy work in connection with the political agitation in most of the districts, labour unrest and strikes, meetings which the Indian National Congress and the various other all India conferences held which added considerably to the work in the year 1927. The political agitation necessitated a great increase in the strength of the Bureau.[109] All enquiries connected with forged currency notes and cases of intricate and difficult nature were also entrusted to this department.[110] For the Criminal Investigation Department, a post of Inspector of Police for special duty was sanctioned in the year 1944.[111]

Temporary staff was sanctioned for investigation of a case of cheating by Ambiraju of Palakole of the West Godavari district relating to currency notes.[112] In the year 1945, temporary additional staff were recruited by the government in the Northern range for the Guntur District Special Branch to help the regular staff with the additional work due to increase in the crime.[113] Four additional Head Constables were sanctioned to the Kistna district branch.[114] In the year the 1945, the Central Recruit School, Vizianagaram had granted money prizes for outstanding investigation work.[115] The Head Constables officiated as Sub-Inspectors in place of probationary Sub-Inspectors under practical training in the districts.[116] The Criminal Intelligence Bureau worked in close liaison with the District Intelligence Bureau coordinating their work and functioning as the central agency for dealing with organised crimes. In every district of the Northern range, there were District Intelligence Bureau manned by Inspectors and good results were achieved in the use of scientific aids to investigation. There was an increase in the number of calls made on the service of experts, especially in footprints. The footprint experts examined 94 cases and were summoned by courts to give evidence in 21 cases in the year 1947.

Training in footprints work was also given to 23 Inspectors and 33 Head Constables from the districts, to an Inspector of Bangalore and two Sub-Inspectors of the Criminal Investigation Department.[117] The special branch continued to function efficiently and the 'X' branch did useful work in detecting a large number of cases relating to the violations of rules and regulations, control and rationing and in the investigation of corruption cases.[118] To investigate the cases of bribery and corruption in the government departments during the World War II, Special Police establishments were organised. By the end of the year 1942, this establishment had extended to the Railways also.[119]

Services of the Shorthand Bureau

Shorthand instructors were appointed in the language groups of English, Telugu, Tamil, Kanarese and Urdu.[120] Shorthand Bureau reporters attended political, labour meetings, and conferences and they were also deputed to follow certain political agitators. They recorded and translated the abstracts of the seditious speeches and communicated the same to the Secretaries and other superior police officers.[121] They kept the Sub-Inspectors informed about the offences. For the efficiency in their work, periodical examinations were conducted in the Bureau.[122] The shorthand staff attended 77 conferences and 1,165 labour and other meetings as against 139 and 1,6740 in the year 1938-39. Tamil and Telugu shorthand Sub-Inspectors recorded speeches delivered in the Madras Legislature and the evidence of witnesses before the Estates Land Act Committee.[123] The following are some of the interesting cases related to the Criminal Investigation Department.

During the year 1925, a gang of forgers of currency notes from the district of Nellore and Guntur conspired at Madras and got a block made for counterfeiting one hundred rupee currency notes. The police arrested three of them at the Madras Central Station on their way to Kalahasti and two more at Kalahasti. Two persons were convicted in this case by the Sessions Court in Madras.[124]

In the year 1928, a case was recorded regarding currency notes forged in Burma that found their way to the Madras Presidency through steamships. The seizure of such notes in Cocanada led to the captures in Rangoon and averted their wider circulation. Two of the accused in the Cocanada cases were convicted. Another case of interest during the same year 1928 was of two railways carriage Inspectors of goods in East Godavari district, who with some of their associates carried on the currency note duplicating tricks. They used to select a rich young man and convince him that they were able to, by means of photography, duplicate hundred rupee currency notes. All the offenders in the case were convicted.[125]

Three Mohammedans, while using counterfeit rupee coins in the bazaar in Guntur town, were noticed by the police. When they investigated the coins, it was found that they were counterfeited by two brothers who were goldsmiths. One brother was arrested at Narasaraopet, Guntur district and the other at Mogalrajapuram, Kistna district.[126] The counterfeit Rs 100 of T.E.87 series were already in circulation in the districts of Kistna and West Godavari which had then spread all over the Madras Presidency of which the Northern range was a part. Most of these counterfeit notes were found in race course. The criminal branch of the police enquired into the origin of this series and took action to stop further circulation.[127]

In the year 1930, a gang consisting of two goldsmiths and two other persons was formed in the East Godavari district for counterfeiting rupees. A well-to-do man of Annavaram was approached to finance this scheme but he gave information to the Sub-Inspector of police of that place. A raid was arranged in which the head of the gang was caught while in the act of striking counterfeiting rupees, who were later convicted. At Mendapata in the East Godavari district in the year 1936, a gang of 10 rupee notes forger was busted from whom 35 counterfeit notes were seized and all culprits were convicted and chargesheeted.[128]

A case of counterfeiting of rupees in a secluded cave in the Veligunda hills of Nellore was detected. A considerable influx of forged ten rupees notes from Burma was investigated by Criminal Investigation Department. In the same district, one Kondala Rao Chowdry, obtained money from the villagers in the Cuddaph district with the promise of teaching them the art of minting and manufacturing currency notes. When he and his associate appeared with some negatives of five rupee currency notes at Chakrayapet, they were arrested.[129]

In the Vizagapatam district, a banking concern known as the Barathamatha Commonwealth Insurance Bank had made fraudulent transactions and cheated many people. The bank had a number of branches in various parts of India, Burma and Ceylon. This case was investigated by the Criminal Investigation Department.[130] In the year 1931, a person by name of Sri Haridoss, disguised as a social reformer with divine powers, created unrest among the hill tribes of Vizagapatam agency tracks. He was arrested on 25th September and interned in Bellary but managed to escape and again reappeared in the year 1932 in a village of the Vizagapatam Agency with his followers. The police arrested him and four of his followers and they were prosecuted and sentenced to long terms of imprisonment. This fellow again escaped but was recaptured in the year 1933.[131]

An inter-district cheat posing as a *sanyasi* gained the confidence of a government servant in the Nellore district and persuaded him to adorn an idol with Rs 2,000 worth of jewels for a special puja and while the puja was in progress, the cheat absconded with all the jewels. In the same year, a young man of the Guntur district, who posed as a Lieutenant of the Royal Indian Naval Reserve, was found traveling in a first class compartment from Madras to Waltair. He used railway warrants for his journeys and was arrested on suspicion by the railway police. Several forged documents were seized from him and he was sentenced to two years imprisonment.[132]

It was reported that an officer of the Criminal Investigation Department successfully established that three individuals in the West Godavari district were manufacturing and circulating counterfeit rupees. Efficient work by this department led to seizure of 528 incomplete ten-rupee counterfeit notes and the materials used for making them.[133] During the year 1932, a house of a Vyasaya (Komati) banker was attacked by dacoits who were armed with guns in the Garagaparru village of the West Godavari district and an amount of six lakh rupees was recovered from the twenty people accused in the case, who were mostly the debtors. It shows that the dacoits were not professionals and out of their distress, they attacked and were caught.

A notorious cheat and inter-provincial criminal named Ramanujam alias Sundarsanam, after escaping from the Cochin jail, operated in the city. He issued bogus demand drafts and induced the Bombay Motor Company to deliver cash styling himself as Dr. Desiken, proprietor of Desikan Company; he attempted to cheat the fiat motor agency and P&O bank of Rs 5,400 and Rs 41,000. He was arrested with great difficulty and was convicted and sentenced to undergo two years rigorous imprisonment. He again escaped from the custody of the Vizagapatnam district police, while being escorted to the Presidency jail, Alipore, to stand his trial in a series of cases in Calcutta, Simla, Lahore and other places. The city intelligence department suspected him to be operating in Bombay, and finally, a

Sub-Inspector, deputed from the Northern range, identified him in Cuddapah when he was undergoing another trial.[134] The number of searches regarding moving of criminal gangs and registration under the Criminal Tribes Act and the number of search references received from West Godavari district in the year 1929 was 1,349 cases.[34] The implementation of the Criminal Tribes Act resulted to a large extent in reducing the organised crimes and the crimes by habitual offenders.

Services of the Railway Police

The origin of the Railway Police Force lies in the Resolution of the Indian Police Commission of 1860. It was created in the year 1866 on the orders of the British government. The administrative control of this force was under the charge of Deputy Inspector General of Police of Madras Presidency through which the railway lines passed. The Superintendent of Police of the railway district was not under the control of the District Magistrate unlike the regular Superintendent of Police. On the recommendation of the Indian Police Commission 1902-03, a separate railway police district was formed as the rails passed through various districts. There were several railway police stations in the districts of the Northern range with jurisdiction of 100 miles. The railway police districts were divided into police circles and police stations and outposts.

With the development of railways in the Madras Presidency, the British government had ordered for the creation of Railway Police Force in the Northern range in the year 1893 with the recommendation of the Inspector General of Police of Madras Presidency for the security of the railway property and railway tracks from criminal gangs. There were a number of criminal activities along the railway lines caused by criminal gangs in the Northern range. The Railway Police was employed for the preservation of law and order within the railway limits.[135] Train guards were drawn from amongst the reserve men on all passenger trains on the South Indian Railways during strike in the months of July and September of 1928.[136]

A scheme was introduced in the Madras Presidency in the year 1895 with a number of Inspectors under control of Superintendents and it became applicable in the Northern range as it was part of the Madras Presidency. A number of Inspectors were recruited for this purpose and the Railway Police Force was responsible for law enforcement on the Northern range railways. They maintained discipline on platform and also inside the trains to keep passengers secure and railway accidents were also handled by them.[137]

The Railway Police was organised to cooperate with the police force in the Northern range and it was divided into two divisions. One was stationary platform staff to preserve order within the railway limits and maintained law and order at the railway stations and this force was armed and unarmed.[138] The second division was for detective work and protecting the travelling staff and the railway companies contributed towards its maintenance.[139] These special branches of Railway Police were under the control of a separate Deputy Inspector General of Police.[140] The Railway Police was part of the Bengal-Nagapur Railway line in the Orissa Province until 1st April, 1938.

The former Presidency General Reserve and the two Special Emergency Forces stationed at Vizianagaram and St. Thomas Mount were amalgamated and formed into two new formations. One formation was known as the Range Armed Reserves which were local strategic forces at the disposal of the concerned Deputy Inspector General of Police. The other formation was known as the Railway Police Armed Reserves intended for railway protection duty, which were at the disposal of the concerned Superintendent of Railway Police.[141] The most important railway was the East-Coast line connecting Madras in the south and Calcutta in the east. For travelling the taluks of Eluru, Tadepalligudem, and Kovvur, a total distance of 92 kilometers railway lines were opened for the traffic up to the Godavari river in the year 1893. In the year 1928, under the Madras and Southern Mahratta Railway, the Gudivada-Bheemavaram railway line of 41 miles length was laid in September. In the year 1929, under the Madras and Southern Maharatta Railway, the Nidadovolu-Narsapur line of 47.25 miles length was laid in February, 1928.[142]

The Railway Police dealt with different forms of thefts in running trains — from passengers, mail and baggage vans, goods trains, stationary wagons, goods sheds, platforms, passenger sheds, and railway material — which frequently occurred in the Railway Police District of the Northern range.[143]

The District Superintendent of Police regularly instructed their subordinates in the matter of preventing trespass on railway lines and circulars were issued to warn people of the danger of using railway lines as footpath. [144] An important development during the year 1931 was the preparation of the railway strike schemes. These schemes were prepared and approved by the government. In additions to these, detailed schemes for every district were prepared and approved.

The Station House Officers were directed to create public awareness and to warn the villagers during their village visits of danger of walking on the railway tracks. The District Superintendents of Police of the districts of the Northern range had issued instructions to the village officers to this effect. A number of cases of theft were dealt successfully by the Railway Police. There were many attempts to wreck or damage the trains and those culprits who were responsible were punished. In Rajahmundry of the East Godavari district, there was a Railway Police outpost and a railway police station.[145] Sergeants were attached to Godavari railway bridge for guarding the bridge in the East Godavari district of the Northern range.[146] The Railway Police force consisted of District Superintendent, Inspectors, Sub-Inspectors, Head Constables and Constables. Discipline was maintained in the department and these officers were also liable for punishments departmentally and judicially in their private and official capacities. An interesting case had occurred in the year 1928, when two railway carriage Inspectors of good status in East Godavari district with some associates carried on currency note duplicating tricks. They selected rich men and convinced them that they were able to, by means of photography, duplicate hundred rupee currency notes and the process and the materials required would be very costly; after the duped person had paid money, process was professed to fail. The case was successfully handled and the chief offenders were convicted.[147]

In the year 1939, there was reduction in the strength of the Railway Police due to the transfer of some of the police officers to the Orissa Province in respect of railway lines lying within the area of that province.[148] Temporary additional staff of two Constables retention was sanctioned for the year 1939 in Vizianagaram railway police station.[149] The proportion of strength of the Railway police officers maintained in the year 1924, till the independence in 1947, was almost same. The following cases are of interest which had occurred during the years 1924-47 in the Northern range.

There were many cases of stone pelting recorded in this range and the young boys who were responsible for these offences, many of them were convicted and their parents warned. In the West Godavari district at Bheemavaram railway station, 27 different types of theft cases were recorded in the year 1929. In Eluru Railway Police outpost of the West Godavari District in the year 1935, a Constable was caught and sentenced to two and haft months rigorous imprisonment for stolen property according to the police record. During the year 1938, three train collisions occurred, of which two were with carts owing to the negligence of level-crossing gate keepers and the third was between two trains. There were three cases of derailment, of which, only in one there was loss of life.[150]

The police travelled in the guards van and line patrols were instituted at particularly criminal parts of the line to prevent crime. Theft was mostly recorded from trans-shipment yards and goods shed. To prevent theft on goods train especially in the nights, Constables travelled to watch loading and unloading at transshipment yards.[151] One Beat Constable travelled by every passenger train day and night. The cases were usually reported to the Criminal Investigation Department, but the railway police took action only when culprit was handed over. The Constables were recruited separately from district police accordingly to rules laid down in the police order. Here is a case of interest in this regard: A young man of the Guntur district, who posed as a Lieutenant of the Royal Indian Naval Reserve, was found travelling in a first class compartment from Madras and Waltair. He used railway warrants for his journeys and was arrested on suspicion by the Railway Police. Several forged documents were seized from him and he was sentenced to two years imprisonment.[152] There was no occurrence of any special railway crime, and local crimes and railway crimes were very closely related.

During the political unrest in the Northern range, especially in the year 1942, there was massive destruction caused to the railways by the agitators of the Quit India Movement. They sabotaged with railway lines, railway telegraph wires were cut near stations, fish plates and bolts were removed, engine and bogies were derailed for which the police imposed fines on the nabbed culprits.[153] There was a marked increase of crime in the Railway Police districts which was to a great extent due to smuggling of foodgrains and due to registration of shortages in sealed wagons, especially during the year 1947.[154] The general increase in the crime related to the railways was attributed to unfavourable seasonal conditions, unemployment due to demobilisation, sporadic communal tensions, widespread labour and agrarian unrest, the abrogation of the Criminal Tribes Act, the general upward trend of prices of essential commodities and better reporting and registration of crimes consequent upon reallocation of areas in several districts of the Madras Presidency including Northern range.

Services of the Traffic Police

Under the Section 31 of the Police Act of 1861, the duties of the police were mentioned. The main functions of the police were to preserve order on the public roads, streets, *ghats*, and other public places. They prevented crime, regulated assemblies, processions, controlled criminal activities, protected life and property of the public and also controlled traffic and offences related to it under the Motor Vehicles Act. The Traffic Police were responsible for maintenance of the smooth flow of traffic and were also responsible for securing the roads and highways from crimes. They controlled the traffic and arrested the offenders for overspeeding and were mostly organised in the cities and towns of the Northern range. With the introduction of the Motor Vehicles Act, the traffic offences reduced to a great extent. Those persons who drove on any public way in a manner considered rash or negligent as to endanger human life or to cause hurt or injury to any other person, was punished with imprisonment of either description for a term which extended to six months, or with fine of maximum one thousand rupees, or with both. [155] Traffic control was important in order to avoid accidents, overloading, smuggling, etc., and measures were taken through rules and regulations to assure safety to the people and the Indian Motor Vehicles Act was enacted for this purpose.[156] Traffic control signals in the Northern range had decreased the number of traffic crimes. The main object of prosecutions under the Indian Motor Vehicles Act was public safety.

The punishments for an offence, deliberately or knowingly committed, under the law were imprisonment and liabilty to pay fine. Under the Motor Vehicles Act, persons were convicted for rash and negligent driving, for causing obstruction for driving without licence, violating the traffic rule by driving on the wrong side or standing without lights, for breach of permits issued for plying for hire, and for offences under the taxi cab rules. The problem of glaring headlights was tackled by enforcing the rules rigorously at the time of registration of cars and buses. Motor bus traffic had increased in the Northern range with the increase in the numbers of motor vehicles and consequently, the number of cases under the Motor Vehicles Act also had increased.[157] Under this Act, the District Superintendents of Police maintained a record of the convictions secured against the holders of licences and permits.[158]

There was a rapid increase in the number of motor vehicles which added to the work of the police force during the years 1924 and 1947. Overloading and errant driving was the chief offence and police staff had exercised efficient control during the period in the districts of the Northern range. In the year 1924, several schemes for regulation and control of traffic were introduced by the police, such as fixing speed limits for buses, making the pedestrians to stick to footpaths and pavements, and to walk on the extreme left of the road. The buses plying for hire in the districts were well-maintained for the public. Overloading and errant driving continued to be chief offence and police staff were increased to exercise efficient control. In many places, there were unhealthy competitions between rival companies and this was solved by regulating the issue of licences. The District Magistrates had been asked to instruct the magistracy to pass deterrent sentences on the traffic offenders.[159]

Sergeants were sanctioned from this range for regulating the starting of buses at various terminals and for directing the bus drivers against overtaking. Also, from this range, two more Sergeants were provided with motor cycles for enforcing speed regulations and for dealing with other matters, four constables were sanctioned. In this range, traffic congestion was due to piling of buses at important junctions and so, the buses that remained stationary for long thus causing obstruction, were prosecuted and fines imposed. All these cases under this Act and Rules came under category of cognizable offences.[160] The regulation of motor passenger bus routes and the control of bus traffic was transferred from the District Magistrates to District Superintendents during the year 1934 and with this change, the staff of motor vehicle Inspectors came under the disciplinary control of the Police Department.[161] In the Northern range, accidents were primarily due to rash and negligent driving, the vagaries of the meandering pedestrians, irresponsible children and ignorance of the ordinary traffic regulations and rules.

After the promulgation of the new Motor Vehicles Rules, the rules empowered the police to exercise stricter and more effective control over all motor vehicles and regulation of traffic and to reduce road accidents. The administration of the Act and the issue of the licences, permits, etc., was vested in a Central Road Traffic Board, constituted in the Madras city, under which Road Traffic Boards were formed in districts with District Superintendents of Police as Secretaries. In spite of the increase in the number of vehicles in the Northern range on the roads and the absence of adequate police staff for traffic control, the number of accidents and fatalities decreased over the years.[162] This decrease was due to special measures taken by the traffic police to prevent accidents on roads in the Northern range under which instructions were issued to check the warning signs on the electric and telegraph poles or lamps posts.[163]

Also deterrent punishments were meted out to rash drivers and instilling traffic sense was made compulsory curriculum in all schools and colleges.[164] A notable feature of the year 1938 was the introduction of the Madras Traffic Control Act and the rules framed thereunder had a positive effect on increase in control over transport vehicles. There was a fall in the number of vehicles newly registered from 1,718 to 1,204. The staff for traffic was increased to control the growing traffic in the Northern range in furtherance of which an additional staff was sanctioned in the years 1938-39 for traffic control in the districts of Vizagapatam and East Godavari.[165] The new Motor Vehicles Rules gave the police more effective control over motor vehicles and the regulation of traffic as a result of which there was a decrease in the number of accidents due to motor vehicles. Pedestrians and cyclists were the usual offenders and were responsible for almost 50 per cent of the accidents.

Services of the Fire Fighters

The Auxiliary Fire Service was organised as a volunteer service in the Madras Presidency which was introduced in the year 1908. It consisted of some steam or manually operated engines stationed at important parts of the city. The police and the fire service officers dealt with outbreaks of fire.[166] The fire fighting personnel were drawn from the Reserve and the Fire Brigade was under the charge of the Commissioner of Police. This service was a part of the Air Raid Precaution and was set up in the Vizagapatam and Coconada districts in the Northern range.[167] The Fire Service section was organised under the charge of the Air Raid Precaution Controller, as the Air Raid Precaution organisation expanded in the districts of the Northern range and it was placed under the Deputy Inspector General of Police, Civil Defence. The municipal water vans were used as elementary fire engines in case of occurrence of a fire. The surplus equipment necessary for war time protection was maintained after the war and used for the protection. The surplus Air Raid Precaution ambulances were also transferred to the fire service and it became a Fire and Ambulance Service.

The year 1941 was most arduous one as a heavy additional burden was placed on the police force. Extra war duties which included air raid precaution, coastal patrol, guarding of vulnerable points and important railway bridges, escort of internees and surveillance of the foreigners, verification of antecedents of a large number of Army recruits, training of regular police, arrest of Army deserters and numerous other special branches and miscellaneous duties occasioned by the war, had imposed a heavy strain on all ranks of the police. The extra duties and normal duties of detection and prevention of crime and maintenance of law and order were discharged efficiently with high discipline and morale.[168] The progress of the war in 1941 found police officer in several new jobs. H.D. Lathanm I.P., was Air Raid Precaution officer, Madras in place of C.R. Charsley and G.F. Harrison I.P. was appointed Deputy Commissioner, Madras Fire Service. These two sub-divisional officers became special Air Raid Precaution officers at Vizagapatam and Cocanada. With the deterioration in the war conditions in 1942, it became necessary to have fire fighting units in large number in the other districts range. In the year 1942, on the request of the Madras government, Thiru. W.A Tozer, the Director of Fire Service, Burma, was appointed as head of Fire Service in Madras.

Fire Service was organised as an adjunct of the Air Raid Precaution Service during the World War II. It became a peacetime organisation in 1943. The British government had approved the establishment of Fire Service in 60 municipal towns apart from 24 which already existed in the Madras Presidency.[169]

The important fire stations were under the charge of Station Officers and other stations were under sub-officers. There were eight fire services in the Northern range and the headquarters was at Bezwada.

The fire services workshop at Bezwada attended to all minor repairs and replacements to vehicles within their region. An emergency breakdown van was acquired for this department. It was fitted with necessary equipment for towing or lifting crashed vehicles and for picking up overturned vehicles and was capable of dealing with all emergencies relating to fire, and accidents. The entry of Japan into the war brought threat to India to counter which air raid precautions were organised and C.R. Charsley was appointed Air Raid Precautions Officer. To strengthen internal security, a temporary Special Emergency Force consisting of two companies of five platoons each and officered by two Assistant District Superintendents of Police was formed in 1940. One of the companies was stationed at Vizagapatam to aid the police. These guards were raised on an entirely voluntary basis and organised in groups of ten persons with a Commander for each group. Initially, this organisation functioned only in Madras city in the Madras Presidency. Later, the Madras Fire Services took over the responsibilities of fire protection of the Vizagapatam harbour and a new section called the "Vizagapatam port section" was opened with effect from the 1st July, 1947.[170] The services of this organisation were beneficial to the public during fire emergencies.

Services of the Port Police

The Northern range was a coastal region and had major river trading activities, so, a separate Port Police Force was organised by the British under the charge of Superintendent.[171] The port police functioned for prevention and detection of serious crimes, including smuggling and regulated traffic in navigable areas and they had cordial relations with the port trust authorities and the police.[172] Under the Indian Police Act of 1861, along with the general police force, the Port Police Force was organised in the Northern range to assist the regular police. The Harbour Police was established at Vizagapatam in the Vizagapatam district, Machillipatnam in the Kistna district and Cocanada port in the East Godavari district.[173] They maintained harmonious relations with the Port Trust authorities.

There were a number of criminal activities, like smuggling, house-breaking, house thefts, cycle thefts and stealing of scrap iron and brass material in the port areas. The harbour police worked along with the customs department to regulate the admissions of people into the harbour and for the preservation of law and order in the port limits.[174] Sergeants, engaged with fixed duties at the gates in connection with floating duty, were given more responsibility for patrolling the harbour and supervising subordinates. A change in uniform was introduced in the Boat Crew establishment during the year 1839. They were supplied with three pairs of blue shorts, three vests, a sailor cap, a sailor blouse and a woolen jersey. [175]

Reserve Police companies were stationed at the ports for security. In the year 1939, H.M.I.S., Indus Lawrence, and Clive ships had visited the Vizagapatam harbour and communication between the naval signallers on board the vessels and the reserve signallers on shore was constantly maintained. The naval authorities complimented the police signallers for their high standards of efficiency.[176] In the year 1939, for maintenance of security for a further period of one year, police force was sanctioned for Cocanada and they continued to work satisfactorily.[177] A reward of Rs 100 was granted by the Chamber of Commerce to the Sub-Inspector of the Port Police of Cocanada port in the East Godavari district in recognition of good work in prevention of cargo thefts.[178]

Services of the Police *Talaiyaris*

A peculiar feature of the year 1926 was the introduction of a new police *talaiyari* scheme.[179] Road patrols were enforced throughout the districts of the Northern range with the appointment of *Ghat* police force as a preventive measure who patrolled the country roads day and night. Travelling by night was common in the Northern range and road dacoities were frequent offences. To provide safety to the public by preventing crimes, road *talaiyaris* were appointed on the important roads and outposts. The presence of these *talaiyaris* provided safety and security to the travelling public on roads in the hilly areas.[180] With regular system of patrol, the roads were made secure and the *talaiyaris* on the patrol duties were armed.[181]

In the towns and villages of the districts of the Northern range, there were a number of village servants known as *talaiyaris* who were responsible for preservation of order and detection of crime. They were employed on various duties which were carried out by police Constables. In special localities, *ghat talaiyaris* were enlisted and controlled by the police department and they were employed to supplement the police in guarding roads in hilly tracts. They were useful in rendering road safety in the backward parts of the range and the government provided them with huts.[182] They were granted rewards by the officers of the police department. The general strength of the police *talaiyaris* in East Godavari district during the year 1926 was 673 [183] which increased to 1,416 in the year 1933.[184] In the West Godavari district, there were no police *talaiyaris* during the year 1934.[185] In the Guntur district, during the year 1931, there were 12 police *talaiyaris.*[186] In the year 1946, four *ghat talaiyaris* each, were abolished in the districts of Guntur and Nellore.[187] The *talaiyaris* and the village officers cooperated with the police in the matter of prevention and detection of crime throughout the Northern range.[188] They successfully mastered the technique of dealing with prohibition crime which was well under control.

Services of the Village Police

On the recommendations of the Police Commissions of 1860 and 1902-03, the village police were placed under the regular police. In the vastness of the range and Agency tracts, the old system of village watch and ward continued for the safety and security of the village community.[189]

The village headmen were placed under the control of the District Magistrate. He had magisterial powers to try petty offences and village watchman was under his charge.[190] To carry out efficient police administration, it was essential to secure the aid of the village community. It was impossible for the police force to obtain information regarding crime over the extensive area and along the vast population without securing the co-operation and enforcing the responsibilities of the village authorities. The British government had retained the system of policing prevailing in the Madras Presidency with some modifications. They apprehended offenders and forwarded them to district authorities. In petty cases, however, they themselves dealt with the criminals. The village police was established in the Northern range with the Regulation Act XI of 1816, and the heads of villages were invested with police duties and also with civil and criminal powers. The main function of the village police was to carry out efficient police administration for the aid of village community. The Police Commission of 1860 recommended continuance of the prevailing system of rural policing with minor changes.

The important officers were the village watchmen and the village headmen. The village headmen were invested with police duties and also had magisterial powers. In the *ryotwari* area, the village headman was the revenue head of the village.[191] The Police Act of 1862 had empowered the village headman with the police powers and they were assisted by the village *panchayat* to dispose of simple civil suits of small value. The village police were under the control of the District Magistrates and their main function was to assist the police in the investigation and detection of crime.[192] The village police in Northern range was improving their administration by educating the village communities to take active part in their own affairs. The village headman represented the village community and effective police administration was based on the recognition and enforcement of the responsibility of the headman. He was the man who could help the police and the police looked for his co-operation in their work.

The responsibilities of the village headmen in the performance of the village police duties were recognised and enforced in the Northern range of the Madras Province. The village watchman was also the village servant subordinate to the village headman and not to the regular police. The supervision and control of village headmen were entrusted with the District Magistrate of the district.[37] Under Section 45 of the Criminal Procedure Code, the village headmen were responsible for the communication to the Magistracy or the police information concerning certain crimes and criminals. The District Magistrate and the District Superintendent of Police issued circulars to village officers regarding proper discharge of their police duties.[193]

For public cooperation, these organisations voluntary trained social workers who came forward to assist the authorities during the important local festivals when very large crowds of people and pilgrims gathered. As auxiliaries to the police force in the regulation of crowds during religious festivals and in the maintenance of order, their help was invaluable. As friends of the pilgrims, guiding and advising them, supplying them with necessary information, and providing them with all services sought, were of great public value.[194]

Rewards were given to the police and also to the private individuals for helping in the reduction of the crime. The British government had abolished the system of granting money rewards to police officials except Constables and Head Constables.[195]

During the year 1938-39, there was an increase in the number of private persons, including village officers, rewarded which represents an improvement in relations between the public and the police. In the Northern range, special steps were taken by printing and posting notices in all the villages to ensure that crime was well-reported. By these measures, offences such as traffic irregularities, street nuisances, petty quarrels, and rowdyism were brought on the police registers.

In West Godavari district of the Northern range, a village magistrate personally helped a Sub-Inspector in chasing and arresting criminal tribe members who had escaped from settlements despite the fact that his own house had been attacked by burglars on account of his zeal in assisting the police.[196] The village officers were rewarded and specific instances of neglect of duty and other offences were reported to the revenue authorities to be suitably dealt with.

In the East Godavari district, the village officers had acted on their own whenever a crime was detected. In the Vizagapatam district, many village officers had acted efficiently in dealing with the criminal tribes registered under the Criminal Tribes Act.[197] During the festive seasons, gambling was most common offence; a number of gambling cases had taken place in the Northern range and many gambling houses were attacked and arrested. The village police, with help of police, had reduced the crime rate and criminals and known depredators were informed about. Crime was well-reported by the villager officers but they were poor in surveillance of village criminals and village patrols.[198] Any failure to report the arrival of gang members and the neglect of duty in the working of the Criminal Tribes Act were some of the offences under which the village officers were punished. The co-operation of the village officers with the police in the matter of controlling crimes continued to be satisfactory throughout the Northern range during the period of study, viz., 1924 to 1947.

Services of the Village Vigilance Committees

In the year 1935, as an auxiliary agency of the police, the Vigilance Committees were formed in the districts of the Northern range. These committees rendered notable public service. They constituted a liaison between the authorities and the village populations, and this, resulted in the control of crime and detection of offences.[199] A District Superintendent of Police has reported in reference to these committees as 'When we thus sought to create a higher sense of civic responsibility and met with a very encouraging response, we were also benefitted by a subjective influence on ourselves. For which we preached the utility of good police, we took every care to make ourselves 'good' and definitely 'good'. Police officers during their tours continued to impress the village police for close co-operation and in many instance they were suitably rewarded for their good work'.

Members of these committees were chosen and selected personally by gazetted officers. Village headmen were always included in such committees as *ex-officio* members and the increased thrust and responsibility was imposed on them. There was a president as the head for the maintenance of the committee. Any cases of misconduct and neglect of duty by the village officers were reported to the revenue authorities. The responsibilities of the village headmen in the performance of the village police duties was recognised and enforced in every district of the Northern range and the village watchman was village servant subordinate to the village headman and not to the regular police. The supervision and control of the village headmen was entrusted with the district magistrate.[27]

The role and importance of these committees was well-understood by the administration, and in some districts of the Northern range, District Magistrates at the instances of District Superintendents of Police, issued circulars to village officers regarding proper discharge of their police duties. Under the welfare programme, the experimental scheme of sports and games in selected villages was introduced in the year 1938; this scheme had continued to work satisfactorily through the period. Additional centres were started during this year 1939, and in almost all of them, the villagers and the public cooperated to make the scheme a success.[200] There existed co-operation between the village vigilance committees officers and the *talaiyaris* with the police in the matter of prevention and detection of the crime.[201] Gazetted officers used to inspect these committees, and during their tours, impressed on village officers the need for close co-operation with the police subordinates.

The village officers were frequently rewarded whenever they did a good work. A number of village officers were rewarded in the years 1938 and 1939 for good work and number of officers rewarded and the amount spent on the same for the year 1938 was 565 and Rs 2,718 respectively. For the year 1939, the number of village officers rewarded were 535 and the amount spent was Rs 2,453. During the year 1946, the number of officers rewarded were 690 and the amount spent was Rs 4,912 while, in the year 1946, the number of village officers rewarded were 580 and the amount spent on the same was Rs 4,161.[202] The village vigilance committee members were also liable for punishmente for their misconduct and neglect of duty by bringing them to the notice of their superior officers.

Village Vigilance Committees continued their good work in detection and prevention of crimes. Village Vigilance Committees in non-factious areas rendered good service in the prevention of crime and the apprehension of offenders.[203] Village officers continued to cooperate satisfactorily with the police in combating crimes. Village Vigilance Committees constituted a link between the authorities and the village population. They established a sound footing in most of the districts of the Northern range and rendered great help. The formation of the Village Vigilance Committees and the introduction of stranger days each month in many districts of the Northern range had produced closer contact with the villagers resulting in a number of cases coming to light and getting registered.

In the year 1937, a government *talaiyari*, who was taking *kist* collection of over Rs 400 to the Sankaranainarkoyil sub-treasury, was knocked off his bicycle and murdered and all the money was stolen. A local Village Vigilance Committee member organised a search party and the offender was arrested. The entire money was restored and death sentence was imposed on the culprit.[204] A villager in the Nellore district evinced public spirit and initiative in promptly giving information to the local Village Vigilance Committee members of the presence of a few suspects in the vicinity leading to the arrest of three armed absconders from the Siddhapuram criminal settlement.[205] Boy Scouts troop of Nellore town used to render assistance during big religious festivals and the public were educated in queue formations.[206]

These troops were responsible for the arrest of an accused with property in 1,367 Penal Code cases, including 317 cattle theft cases for tracing or arrest of a number of bad characters and criminal tribe members and for putting up 1,078 gambling cases in the year 1938-39.[207] Number of Village Vigilance Committees and cases, including those realted to property, cattle theft and gambling, dealt by them in the Northern range during the years 1935 to 1947 are as under:[208]

Years	*No. of Village Vigilance Committees*	*No. of Cases*
1935	-	179
1936	3743	703
1937	5347	1006
1938	4733	973
1939	5544	846
1940	5651	1102
1941	5764	1682
1942	5101	1275
1943	4937	1181
1944	5218	961
1945	4879	1134
1946	4564	473
1947	5219	1840

The number of cases dealt by Village Vigilance Committees are shown graphically as follows:

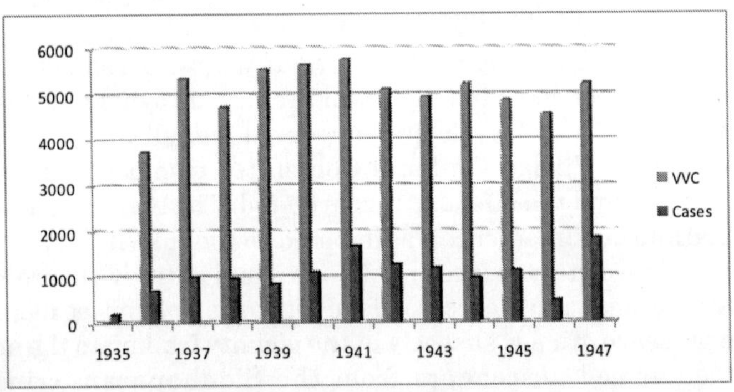

The village headmen represented the village community and effective police administration was based on the recognition and enforcement of the responsibility of the headman. He was the man who helped the police and the police looked at him for co-operation in their work. The growth of this new non-official agency of cooperation, its magnitude and the volume of effective public service which it was rendering can be gauged from the figures in the above graph. The above table shows the number of Village Vigilance

Committees in districts of the Northern range and the effective work done by them in co-operation with the police.[209] It was recorded in the year 1937 that the quantum work done by the Village Vigilance Committees was 490 cases in the West Godavari district out of which 29 accused persons were arrested with property and 56 cases related to cattle theft. Cattle were mostly stolen by the tribes and the lower caste people for hides or for consumption.

The special and auxiliary police forces were units of the regular police force that were organised to maintain law and order. The Special Police were recruited mostly from the ex-military men and they assisted the regular police. These police forces were paramilitary in nature and were trained to maintain internal security and were armed or unarmed depending on their duties. The Presidency General Reserves, Malabar Special Police, East Coast Special Police, Emergency Police Forces, and Armed Reserve Police were kept as reserves at all the district headquarters in the Northern range. These forces functioned under the supreme command of the Inspector General of Police of the Madras Presidency and their superior cadres were Europeans.

The East Coast Special Police was organised on the lines of the Malabar Special Police and was employed for agency operations and for suppressing political unrest and rebellions. These Special Police Forces were well-trained in arms, physical training, signalling and bayonet fighting by a military officer. These special police forces were not intended to be military in nature and were armed to control the riots and perform guard and escort duties. They were activated only on orders from the higher level authorities. They came into contact with the public when they were assigned the duty of maintaining order during political unrest, fairs, festivals, elections, and natural calamities. They were also deputed to quell outbreaks of unrest, organised crime, and depending on their assignment, they carried *lathis* or lethal weapons.

These police forces were mostly temporary in nature and were deputed only under emergencies. These forces lacked quality in performance and discipline, and so, the East Coast Special Police and the Civic Guards were disbanded except for the Presidency General Reserve Police Forces which was organised as a temporary force and later became permanent. During the political unrest in the Northern range, a new force called as Presidency General Reserve Police Force was formed. It had recruited a number of young men and ex-military men and had trained them with discipline and these recruirts were equipped with muskets and smoothbores.

The auxiliary units were a part of the regular police and they were highly specialised branches of the main police. The Criminal Investigation Department, Railway Police, Traffic Police, Port Police, Fire Services, Village Vigilance Committees, and *Ghat Talaiyaris* formed the auxiliary branches of the police to deal with crimes of special nature which spanned across multiple districts of the ranges. The Criminal Investigation Department investigated complex and complicated cases, such as those of counterfeit currency, postal fraud, false impersonation, bogus banking, cheating, coinage, forgery, fraud, complicated murder cases and other offences that required intricate detection. This department consisted of District Intelligence Bureaus, Fingerprint Bureau, Police Wireless Grid, Short hand Bureau and X-Branch.

The Railway Police preserved order within the railway limits and maintained law and order at the railway stations. They dealt different forms of thefts in running trains, platforms, goods sheds, passenger sheds and other railway material. During the political unrest under influence of the freedom struggle in the Northern range, there was massive destruction to the railways by the agitators.

The Traffic Police maintained smooth flow of traffic and secured the roads and highways from crime. They controlled the traffic, arrested the overspeeding offenders and they were mostly organised in the cities and towns of the Northern range. The Auxiliary Fire Service was organised as a volunteer service and it was a part of the Air Raid Precaution. It was placed under a police officer carrying designation of Deputy Inspector General, Civil Defence. During the war times, their extra duties included air raid precaution, coastal patrol, guarding of vulnerable points and important railway bridges. The Northern range was a coastal region; so, a separate police force called Port Police Force was organised for prevention and detection of serious crimes on the navigable waters. They worked in tandem with the customs department to regulate the admissions of people into the harbour and for the preservation of law and order in the port limits. Travelling by night was common in the Northern range and road dacoities were frequent offences. To provide safety to the public on the roads, *Ghat talaiyaris* were appointed who patrolled the countryside roads day and night.

The police force, in order to obtain information regarding crime over the extensive area with vast population in the Northern range, secured the co-operation of the village officers. They assisted the police in the investigation and detection of crimes, regulating crowds during fairs and festivals for the aid of village community and disposed of simple civil suits of trivial nature. They were under the control of the District Magistrates. The Village Vigilance Committees constituted a liaison between the police authorities and the village populations in the control of crime and detection of offences. The police forces were mostly kept up to their sanctioned strength throughout the period 1924-47 in the Northern range. The natives formed the most part of theses police forces. The communal and labour tensions, agrarian disputes, railway strikes, and political unrest which were the result of freedom struggle imposed a very heavy strain on these police forces but they discharged their duties efficiently on all these occasions.

The other auxiliary police forces patrolled the countryside and public roads, the prevented nuisances, and escorted and guarded treasury and convicts.[210] They were also entrusted with the guarding of railway tracks, prevention of smuggling on foreign frontiers, guarding of distilleries under the Excise Act and cantonments and ensuring implementation of Contagious Diseases Acts. The Special Police Forces preserved order and restored peace especially during the emergencies, such as political unrest, agrarian strikes, communal disturbances, and natural calamities. Their services were used in control of crime and in maintenance of law and order.

The Special Police Forces were sanctioned to prevent unlawful assembly, riots and disturbances in cases where the ordinary police appointed were not sufficient for preservation and protection of the public and security of the property. These Special Police Forces had opened fire, lathi-charged, used muskets and tear gas to control the rioters in many places in the Northern range during 1924-47. They had performed the task of suppressing the disturbances which enabled the British Authority to continue their rule. The Presidency General Reserve Police and District Armed Reserves worked successfully in suppressing the political agitations. As these services of the Special Police were under public criticism for their role, the British government, in order to keep up their morale high and incentivise them, granted them rewards lavishly. With the Government of India Act of 1935, the services of the Malabar Special Police, the Presidency General Reserve, and the District Reserves were increased in their numbers and they were reorganised for improvement. These forces successfully kept the mass agitations under control during the political struggle in the Northern range and few troops were used for internal security whenever there was unrest in repressive capacity.

The British government, in the districts of the Northern range, had utilised services of the paramilitary police forces and auxiliary forces for effective control of law and order. These forces were kept in reserve for major emergencies and this led to the creation of Special Police Forces. With the increasing political unrest due to freedom struggle in the Northern range, the British had sanctioned and strengthened the armed special police to protect their rule from the assaults of communal, political, labour, and agrarian agitations. These Special Police Forces in the Northern range had performed the task of suppressing the disturbances by which they enabled the British Authority to continue their rule in India. These Special Police Forces were retained for their services throughout the period 1924-47 in the districts of the Northern range. These Special Police Forces had performed their duty successfully and loyally with unshaken morale. This shows that the British had protected their rule with the help of services of the Special Police Forces and the Auxiliary Police Forces for maintaining law and order.

References

1. Government of Madras, Legal Department, The Madras District Police Act XXIV of 1859, printed by Superintendent, Government Press, Madras, 1937, pp. 4-6.
2. G.O.No.1407, Home, dated 1st April, 1942, Home Department, Madras Government.
3. G.O.No.3728, Home, dated 11th September, 1940, Home Department, Madras Government.
4. Report of Indian Police Commission 1902-03, printed at Government Central Printing Office, Simla, 1904, p. 140.
5. Handbook of Information on the Administration of the Province of Madras, 1945-46, printed by Superintendent, Government Press, Madras, 1947, p. 33.
6. Report on the Administration of the Police of the Madras Province, 1925, printed by Superintendent, Government Press, Madras, 1926, p. 6.
7. *Ibid.*
8. Letter No. 215/A R dated 15th July, 1926, from Inspector General of Police to the Chief Secretary to Government, Judicial Department, Madras.
9. Report on the Administration of the Police of the Madras Province,1939, printed by Superintendent, Government Press, Madras, 1940, p. 6.
10. Gazetteer of South India, Vol. I, Superintendent of Government Printing, Madras, 1909, p. 297.

11. Report of the Administration of the Madras Presidency for the rear 1921-22, printed by Superintendent, Government Press, Madras, 1923, pp. xiii,xiv.
12. Venkatarangaiya M, *The Freedom Struggle in Andhra Pradesh* (1921-31) Vol. III, printed by Commissioner, Andhra Pradesh State Archives and Research Institute, Hyderabad, 1997, p. 90,91.
13. Letter No. 215/A R, dated 15th July, 1926, from Inspector General of Police to the Chief Secretary to Government, Judicial Department, Madras.
14. G.O.No.4656, Home, dated17th December, 1947, Home Department, Government of Madras.
15. Report on the Administration of the Police of the Madras Presidency, 1946, printed by Superintendent, Government Press, Madras, 1947, p. 5.
16. G.O.No.4112, Home, dated 7th November, 1947, Home Department, Government of Madras.
17. Report on the Administration of the Police of the Madras Presidency, 1947, printed by Superintendent, Government Press, Madras, 1948, p. 6.
18. Report on the Administration of the Police of the Madras Province, 1925, printed by Superintendent, Government Press, Madras, 1926, p. 6.
19. Report on the Administration of the Madras Presidency for the years 1924-25, printed by Superintendent, Government Press, Madras, 1926, p. 22.
20. G.O.No.432, Judl. (Police), 18th August, 1923, Judicial Department, Government of Madras.
21. G.O.No. 232, Judl., 17th February, 1922, Judicial Department, Government of Madras.
22. Handbook of Information on the Administration of the Madras Presidency, 1941, printed by Superintendent, Government Press, Madras, 1942, p. 23.
23. Report on the Administration of the Police of the Madras Province, 1925, printed by Superintendent, Government Press, Madras, 1926, p. 7.
24. Frederick G. Bailey, *Tribe, Caste and Nation: A Study of Political Activity and Political Change in Highland Orissa*, Manchester, 1960, pp. 175,83.
25. G.O.No. 259, Judl. (Conf.), dated14th May, 1928, Judicial Department, Government of Madras.
26. Police Administrative Report of the Madras Presidency, 1925, printed by Superintendent, Government Press, Madras, 1926, p. 7.

27. Report on the Administration of the Police of the Madras Presidency, 1926, printed by Superintendent, Government Press, Madras, 1927, p. 7.
28. Report on the Administration of the Police of the Madras Presidency, 1927, printed by Superintendent, Government Press, Madras, 1928, p. 7.
29. Report on the Administration of the Madras Presidency, 1925, printed by Superintendent, Government Press, Madras, 1926, p. xix.
30. G.O.No.467, Judl., dated 25th September, 1928, Judicial Department, Government of Madras.
31. Report on the Administration of the Police of the Madras Presidency, printed by Superintendent, Government Press, Madras, 1927, p. 7.
32. G.O.No.425, Public (Police), dated 6th August, 1929, Home Department, Government of Madras.
33. Report on the Administration of the Police of the Madras Presidency for the year 1929, printed by Superintendent, Government Press, Madras, 1930, p. 7.
34. The Imperial Gazetteer of India, The Indian Empire, Vol. IV, Clarendon Press, Oxford, 1907, p. 389.
35. G.O.No.354, Public (Police), dated 24th June, 1930, Public (Police) Department, Government of Madras.
36. Madras Legislative Council Proceedings, Vol. VII, dated 22nd March, 1922.
37. G.O.No.1426, Home (Judl.), dated 15th June, 1918, Home Department, Government of Madras.
38. Report on the Administration of the Police of the Madras Presidency, 1925, printed by Superintendent, Government Press, Madras, 1926, p. 26.
39. Report on the Administration of the Madras Presidency for the year 1929-30, printed by Superintendent, Government Press, Madras, 1931, p. 36.
40. Report on the Administration of the Police of the Madras Presidency for the year 1929, printed by Superintendent, Government Press, Madras, 1930, p. 6.
41. Administrative Report of the Inspector General of Police for the year 1926, printed by Superintendent, Government Press, Madras, 1927, p. 11.
42. Report on the Administration of the Police of the Madras Presidency, 1927, printed by Superintendent, Government Press, Madras, 1928, p. 3.

43. Report on the Administration of the Police of the Madras Presidency, 1928, printed by Superintendent Government press, Madras, 1929, p. 46.
44. Report on the administration of the Police of the Madras Presidency, 1927, printed by Superintendent, Government Press, Madras, 1928, p. 6.
45. Report on the Administration of the Police of the Madras Province, 1925, printed by Superintendent, Government Press, Madras, 1926, p. 6.
46. Ayyar K.N.K., Madras District Gazetteers, Statistical Appendix (together with a supplement to the District Gazetteer, 1907 for Godavari district), Superintendent, Government Press, Madras, 1935, p. 91.
47. Report on the Administration of the Police of the Madras Province, 1929, printed by Superintendent, Government Press, Madras, 1930, p. 7.
48. The History of the Andhra Pradesh Police, 1861-1961, published by Inspector General of Police, Andhra Pradesh, Hyderabad, 1961, p. 222.
49. G.O.No.354, Public (Police), dated 24th June, 1930, Home Department, Government of Madras.
50. Administrative Report of the Inspector General of the Police for the year 1926, printed by Superintendent, Government Press, Madras, 1927, p. 13.
51. Police Administrative Report of the Madras Presidency, 1925, printed by Superintendent, Government Press, Madras, 1926, p. 6.
52. Report on the Administration of the Police of the Madras Presidency, 1926, printed by Superintendent, Government Press, Madras, 1927, p. 6.
53. Police Administrative Report of the Madras Presidency, 1925, printed by Superintendent, Government Press, Madras, 1926, p. 6.
54. Madras Administrative Report for the years 1938-39, printed by Superintendent, Government Press, Madras, 1940, p. 28.
55. The History of The Andhra Pradesh Police, 1861-1961, published by Inspector General of Police, Andhra Pradesh, Hyderabad, 1961, p. 224.
56. G.O.No.168 (Ms), Pub. (Police) 25th March, 1931, Public (Police) Department, Government of Madras.
57. G.O.No.I426, Home (Judicial), dated 15th June, I918, Home Department, Government of Madras.

58. Report on the Administration of the Police of the Madras Province, 1939, printed by Superintendent, Government Press, Madras, 1940, p. 6.
59. G.O.No.2407, Home (Ms), dated 1st May, 1939, Home Department, Government of Madras.
60. G.O.No.4376, Home (Ms) (Confdl.), dated 10th December,1945, Home Department, Government of Madras.
61. G.O.No.754, Home (Ms) (Confdl.), dated 27th Febrarury, 1945, Home Department, Government of Madras.
62. G.O.No.5273, Home (Ms), dated 4th October, 1939, Home Department, Government of Madras.
63. G.O.No.4075, Home (Ms), dated 9th November, 1945, Home Department, Government of Madras.
64. G.O.No.1353, Home (Ms), dated 28th April, 1945, Home Department, Government of Madras.
65. G.O.No.3905, Home (Ms), dated 19th July, 1939, Home Department, Government of Madras.
66. G.O.No.1407, Home, dated 1st April, 1942, Home Department, Madras Government.
67. G.O.No.151, Home (Ms), dated 16th January, 1945, Home Department, Government of Madras.
68. G.O.No.553, Home (Ms), dated 20th February, 1945, Home Department, Government of Madras.
69. G.O.No.1951, Home (Ms), 21st June, 1945, Home Department, Government of Madras.
70. G.O.No.3019, Home (Ms), dated 3rd September, 1945, Home Department, Government of Madras.
71. Report on the Administration of the Police of the Madras Province, 1946, printed by Superintendent, Government Press, Madras, 1947, p. 5.
72. G.O.No. 3701, Home, 6th October, 1948, Home Department, Government of Madras.
73. Report of the Administration of the Madras Presidency for the year 1947, printed by Superintendent, Government Press, Madras, 1948, p. 9.
74. Madras in 1947, Outline of Administration, Part-I, printed by Superintendent, Government Press, Madras, 1948, p. 23.
75. G.O.No.467, Judl., dated 25th September, 1928, Judicial Department, Government of Madras.
76. G.O.No. 354, Judicial (Conf.), dated 24th June, 1930, Judicial Department, Government of Madras.

77. G.O.No. 485, Public (Police), dated 12th September, 1931, Public Department, Government of Madras.
78. G.O.No.1197, Public (Military) (Conf.), dated 22nd July, 1935, Public Department, Government of Madras.
79. G.O.No.206, Judicial (Conf.), dated 16th April, 1929, Judicial Department, Government of Madras.
80. G.O.No.3391, Home (Conf.), dated 14th August, 1940, Home Department, Government of Madras.
81. The History of the Andhra Pradesh Police 1861-1961, published by Inspector General of Police, Hyderabad, 1961, p. 225.
82. G.O.No.485, Public (Police), dated 12th September, 1931, Public (Police) Department, Government of Madras.
83. G.O.No.600, Public (Police), dated 7th November, 1935, Public (Police) Department, Government of Madras.
84. G.O.No.2724, Home (Conf.), dated 25th June, 1940, Home Department, Government of Madras.
85. G.O.No.1407, Home (Conf.), dated 1st April, 1942, Home Department, Government of Madras.
86. Report on the Administration of the Madras Presidency for the years 1938-39, printed by Superintendent, Government Press, Madras, 1940, p. 11.
87. Report on the Administration of the Police in the Madras Province for the year 1941, printed by Superintendent, Government Press, Madras, 1942, p. 12.
88. G.O.No.2424, Home (Ms), dated 23rd July, 1945, Home Department, Government of Madras.
89. Report on the Administration of the Police of the Madras Presidency for the year 1941, printed by Superintendent, Government Press, Madras, 1942, p. 7.
90. Ramesan N, Andhra Pradesh District Gazetteers, East Godavari, printed by Director of printing and stationery at Government Secretary Press, Hyderabad, 1979, pp. 160,161.
91. Report on the Administration of the Police of the Madras Presidency, 1941, printed by Superintendent, Government Press, Madras, 1942, p. 4.
92. G.O.No.1087, Home (Ms), dated 8th April, 1945, Home Department, Government of Madras.
93. G.O.No.4656, Home, dated 17th December, 1947, Home Department, Government of Madras.
94. Royal Commission on Public Service in India, Appendix to the Report of the Commissioners, Vol. XIII, Police Department, London, 1915, p. 174.

95. Ramesan N, Andhra Pradesh District Gazetteers, Krishna District Gazetteer, printed by Director of printing and stationery at Government Secretary Press, Hyderabad, 1977, p. 145.
96. Devi Dayal Aggarwal, *CBI and Policing in India*, Kaveri Books, New Delhi, 2000, p. 92.
97. Report on the Administration of the Madras Presidency for the years 1938-39, printed by Superintendent, Government Press, Madras, 1940, p. 23.
98. Report on the Administration of the Police of the Madras Province, 1927, printed by Superintendent, Government Press, Madras, 1928, p. 22.
99. Report on the Administration of the Madras Presidency for the year 1930, printed by Superintendent, Government Press, Madras, 1931, p. 39.
100. The History of the Andhra Pradesh Police, 1861-1961, published by Inspector General of Police, Hyderabad, p. 226.
101. *Ibid.*, pp. 224, 225.
102. Report on the Police Administration of the Madras Presidency, 1925, printed by Superintendent, Government Press, Madras, 1926, p. 23.
103. G.O. No. 4656, Home, dated 17th December, 1947, Home Department, Government of Madras.
104. Report on Administration of the Police of the Madras Presidency for the year 1932, printed by Superintendent, Government Press, Madras, 1933, p. 22.
105. G.O. No. 1449, Home (Ms), dated 5th May, 1945, Home Department, Government of Madras.
106. G.O.No. 3701, Home, 6th October, 1948, Home Department, Government of Madras.
107. G.O. No. 2092, Home, dated 30th June, 1945, Home Department, Government of Madras.
108. G.O. No. 567, Judl., dated 28th August, 1926, Judicial Department, Government of Madras.
109. G.O. No. 171, Judl., dated 1st November, 1929, Judicial Department, Government of Madras.
110. G.O.No. 467, Judl., dated 25th September, 1928, Judicial Department, Government of Madras.
111. G.O. No. 1083, Home, dated 4th April, 1944, Home Department, Government of Madras.
112. G.O. No. 3716, Home (Ms), dated 7th October, 1945, Home Department, Government of Madras.

113. G.O.No. 1897, Home (Ms), dated 18th June, 1945, Home Department, Government of Madras.
114. G.O.No.1376, Home (Ms), dated 1st May, 1945, Home Department, Government of Madras.
115. G.O.No. 2994, Home (Ms), dated 30th December, 1945, Home Department, Government of Madras.
116. G.O.No.1250, Home (Ms), dated 19th April, 1945, Home Department, Government of Madras.
117. Report on Administration of the Police of the Madras Presidency for the year, 1947, printed by Superintendent, Government Press, Madras, 1948, p. 13.
118. *Ibid.*, p. 14.
119. Devi Dayal Aggarwal, *CBI and Policing in India*, Kaveri Books, New Delhi, 2000, p. 96.
120. Report on the Police Administration of the Police of the Madras Presidency 1925, printed by Superintendent, Government Press, Madras, 1926, p. 23.
121. C.I.D. Report, Confidential, dated 7th November, 1909.
122. Report on the Administration of the Police of the Madras Province, 1927, printed by Superintendent, Government Press, Madras, 1928, p. 22.
123. Report of the Administration of the Madras Presidency for the years 1938-39, printed by Superintendent, Government Press, Madras, 1940, p. 34.
124. Report of the Administration of the Madras Presidency for the year 1925, printed by Superintendent, Government Press, Madras, 1926, p. 12.
125. Report of the Administration of the Madras Presidency for the year 1928, printed by Superintendent, Government Press, Madras, 1929, p. 12.
126. Report of the Administration of the Madras Presidency for the year 1929, printed by Superintendent, Government Press, Madras, 1930, p. 15.
127. Report on the Administration of the Police of the Madras Presidency, 1929, printed by Superintendent, Government Press, Madras, 1930, p. 19.
128. Report on the Administration of the Police in the Madras Province for the year 1938, printed by Superintendent, Government Press, Madras, 1939, pp. 18,19.
129. Report on the Administration of Police in the Madras Province for the year 1939, printed by Superintendent, Government Press, Madras, 1940, p. 17.

130. Report on the Administration of the Police in the Madras Province for the year 1937, Government Press, Madras, 1938, p. 16.

131. The History of the Andhra Pradesh Police, 1861-1961, published by Inspector General of Police, Andhra Pradesh, Hyderabad, 1961, p. 229.

132. Report on the Administration of the Police of the Madras Province, 1937, printed by Superintendent, Government Press, Madras, 1938, p. 15.

133. Report on Administration of the Police of the Madras Presidency for the year 1937, printed by Superintendent, Government Press, Madras, 1938, p. 16.

134. G.O.No. 467, Judl., dated, 25th September, 1928, Judicial Department, Government of Madras.

135. Report on the Administration of the Madras Presidency for the years 1938-39, printed by Superintendent, Government Press, Madras, 1940, p. 51.

136. Report on Administration of the Police of the Madras Presidency for the year 1928, printed by Superintendent, Government Press, Madras, 1929, p. 6.

137. Ramesan N, Andhra Pradesh District Gazetteers, East Godavari, printed by director of printing and stationery at Government Secretary Press, Hyderabad, 1979, p. 160.

138. G.O.No. 425, Public (Police), dated 6thAugust, 1929, Public (Police) Department, Government of Madras.

139. Gazetteer of South India, Vol. I, Superintendent of Government Printing, Madras, 1909, p. 116.

140. Abdul Waheed Khan, Brief History of Andhra Pradesh State Archives, Hyderabad, 1972, p. 112.

141. Report of the Administration of the Madras Presidency for the years 1938-39, printed by Superintendent, Government Press, Madras, 1940.

142. Report on Administration of the Police of the Madras Presidency for the year 1929, printed by Superintendent, Government Press, Madras, 1930, p. 27.

143. Report on the Police Administration of the Police of the Madras Presidency 1928, printed by Superintendent, Government Press, Madras, 1929, p. 16.

144. Report on the Administration of the Police of the Madras Presidency, 1925, printed by Superintendent, Government Press, Madras, 1926, p. 23.

145. G.O.No. 474, Home (Ms), dated, 14th February, 1945, Home Department, Government of Madras.

146. G.O.No. 2424, Home (Ms), dated 23rd July, 1945, Home Department, Government of Madras.
147. Report on the Administration of the Police of the Madras Presidency, 1928, printed by Superintendent, Government Press, Madras, 1929, p. 12.
148. G.O.No.1107, Home (Ms), dated 1st March, 1939, Home Department, Government of Madras.
149. G.O.No.6249, Home (Ms), dated 5th December, 1939, Home Department, Government of Madras.
150. Madras Administration Report, 1938-39, printed by Superintendent, Government Press, Madras, 1940, p. 51.
151. Government of India, Letter No. E-78-26-Police, dated 7th January, 1927, to all local Governments, p. 22.
152. Report of the Administration of the Police of the Madras Province, 1941, printed by Superintendent, Government Press, Madras, 1942, p. 15.
153. Ramesan N, Andhra Pradesh District Gazetteers, Srikakulam, printed by Director of printing and stationery at Government Secretary Press, Hyderabad, 1979, p. 37.
154. Report on the Administration of the Police of the Madras Presidency, 1947, printed by Superintendent, Government Press, Madras, 1948, p. 7.
155. The Indian Penal Code, 1860, Act 45 of 1860, 6th October, 1860.
156. Madras Administrative Report, 1945-46, Part-II, printed by Superintendent, Government Press, Madras, 1947, p. 52.
157. G.O.No. 467, Judl., dated 25th September, 1928, Judicial Department, Government of Madras.
158. Collector's Standing Orders of Nellore District, M.R. Ry. Rai Bahadur, printed by Superintendent, Government Press, Madras, 1931, p. 147.
159. G.O.No. 172, Judl. (Ms), dated 28th March, 1928, Judicial Department, Government of Madras.
160. Report on the Administration of the Police of the Madras Presidency for the year 1927, printed by Superintendent, Government Press, Madras, 1928, p. 51.
161. The History of the Andhra Pradesh Police 1861-1961, published by Inspector General of Police, Andhra Pradesh, Hyderabad, 1961, p. 231.
162. Report on the Administration of the Police of the Madras Presidency, 1938, printed by Superintendent, Government Press, Madras, 1939, p. 29.

163. G.O.No. 3940, Home (Ms), dated 19th July, 1939, Home Department, Government of Madras.
164. G.O.No. 467, Judl., dated 25th September, 1928, Judicial Department, Government of Madras.
165. Report of the Administration of the Madras Presidency for the years 1938-39, printed by Superintendent, Government Press, Madras, 1940, p. 46.
166. Madras in 1947, Part-I, printed by Superintendent, Government Press, Madras, 1948, p. 5.
167. Report on the Administration of the Police of the Madras Province, 1941, printed by Superintendent, Government Press, Madras, 1942, p. 1.
168. Report on the Administration of Police in the Madras province for the year 1941, printed by Superintendent, Government Press, Madras, 1942, p. 24.
169. G.O. Ms. No. 2530, Public (Civil Defence) Department, dated 4th September, 1943, Public (Civil Defence) Department, Government of Madras.
170. Report of the Administration of the Madras Presidency for the year 1947, printed by Superintendent, Government Press, Madras, 1948, p. 30.
171. Report of Indian Police Commission 1902-03, printed at Government Central Printing Office, Simla, 1904, p. 141.
172. Report on the Administration of the Police of the Madras Province for the year 1939, printed by Superintendent, Government Press, Madras, 1940, p. 52.
173. G.O.No. 1693, Home (Ms), dated 25th March, 1939, Home Department, Government of Madras.
174. Report on the Administration of the Police of the Madras Province,1941, printed by Superintendent, Government Press, Madras, 1942, p. 43.
175. Report on the Administration of the Police of the Madras Province for the year 1939, printed by Superintendent, Government Press, Madras, 1940, p. 52.
176. Report on the Administration of the Police of the Madras Province,1939, printed by Superintendent, Government Press, Madras, 1940, p. 6.
177. Report of the Administration of the Madras Presidency for the years 1938-39, printed by Superintendent, Government Press, Madras, 1940, p. 51.
178. Report on the Administration of the Police of the Madras Presidency, 1925, printed by Superintendent, Government Press, Madras, 1926, p. 24.

179. G.O.No. 753, Judl., dated 28th December, 1925, Judicial Department, Government of Madras.
180. Report on Administration of the Police of the Madras Presidency for the year 1928, printed by Superintendent, Government Press, Madras, 1929, p. 7.
181. History of Police Organisation in India and Indian Village Police, published by the University of Calcutta with the permission of Government of India, University Press, Calcutta, 1913, p. 47.
182. Report on the Administration of the Police of the Madras Province, 1929, printed by Superintendent, Government Press, Madras, 1930, p. 9.
183. Ayyar K.N.K., Madras District Gazetteers, Statistical Appendix (together with a supplement to the District Gazetteer, 1907 for Godavari district), Superintendent, Government Press, Madras, 1935, p. 91.
184. Statistical Record of West Godavari District, 1934, printed by Superintendent, Government Press, Madras, 1934, p. 176.
185. *Ibid.*, p. 45.
186. Madras District Gazetteers, Guntur district, Vol. III, published by District Gazetteers, 1933, p. 59.
187. Report on the Administration of the Police of the Madras Province, 1946, printed by Superintendent, Government Press, Madras, 1947, p. 6.
188. Report on the Administration of the Police of the Madras Province, 1936, printed by Superintendent, Government Press, Madras, 1937, p. 8.
189. Devi Dayal Aggarwal, *CBI and Policing in India*, Kaveri Books, New Delhi, 2000, p. 89.
190. Chande M.B., *The Police in India,* Atlantic Publishers and Distributors, New Delhi, 1997, p. 199.
191. Bhaskara Rao T, Collector's Standing Orders of Krishna District, printed by Government Press, Madras, 1939, p. 101.
192. Report of the Administration of the Madras Presidency for the years 1938-39, printed by Superintendent, Government ress, Madras, 1940, p. 51.
193. Report of the Administration of the Madras Presidency for the year 1929, printed by Superintendent, Government Press, Madras, 1930, p. 9.
194. Report of the Administration of the Madras Presidency for the year 1935, printed by Superintendent, Government Press, Madras, 1936, p. 8.
195. G.O No. 2412, Home, dated 9th May, 1938, Home Department, Government of Madras.

196. Report on the Administration of the Madras Presidency for the year 1925, printed by Superintendent, Government Press, Madras, 1926, p. 7.
197. Report of the Administration of the Police of the Madras Presidency for the year 1929, printed by Superintendent, Government Press, Madras, 1930, p. 9.
198. Village Officers Manual, Vol. I, prepared under the order of Government, printed by Superintendent, Government Press, Madras, 1893, p. 19.
199. Report of the Administration of the Police of the Madras Presidency for the year 1935, printed by Superintendent, Government Press, Madras, 1936, p. 8.
200. Report of the Administration of the Madras Presidency for the year 1939, printed by Superintendent, Government Press, Madras, 1940, p. 7.
201. G.O.No. 2344, Home, dated 21st September, 1936, Home Department, Government of Madras.
202. Report of the Administration of the Madras Presidency for the year 1939, printed by Superintendent, Government Press, Madras, 1940, p. 42.
203. Report of the Administration of the Madras Presidency for the years 1938-39, printed by Superintendent, Government Press, Madras, 1940, p. 9.
204. Report on the Administration of the Police in the Madras Province for the year 1937, Government Press, Madras, 1938, p. 12.
205. Report on the Administration of the Police of the Madras Presidency for the year 1938, printed by Superintendent, Government Press, Madras, 1939, p. 5.
206. *Ibid.*, p. 8.
207. Report of the Administration of the Madras Presidency for the years 1938-39, printed by Superintendent, Government Press, Madras, 1940, p. 14.
208. Report on the Administration of the Police of the Madras Presidency for the years 1924-47, printed by Superintendent, Government Press, Madras.
209. Government of Madras, Legal Department, The Madras District Police Act No. XXIV of 1859, printed by Superintendent, Government Press, Madras, 1937, p. 5.

6

Police-Public Relations

Man is a social being and he lives in a society which has a set of institutions related to each other and both depend on one another. The society needed enforcement of law to protect the life and property of the people and people had to depend on such institutes. There was a need to establish institutions with a set of rules and regulations which would strictly enforce the law and punish the public who do not obey. Laws were written statements which gave directions to the administration for public peace with common justice. The people had to live and behave accordingly and the society had to function according to definite law and order.[1] Without a definite and unified law, there cannot be public order and agencies of law cannot function without a government.[2] The police were persons empowered to enforce the law, protect life and property and maintain public order.

A study of police-public relations is important for the police administration without which it remains incomplete.[3] The police force cannot discharge satisfactorily its functions without public co-operation and public peace and prosperity cannot be preserved without police administration, so, both depend on each other. The success and failure of the police is largely dependent on the cordiality of police-public relations and the extent of co-operation the police get from the public in its day-to-day functions. The principal arm of the British government was police for the preservation of order.[4]

In the Northern range, under the British rule, the police force was maintained mainly as an instrument to enforce law and order; it was a force rather then a service.

With the changing socio-political and economic situation, the British government had enacted a number of rules and regulations for the police administration. The police was exercised by the British authority through these enactments and ordinances which the public had to follow. The police had the power to promote security to the public life and property, peace and security from crime, safety and health, public order and comfort, public morality by regulation of gambling and intoxicating liquors and they also promoted the economic interests of the people by protecting them against fraud. All these powers and functions were stated in the Police Acts and the police had functioned accordingly in the Northern range.

The attitude of the police was getting endorsed according to the changing social and political times. The relationship between the police and public was not that good, they had strained relationship. The cause for this nature of relationship between the public and the police has a long historical background. During the Mughal period, the government representatives were given the responsibility of maintaining order and good relationship with the public. With the advent of the British, they began to rule with an objective of collecting revenue and maintained their supremacy by keeping the natives under their control. They converted the office of the Ziladar into that of the district officer who had the functions of a magistrate, collector of revenue and that of the chief executive officer of the district. This system was based on a combination of judicial, revenue, and executive powers. When these powers got vested in the hands of the British officers, there was misuse of power and authority. The police under the British government resorted to torture for the collection of revenue and this lead to the establishment of the Torture Commission of 1855.[5]

This Commission recommended for the separation of judicial and executive powers of the district officers. Before this recommendation could be implemented, the revolt of 1857 broke out and the British once again decided in favour of concentration of powers in the hands of the district officers. The Police Act of 1861 was patterned after the law that established the Ulster Constabulary in Northern Ireland. The significant characteristic of this model was that it established the principle that the Constable was answerable to the Chief Constable rather than the law, the Chief Constable, being himself responsible to the British government. The police administration in the Northern range was reorganised on this model. The police in the Northern range were under the direction and control of the Madras government under the charge of European Inspector General of Police. The European Deputy Inspector General of Police was the chief of the police administration in the Northern range and the superior police officers were Europeans. Indians occupied subordinate positions in the police administration.

In this conception, the entire range of police-public relationship needs to be viewed. It is clear that the police organisation evolved principally in response to the political realities of the times. During the British period, the basic objective of the system designed by them was to create an instrument to control their colonies.

Role of the Police in Preventive and Punitive Functions

Under the British rule, there was a unified system of rules and regulations for the *preservation* of order and enforcement of law as punitive method. For this purpose, the policemen were recruited to perform these duties. The police performed preventive and punitive functions to protect the public and the government. The police had the preventive powers under the Code of Criminal Procedure. The legal limits of arrest and detention of suspects were defined in this Code. The police in the Northern range apprehended suspicious characters, detected and brought the offenders to the justice, collected and communicated the intelligence affecting the public peace to the concerned quarters, and obeyed and executed all the orders and warrants lawfully issued to them for preservation of peace, protection of life and property of the public. They had dealt with all aspects of the society, such as socio-political, economical, and religious.[6] Any offence against the society was dealt by the police. The most important preventive functions of the village officers were to watch the arrival of the strangers which evoke suspicion, movements of the criminal tribes, known as depredators, and that of notorious suspects, residents in his village.[7]

Police and the Crimes

The general crimes in the Northern range were murder, theft, robbery, dacoity, communal disturbances, etc. The motives of these crimes were family disputes, sexual jealousies, economic causes, religious differences, among others. The political unrest also prevailed due to the policies of the British government: there were labour strikes, agrarian agitations besides the offences related to the freedom movement. The police were recruited from the eligible families for the protection of life and property and to maintain public peace. The policemen were considered to be on duty all the time and had power in every part of the General Police Districts of the Northern range and they prevented all crimes, offences, and public nuisances to preserve public order.

The police in the Northern range also dealt with the offences which affected the public health, safety and convenience, spread of infection of any disease dangerous to life, sale of unwholesome food or provisions, adulteration of food and drink and the punishment for such crimes was imprisonment.[8] These offences came under Special and Local Laws and nuisance-related Sections of the Indian Penal Code. These offences numbered much in the year 1939 in the districts of Vizagapatam, Nellore, West Godavari, Guntur and the police kept them under control by vigorous police activity in the municipal areas and on the roads in interests of public safety and sanitation. The Boy Scout troop of Nellore town rendered assistance during festivals. The public were educated in the queue formation and order, whenever necessary and possible.[9]

The Special Police Force was organised along with the regular police force as an emergency force to quell any unrest in the Northern range. They followed all the rules and regulations and were well-trained to handle any unrest for crime control. They were of two types—unarmed and armed police; the armed police used the weapons on the orders of their superior police officers to quell any crowd unrest. These reserve police also performed functions of guarding railway bridges, canals and provided *bandobasts* during elections, fairs, festivals, etc. They maintained law and order and preserved peace during industrial strikes, agrarian unrest, and political agitations. The additional police force was also sanctioned during emergencies to maintain law and order and to protect the public peace. The police in many instances used lathis and also opened fire and used tear gas to control the rioters for creating public disturbances. The government property was guarded and protected by the auxiliary police forces, such as railway police, port police, *ghat* police, traffic police, etc. The offenders were judicially punished under the Indian Penal Code and the Criminal Procedure Code.

Police and the Freedom Struggle

The political unrest in the Northern range during the period 1924 to 1947 was at its peak. The Northern range was in the forefront during the freedom struggle, people there had agitated against the British rule peacefully and violently. The police in order to control the unrest and to restore law and order, used tear smoke, lathi charge and opened fire, as the situation demanded. Under this situation, the relation between the people and the police had become strained. The British government had given extra powers to the police force in the Northern range during the freedom struggle to suppress the political unrest to maintain law and order. During this period, the police force in the Northern range had come into the public criticism by the Press. The government had imposed restriction on the Press to protect the police from public criticism, and to lift the morale of the police force, they were rewarded frequently for their good work.

Police and the Village Community

To carry out efficient police administration by the policemen, it was essential to secure the aid of the village community. The village watchmen and the village headmen maintained the records of the old offenders, criminal tribes, habitual offenders and those of the known depredators; also, movements of such elements were watched from time to time to prevent crime. *It was impossible for the police force to obtain information regarding crime over the extensive area and on the vast population of the Northern range without securing the co-operation and enforcing the responsibilities of the village authorities and the public. These policemen were provided government quarters to reside in the vicinities of these places to attend for the security of the public. The Constables were provided accommodation in almost all the faction-ridden places of the Northern range to maintain law and order.*

The Inspector General of Police, Deputy Inspector General of Police and the gazetted officers had conducted tours as a part of their duty in the Northern range to inspect the functioning of the police administration at the district police offices, sub-divisional police stations, police circles, police stations, and also that of the village vigilance committees. The village police officers and the general public extended their co-operation in the prevention and detection of crimes.[10] *They had encouraged the public to report the occurrence of any crime and the British rewarded the public for the assistance given in the crime control.*

For better policing in the villages of the Northern range, the Village Vigilance Committees were organised in the year 1935 as an auxiliary agency of the police. The Village Vigilance Committees were formed in all the districts of the Northern range and they rendered notable public service. They had constituted a liaison between the authorities and the village populations in the crime control and detection of offences. As the result of their co-operation with the police, crimes in the Northern range were better reported and detection improved. A District Superintendent of Police has reported in reference to these committees as "When we thus sought to create a higher sense of civic responsibility and met with a very encouraging response, we were also benefitted by a subjective influence on ourselves. For which we preached the utility of good police, we took every care to make ourselves 'good' and definitely good".[11] *Police officers, during their inspections to the villages impressed the village police for close co-operation, and in many instances, public and the village officials were suitably rewarded for their good work.*

The village police in Northern range had improved their administration by educating the village communities to take active part in their own affairs. In the subject of public cooperation, these organisations voluntary trained the social workers who had come forward to assist the authorities during the important local fairs and festivals, when very large crowds of town people and pilgrims had to be dealt with. There was co-operation between the village officers, ghat talaiyaris, and the police in the matter of prevention and detection of the crime. Gazetted officers used to inspect these vigilance committees to check their performance and during their tours, impressed on village officers the need for close co-operation with the police subordinates.

As auxiliaries to the police, these vigilance committees rendered assistance in regulation of crowd and maintenance of order; their help was invaluable during religious occasions. These committees were like friends of the pilgrims and guided, advised, and supplied them with necessary information and their services were of great public value.[12] Their role and importance was so well-understood by the administration that in some districts of the Northern range, District Magistrates at the instances of District Superintendents of Police issued circulars to village officers regarding the proper discharge of their police duties. The Village Vigilance Committee's misconduct and neglect of duty were brought to the notice of their superior officers and they were punished.[13] The growth of this new non-official agency had rendered public co-operation in the crime control. The magnitude and the volume of effective public service which these Village Vigilance Committees rendered in districts of the Northern range could be gauged from the figures in the following paragraph.

The types of crime that were common in the villages were agricultural disputes regarding cattle or possession of land, village quarrels, family disputes, cheating, election rivalries, misappropriation of funds besides dacoities, robberies, murders, etc. The number of cases, such as stolen property cases, cattle thefts, gambling cases and other thefts were dealt by the Village Vigilance Committees in the Northern range during the years 1935 to 1947.[14]

These figures for the year 1935 were 179, for 1936 were 703, for 1937 were 1,006, for 1938 were 973, for 1939 were 846, for 1940 were 1,102, for 1941 were 1,682, for 1942 were 1,275, for 1943 were 1,181, for 1944 were 961, for 1945 were 1,134, for 1946 were 473, and for year 1947 were 1,840.

These figures illustrate that performance of these committees was remarkable, a number of cases were dealt successfully but towards the last two years, the number of cases reduced which shows that these committees in few districts did not work efficiently. *Under the welfare programme of the Village Vigilance Committees of the Northern range, the experimental scheme of sports and games were introduced in selected villages in the year 1938. Later, additional centres were started during the year 1939, and in almost all of them, the villagers and the public cooperated to make this scheme a success.*[15] *These sports brought mutual co-operation among the people and the police authorities of the Northern range.*

The village officers were frequently rewarded whenever they did a good work. A number of village officers were rewarded in the Northern range in the years 1938 and 1939 for good work. For the year 1938, number of officers rewarded was 565 and the amount spent by the government on the rewards was Rs 2,718. For the year 1939, the number of village officers rewarded were 535 and the amount spent on these rewards was Rs 2,453. During the year 1946, the number of officers rewarded was 690 and the amount spent for the reward was Rs 4,912, and in the year 1946, the number of village officers rewarded was 580 and the amount spent by the British government on these rewards was Rs 4,161.

Here is a citation in which a villager in the Nellore district evinced public sprit and initiative in promptly giving information to the local Village Vigilance Committees members about the presence of a few suspects in the village vicinity. This information given by the villager led to the arrest of three armed absconders from the Siddhapuram criminal settlement.[16] This case was recorded in the year 1937 and shows that the crime was well-reported and the authorities reacted equally promptly. In the year 1938, a villager and a member of Yanadi tribe from the Nellore district were rewarded for giving information to the Village Vigilance Committee members about the culprits in a case of house-breaking and theft.[17] Whenever public witnessed any crime in village, they informed these committees who took their assistance for crime control. The Village *Vigilance Committees were very useful to the public and the police equally in the Northern range for prevention and detection of crimes.*

Police and Public Safety

The police administration in the Northern range had functioned for the public safety to prevent crime. The police provided security to the public by constant beat and patrol system in the villages and also in the towns. The public places, bridges, canals, and roads were watched and secured for the protection of the people. The police, by residing near the police stations, were readily available during emergencies. The police functioned under various Acts for the safety of the public. The opium and gambling houses were regularly raided to prevent nuisance cases. They checked immoral traffic, smuggling and other offences which created nuisance and public disturbance.

Traffic Police and Public Safety

The traffic police was organised in the towns of the Northern range for regulating the traffic for the safety of the public. The traffic police had prevented accidents and protected the health of the people by educating them about importance of following the traffic rules and regulations. Traffic Police were responsible for maintenance of the smooth flow of traffic and they were responsible for securing the highways and for catching overspeeding drivers. With the enactment of the Motor Vehicles Act, traffic offences came to be well-controlled in the Northern range. The buses plying for hire in the districts were well-maintained for the public. Overloading and errant drivers were the chief offenders and police staff was increased to exercise efficient control.[18] The public were educated about their safety by following the traffic rules and the public had cooperated with them. As the motor bus traffic increased in the Northern range with passage of time, the government sanctioned additional traffic staff to tackle the offenders by enforcing the rules rigorously to deal with the nuisance on roads. The British government ordered the District Magistrates of the districts to remove the incompetent and dishonest men from the department giving special importance to the matter and held the department as responsible for the protection of life and property of the common man.[19] The British government took steps through legal procedures to punish the officials involved in corruption.

Railway Police and Public Safety

The Railway Police prevented various forms of thefts from passengers, luggage vans, goods sheds etc., which frequently occurred in the railway districts of the Northern range. There were railway police stations in Bezwada, Rajahmundry, Gudivada, Bheemavaram, and Vizagapatnam districts of the Northern range. The railway Station House Officers were directed to warn the villagers during their village visits about the danger of walking on the railway tracks. The District Superintendents of the districts of the Northern range, issued instructions to the village officers for proper discharge of their duties to prevent crimes and to preserve order and they also instructed their subordinates regularly in the matter of preventing trespass on railway lines. Circulars were issued to warn the people of the danger of using railway lines as footpath thus preventing their trespass.[20] The parents of the mischievous children were warned about the danger of throwing stones at the running trains which was a common offence.

The other auxiliary police forces were organised for public safety and security and to take care of their property. The *Ghat* police were sanctioned on all important roads in the Northern range for public safety. For the people travelling on lonely roads and passing through mountainous countryside where dacoity and robbery was prevailing, the *Ghat talaiyaris* were appointed, to provide them with safety; these officials patrolled the countryside roads day and night.[21] The Civic Guards voluntarily helped the public during emergencies and provided *bandobast* in fairs and festivals. The auxiliary and special police forces in the Northern range provided valuable services such as escorts, guards and protected the public from emergent circumstances. They had protected the public during the socio-political unrests and also during the natural disasters, such as, floods. Police is an institution set up for securing itself from disorder to make peaceful progress. The Special Police Forces usually did not came into contact with the general public unless they was assigned duty to maintain order during political unrests, fairs, festivals, elections, and natural calamities. They were sanctioned to quell outbreaks of any unrest, deal with organised crimes, and to guard and provide security. Depending on the type of assignment, they carried lathis or lethal weapons.

Police and Criminal Tribes

The tribal community was a part of the society and the police took special care for the protection and welfare of these primitive groups. In the districts of the Northern range, some tribes committed habitual non-bailable offences and these tribes were registered under the Criminal Tribes Act. For the welfare of these criminal tribes, special settlements and reformatories were constructed in various places of the Northern range. The reformation of these criminal tribes was taken by the British government for a better society. A number of crimes were recorded in the Northern range which were committed mostly by the criminal tribes as this range was largely inhabited by nomadic tribes. When compared with the crimes committed by general offenders, like the known depredators, habitual offenders, and others, the crimes committed by the criminal tribes were found to be more in numbers.

With the introduction of Criminal Tribes Amendment Act of 1924, the police administration in the Northern range had taken up seriously the work of registration, surveillance and settlements of the criminal tribes in the form of preventive programme. With proper measures of the government, these crimes were controlled. In this connection, the Criminal Investigation Department had played an important role by proper registration and surveillance of the criminal tribes. The public also provided useful information about the offences and the offenders. With co-operation of the public and police, the crime was better reported and was under control. Here is a case of interest in this regard: A Yanadi in the Nellore district assisted the police in tracking the culprits in a case of house-breaking and theft who were member of his tribe. He was suitably rewarded.[22] Rewards were granted to the public to encourage them to report the occurrence of crime. The duty of the police was to ensure that no registered member of the tribe was absent without notice. For the good behaviour, certain registrations were cancelled in respect of the registered criminal tribe members. Some of the criminal tribes who were not declared in the Ganjam and Jeypore district as such under Section 3 of this Act were Dandasis,[23] Donga Yenetis,[24] Munda Pottas,[25] Oriya Dombs [26] of the Ganjam district and Dombs, commonly known as, Audiniya Dombs [27] and Ghasis [28] of the Jeypore district.[29]

Criminal Tribes Settlements

To control the criminal activities of the criminal tribes, reformatories and settlements were established. They were managed initially by private individuals while later, by the British government. Under the preventive functions, the Act of Criminal Tribes was passed in the Northern range and a number of habitual criminal tribes of the Northern range were registered under this Act. Their movements were restricted to prevent them from committing crimes. They were confined in the settlements under police surveillance. Efforts were made to reclaim the criminal tribes by some private benevolence earlier and this reformatory function was taken up by the government as a preventive measure.[30] The British government had maintained criminal settlements and reformatories at various places in the Northern range for prevention of crimes committed by the criminal tribes.

The Deputy Inspector General of Police of the Northern range and the Criminal Investigation Department was entrusted with the supervision and control of all the settlements. The Sitanagaram and Stuartapuram in the Guntur district, Kalechedu and Kavali in the Nellore district were some such settlements. The general control and management of these settlements was transferred from the Deputy Inspector General of Police, Railways and Criminal Investigation Department to the Labour Commissioner.[31] The conduct of other operations which were under the Criminal Tribes Act continued to be with the magistracy and police, while the matters of scrutiny of accounts and the preparation of budget remained with the District Magistrates.

The object of criminal settlements was to reform the members of the criminal tribes by providing them with means for earning an honest livelihood under the supervision of the police. Under the orders of the British, the Madras Presidency government had taken up reform of some of the tribes who were notified in the Northern range under the Criminal Tribes Act as they were habitual criminals who had committed a number of crimes in the range.[32]

The system of "Holding in Abeyance" the British government orders issued under Rule 10 relative to Section 10 (1) (a) of the Criminal Tribes Act was introduced in the year 1929.[33] Under this scheme, the criminal tribe members who were not particularly dangerous and were reporting at the check-posts were exempted from reporting on condition that if at any time thereafter their conduct gave room for suspicion, or was unsatisfactory in any way, they would again have to report attendance twice every night at the police station. This system enabled the police to concentrate their attention on the actually bad criminals.

The reformation movement made good progress in the Northern range and an Inspector of Police was appointed to establish communal *panchayats* among the members of these tribes. As a preventive measure, the registered criminal tribes were provided with reformatories and settlements and were also assisted with in lawful occupation.[34]

The government built houses for them and land was provided for their livelihood and all these settlements and reformatories were under the supervision of the police. The children of these families were given education, mid-day meal and books free of cost and they were also trained in technical fields.

The Donga Dasaris and Donga Yerakalas, refractory inmates from other settlements outside the districts, which belonged to other gangs, were bought into the reformatory settlements at Kavali in the Nellore district and they were kept under strict police watch because they were wander-lust and chronic absconders.[35] Registered members, who led honest lives or those who were too old or too weak to commit crime, for them, the restrictions imposed under Section 10(1) (a) of Criminal Tribes Act was relaxed.[36] In the year 1937, the government directed the District Magistrate, Vizagapatam to register the members of Oriya Dombs, Dandasis, and Donga Yanadies and such other members of each tribe for the reason of committing or abetting the commission of non-bailable offences.[37]

To mention a few, there was Stuartpuram settlement and Sitanagaram settlement in Guntur district, Bitragunta settlement, Bitragunta reformatory and Chintaladevi settlement in Nellore, Kalichedu, Kavali and Allur settlements. In the year 1936, for the Bitragunta settlement, the strength of the police were 10 Inspectors, one Charge Sergeant, four Sergeants, 64 Sub-Inspectors, two Havildars Majors, 105 Head Constables and 788 Constables and four *talayaries* for 45 stations and outposts.[38] The Stuartpuram settlement in Guntur district was managed by the Salvation Army and the rest of the settlements by the government. A new settlement was opened at Chintaladevi in the Nellore district for the *kanjar bhats* and these tribes contributed to the increase in the population of these settlements. The Madras government established and maintained reformatory settlements for the members of the criminal tribes.[39] The criminal tribes convicts of good conduct were transferred to these settlements for the unexpired periods of their sentences.[40] Money advances for purchasing bullock carts to the settlers were sanctioned to the Siddhapuram settlement.[41]

Fresh registrations under the Madras Registration of Habitual offenders Act XXX of 1943 numbered 3,027, while 3,516 numbers were removed from the registers on account of good conduct or other causes. The provisions of the Act were worked with great consideration so as to avoid undue hardship to the members. The restriction under Section 10 (1) (a) of the Criminal Tribes Act were imposed in suitable cases and to curb the criminal tendency of the active members. Those who conducted themselves properly and proved worthy of the concession, temporary exemption was granted to them and they were recommended for entire removal from the registers. In deserving cases, lands were assigned to exempted criminal tribe members. With these measures, the numbers of criminal tribes on the rolls decreased and only hardened criminals remained on the registers. The communal *panchayat* system had worked well among the Dandasis and Panoes of the Ganjam district.[42]

New houses were built and land was given which provided an opportunity for cultivation for earning livelihood in many of these colonies. The other inmates of these settlements made a livelihood out of charcoal burning and by marketing of their produce. These colonies were reported to have been settled down happily and many of these were reformed from their previous criminal lives.[43] There was a growing band of young men in the Bitragunta settlement who disliked agricultural labour, and to prevent them from committing crimes, an alternative employment was provided for them in industrial and non-agricultural areas. They were also employed in cottage industries [44] in the Northern range. For the reclamation of the Dandasis of the Ganjam district, the Rajah of Bobbili donated Rs 100 and granted lands through the District Superintendent of Police in the year 1929.[45] Not only government, but some private individuals also encouraged for the rehabilitation of these tribes.

Punitive measures of the police were by means of assisting the courts in convicting the criminals. By providing special settlements to the criminal tribal members, numbers of crimes committed by these members were reduced in the Northern range. The police had enlisted the criminals by maintenance of records and thus prevented most of the crimes committed by these habitual criminals. With the Criminal Tribes Act, most of the criminal tribe members were registered to prevent the crimes. Many times, these tribals were enlisted for selection into the police. The reformation movement made good progress in the Northern range as the range was largely covered by Agency area which was inhabited by many tribes. The reclamation and rehabilitation of criminals and criminal communities was one of the functions of police administration. The police took the census of the criminal gangs and communities and attempted to make them settle in particular areas for better surveillance. [46] Many of these tribal members had settled down happily by taking up legal occupations.

The police inspections of the settlements prevented the offence of concealed stolen property.[47] Discipline was maintained in the settlements and they were punished under the Section 18 of Criminal Tribes Act for violating any rule whereby the offenders were punished with rigorous imprisonment for a term of six months or fine or whipping or all of them. The periodic inspections of such settlements and the *panchyat* system proved beneficial.[48]

The Pano *panchyats* in Gumsur Udayagiri circle of the Ganjam district was established.[49] Most of the criminal tribes of these settlements had eschewed committing crimes and were settled.

The main objective of the Criminal Tribes Act was to safeguard the rights of the society against anti-social influence and its secondary aim was the reformation of the Criminal Tribes.[50] In the year 1932, on the recommendations of Charles Cunningham, the Inspector General of Police of the Madras Presidency, each District Superintendent of Police was made responsible for reclamation work within his jurisdiction. For efficient surveillance and for reclamation work, the administrative control of the settlements was again transferred to the Deputy Inspector General of Police, Railways and Criminal Investigation Department in the year 1944. The Habitual Offenders Act of 1943 was introduced for better reformatory and penal needs, which repealed the Criminal Tribes Act. An accurate registration of known depredators, wandering gangs, and criminal classes were maintained by the police. After the enactment of Criminal Tribes Act, many wandering gangs of the criminal tribes were watched by the police and the members of the criminal tribes were restricted in their movement and this prevented the crimes committed by these tribes.[51] The introduction of this Act had resulted in a considerable decrease in crimes against property in the Northern range.

Police-Public Relations

The police was accountable for their actions, relations and co-operation with the public and good police-public relations played an important role. The police had to deal with different groups of people and they had to establish a specific relation with them. They adopted different approaches for those who violated the law and for those, who did not violate the law. The police and the public were equally responsible for their relations. The vast area, large population and the rapid economic development in the Northern range depended on the successful and efficient operation of the police administration which was constantly under the critical public eye. Public relations were an inseparable factor of police work. Education and training also played an important role for the successful performance of the police work, while culture was also necessary for their professionalism and skills for dealing with the natives. The higher grades of police officers were mostly the Europeans which aptly indicates the intentions of the British rule. Though the police of lower grade were natives and had close contacts with the public but they had to follow the orders of their superiors. The police had many kinds of relationships with the public which was mostly negative in its nature.

Public-Police Cooperation

According to the Police Commission of 1902, "it was impossible to carry on the police administration only by regular police and it was essential to secure the aid of village community through the agency of *Chaukidars*. Any other alternative of employing regular policemen at villages could be too expensive." The need for public co-operation was felt by the British government and measures were taken to get their co-operation for efficient police functioning. The police auxiliary force, such as the Village Vigilance Committees, village regular police force in the rural areas of the Northern range, Railway Police, Traffic Police, Criminal Investigation Department and the Special Police Forces in the urban set up had contributed in the crime control with the co-operation and help extended by the public. The British had taken steps to secure public co-operation and whenever the latter had assisted the police in crime control, they were suitable rewarded.

For performing such functions, the police and the public had to be cooperative to control crime. The police can function effectively with the public cooperation. Crime cannot be controlled without proper support from the public, the police become helpless if people hesitate to give useful information regarding the crime and the criminals.[52]

In the prevention and detection of the crimes, the public co-operation played an important role in the Northern range. There were many incidences where the people had extended their help in prevention of crimes.

Here is a theft case of interest which shows how the police were able to find the culprit with the help of public after a year of committing the offence. In the year 1935, theft occurred in the Nurses' quarters at Mission Hospital in the Nellore district in which the property stolen was a ring; no evidence was found and the case remained undetected for some time. In the year 1936, the owner of the ring noticed her property being sold in a shop in Nellore town, she informed the police and the offender was arrested.[53] A case was recorded in Setarampuram of Nellore district in the year 1936 wherein a man had murdered his wife's lover and faked the incident as a suicide. A farmer of that place informed the police about the murder and the culprit was arrested and convicted.[54] In the year 1937, a government *talaiyari* was carrying tax collection of Rs 400 to the Sankaranainarkoyil sub-treasury. On the way, he was knocked off his bicycle and murdered and all the money was stolen. The local

Village Vigilance Committee members organised a search party and the offenders were arrested.[55] In the year 1939, a case was filed against a female coffee hotel keeper in the Nellore district who robbed an eight-year-old girl for her jewels worth Rs 101 and locked the girl in a room. A boy heard the cries of the girl and informed the police, the girl was rescued and the offender was arrested.[56] It shows that the police took action immediately whenever the public reported the incident, both the police and the public cooperated with each other and controlled the crime.

Rewards for Police and Public

Special instructions were given to the District Superintendents of Police by the British government to incentivise for the good work on the part of the village police, village officers, the regular police, and the public.[57] By rewards, the advantage was taken by the police to impress upon public the need for their cooperation.[58]

The British government granted rewards to the police officers and private individuals who helped in prevention and detection of crime.[59] Titles and honours were conferred on Police officers and medals were bestowed on them for capturing notorious criminal or for their conduct in dealing with the riots that had occurred in the Northern range. Rewards were freely granted to village officers, private individuals and also to the members of criminal tribes for their valuable assistance and co-operation in crime control.[60] These occasions served as a platform to impress on public the necessity of mutual co-operation between the police and the public.

Under the orders of the British government, the grant of money rewards to all the police officials except Constables and Head Constables was abolished in the year 1938.[61] This had increased the number of private individuals rewarded and the amount expended on this item. The good work by police officers was recognised by grant of good service entries and by promotions. In the case of private individuals, the government issued letters of appreciation or parchment certificates. There was an increase in the number of rewards granted to the private persons, including village officers indicating improvement in relations between the public and the police.[62] The rewards were considered as a honour and they also encouraged the common people to react against the crimes in the society. Rewards were distributed in the shape of some useful articles of value to private persons after consulting them beforehand.[63] This method was useful to the public because they could choose the article required. The following were the rewards granted by the British government to the private persons, who assisted the police during the years 1924 to 1947 in the Northern range.

Among the rewards offered to private persons, the presentation of a gold bangle to a woman in the West Godavari district for her courageous conduct in holding up the burglar, who was trying to escape after committing burglary, till the neighbours came in, needs to be mentioned. The burglar was arrested with the stolen property.[64] In the same district, the government had granted 10 parchment certificates to the persons in recognition of their assistance to the police in the year 1929.[65] The village magistrate of Doddipatla in the West Godavari district got information of arrival in his village of a known depredator who had been out of village for a long time. He and four others chased down the depredator and jumped into the canal at the risk of their own lives and captured him. For their successful and act of valour, the village Magistrate and his followers were suitably rewarded. This case was one of a peculiar type where a District Magistrate was rewarded for his prompt act of bravery. This shows that the government had encouraged every person of the society for their help in crime control. In the year 1928, three students from the same district, while returning from school, noticed four men trying to conceal themselves by the roadside with a bull. The boys suspected them of being miscreants and informed the police who arrested all of them. The case ended in conviction and each boy was gifted with a fountain pen for their smart act.[66]

In the East Godavari district during the year 1924, a sum of Rs 100 was offered by the villagers of Koyyalagudem to the Sub-Inspector of that station for tracing and arresting a gang of members who had escaped from criminal settlements.[67] In the same year, and in the same district, a case was recorded about the zamindar of Katravulapalli who presented a silver cup to the Head Constable for detective work performed by him in the district during the district sports of November, 1924. These cases indicate that the private individuals also encouraged the police for their good work in detecting and controlling crime. The police and private individuals were rewarded Rs 650 by the government in connection with a case of counterfeiting currency notes in the Kistna district in the year 1925 and expressed their appreciation to the temporary Deputy Superintendent of Police, Mr Ry. Rao Sahib K. Brahmayya Pantulu. A reward of Rs 250 was granted by the District Magistrate of Guntur district to the villages of Isukatripuravaram for attacking the gang headed by the notorious Yerakala dacoit Kondigadu and killing him and two other members of the gang. A reward of Rs 500 was offered by Zamindar of Udaiyarpalaiyam in the year 1925 for apprehension of Kodukkur Arumugam, which was distributed amongst one Inspector, six Sub-Inspectors, one Head Constable, four Constables, one *Karnam* and three private individuals.[68]

A villager and a Yanadi tribal fellow from the Nellore district were rewarded for giving information to the Village Vigilance Committee members about the culprits in a case relating to house-breaking and theft.[69] In the year 1927, in the district of East Godavari, a woman was rewarded for her presence of mind in arresting a thief who entered her house.[70] In the same district Mr Ry. D. Sitaramaswami offered a silver cup to a police officer for good detective work and the Maharajah of Pithapuram paid Rs 100 to a Sub-Inspector for recovering a valuable emerald.[71]

A reward of Rs 830 was sanctioned to the police officers of Guntur district and the Criminal Investigating Department and Rs 250 to private individuals for rounding up a gang of Erukala absconders.[72] In another case recorded in the West Godavari district, a private individual was awarded with a cash amount of Rs 100 for arresting a prisoner Lakshmikantham C.N. who escaped from police custody.[73] In the year 1927, in the district of Jeypore, a group of villagers were rewarded for the help rendered to the police in a detection case of housebreaking.[74] Two Inspectors, four Constables and seven private individuals of the West Godavari district and two coin and currency experts of the Criminal Investigation Department earned a cash reward of Rs 343 for well-co-ordinated work in bringing the offenders to justice.[75] The reward system was beneficial to the police, the public, and the government. The British freely granted rewards to the police and private individuals to impress upon them the need for mutual co-operation between the police and the public. The British government rewarded both the police and the public with honours, titles, and money to maintain law and order in the district. These rewards gradually increased from the year 1924 to the end of 1947, and it reflects existence of mutual co-operation between the police and the public.

In many cases, when the public had not co-operated with the police, the police had faced many difficulties while discharging their duties. Here are few cases of interest where the public were not cooperative with the police. In Rajahmundry of the East Godavari district, a Constable while performing his beat duty was hurt by a bullock cart puller, the Constable was beaten badly and his finger was bitten by the cart puller; the accused was finally sentenced to the Rajahmundry Central jail. This indicates that the law and order was not strictly followed by the public and police faced many difficulties while performing their duties.[76]

Good relations between the police and public depended on the sense of responsibility in both police and public towards proper maintenance of law and order.

On 15th January, 1936, in the East Godavari district of Northern range, police had received information that gambling and cockfighting was going on in the festival at Amalapuram Taluk. A Head Constable, who was acting as the Sub-Inspector of Uppalaguptam station in Amalapuram Taluk, went to apprehend the offenders, taking with him three Constables and four members of the Village Vigilance Association, its President, and five residents. The Sub-Inspector took with him a revolver and the staff were also equipped with lathies while going to that place. On seeing the police, the gamblers and the cock-fighters ran away. While the police were awaiting for the village *munsiff*, at that juncture, the gamblers and the cock-fighters came back and attacked the police party with sticks and injured them badly and ran away. Later, they were caught and were charged for the offences under Section 147 of Indian Penal Code and some of them for individual offences under Sections 149, 332 and 333 of Indian Penal Code for forming themselves into unlawful assembly with the common object of attacking the police party who were engaged in the lawful discharge of their duties in arresting the culprits; the accused were sentenced to rigorous imprisonment.[77]

There existed land dispute between Koyas tribes and the zamindars of Nandigudem in the West Godavari district of the Northern range. The Sub-Divisional Magistrate ordered both the parties to not enter their lands, but the Koyas with the support from the Communist party, violated the government order, committed theft of paddy and attacked the police party with their bows and arrows injuring three police officers. The police opened fire which killed five persons and injured four persons.[78] In the village of Kalikova in the Kistna district, fire was opened by the police on a riotous mob who disobeyed an order under Section 144 of the Criminal Procedure Code and tried to attack the police with lethal weapons. In this incident, two men were killed and others were injured; later, cases were filed against some of the communists.[79] This shows the police played a crucial role in the maintenance of law and order and peace prevailed in this district.

There was indigent relationship between the police and the public during the political unrest in the Northern range. In spite of the public criticism and abuse from the Press, the police had performed their duty faithfully and loyally with their morale unshaken.[80] The department of the police had much additional work as a result of the Civil Disobedience Movement in the year 1930. The police were frequently called upon to maintain law and order by the British. The activities of this Movement led to serious riots, disturbances, *hartals*, and demonstrations in several places of the Madras Presidency which included the Northern range; several people lost their life and there was much abuse and also social boycott of the police in many districts. Yet, the police remained loyal throughout and courageously and effectively dealt with every serious situation.[81] The police were rewarded for their courage and discipline in dealing with serious riots which resulted from freedom movement. The police forces were exempted from ten per cent cut in their salaries in the year 1931 unlike other government employees when the economic depression showed up. To prevent the police force from public criticism, they were well-trained and maintained strict discipline. With the growth of freedom movement, such as Civil Disobedience Movement, and Quit India movement, large number of people participated in the national agitation which involved violent activities and political unrest throughout the Northern range. For combating the political unrest, the police were specially trained in lathi charge, firing, and use of tear gas to maintain law and order and collective fines were imposed on the public for the offences.[82] The trivial nature of some of them show that the public were more inclined to seek the help of the police.

All the Congress meetings, anti-British symbols, such as Gandhi caps, Indian national flags, *khaddar* dress, singing national songs were not tolerated by the police and these were regarded as offences.[83]

The people of the Northern range had violated these rules, and for this, they were severely punished. The people of the Northern range, along with othe people of the nation, had boycotted during the Civil Disobedience Movement of 1932, by thwarting working of railways, post and telegraphs, etc., and picketing of shops that dealt in imported goods and liquor shops.[84]

In this regard, the Inspector General of Police had issued a circular to all the District Superintendents of the Northern range to use force on these demonstrations to preserve public peace. (Moveable property, possession of building the government declared all the congress associations as unlawful).[85] The British had passed the orders through the District Magistrates to collect fines from the inhabitants for offences related to political activities. No freedom fighter was prepared to obey the ordinance and continued with the agitations; several of them were imprisoned for public seditious speeches, for display of Indian flag, for singing the national song, for wearing *khaddar* caps. The British government had imposed restriction on the Press for propaganda. All those who disobeyed were arrested and had to undergo rigorous imprisonment.[86] For violation of orders passed under Section 144 of the Criminal Procedure Code, the people were arrested in large numbers during the freedom movement. To suppress this movement, the British government enacted a number of ordinances that could take away the liberties of the people and armed the police with necessary legal measures. One of the two important measures in this regard was the special ordinance power which could enable the police to arrest, detain and even confiscate the property temporarily or permanently. The second ordinance was clamping of the Marshall Law thereby suspending ordinary laws. Under this situation, the British government had sanctioned additional police force and Special Police Force to suppress the Freedom Movement; in many instances, the police carried out lathi charge, opened fire, and also used tear gas on the crowd in the assembly.[87] There were many instances where the police in order to recover the fines even went to the extent of taking away utensils, buffaloes, clothes, cots, trunks, tables, etc.[88] The government collected fines from the inhabitants to recover the cost of police stationed in those places to quell the riots. To keep up the strength of the jails, the political prisoners were taken to far off distances and used to leave them there. The women agitators were the special target of the police during the struggle, they were badly treated.[89] The police had lathicharged the agitators even in the police lock-ups and in jails.[90] The police used all methods to suppress the political movement. The role of the police was punitive, the methods of interrogation in the lock-ups was harsh and the behaviour of the police during law and order disturbances was beastly where they restored to violence and force; this developed a gap between the public and the police.

In the last phase of freedom struggle, which was a massive agitation, both peaceful and violent, it permeated to every village of the Northern range. The educated and economically rich people went up in violent agitation when Congress leaders were arrested. With the imprisonment of national leaders, political situation had worsened in the country and underground movements, stoning, arsoning, and bombing became recurrent features in the Northern range.

The Inspector General of Police commanded the use of powerful force against labour and national agitators.[91] This activity of the police in handling the common masses was disliked by the people due to which they had developed hatred against them. The Presidency General Reserve Police and District Armed Reserve Police of the Northern range worked successfully in suppressing the political agitations. They had used lathis, opened fire, used tear gas, and other harsh measures to suppress the unrest.[92] The use of tear gas had caused suffocation to the agitators and the ordinary public and also the police themselves.[93] In this situation, both the police and public relations had got strained abundantly, especially during this period.

Besides the general crimes, the labour unrests, agrarian strikes, and communal troubles had caused disturbance to the public peace and the police had handled these situations with tact and firmness. The communal tensions in the Northern range prevailed since long time and they had aggravated during this period, especially in the district of Nellore. In spite of magistrate's orders and police intervention, the communal tensions during the festival season continued. The agrarian strikes in the Northern region were due to British economic policies. The labourers had agitated for improvement in the working conditions and also for increase in the wages.

In these situations, the relationship of the police with the public had severely strained.[94] The police during this period were under constant pressure, but they were loyal throughout the period and performed their duties. Under the political unrest, the police had to resort to most repressive methods to maintain order. These activities of the police towards the public, who were fighting against the British rule, were badly treated by the police. The British government, for economic and political reasons, had suppressed all those who revolted against them; the police force was used as an instrument to protect their rule. During the war time, when there was threat of Japan attack, the Indian political parties pleaded the British government to reduce the strength of the Special Police Force and the cost of maintenance on the local people. Well trained special and additional police with extra powers were sanctioned to deal with the agitators of the freedom movement and the cost of expenditure in this regard was borne by the public. The political unrest due to the freedom movement had ended after India achieved Independence.[95] The principal arm of the British government was police for the preservation of order in the society among the public.[96] The police were obliged due to the nature of their duties to use violence as a measure to control and apprehend criminals in the prevalent continuing violence.

In the Indian Police Act V of 1861, the rules and regulations were laid for the police according to which they were not supposed to accept any kind of gifts and favours or have any monetary transitions with the public or within the police administration. But over the years, the public and police got involved in corruption. Low salary of the police and the people's hesitation to approach the police and courts might have been a reason for the corruption. The Indian Police Commission had stated in their report that there was dishonesty existent in the police. It was observed that the constabulary got more chance to have intimacy with people. The living conditions and inadequacy of pay scales were also responsible for corruption.[97] No police officer of the district was allowed to take part in any trade or calling unless permitted and also no police officer was allowed, under any pretext, to have any money transaction with any other police officer. They were not permitted on any occasion, directly or indirectly, to take or receive any present, gratuity or fee without the express permission of the District Superintendent.

The Station House Officers and the officers in police stations in the Northern range had close contacts with the people. The police stations were the place where people came into contact with the police;, for speedy investigation or for eliciting false evidence or to escape from punishment, people seek the help the police and the bribe them. There was widespread inefficiency and corruption in the police administration during that period. In the Jeypore district of the Northern range, the District Superintendent of Police, while touring dismissed two Sub-Inspectors, three Head Constables and fourteen Constables on charges of corruption. One of the Sub-Inspectors was subsequently reinstated by government.[98] A Constable of the Guntur district was fined Rs 50 for extorting bribe from a cartman.[99]

These cases show that the police, right from the higher ranks upto the lower ranks, were charged for corruption. There was a wide gap between the police and the public, which made the police unpopular. The unhappy relationship was attributed to the frequent abuse of power by policemen.

In case of grave offences committed by the police officers, they were judicially punished. They were convicted for offences committed either in their official capacity or in their private capacity. Here is a citation in which the rules were violated: In the year 1925, in the West Godavari district, a Yanadi fellow who belonged to an identified criminal tribe, was made forcefully to accept a theft that occurred in a Sub-Inspector's house that later proved to be wrong. For this, the Sub-Inspector was punished with six months rigorous imprisonment and other Constables who worked with the Sub-Inspector, were also sentenced to four months rigorous imprisonment. In the same year, a Constable of Guntur district, was fined Rs 50 for extorting bribe from a bullockcart-puller. In the Ganjam district, a man who was suspected to have committed a murder, was roughly handled by the police in their attempt to make him confess his crime during course of which he died. The station police reported the occurrence as a case of suicide and all those who were responsible were punished.[100] During this year, the Inspector General of Police had appreciated Saunders, the District Superintendent of the Jeypore district for putting laborious effort in putting down corruption and protecting the interests of the people.[101] Following the orders from the British government, the police officers had tried to stop corruption among the police in other districts of the range.

The districts of the Northern range of Madras Presidency were economically rich, so, the range became administratively demanding. Though police, as a weapon, was used mercilessly on the people opposed to the British rule, the police administration and the British rule in many ways proved advantageous to the Northern range. During the British rule, the police were powerful and the common people were afraid to approach them; this situation continued even after Independence. The people, in general, were reluctant to come forward as witness and assist the police in apprehending criminals. The British government, European supremacy, poor payments, and the non-cooperative attitude of the public made the police demoralised and detached from the public. {The police had functioned under the guidance of the British rules and regulations which were made miles apart from the public and often turned it into a target of emotional abuse by those who were pitted against the British}. Within the police, emergency duties and internal organisational pressure had strained its relations with the public.[102] Police were faithful and loyal towards the British government, but by their performances, they had strained their relation with the public. The police performed both, destructive as well as constructive functions, they were helpful to the people and the government, while at the same time, exploited the people by using their powers. The public were against the police for their rude behaviour and exploitation, though they were helpful towards the protection of life, property, crime control, maintenance of law and order, and for preservation of public peace.

The political, communal and other social tensions were also the causes of crime due to which public order got disturbed and violence broke out. The major role of the police force was prevention of crime and maintenance of public order. The police functions were to prevent commission of offences and public nuisances, bring offenders to justice, collect information affecting public peace, and keep order in all public places keeping in view the changing political and social scenario.

The relations between the police and public was important without which the crime control was not possible. The police force cannot discharge satisfactorily its functions without the public co-operation and public peace and prosperity cannot be preserved without police administration; both, vitally depend on each other. The principal arm of the British government for the preservation of order was the police though they used it as an instrument to enforce law and order. The public were cooperated by the police and the police were also assisted the public; however, towards end of freedom struggle, due to severe political unrest, the relations between the two got disturbed. The success of the police administration during the period of study 1924-1947 was dependent on the public co-operation which the police had sought and secured.

References

1. Law Commission of India, Report on Section 44, Code of Criminal Procedure of 1898, Government of India, Minister of Law, New Delhi, 1967.
2. Sultan Akbar Khan, *Power, Police and Public*, Vikas Publishing House Ltd., Delhi, 1979, p. 163.
3. Bhardwa K.K., *Indian Police Administration*, National Publications, 1978, p. 196.
4. Rushbrook Williams L.F., *India in 1923-24*, Central Publication Branch, Calcutta, 1924, p. 73.
5. Ramesan N, Andhra Pradesh District Gazetteers, Srikakulam, printed by Director of printing and stationery at Government Secretary Press, Hyderabad, 1979, p. 135.
6. Government of Madras, Legal Department, The Madras District Police Act, 1859, Act XXIV of 1859, printed by the Superintendent, Government Press, Madras, 1937, p. 7.
7. Mr Ry. Rai Bahadur N Gopalaswami Ayyangar, Collector's Standing Orders of Nellore District, printed by Superintendent, Government Ppress, Madras, 1931, p. 139.
8. Second Report of the Indian Penal Code, W. Ridsdale Military Orphan Press, Calcutta, 1847, pp. 84, 85.

9. Report on the Administration of the Police in the Madras Province for the year 1939, printed by Superintendent, Government Press, Madras, 1940, pp. 8,9.
10. G.O.No.467, Judl., dated 25th September, 1928, Judicial Department, Government of Madras.
11. Report on the Administration of the Police of the Madras Presidency for the year 1935, printed by Superintendent, Government Press, Madras, 1936, p. 8.
12. *Ibid.*
13. Report on the Administration of the Police of the Madras Presidency for the year 1939, printed by Superintendent, Government Press, Madras, 1940, p. 7.
14. Report on the Administration of the Police of the Madras Presidency for the years 1935 to 1947, printed by Superintendent, Government Press, Madras.
15. Report on the Administration of the Police of the Madras Presidency for the year 1939, printed by Superintendent, Government Press, Madras, 1940, p. 7.
16. Report on the Administration of the Police in the Madras Province for the year 1937, printed by Superintendent, Government Press, Madras, 1938, p. 12.
17. Report on the Administration of the Police of the Madras Province, 1938, printed by Superintendent, Government Press, Madras, 1939, p. 5.
18. G.O.No. 172, Judl. (Ms), dated 28th March, 1928, Judicial Department, Government of Madras.
19. Letter No. 215/A R dated, 15th July, 1926, from Inspector General of Police to the Chief Secretary to Government, Judicial Department, Madras.
20. Report on the Administration of the Police of the Madras Presidency for the year 1928, printed by Superintendent, Government Press, Madras, 1929, p. 24.
21. Handbook of Information on the Administration of the Province of Madras, printed by Superintendent, Government Press, Madras, 1947, p. 29.
22. Report on the Administration of the Police of the Madras Province, 1930, printed by Superintendent, Government Press, Madras, 1931, p. 5.
23. G.O.No.116, Judl.(Police) dated 13th March, 1923, Home Department, Government of Madras
24. G.O.No.28, Judl., dated 15th March, 1926, Judicial Department, Government of Madras
25. G.O.No.5421, L, dated 10th November, 1933, Law Department, Government of Madras.

26. G.O.No.439,Home(Judl),dated16thFebruary1920, Judicial Department, Government of Madras,
27. G.O.No.1386, L, dated 27th June, 1927, Law Department, Government of Madras.
28. G.O.No.2169, L ,dated 25th July, 1930, Law Department, Government of Madras.
29. G.O.No.294, Home, dated 2nd January, 1937, Home Department, Government of Madras.
30. History of Police organisation in India and Indian village police, published by the University of Calcutta, with the permission of Government of India, University press,Calcutta1913,p. 53
31. G.O.No.338, Judl., dated 6th February, 1920, Judicial Department, Government of Madras.
32. G.O.No.523, Home (Judl.), dated 5th March, 1917, Home Department, Government of Madras
33. Report on the Administration of the Police of the Madras Presidency for the year 1932, printed by Superintendent, Government Press, Madras, 1933, p. 22.
34. *Ibid.*, p. 349.
35. Report on Administration of the Police of the Madras Province for the year 1928, printed by Superintendent, Government Press, Madras, 1929, p. 18.
36. Report on Administration of the Police of the Madras Province for the year 1927, printed by the Superintendent, Government Press, Madras, 1928, p. 18.
37. Letter No. 768/36 C-4, dated 21st October, 1936, from E.C. Wood, District Magistrate, Vizagapatam, to the Inspector General of Police, Madras.
38. Gazetteer of the Nellore District, 1938, Vol. A, printed by Superintendent, Government Press, Madras, 1942, p. 278.
39. G.O.No.2764, Home (Judl), dated 23rdNovember, 1916, Home Department, Government of Madras.
40. G.O.No.290, Home, dated 1st Febraruary, 1945, Home Department, Government of Madras.
41. G.O.No.3218, Home (Ms), dated 17th September, 1945, HomeDepartment, Government of Madras.
42. Report on Administration of the Police of the Madras Province for the year 1928, printed by Superintendent, Government Press, Madras, 1929, p. 18.
43. Administrative Report on the Madras Presidency for the year 1936, printed by Superintendent, Government Press, Madras, 1937, p. 28.
44. Administrative Report on the Madras Presidency for the year 1938, printed by Superintendent, Government Press, Madras, 1939, p. 24.

45. Report on Administration of the Police of the Madras Province for the year 1929, printed by Superintendent, Government Press, Madras, 1930, p. 24.
46. Handbook of Information on the Administration of the Province of Madras, 1945-46, printed by Superintendent, Government Press, Madras, 1947, p. 33.
47. John Marriott and Bhaskar Mukhopadhyay, *Britain in India, 1765-1905, Justice, Police, Law and Order,* Vol. I, Pickering and Chatto, London, 2006, p. 234.
48. *Ibid.*, p. 353.
49. Report on the Administration of the Police in the Madras Province for the year 1929, printed by Superintendent, Government Press, Madras, 1930, p. 24.
50. Report of the Criminal Tribes Act Enquiry Committee, printed at the Government Press, Bombay, 1939.
51. Francis W, Gazetteer of South India, Vol. II, Mittal Publications, New Delhi, 1989, p. 116.
52. Bhardwaj K.K., *Indian Police Administration,* National Publications, 1978, p. 2.
53. Report on the Administration of the Police in the Madras Province for the year 1936, printed by Superintendent, Government Press, Madras, 1937, pp. 18,19.
54. Report on the Administration of the Police in the Madras Province for the year 1938, printed by Superintendent, Government Press, Madras, 1939, p. 6.
55. Report on the Administration of the Police in the Madras Province for the year 1937, printed by Superintendent, Government Press, Madras, 1938, p. 12.
56. Report on the Administration of the Police in the Madras Province for the year 1939, printed by Superintendent, Government Press, Madras, 1940, p. 15.
57. Report on the Administration of the Police of the Madras Presidency, 1927, printed by Superintendent, Government Press, Madras, 1928, p. 5.
58. Report on the Administration of the Police of the Madras Presidency, 1928, printed by Superintendent, Government Press, Madras, 1929, p. 5.
59. G.O.No.765, Public (Police),dated 1st July, 1932, Public (Police) Department, Government of Madras.
60. Administrative Report on the Inspector General of Police for the year 1926, printed by Superintendent, Government Press, Madras, 1927, p. 14.
61. G.O. No. 2412, Home, dated 9th May, 1938, Home Department, Government of Madras.

62. Administrative Report of the Madras Presidency for the year 1938-39, printed by Superintendent, Government Press, Madras, 1940, p. 11.
63. G.O.No.467, Judl., dated 25th September, 1926, Judicial Department, Government of Madras.
64. Administrative Report on the Madras Presidency for the year 1926, printed by Superintendent, Government Press, Madras, 1927, p. 5.
65. Administrative Report of the Madras Presidency for the year 1929, printed by Superintendent, Government Press, Madras, 1930, p. 6.
66. Administrative Report of the Madras Presidency for the year 1928, printed by Superintendent, Government Press, Madras, 1929, p. 5.
67. Report on Administration of the Police of the Madras Province for the year 1925, printed by Superintendent, Government Press, Madras, 1926, p. 2.
68. *Ibid.*, p. 5.
69. Report on Administration of the Police of the Madras Province for the year, 1938, printed by Superintendent, Government Press, Madras, 1939, p. 5.
70. Report on Administration of the Police of the Madras Province for the year 1927, printed by Superintendent, Government Press, Madras, 1928, p. 5.
71. Report on Administration of the Police of the Madras Province for the year 1929, printed by Superintendent, Government Press, Madras, 1930, p. 6.
72. Report on Administration of the Police of the Madras Province for the year 1933, printed by Superintendent, Government Press, Madras, 1934, p. 5.
73. *Ibid.*, p. 47.
74. Report on Administration of the Police of the Madras Province for the year 1927, printed by Superintendent, Government Press, Madras, 1928, p. 5.
75. Report on the Administration of the Police of the Madras Province, 1935, printed by Superintendent, Government Press, Madras, *1936,* p. 5.
76. Letter to the Secretary to Government, Home Department, Madras, Ref. No.1139/36, dated 11th September, 1936 (also see Madras Mail, dated 11th August, 1936).
77. Madras Mail, dated 11th August, 1936.
78. Report on the Administration of the Madras Presidency for the years 1938-39, Madras, Superintendent Government Press, 1940, pp. 46,49.
79. Report on the Administration of the Madras Presidency for the year 1947, printed by Superintendent, Government Press, Madras, 1948, p. 8.
80. G.O.No. 485, Public (Police), 12th September, 1931, Public Department, Government of Madras.

81. Report on the Administration of the Madras Presidency for the year 1930, printed by Superintendent, Government Press, Madras, 1931, pp. xxiii-xxiv.
82. G.O.No.3391, Home (Conf.), dated 14thAugust, 1940, Home Department, Government of Madras.
83. The Hindu, dated 26th September, 1932.
84. The Hindu, dated 17th January, 1932.
85. Venkatarangaiya. M, *The Freedom Struggle in Andhra Pradesh*, Vol. IV, published by Andhra Pradesh State Committee, Hyderabad, 1974, p. 16.
86. The Hindu, dated 7th January, 1932.
87. The Hindu, dated 29th January, 1942.
88. The Hindu, dated 26th February, 1932.
89. The Hindu, dated 23rd January, 1932.
90. G.O.No.2060, L (General), dated 23rd May, 1932, Law Department, Government of Madras.
91. G.O.No.275 A (S-I) Public (Police)(Conf.), dated 12th May, 1930, Public(Police), Government of Madras.
92. G.O.No.1197, Public (Military)(Conf.), dated 22ndJuly, 1935, (Military) Department, Government of Madras.
93. G.O.No. 206 Judl. (Conf.), dated 16th April, 1929, Judicial Department, Government of Madras.
94. Report on the Administration of the Police in the Madras Province for the year 1939, Government Press, Madras, 1940, p. 63.
95. G.O.No. 3701, Home, 6th October, 1948, Home Department, Government of Madras.
96. Rushbrook Williams L.F., *India in 1923-24*, Central Publication Branch, Calcutta, 1924, p. 73.
97. Report of the Indian Police Commission 1902-03, Government Central Printing Office, Simla, 1904, p. 21.
98. Report on the Administration of the Police of the Madras Presidency, 1925, printed by Superintendent, Government Press, Madras, 1926, p. 3.
99. Report on the Administration of the Police of the Madras Presidency, 1925, printed by Superintendent, Government Press, Madras, 1926, p. 4.
100. Administrative Report of the Police of the Madras Presidency, 1925, printed by Superintendent, Government Press, Madras, 1926, pp. 5,6.
101. Report on the Administration of the Police of the Madras Presidency, 1925, printed by Superintendent, Government Press, Madras, 1926, p. 25.
102. G.O.No. 3701, Home, 6th October 1948, Home Department, Government of Madras.

7

Conclusion

Police administration is an executive arm of the government to perform the duty of maintaining law and order. It plays an important role in the field of judicial administration and its functions are multifaceted and varied. The control of the police administration was an important task of the British in maintaining their rule. For this purpose, the British had divided the geographical area of Madras Presidency into police ranges and the Northern range was one of the police divisions. This range included the districts of Ganjam, Jeypore, Vizagapatam, Godavari, Kistna, Guntur, and Nellore. Each district of the range was further divided into police sub-divisions and again into police circles which consisted of police stations and outposts. The clear divisions of the geographical areas into well-defined smaller areas of police administration provided the British for better control of the natives. These divisions of the Northern range were easily managed and there was a flow of information from the police stations to the sub-divisions, from sub-divisions to the district, and from district to the range for purpose of police administration which had benefitted the range as a whole.

The Northern range of the Madras Presidency is a vast area with large tracts of fertile lands which contributed to the economy of the range, this coupled with the factor of dense population of this range, had made it administratively demanding. Prior to the advent of the British, the police system in Southern India was local in scope and reactive in nature. There was no unified system of police administration; instead, there were many police agencies with a wide variety of organisational patterns functioning at different levels of the local rulers. The British, on acquiring the districts of the

Northern range, after a number of experimentations finally designed and organised the Irish model of police administration and used it as an instrument to prevent crime and enforce law and order. The British brought the English institutionalised forces and introduced them, and in course of time, this police systems and proceedings became a part and parcel of police administration. The British constructed the police administration machinery in a planned manner and the Indian Police Act of 1861 acted was the legal backbone of the police system. This Act stipulated the organisational structure, functions and constitution of the police force. The Indian Police Act stated that the entire police force was established under the Madras Presidency and this police system was extended at the levels of the range and its districts. The primary function of the police was maintenance of law and order, crime control, and surveillance. The arrangement of police at the range level had the advantage for the police force to move from one district to another to meet any emergency situation. The changeover from the Indian to the English system did prove advantageous to this Northern range. It is observed that the position of the police organisation in the Northern range was same as that of any other range in the Madras Presidency.

The geographical background, historical background and the course of implementation of police administration in the erstwhile Northern range has been elucidated which formed the basis for its further continuation. The police administration, selection, recruitment, training, powers and functions, constitution, discipline, dismissals, promotions, rewards, prevalence of crimes, services of special and auxiliary police forces, and the police-public relationship have been brought to light for the period of study from 1924 to 1947 in the Northern range.

By the study, it is understood that the Deputy Inspector General of Police was the head of the Northern range and was a subordinate to the Inspector General of Police of the Madras Presidency. The constitution of the police organisation, their powers and functions, and their facilities right up to the police station, which were according to the Police Acts, have been detailed from the administrative angle in this range. During the period 1924-47, there were four major administrative changes — the division of Godavari district into two districts, West and East Godavari in the year 1925; the Nellore district, which was transferred to the Central range in the year 1929, was incorporated again in the Northern range in the year 1936; the transfer of the districts of Jeypore and Ganjam along with some parts of the Vizagapatam to the Orissa Province in the year 1936;

and the bifurcation of the Vizagapatam police jurisdiction into two parts, North and South Vizagapatam, in the year 1946. All these have been brought to light in this study. Each district of the Northern range was placed under the charge of a District Superintendent of Police who was assisted by Inspectors, Sub-Inspectors and the constabulary.

It is observed that the hierarchy of the police administration was same as in the other ranges of the Madras Presidency. The police stations were the basic units of police administration. The police stations were the most important administrative units and they were the lowest of the police executive wing. The police station was a place for the police power and functions. The complaint of the public against any crime and the First Information Reports were first recorded, and after this initial step, the whole police machinery started functioning. There were many police stations in the Northern range and each police station was under a Sub-Inspector who was assisted by Head Constables and Constables. The Station House Officers and the Constables came into direct contact with various sections of people which left behind the image of the police administration in the Northern range.

It is known from the study that the police stations and police outposts were more in the Northern range during the period 1924-47 as the population was high and the area had vast agency tracts inhabited by criminal tribes. It is observed that from the year 1936 onwards, the number of police stations and police outposts were reduced due to the transfer of two districts of the Northern range to the Orissa Province. The numbers of these provinces remained almost steady for a few years, and then later, their numbers were slightly increased due to the political agitations and mass movements seeking independence. The police stations and outposts in the Northern range were advantageous as the public freely reported the occurrence of crime and sought police assistance. This co-operation between the police and the public resulted in prevention of crime and its control during the period of study in the Northern range.

From the study, it is understood that there were special and auxiliary police forces organised along with the regular police, who assisted the latter in many instances during the period 1924-47. The Wireless and Fire Service were also introduced during this period. The British government had used their services to the maximum in crime control and in maintenance of law and order throughout the period of study. They had preserved peace, prevented crimes, detected and apprehended the offenders and their services proved beneficial to the Northern range in the maintenance of law and order. The performance of the Special Police Forces can be gauzed from the suppression of Rampa rebellion in the year 1924, where law and order was restored in the Agency regions of the Northern range. The Special Police Forces of the Northern range dealt with many cases to restore law and order during political unrests, agrarian and industrial strikes, communal disputes and other riots and disturbances. These paramilitary forces were deputed many times in the Northern range to quell crowd unrests, had maintained security, and helped the public in contigencies, such as natural calamites, fairs, and festivals. For the Krishna Pushkaram festivals, the Special Police Forces were deputed for *bandobast* duty in the year 1945. The percentage of natives in the reserve out of total strength, in the headquarters was kept as low as possible to avoid communal and labour tensions. It is understood that the Civic Guards were formed on voluntary basis and they provided valuable services during Quit India Movement of 1942 by guarding government property, viz., telegraph and railway lines, amongst others.

It can be seen that the Lee Commission of 1924 was appointed to study about the general conditions of services and also the methods of recruitment for Europeans as well as Indians. On its recommendations, the quota was raised from 33 per cent to 50 per cent in the Indian Civil Services, but the superior positions in the police force remained in the European hands until independence. It is observed that on pressure from the Indian political leaders for the set up of Public Services Commission at the provincial level, it was in the year 1929 that the Madras Service Commission came to be first established for the province of Madras in India; later, this Commission emerged as Madras Public Service Commission. The benefit of this change was that the educated men from this range started showing interest in police jobs by competing for these examinations as the conditions of the services were improved.. It is brought to light in the study that the recruitment through competitive examination has provided an opportunity for many Indians to join the police forces in the Northern range.

It is understood that the recruitment of the police officers and policemen was made easy throughout the period 1924-47. The sanctioned and actual strength of the police officers and policemen recruited for almost all the years was nearly equal. The increase in the initial years of the period was more as whenever the workload increased, additional forces were recruited. On transfer of the Ganjam and Jeypore districts in the year 1936, the strength of the police force was reduced. During the last few years, the strength was more as additional policemen were recruited to contain the numerous disturbances associated with freedom struggle. The functioning of the police administration can be seen by comparing the police performance with the rate of crime control. The value of the property stolen by robbery, burglary, and theft cases was considerable and percentage of recovery varied from district to district in the Northern range. The average percentage of recovery of the stolen property was nearly 30 per cent which reflects the good work of the police taking into account the huge population of the range which was inhabited with large number nomadic criminal tribes. The economic well being and public peace and order in the range was preserved by good performance of the police during the period of study.

From the study, it is known that the Superintendents and the subordinate officers were required to pass an examination in the vernaculars along with other subjects for better grasp of administration. With this, it is understood that the British wanted the police officers to know and understand the people and their culture and habits for better performance of their duties. This led to a cordial relationship among the village officers, village community, and the police themselves in the Northern range which benefitted the public. It is observed that the selected candidates without police experience underwent a course of training at the Recruits Schools in the Madras Presidency. It is learnt that there was a Provincial Police Training School at Vellore for the training of the police officers and at the Central Recruits Schools at Vellore, Anantapur, Coimbatore, and Vizianagaram districts for the training of the constabulary. The Central Recruits School at Vizianagaram established in the Northern range which was closed in the year 1921, but was reopened in the year 1929 to train the additional recruits. Later, it remained closed and again opened in the year 1939; large numbers of recruits were trained and sent for war duties and this school was again closed in the year 1940. This shows that the schools were opened for training only when additional recruits needed for selected police duties.

Further from the study, it is known that the officers were drawn from the districts of the range and sent to the Central Recruits Schools in order to get in-service training. These officers, who came from different parts of the range to the Madras Presidency, shared experiences, discussed various problems and exchanged their opinions while they were undergoing training. This kind of continuous in-service training improved the efficiency of the trainees and made them up to date in their professional knowledge and career. It is understood that the recruits were taught the subjects like Criminal law and Law of Evidence, police procedures and practices, habits and customs of the criminal gangs along with physical training. In specialised areas, the Sub-Inspectors were trained by experts in scientific investigation in footprints, Facial Index System, fingerprints, precis writing, and recording and classification of fingerprints. This proved advantageous as this training improved their investigating skills and solved complicated crimes which resulted in better crime control in the range.

They regularly drilled in manual and platoon exercises in addition to baton exercises and lining streets to clear crowds during the emergencies. This was useful as they dealt with a number of riots and disturbances in the Northern range during the period 1924-47 to maintain law and order. It is found that the training of the constabulary in the Northern range was in elementary practical education besides drill, physical training, musketry, and the use of arms. It is brought to light that all the weapons were kept in the police stations and were not carried by policemen when posted on ordinary duties. The police officers carried revolvers, the constabularies were equipped with rifles and smoothbores, and the armed reserves with long snider rifles. These armed police forces secured the roads, railways, canals, and bridges for the safety of the public and to protect the government property.

In the Northern range, earlier, most of the constabulary were illiterates, but through proper training, they were provided with minimum education and illiterate men were gradually weeded out. It is known from the government reports that the rate of illiteracy amongst the policemen was high in the initial years of the period 1924-47, as they were not many educated men available. Later, the police were recruited from educated classes, and with proper training, illiteracy was gradually reduced. This reflects the progress of literacy in the Northern range which has been impressive in the context of the growing population.

It is known that the British appreciated and encouraged the police for their performance and this was recognised by way of grant of good service entries and accelerated promotions. Also, veteran sports men were given promotions for outstanding achievements. Only on five occasions, the police officers were promoted in recognition of their good work in the Northern range during the period 1924 to 1947. In the year 1932, two police officers in the

Vizagapatam district; in the year 1935, one police officer in West Godavari district; in the year 1939, two from Vizagapatam district and one from Guntur district; one in the year 1941 in the East Godavari district and one in the Nellore district in the year 1946, were promoted. This shows that the police officers' performance was poor and this also indicates the British had implemented strict rules of services.

It is observed from the study that for good work, the police officers, subordinate officials, and private individuals were rewarded to keep up their morale high. The good work done by the police officers was recognised by grant of good service entries and the cash rewards were stopped in the year 1938 to all police officers except for Head Constables and Constables. The rewards to the police were in the form of medals, honours, titles, and certificates for their gallantry and merit whenever they performed good work in capturing notorious criminals and for their conduct in dealing with riots and disturbances. It is brought to light some of the titles bestowed by the British government to the police, viz. Order of British Empire, Member of British Empire, Rao Bahadur, Khan Sahib and Rao Sahib, King's Police Medal, Bar to the King's Police Medal, Indian Police Medal, Bar to the Indian Police Medal, and Kendall Humanity Medal awarded for gallantry and also for meritorious service.

From the study, it is understood that the British government also rewarded private individuals for their valuable co-operation and to impress on public the necessity of mutual co-operation between the police and the public. Letters of appreciation and parchment certificates were issued and they were given the choice between articles of daily use and money. Besides the British government, magistrates, zamindars, private individuals and other government departments also rewarded the police and public for their good work. Here is a citation of interest where a woman in West Godavari district was presented with a gold bangle of her choice as reward for her courageous conduct of helping the police in capturing the burglar. In another case in the same district, three school students were gifted with a fountain pen each for arresting four suspected culprits and handling them over to the police. This shows that the private individuals were rewarded with articles of choice and for daily use. It is found from the study that the police officers of Guntur district and the Criminal Investigation Department were rewarded with Rs 830 for rounding up a gang of Erukala absconders from the Sitanagram settlement who were responsible for many burglaries in the districts of Guntur, Kistna, and West Godavari. This system of cash rewards to police officers was abolished in the year 1938 by the government.

Rewards to the police force and village officers proved to be advantageous as through them, the crime could be better controlled and reported. The rewards to private individuals brought co-operation between the police and the public which resulted in crime control and detection. The system of rewards encouraged the common people to react against the crimes in the society. It is known from the study of the records during the period 1924-47, that a number of rewards were given to the individuals including the criminal tribes and the police officials and this number increased later. This reflects that the government, private individuals, zamindars, and other public departments had encouraged both the public and police co-operation in crime control and enforcing the responsibilities on the public. Here is a citation of interest: A reward of Rs 500 was offered by zamindar of Udaiyarpalaiyam for apprehension of Kodukkur Arumugam, a notorious criminal, and this amount was distributed among one Inspector, six Sub-Inspectors, one Head Constable, four Constables, one *Karnam* and three private individuals. The Chamber of Commerce rewarded Rs 100 to the Sub-Inspector of the Port Police of Cocanada port in the East Godavari district in recognition of his good work in prevention of cargo thefts. In another case of interest, a villager and a Yanadi tribal from the Nellore district were rewarded for giving information about the culprits in a case of house-breaking and theft to the Village Vigilance Committee. This reflects that the rewards were freely granted and this rewarding system improved the public-police relationship and played an important role in prevention and detection of crimes in the Northern range.

It is observed that the police were punished departmentally and judicially for violating the rules under their personal or official capacity. The police were punished for violating the police rules which were met with disciplinary proceedings. The predominance of the natives in the ranks of the police force called for a capacity to discipline and control of the recruited natives to serve the British administration. They were punished by dismissal from service, reduction in cadre, loss of pay, and black marking for offences committed in their official capacity and they were judicially punished for offences committed under private capacity through Criminal Procedures Code and Indian Penal Code. The number of dismissals of policemen in the Northern range which were very high in the initial years of the period 1924-47, were due to absence without leave as there was laxity of discipline. During the following years, there was gradual decline in dismissals as instructions were issued to the district officers to use discretion in matter of granting leave by Inspector General of Police, and this indicates that, there was good disciplining in the police force of the Northern range.

It is identified from the records that the East Coast Special Police Force and the Civic Guards were disbanded for lack of discipline. This discipline among police made them obedient to the command and control of the police structure and to work in coordination in the Northern range. Here is a citation of interest: The Assistant Armourer of the East Coast Special Police had stabbed to death the Havildar-Armourer and the Commandant of the Force, Peterson and then shot himself. The government then ordered a joint enquiry by the District Magistrate, Vizagapatam and the Inspector General of Police. The government had concluded that the East Coast Special Police lacked discipline and so, it was disbanded. The following are the cases where the police officers and police men were punished for lack of discipline: In the district of Ganjam — an Inspector, for misuse of railway warrants, and a Sub-Inspector, for neglect of duty in a case of murder — were dismissed from service. In another case from the West Godavari district, a Yanadi tribal was made forcefully to accept a theft that occurred in a Sub-Inspector's house and when this case was proved wrong, the Sub-Inspector and the Constables who were associated with this case, were sentenced to rigorous imprisonment. This proves that the government did not tolerate any indiscipline, both in the ranks of police officers and subordinate policemen.

It is understood that the Northern range was no exemption to crime as this range was vast, highly populated, and economically rich and most of the range was covered with Agency tracts. The common crimes prevalent there were murder, dacoity, robbery, theft and other crimes like cheating, forgery, counterfeit of currency, factional riots, labour troubles, agrarian strikes, communal tensions, culpable homicide occurred which were related to political, socio-economical and religious animosity. It is understood that the motives for these crimes were socio-economic reasons, communal causes, faction feuds, family disputes, sexual jealousy, and other motives.

It is found that the theft cases in the Northern range during the period 1924-47 were mostly jewellery thefts, cycle thefts, and cattle thefts. It is analysed that these offences were high in the initial years of the period 1924-47, but later decreased, and their numbers rose towards the end of the period. The increase in the initial years was due to economic stress, agrarian disputes, famine conditions and unfavourable seasonal conditions. With better reporting and registration of crimes and measures taken by the police, the number of cases decreased in the middle years and the increase towards the end of the period was due to the political unrest. There was an increase in cattle thefts during the war period due to huge demand for hides, but later, the cases of cattle thefts were less because the government issued orders to the District Magistrates in the Northern range to give deterrent sentences to the cattle thieves. Since the cattle were considered as valuable property to the agricultural classes of the Northern range, these offences caused economic loss to them. It is found that these offences were mostly committed by the nomadic tribes in the Northern range.

It is observed that cases of robbery in the Northern range were highway robberies, field robberies, house robberies, and mail robberies. The distinct rise in the number of reported robbery cases, as was case with dacoity, were due to economic conditions, activities of criminal tribes, failure of crops, floods, and unemployment in almost all the districts of the Northern range. From the records, it is known that the cases were high in the initial years of the period of the study, i.e., 1924-47 due to activities of criminal tribes, and over the years these cases had gradually decreased due to strict enforcement of the Criminal Tribes Act and better reporting. It is found that the police had organised day and night patrols as a result of these organised measures, the cases of robbery had decreased over the years.

It is known that the highway dacoities, field dacoities, and house dacoities were common in the Northern range during the period 1924-47. It is found that these offences were committed by local organisations of bad character and also by the criminal tribes. From the statistics, it is found that the dacoities were high in the initial years of the period 1924-47 and these cases had gradually reduced towards the end. The increases in the dacoity cases were mostly due to rise in the prices of staple food grains. It is also found that decrease in dacoity was due to the special action taken by the police administration by constructing special settlements for the notified criminal tribes, concentration of the police in certain areas, and appointment of road *talaiyaris*. The separation of large Agency areas of Ganjam and Jeypore contributed in this decline and apart from the factors of growing population and proper street lighting.

It is understood that the cases of house-breaking were committed habitually by old offenders and criminal gangs. It is found that these cases were high in the initial years of the period 1924-47 and had reduced for few years, but thereafter increased. The high increase in the initial years was due to unfavourable seasonal conditions and also due to rise in food prices after the declaration of war. It is known from the reports that there was co-operation between the Village Vigilance Committees, Criminal Investigation Department, and the District Intelligence Bureaus that reduced the number of house-breaking crimes in the Northern range. In the last few years, the police were preoccupied with the extra duties due to political unrest and this led to the increase in these crimes.

Murder is an offence where the police have very little power to prevent and it is found that, a number of murders were committed in the Northern range due to sexual matters, family disputes, factionalism, robbery and other causes. According to the statistics, the offence of murder showed increase mostly due to family and petty quarrels, drunken brawls and due to large number of people without employment due to demobilisation. The other factors that had also contributed to the increase were acute economic conditions, scarcity of food grains, high cost of living, and prevalence of communal and labour troubles throughout this range. It is found that the increase in the last few years was due to increasing urbanisation and population in the range during this period of study.

It is understood that besides the grave offences, the police also dealt with counterfeiting currency notes, cheating, forgery, and postal fraud offences. All such cases were firmly detected by the Criminal Investigation Department and its branches. In the year 1946, a separate unit called 'X' Branch was formed in the Department. The manufacture of counterfeit rupees and coins of different values was a constant offence throughout the Northern range. These offences were mostly carried out by criminal tribes and professional gangs. It is brought to light that the police were successful in seizing the collections of false coins, moulds, and apparatus used for making them and also arresting the false coiners and forgers of currency notes. Here is a citation of interest. Currency notes forged in Burma were brought through steamships and circulated in the Madras Presidency. The Criminal Investigation Department police seized these notes in Cocanada and this led to captures in Rangoon thereby preventing wider circulation of such notes. This shows how Criminal Investigation Department solved such complicated international cases of counterfeit. This Department played an important role in solving a number of complicated cases which resulted in reduction in crime in the Northern range during the period 1924-47. Here is another citation where the Fingerprint Bureau of the Criminal Investigation

Department solved an intricate case: An ex-convict had developed intimacy with his neighbour's wife and this had enraged her husband; he went with several others to the ex-convict's house and hacked him to death. The parts of his body were burnt and the remaining was buried but the left hand of the deceased was found by the police. With the help of the Fingerprint Bureau, the police established the identity of the deceased. It proves that the Criminal Investigation Department had helped to solve this case with scientific methods of investigation.

It is also known that the Northern range had contributed significantly in the freedom struggle and this led to a number of agitations against the British rule which created unrest throughout the range. As the period 1924-47 was the peak period for the Indian freedom struggle, many people were arrested and send to jails for assembling, holding Indian flags, singing the national song, public speeches, and for attending congress committees. In many instances, the police had lathicharged, opened fire, and used tear smoke to restore order. In the year 1932, two serious collisions occurred during the Civil Disobedience Movement , one at Gudivada and the other at Eluru, between the police and riotous mobs. At Gudivada, a mob attacked a party of Reserve Police under W.F.A. Hamilton, probationary Assistant Superintendent of Police, who was protecting certain Civil Disobedience Movement prisoners; the police opened fire to disperse the mob and 118 persons were arrested, charged, and convicted in this incident. In Eluru taluk of the West Godavari district, a mob of about 3,000 labourers and others who were armed with sticks had attacked upon the Armed Reserve Police under the District Superintendent of Police, Sanjeevi Pillai. The police opened fire in which 25 men were injured and one died. Eighteen of the rioters were convicted and sentenced to imprisonment. This shows that the police were loyal towards their duties under the command and control of the British which proved disadvantageous to the people of the Northern range as they were fighting for a cause.

From this study, it is understood that the districts in the Northern range had abundant agricultural lands and the revenue collection was high. The *ryots* of the Northern range revolted against the zamindars and the British for their coercive revenue polices and illegal taxation and they advocated the abolition of zamindari system. From the reports, it is brought to light that there were propaganda demonstrations throughout the villages of the range which resulted in the formation of several peasant associations and taluk ryots associations in the East and West Godavari districts. It is found that in the Northern range, the labour disputes were staged mostly in the towns of Chirala in the Guntur district and in Chittavalasa of the Vizagapatam district by the factory workers for enhancing their wages. In many instances, the police had opened fire on the rioters to restore law and order. From the study of records, it is known that there were sporadic communal clashes between the Hindus and the Muslims during religious festivals in most of the districts of the Northern range. It is found that the Nellore district was dominated by communal riots due to the existence of large Muslim population along with Hindus. There were frequent clashes between high caste and low caste Hindus over caste superiority. The persistence of inter-communal bitterness accounted for the increase in number of public disturbances in the Northern range and these existed throughout the period 1924-47.

It is understood that the Northern range was large, covered with Agency tracts and inhabited by numerous tribes. The most troublesome criminal tribes, such as Donga Lambadis, Donga Yanadis, Donga Dasaries, Donga Yerukalas, Dommaras, Donga Woddars, Jogulas, Donga Yanadis, were registered under the Criminal Tribes Act. These nomadic tribes were enlisted as criminal tribes under this Act with the objective to safeguard the rights of the society against anti-social influence and the reformation of the criminal tribes. They had committed a number of crimes for the reasons of lack of property, vagrancy, wanderlust, lack of stability and general purpose in life, restlessness, and aimlessness. It is found that the British government provided reformations and special settlements which resulted in a large reduction of organised crimes and crimes by habitual offenders in the Northern range. The reformation movement provided these tribes an alternative means of livelihood. It is also known that communal *panchayats* were organised among the members of these tribes for the aid of the tribal community.

Further from the study, it is known that the settlement areas of the criminal tribes in the districts of the Northern range were Stuartpuram and Sitanagaram in Guntur district and Kavali, Allur and Bitragunta in Nellore district. The criminal tribes convicted, but later showed good conduct, were transferred to these settlements for their unexpired periods of sentences and money advances were given for purchasing bullock carts to the settlers. Further, these settlers were supplied free agricultural land, seeds, and money advances by the Agriculture Department. Besides, the government, even private individuals also helped for the reclamation of the criminal tribes. Here is a citation in this regard where the Rajah of Bobbili gave money donations and granted lands for the reclamation of the Dandasis tribes of the Ganjam district. The inmates of these settlements were also given training in industry skills, such as chapli-making, weaving, stone quarrying, and manufacture of matches for earning their livelihood. The health of these settlers was taken care by the Rural Medical Officers and anti-malaria operations were regularly undertaken. The children, aged between eight to 14 years of age, of registered members were also placed in these settlements. All the boys and girls received education in the schools; the Commissioner of Labour granted them with books, clothes, and mid-day meals to encourage the attendance of school going children.

The reclamation and rehabilitation of criminals and criminal communities was one of the functions of police administration. The police took the census of criminal gangs and communities and attempted to make them settle in particular areas for better surveillance. To control the criminal activities of the criminal tribes, reformatories and settlements were established. They were managed initially by private individuals, but later by the British government. Under the preventive functions, the Act of Criminal Tribes was passed in the Northern range and a number of habitual criminal tribes of the Northern range were registered under this Act. Their movements were restricted to prevent them from committing crimes. They were confined in the settlements under the police surveillance. The British government had maintained criminal settlements and reformatories at various places in the Northern range for prevention of crimes committed by the criminal tribes. The Deputy Inspector General of Police of the Northern range and the Criminal Investigation Department was entrusted with the supervision and control of all the settlements.

In the year 1947, the government had repealed the Criminal Tribes Act and fresh registrations were made under the Habitual Offenders Act. The restrictions imposed on members of the tribes were also relaxed after the suspension of working of the Criminal Tribes Act. The removal of surveillance over wandering gangs had no perceptible effect on the control of such gangs or on the state of crime.

It is brought to light that grave crimes were noticeable in all the districts of the Northern range during the period of the study. The total crimes recorded in the years 1924 to 1927 were less due to good foundation of the police administration in the Northern range. The proportion of offences against persons and property was highest in the districts of Jeypore and West Godavari among other districts of range and also in the Madras Presidency. It is found that the volume of crime in the years from 1929 to 1931 was low as there was a notable decrease in ordinary thefts and railway thefts by nearly 50 per cent. For the next five successive years, the percentage of detection of total crimes had increased to 45.3 per cent to which the West Godavari district contributed about 8.4 per cent. In the year 1937, there was a very large increase in the number of factious murders in the districts of Guntur and Nellore of the range. In the range where the standard of living was low, it is known thing that the crime would have varied with prices; whenever there was an unfavourable season, the prices of the grains increased consequent to which, the crimes were also high during these seasons. It is found that these unfavourable seasonal conditions of the year 1938 had an inevitable effect on the volume of crimes which increased in the districts of Vizagapatam and East Godavari, each recording highest with 14.6 per cent and 11.1 per cent respectively, and this was due to better reporting and registration of crimes. The active co-operation of Village Vigilance Committees, adequate control by the police over looting gangs and bad characters, the enforcement of the system of joint responsibility for the good conduct of criminal tribe members, and effective help rendered by the Central Crime Branch of the Criminal Investigation Department and District Intelligence Bureau kept the professional crimes under control. The trend of crime and its relation to the prices of two staple food grains, rice and sorghum, had steadily increased since the year 1940.

In the years 1941-42, it is understood that there was an increase in the volume of crime and it was due to the general economic conditions of the years. Distress was prevailing throughout Northern range during this period as there was blackout restriction, panic and evacuation, movements of refugees from Burma and Malaya and the congestion on the railways. It is found that the Nellore district alone contributed 61.0 per cent of the total grave crimes in the Madras Presidency which was the highest in the year 1941 and this increase was mostly due to communal disturbances. The districts Kistna and East Godavari were lowest in crime rate standing at 17.9 and 13.4 per cent respectively in the presidency and this was due to breaking up of several criminal organisations in these districts. There was increase in number of crimes in the year 1944 and this was due to the adverse conditions created by the war. There was an increase in crime in all districts of the Northern range which was most noticeable in the district of Nellore which recorded 24.0 per cent while in West Godavari district, it was 20.2 per cent. There was an increase in crime during the year 1946 because the prices of staple foodgrains and essential commodities continued to remain at a very high level throughout the Madras Presidency. This year, the south-west monsoon was above normal in the Nellore district, the north-east monsoon set in late and caused heavy rains locally in the Guntur and Nellore districts. The increase also contributed to labour unrest in most of the districts resulting in strikes and consequent dislocation of normal police work.

It is found that the crime was high in the year 1947 in all the ranges of the Madras Presidency. The highest crime in the Northern range and in Madras Presidency was recorded in the districts of Kistna with 35.84 per cent and Nellore with 38.10 per cent. There were 65 cases of riots and disturbances during this year in the Madras Presidency most of which were of a minor nature, but on 24 occasions, the police had to open fire to restore law and order. The Hindu-Muslim clashes in the districts of Guntur and Nellore in the Northern range were highest in the presidency. The reasons that contributed to increase in crimes were that the prices of the staple food grains continued to remain high and bad seasonal conditions in all the districts of the Madras Presidency, which were parts of the Northern range. Unemployment followed the demobilisation of military personnel and also there was a widespread labour, agrarian and communal unrest which diverted the police from their normal functions. The political unrest due to the freedom movement also contributed to the increase in crimes along with the activities of the communists and the local factions in most of the districts of the range. It is understood that much free reporting and registration of crimes, active co-operation of Village Vigilance Committees, adequate control by the police over looting gangs and bad characters, enforcement of the system of joint responsibility for the good conduct of criminal tribes' members and the effective help rendered by the Criminal Investigation Department and District Intelligence Bureaus kept professional crime under check. It found from the study that the police administration in the Northern range had functioned successfully during the period 1924-47 as the crime was better controlled and detected then when compared to the other ranges of the Madras Presidency.

It is understood that the British government, through the police, collected and collated the crime statistics on all offences from the districts of the Northern range. This crime statistics were used as a tool of management to understand the cause of crime and as an index of efficiency of the police organisation and the action taken under various Sections of the Indian Penal Code and the Criminal Procedure Code. The reports and crime figures gave the British superior officers at the district headquarters a clear picture of the developments in the range.

The study of police-public relations is important for the police administration without which it remains incomplete. The success and failure of the police is largely dependent on the cordiality of police-public relationships and the extent of co-operation that the police gets from the public in its day to day functions. The police administration in the Northern range had discharged its functions satisfactorily with public cooperation. The public peace and prosperity was preserved by the proper functioning of the police administration in the districts of the Northern range. It is understood that the relationship between the public and the police had strained during the freedom struggle movement as the police performed their functions under the command of the British and the public were fighting against the British rule. The British government had used the police as principal arm for the preservation of law and order; it worked a force rather then a service.

The police administration in the Northern range has a long history, and it came into existence under the British rule. The police systems introduced by them, in course of time became a part and parcel of the police administration. This changeover from the Indian to the British system had proved advantageous to this range. The Northern range formed the largest range in the Madras Presidency; with growing population and rapid urbanisation, it became administratively challenging to manage it. Thus, the police administration played an important and a positive role in maintaining law and order, and in controlling crime.

The British, in order to protect the interests of European trade, controlled the general administration and used the police as a weapon against the people who opposed them. It is also found that the police administration under the British rule in the Northern range of Madras Presidency during the period 1924-47 had functioned successfully as indicated by the proportion of crimes dealt by the police, which was high, when compared to the neighbouring ranges. It is also noted that the proportion of police to the area and population was higher than the other ranges of the presidency. The British police administration was almost the same all over India except for some differences with varying local conditions. In the beginning, the higher posts were monopolised by the British as there was a minimal natives participation. It was through the police that the

British exercised control over the range and faced the challenges against their rule. A detailed analysis of the nature and functioning of the police in their various aspects gives a better perspective regarding the working of the police administration in this Northern range. Therefore, the police administrative system has had far-reaching impact on the general administration in Northern range as the system has continued unchanged even after India attained Independence.

Appendix

Murders Cases in the Northern Range District-wise[1]

Years	*Gan-jam*	*Vizag-apatam*	*Jeypore*	*East Goda-vari*	*West Goda-vari*	*Kistna*	*Gun-tur*	*Nell-ore*
1924	21	28	07	21	-	27	31	27
1925	24	19	14	30	14	21	44	24
1926	18	17	09	23	12	21	32	29
1927	25	22	13	35	09	09	30	35
1928	29	21	06	30	18	15	20	-
1929	31	17	07	22	19	15	37	-
1930	35	29	11	49	19	16	31	26
1931	30	21	14	32	28	20	51	27
1932	38	23	10	18	22	13	39	38
1933	28	34	06	28	21	15	46	26
1934	46	50	12	38	17	15	46	29
1935	37	20	10	35	29	17	42	22
1936	10	34	03	21	18	22	41	22
1937	-	36	-	34	34	20	46	22
1938	-	44	-	27	24	33	57	22
1939	-	51	-	41	25	20	63	24
1940	-	46	-	56	18	32	45	17
1941	-	52	-	40	24	23	52	41
1942	-	48	-	49	28	28	38	24
1943	-	36	-	38	30	37	49	28
1944	-	50	-	35	26	21	52	32
1945	-	47	-	33	28	25	47	34
1946	-	51	-	43	32	38	54	20
1947	-	46	-	40	31	59	50	22

Dacoity Cases in the Northern Range District-wise[2]

Years	*Gan-jam*	*Vizaga-patam*	*Jey-pore*	*East Goda-vari*	*West Goda-vari*	*Kistna*	*Gun-tur*	*Nellore*
1924	11	08	01	14	-	33	28	22
1925	04	03	02	08	-	06	10	20
1926	03	01	04	03	06	03	09	11
1927	02	01	03	05	05	-	17	08
1928	04	-	01	02	-	-	12	-
1929	04	04	02	05	02	05	04	-
1930	07	01	-	05	04	06	03	05
1931	08	04	-	04	03	10	11	10
1932	09	02	04	03	05	01	06	05
1933	02	02	04	05	01	-	05	06
1934	17	01	01	03	01	-	03	11
1935	02	01	07	05	03	01	02	08
1936	01	03	-	03	01	-	05	03
1937	-	05	-	02	02	-	-	01
1938	-	05	-	01	07	01	01	03
1939	-	07	-	10	01	01	04	05
1940	-	08	-	03	01	01	01	02
1941	-	07	-	04	-	-	09	03
1942	-	04	-	09	02	02	01	02
1943	-	01	-	04	04	-	03	05
1944	-	06	-	08	01	01	-	03
1945	-	01	-	03	01	-	-	01
1946	-	-	-	01	-	-	-	05
1947	-	10	-	01	-	02	12	02

Robbery Cases in the Northern Range District-wise[3]

Years	*Gan-jam*	*Vizaga-patam*	*Jey-pore*	*East Goda-vari*	*West Goda-vari*	*Kistna*	*Gun-tur*	*Nellore*
1924	16	36	10	27	-	56	46	51
1925	09	16	05	27	12	14	29	49
1926	07	17	20	13	14	11	30	34
1927	12	13	06	31	22	15	40	24
1928	10	09	06	21	17	09	30	-
1929	11	25	04	16	07	13	20	-
1930	14	04	02	34	14	17	36	23
1931	06	08	-	23	12	14	30	27
1932	15	21	03	17	21	13	24	25
1933	20	08	04	31	09	03	35	25
1934	08	15	01	09	09	03	20	24
1935	13	17	01	09	10	04	13	32
1936	02	15	01	07	07	05	23	20
1937	-	14	-	09	04	01	09	15
1938	-	21	-	20	07	04	09	10
1939	-	20	-	07	11	01	11	12
1940	-	18	-	19	09	01	16	08
1941	-	20	-	10	04	01	15	12
1942	-	15	-	16	06	09	11	07
1943	-	21	-	18	11	13	09	17
1944	-	13	-	11	17	06	13	09
1945	-	22	-	05	02	09	13	11
1946	-	14	-	08	04	04	11	07
1947	-	31	-	07	08	09	21	06

House-breaking Cases in the Northern Range District-wise[4]

Years	*Gan-jam*	*Vizaga-patam*	*Jey-pore*	*East Goda-vari*	*West Goda-vari*	*Kistna*	*Gun-tur*	*Nellore*
1924	320	312	196	442	-	802	447	401
1925	214	268	248	351	277	476	316	358
1926	232	292	313	362	229	340	282	268
1927	191	270	251	382	280	309	315	297
1928	206	265	159	409	206	202	251	-
1929	265	308	135	371	238	324	251	-
1930	201	303	167	330	249	477	242	219
1931	208	297	176	378	321	442	330	171
1932	239	223	184	344	235	273	310	195
1933	199	227	141	307	247	158	251	198
1934	218	200	90	264	222	178	310	179
1935	249	200	81	200	191	160	309	176
1936	61	231	26	175	206	114	255	174
1937	-	226	-	183	208	160	247	130
1938	-	297	-	202	268	155	245	152
1939	-	312	-	253	282	278	271	211
1940	-	286	-	328	296	211	339	183
1941	-	295	-	241	220	154	312	341
1942	-	221	-	335	216	132	281	144
1943	-	217	-	313	285	186	249	281
1944	-	251	-	287	291	195	322	205
1945	-	305	-	229	173	340	268	136
1946	-	373	-	267	238	399	362	271
1947	-	571	-	301	273	422	548	400

Theft Cases in the Northern Range District-wise[5]

Years	*Gan-jam*	*Vizaga-patam*	*Jey-pore*	*East Goda-vari*	*West Goda-vari*	*Kistna*	*Gun-tur*	*Nellore*
1924	623	774	219	1206	-	1261	691	548
1925	564	687	239	1194	641	720	547	557
1926	556	653	350	1098	670	636	568	468
1927	557	603	285	1154	739	610	715	483
1928	611	738	265	1123	621	478	648	-
1929	682	935	325	1144	649	624	695	-
1930	496	690	347	1006	584	707	685	404
1931	487	553	322	992	642	789	710	398
1932	565	580	294	935	478	465	684	400
1933	556	617	241	849	567	416	682	343
1934	538	546	192	891	578	393	730	408
1935	564	648	176	791	549	409	756	335
1936	109	573	60	649	601	372	758	320
1937	-	728	-	643	511	384	675	294
1938	-	840	-	643	500	432	593	299
1939	-	803	-	729	594	586	673	366
1940	-	912	-	906	574	543	728	332
1941	-	771	-	827	565	454	362	446
1942	-	148	-	75	121	81	76	87
1943	-	152	-	91	115	89	82	89
1944	-	134	-	87	109	73	91	95
1945	-	1097	-	787	333	632	743	530
1946	-	1256	-	960	522	756	875	563
1947	-	1196	-	872	591	1071	1140	703

Cattle-theft Cases in the Northern Range District-wise[6]

Years	*Gan-jam*	*Vizaga-patam*	*Jey-pore*	*East Goda-vari*	*West Goda-vari*	*Kistna*	*Gun-tur*	*Nellore*
1924	61	72	66	97	-	126	73	109
1925	44	48	50	76	56	67	71	82
1926	80	76	52	107	97	80	65	100
1927	60	68	38	96	111	77	112	137
1928	44	73	34	100	106	71	112	-
1929	36	80	45	104	97	76	90	-
1930	45	77	50	78	76	90	86	92
1931	42	48	20	102	97	106	101	51
1932	40	38	30	72	55	72	88	55
1933	49	65	21	63	57	51	79	63
1934	50	47	25	78	55	47	96	60
1935	69	77	28	62	81	45	78	59
1936	21	87	07	52	96	50	90	76
1937	-	73	-	62	95	51	103	66
1938	-	75	-	82	59	74	62	63
1939	-	77	-	106	93	100	104	88
1940	-	89	-	150	100	94	88	54
1941	-	135	-	110	88	78	96	68
1942	-	82	-	145	103	98	104	64
1943	-	93	-	119	81	99	88	89
1944	-	71	-	93	91	100	65	90
1945	-	102	-	64	55	57	71	77
1946	-	102	-	75	106	79	81	93
1947	-	101	-	104	89	99	118	88

Proportion of Police to Area in the Northern Range District-wise[7]

1924	7.7	6.0	15.0	5.5	6.1	4.7	5.1	7.9
1925	7.7	6.2	15.8	5.8	6.3	4.9	5.6	7.7
1926	8.9	7.5	15.8	5.9	6.5	5.4	6.0	5.0
1927	8.9	7.5	15.1	6.0	6.6	5.2	6.1	3.3
1928	8.9	7.5	15.0	5.5	6.6	5.2	6.1	8.3
1929	8.9	7.1	13.9	5.5	6.6	5.2	6.1	-
1930	8.9	7.1	13.9	5.3	5.4	5.5	6.1	-
1931	9.0	7.5	14.2	5.4	5.5	4.9	5.9	-
1932	9.5	8.5	15.6	5.7	5.4	5.0	6.0	-
1933	9.5	8.6	15.5	5.7	5.4	5.0	5.0	-
1934	9.5	8.6	15.5	5.7	5.4	5.1	6.0	-
1935	9.6	8.6	15.5	5.7	5.4	5.0	6.0	-
1936	-	9.1	-	5.7	5.3	5.0	6.0	8.2
1937	-	9.1	-	5.4	5.3	5.0	6.0	8.3
1938	-	8.9	-	5.6	5.3	5.0	6.0	8.3
1939	-	15.2	-	5.5	12.1	9.6	8.2	6.0
1940	-	8.9	-	5.6	5.3	5.0	6.0	8.3
1941	-	8.9	-	5.6	5.3	5.0	6.0	8.3
1942	-	9.0	-	5.6	5.4	5.0	6.2	8.2
1943	-	9.0	-	5.6	5.4	5.2	6.0	8.4
1944	-	7.0	-	5.2	5.4	3.6	5.2	8.4
1945	-	5.4	-	4.2	5.0	3.6	5.0	7.4
1946	-	5.2	-	3.9	4.3	3.2	4.8	7.2
1947	-	5.1	-	4.1	3.7	3.0	4.1	6.1

Proportion of Police to Population in the Northern Range District-wise[8]

1924	2004	1891	1129	1514	2740	1500	1778	1338
1925	2004	1891	1129	1512	2746	1505	1778	1331
1926	2216	2231	1090	1612	2890	1524	1854	1411
1927	2302	2287	1082	1620	2905	1589	1921	1448
1928	2302	2296	1075	1539	2905	1589	1921	1448
1929	2300	2162	995	1480	2905	1589	1921	-
1930	2300	2162	995	1414	2390	1693	1924	-
1931	2316	2301	1019	1439	1417	1536	1890	-
1932	2734	2746	1452	1759	2818	1784	2134	-
1933	2744	2745	1438	1749	2780	1774	2123	-
1934	2744	2745	1442	1748	2786	1771	2123	-
1935	2756	2745	1441	1746	2780	1774	2123	-
1936	-	2947	-	1762	2755	1779	2127	1534
1937	-	2939	-	1762	2755	1779	2111	1543
1938	-	2894	-	1735	2755	1779	2111	1543
1939	-	2894	-	1735	2755	1779	2123	1543
1940	-	2894	-	1719	2755	1779	2123	1543
1941	-	1097	-	1942	3113	2057	2379	1683
1942	-	1322	-	1846	3027	2012	2190	1625
1943	-	1760	-	1790	2932	1836	2066	1655
1944	-	1766	-	1599	2675	1905	1972	1592
1945	-	2067	-	1375	2490	1462	1902	1500
1946	-	2190	-	1400	2134	1336	1887	1470
1947	-	2146	-	1463	1841	1233	1628	1249

Proportion of Cognizable Crimes investigated by the Police in the Northern range District-wise[9]

Years	*Gan-jam*	*Vizaga-patam*	*Jey-pore*	*East Goda-vari*	*West Goda-vari*	*Kistna*	*Gun-tur*	*Nellore*
1924	2.4	3.6	2.0	4.7	5.9	5.6	4.5	3.5
1925	2.4	3.6	2.0	4.6	5.9	5.6	4.7	3.5
1926	2.8	4.2	2.0	5.6	7.9	5.2	6.4	3.6
1927	2.8	4.3	2.0	5.6	8.3	4.9	7.3	3.4
1928	3.8	3.7	1.9	6.6	7.4	5.3	10.6	3.6
1929	3.7	3.7	1.7	5.8	9.4	4.4	9.9	-
1930	3.9	5.2	1.9	4.6	5.3	8.6	7.1	-
1931	4.1	5.1	1.5	4.0	4.2	6.0	6.7	-
1932	4.7	6.0	2.2	5.4	8.0	6.7	6.0	-
1933	4.5	9.3	2.4	4.8	8.6	5.2	6.6	-
1934	4.5	10.8	1.7	5.0	8.7	7.0	7.2	-
1935	4.1	10.4	2.0	5.4	12.2	7.3	6.8	-
1936	-	12.9	-	6.8	13.3	8.1	7.4	4.9
1937	-	12.8	-	6.7	10.8	8.0	7.7	4.9
1938	-	14.7	-	3.0	7.7	7.7	6.1	4.7
1939	-	15.2	-	5.5	12.1	9.6	8.2	6.0
1940	-	18.7	-	7.3	16.7	12.0	9.7	7.8
1941	-	21.2	-	8.7	15.3	9.4	9.3	7.2
1942	-	21.0	-	8.9	15.1	9.5	9.2	7.8
1943	-	21.8	-	8.9	14.7	9.5	9.0	8.0
1944	-	19.6	-	9.1	12.0	8.9	10.7	8.3
1945	-	19.0	-	10.1	9.9	8.0	16	9.0
1946	-	18	-	11	10	07	18	09
1947	-	20	-	13	08	08	17	08

Number of Police Stations in the Northern Range District-wise[10]

Years	*Gan-jam*	*Vizaga-patam*	*Jey-pore*	*East Goda-vari*	*West Goda-vari*	*Kistna*	*Gun-tur*	*Nellore*
1924	44	49	30	37	17	26	38	46
1925	44	49	30	37	17	26	38	46
1926	44	47	30	41	17	26	38	46
1927	42	47	30	41	19	27	38	45
1928	42	47	30	41	19	27	38	45
1929	42	47	30	41	19	27	38	-
1930	42	47	31	43	19	27	39	-
1931	42	47	31	43	19	27	39	-
1932	39	46	24	41	19	27	39	-
1933	39	46	24	41	19	27	39	-
1934	39	46	24	41	19	27	39	-
1935	39	46	24	41	19	27	39	-
1936	-	49	-	42	19	27	39	45
1937	-	49	-	42	19	27	39	45
1938	-	49	-	42	19	27	39	45
1939	-	49	-	42	19	27	39	45
1940	-	49	-	41	19	27	39	45
1941	-	49	-	41	19	27	39	45
1942	-	49	-	41	19	27	39	45
1943	-	49	-	41	19	27	39	45
1944	-	50	-	41	19	29	45	45
1945	-	53	-	41	22	30	46	45
1946	-	53	-	40	22	30	46	45
1947	-	54	-	40	22	29	47	45

Number of Outposts in the Northern Range District-wise[11]

Years	*Gan-jam*	*Vizaga-patam*	*Jey-pore*	*East Goda-vari*	*West Goda-vari*	*Kistna*	*Gun-tur*	*Nellore*
1924	08	09	06	06	04	05	10	11
1925	08	09	06	06	04	05	10	11
1926	05	06	06	01	02	02	10	11
1927	05	06	06	01	-	03	10	10
1928	04	05	06	01	-	03	10	10
1929	05	06	06	01	-	03	10	-
1930	05	05	06	01	-	03	10	-
1931	04	02	04	01	-	09	07	-
1932	07	02	10	03	-	03	07	-
1933	07	02	10	03	-	03	07	-
1934	07	02	10	03	-	03	07	-
1935	07	02	10	03	-	03	07	-
1936	-	02	-	03	-	03	09	10
1937	-	02	-	03	-	03	07	10
1938	-	02	-	03	-	03	07	10
1939	-	02	-	03	-	03	07	10
1940	-	02	-	03	-	03	07	10
1941	-	02	-	03	-	03	07	07
1942	-	02	-	03	-	03	07	08
1943	-	02	-	03	-	03	07	08
1944	-	02	-	02	-	03	07	08
1945	-	03	-	03	01	03	07	12
1946	-	03	-	02	01	02	07	12
1947	-	03	-	02	02	02	07	07

Number of Policemen Dismissed in the Northern Range District-wise[12]

Years	*Gan-jam*	*Vizaga-patam*	*Jey-pore*	*East Goda-vari*	*West Goda-vari*	*Kistna*	*Gun-tur*	*Nellore*
1924	04	10	22	02	02	02	01	02
1925	04	10	22	02	02	02	01	-
1926	03	10	22	09	02	01	02	04
1927	06	02	09	07	01	01	05	07
1928	17	19	15	03	06	06	02	06
1929	03	03	04	09	04	01	05	-
1930	03	08	04	04	01	04	03	-
1931	12	02	-	05	-	01	01	-
1932	06	03	03	07	-	-	01	-
1933	02	03	03	07	01	01	04	-
1934	02	03	03	03	01	04	03	-
1935	02	06	03	05	-	02	04	-
1936	-	02	-	01	-	03	02	01
1937	-	03	-	05	01	-	02	-
1938	-	02	-	02	01	01	-	-
1939	-	05	-	02	03	02	02	03
1940	-	04	-	05	01	01	02	02
1941	-	05	-	09	02	01	01	05
1942	-	02	-	08	02	01	02	05
1943	-	07	-	09	03	02	02	05
1944	-	07	-	10	-	02	02	07
1945	-	10	-	10	01	04	02	07
1946	-	11	-	10	05	04	05	09
1947	-	16	-	03	01	01	03	03

Number of Policemen Punished Departmentally in the Northern Range District-wise[13]

Years	*Gan-jam*	*Vizaga-patam*	*Jey-pore*	*East Goda-vari*	*West Goda-vari*	*Kistna*	*Gun-tur*	*Nellore*
1924	245	278	201	241	79	320	251	213
1925	236	283	125	189	68	215	267	208
1926	243	299	112	154	53	230	187	156
1927	52	71	52	74	20	49	42	39
1928	58	52	61	89	32	43	34	38
1929	27	27	25	37	38	46	48	-
1930	13	22	10	27	17	31	13	-
1931	13	38	11	27	18	36	13	-
1932	49	31	12	22	10	34	18	-
1933	20	35	19	13	19	22	37	--
1934	29	41	07	31	30	16	13	--
1935	11	30	07	52	20	09	27	-
1936	-	27	-	20	20	14	16	26
1937	-	15	-	18	04	13	08	21
1938	-	06	-	17	10	15	13	21
1939	-	35	-	35	11	20	13	30
1940	-	43	-	36	38	28	18	24
1941	-	35	-	32	16	19	25	30
1942	-	43	-	32	26	23	23	26
1943	-	30	-	29	19	21	28	21
1944	-	32	-	24	21	16	21	17
1945	-	28	-	31	16	28	19	26
1946	-	-	-	-	-	-	-	-
1947	-	31	-	25	22	24	34	22

Number of Literate Policemen in the Northern Range District-wise[14]

Years	Gan-jam	Vizaga-patam	Jey-pore	East Goda-vari	West Goda-vari	Kistna	Gun-tur	Nellore
1924	842	1080	341	802	295	577	861	797
1925	822	1021	366	845	310	556	865	780
1926	832	1099	368	899	300	581	861	719
1927	830	920	367	909	313	564	851	789
1928	820	921	466	947	314	549	852	793
1929	838	1061	526	960	315	548	855	-
1930	830	1105	533	1064	381	519	774	-
1931	866	1080	531	1037	377	577	831	-
1932	800	989	475	980	374	581	818	-
1933	793	987	454	988	377	587	804	-
1934	791	959	656	996	874	608	802	-
1935	787	939	449	996	374	609	797	-
1936	-	1009	-	994	377	614	801	850
1937	-	1001	-	989	386	613	806	844
1938	-	1029	-	1010	384	616	813	843
1939	-	1013	-	1015	387	615	819	852
1940	-	1019	-	1039	382	609	844	871
1941	-	1029	-	1038	379	629	830	848
1942	-	1291	-	1092	356	680	862	892
1943	-	1298	-	1102	470	768	908	906
1944	-	1461	-	1197	587	801	1022	936
1945	-	1509	-	1202	603	957	1152	963
1946	-	1537	-	1270	635	941	1047	957
1947	-	1603	-	1247	342	954	1286	1082

Number of Rewards given in the Northern Range District-wise[15]

Years	*Gan-jam*	*Vizaga-patam*	*Jey-pore*	*East Goda-vari*	*West Goda-vari*	*Kistna*	*Gun-tur*	*Nellore*
1924	129	67	59	201	63	119	186	177
1925	119	80	57	227	70	133	152	153
1926	102	58	47	245	85	162	207	242
1927	127	49	45	222	91	183	188	246
1928	159	192	129	323	115	216	254	309
1929	88	223	220	199	192	247	175	-
1930	103	348	175	227	53	186	272	-
1931	111	286	90	341	233	263	510	-
1932	123	212	96	180	86	182	137	-
1933	99	215	117	191	65	187	195	-
1934	91	238	96	298	116	209	157	-
1935	127	150	81	330	90	385	200	-
1936	-	362	-	286	88	346	206	288
1937	-	419	-	308	196	507	156	330
1938	-	709	-	238	43	264	378	161
1939	-	321	-	160	101	100	187	215
1940	-	372	-	124	89	74	161	280
1941	-	411	-	302	127	226	332	347
1942	-	409	-	381	151	247	316	399
1943	-	571	-	493	103	295	483	409
1944	-	688	-	481	532	305	659	521
1945	-	709	-	510	589	296	740	497
1946	-	694	-	502	653	288	767	542
1947	-	845	-	524	690	287	547	361

Number of Rifles held by the police forces in the Northern Range District-wise[16]

Years	*Gan-jam*	*Vizaga-patam*	*Jey-pore*	*East Goda-vari*	*West Goda-vari*	*Kistna*	*Gun-tur*	*Nellore*
1924	206	535	112	203	-	-	-	-
1925	204	532	109	197	-	-	-	-
1926	201	532	109	153	-	-	-	-
1927	157	492	109	129	-	-	-	-
1928	160	278	109	179	-	-	-	-
1929	160	252	157	179	-	-	-	-
1930	171	217	157	238	-	-	-	-
1931	171	217	157	239	-	-	-	-
1932	171	217	157	233	-	-	-	-
1933	171	217	157	233	-	-	-	-
1934	171	217	157	233	-	-	-	-
1935	171	217	157	233	-	-	-	-
1936	-	211	-	229	-	-	-	-
1937	-	211	-	229	-	-	-	-
1938	-	211	-	228	-	-	-	-
1939	-	211	-	228	-	-	-	-
1940	-	211	-	228	-	-	-	-
1941	-	209	-	226	-	-	-	-
1942	-	209	-	226	122	223	193	124
1943	-	209	-	226	125	223	196	124
1944	-	411	-	387	125	221	195	124
1945	-	411	-	387	125	217	186	124
1946	-	618	-	387	125	217	186	124
1947	-	590	-	387	125	220	192	124

Number of Smoothbores held by the police forces in the Northern Range District-wise[17]

Years	Gan-jam	Vizaga-patam	Jey-pore	East Goda-vari	West Goda-vari	Kistna	Gun-tur	Nellore
1924	267	478	175	258	-	359	321	369
1925	267	474	175	257	-	359	319	336
1926	256	353	190	250	-	339	323	320
1927	256	353	190	250	-	339	323	320
1928	254	330	190	249	95	245	326	320
1929	254	311	175	249	93	245	236	-
1930	254	334	175	249	169	267	391	-
1931	251	334	175	249	169	267	391	-
1932	298	382	223	337	213	311	433	-
1933	292	337	219	331	213	311	425	-
1934	248	293	175	243	173	267	381	-
1935	248	297	175	243	173	267	381	-
1936	-	294	-	243	173	267	381	362
1937	-	302	-	243	173	267	385	362
1938	-	302	-	243	173	267	385	361
1939	-	299	-	243	173	267	386	361
1940	-	592	-	263	182	289	390	365
1941	-	598	-	266	182	293	390	370
1942	-	598	-	266	182	293	390	370
1943	-	572	-	355	263	393	411	454
1944	-	572	-	355	263	454	476	454
1945	-	686	-	359	263	454	476	463
1946	-	686	-	359	263	454	476	463
1947	-	496	-	356	287	454	576	463

Number of Revolvers held by the Police Forces in the Northern Range District-wise[18]

Years	*Gan-jam*	*Vizaga-patam*	*Jey-pore*	*East Goda-vari*	*West Goda-vari*	*Kistna*	*Gun-tur*	*Nellore*
1924	20	49	15	30	-	34	21	24
1925	20	48	15	25	-	29	21	24
1926	28	49	15	25	-	36	21	24
1927	24	57	15	30	-	38	36	30
1928	25	44	15	38	17	27	30	35
1929	30	50	21	43	17	30	32	-
1930	39	53	21	43	18	29	32	-
1931	34	51	23	53	23	31	42	-
1932	34	51	23	54	23	31	43	-
1933	33	49	23	55	23	31	43	-
1934	33	49	28	55	23	31	47	-
1935	36	54	23	63	24	36	50	-
1936	-	60	-	63	34	36	50	51
1937	-	65	-	66	29	41	55	55
1938	-	65	-	66	30	41	46	46
1939	-	67	-	66	30	41	55	65
1940	-	75	-	66	30	41	58	65
1941	-	72	-	66	30	41	58	65
1942	-	82	-	76	35	61	75	60
1943	-	87	-	75	35	65	79	69
1944	-	91	-	84	37	71	82	77
1945	-	101	-	86	51	79	89	84
1946	-	109	-	86	49	79	92	88
1947	-	104	-	86	49	80	92	91

The comparative statement of the average prices of staple Foodgrains and the Crimes during the initial years of the period 1924-27[19]

Year	*Number of Government score per rupee*			*Grave crimes*
	Rice	*Cholam*	*Ragi*	
1924	5.2	8.5	9.0	36,410
1925	5.2	0.4	8.8	33,470
1926	5.0	0.7	10.0	30,631
1927	5.4	8.5	9.1	31,580

Property Lost and Recovered by the police in the Northern range during the year 1944 is as follows[20]

Districts	*Lost*	*Recovered*
Vizagapatam North Vizagapatam South	Rs 1,45,204	Rs 59,677
East Godavari	Rs 1,37,541	Rs 41,474
West Godavari	Rs 1,29,563	Rs 17,854
Kistna	Rs 1,71,749	Rs 57,496
Guntur	Rs 2,20,821	Rs 1,00,640
Nellore	Rs 98,146	Rs. 38,984

Property Lost and Recovered by the police in the Northern range during the year 1945 is as follows[21]

Districts	*Lost*	*Recovered*
Vizagapatam North Vizagapatam South	Rs 1,35,542 -	Rs 55,288 -
East Godavari	Rs 1,31,159	Rs 58,409
West Godavari	Rs 1,00,327	Rs 11,411
Kistna	Rs 95,694	Rs 32,284
Guntur	Rs 1,49,251	Rs 46,249
Nellore	Rs 1,21,571	Rs 59,987

Property Lost and Recovered by the police in the Northern range during the year 1946 is as follow[22]

Districts	Lost	Recovered
Vizagapatam North Vizagapatam South	Rs 1,44,852 Rs 96,731	Rs 37049 Rs 43,742
East Godavari	Rs 1,45,362	Rs 40,782
West Godavari	Rs 1,52,850	Rs 87,697
Kistna	Rs 1,26,181	Rs 38,950
Guntur	Rs 44,19,024	Rs 98,291
Nellore	Rs 1,39,218	Rs 37,896

References

1. Report on the Administration of the Police of the Madras Presidency for the years 1924 to 1947, printed by Superintendent, Government Press, Madras.
2. *Ibid.*
3. *Ibid.*
4. *Ibid.*
5. *Ibid*
6. *Ibid.*
7. *Ibid.*
8. *Ibid.*
9. *Ibid.*
10. *Ibid.*
11. *Ibid.*
12. *Ibid*
13. *Ibid.*
14. *Ibid.*
15. *Ibid.*
16. *Ibid.*
17. *Ibid.*
18. *Ibid.*
19. Report on the Administration of the Police of the Madras Presidency for the year 1927, printed by Superintendent, Government Press, Madras, 1928, p.8.

20. Report on the Administration of the Police of the Madras Presidency for the year 1945, printed by Superintendent, Government Press, Madras, 1946, p. 8.
21. Report on the Administration of the Police of the Madras Presidency for the year 1946, printed by Superintendent, Government Press, Madras, 1947, p. 8.
22. Report on the Administration of the Police of the Madras Presidency for the year 1947, printed by Superintendent, Government Press, Madras, 1948, p. 8.

Bibliography

PRIMARY SOURCES

GOVERNMENT REPORTS

Administrative Reports of the Madras Presidency Police for the years 1894, printed by Superintendent, Government Press, Madras, 1895.

Administrative Report of the Madras Presidency for the years 1924 to 1947, printed by Superintendent, Government Press, Madras.

Administration Report of the Inspector General of Police for the years 1923 to 1947, printed by Superintendent, Government Press, Madras.

Administrative Reports of the Madras Police, 1862 to 1878, printed by Superintendent, Government Press, Madras.

Annual Reports on the Administration of the Madras Presidency for the years 1924 to 1947, printed by Superintendent, Government Press, Madras.

Madras in 1939 to 1940, Outline of the Administration, printed by Superintendent of Government Press, Madras.

Report on the Administration of the Police of the Madras Presidency for the year 1911, Statistics of British India, Part-VI, Administrative and Judicial-Police, printed by Superintendent, Government Press, Madras, 1912.

Report on the Administration of the Police of the Madras Presidency for the years 1924 to 1947, printed by Superintendent, Government Press, Madras.

Report on the Administration of the Police of the Madras Province for the years 1936 to 1947, printed by Superintendent, Government Press, Madras.

Report on the Administration of the Madras Presidency for the years 1923 to 1947, printed by Superintendent, Government Press, Madras.

Reports on the Administration of the Jails in the Madras Presidency for the years 1925 to 1947, printed by Superintendent, Government Press, Madras.

Reports on the Administration of the Civil Justice in the Madras Presidency for the years 1924 to 1947, printed by Superintendent, Government Press, Madras.

Report on the Administration of the Criminal Justice in Madras Presidency for the year 1894, printed by Superintendent, Government Press, Madras, 1895.

Reports on the Administration of the Criminal Justice in the Madras Presidency for the years 1925 to 1948, printed by Superintendent, Government Press, Madras.

Report of the Madras Public Service Commission for the years 1936-37, printed by Superintendent, Government Press, Madras, 1938.

Report of Indian Police Commission, 1886-87, printed by Superintendent of Government Press, Madras.

Report of the Indian Police Commission 1902-03, Government Central Printing Office, Simla, 1904.

Report of the Indian Statutory Commission, Vol. II, Recommendations, Logos Press, New Delhi, 1930.

Report of the Auxiliary and Territorial Forces Committee, Vol. I, dated 23rd January 1925.

Report submitted by the Superintendent of Police, Guntur, Special Branch, C.I.D. in reply to the Government Memo. No. 6-45-l-H-36 dated May 20, 1936.

Report of the District Superintendent of Police, East Godavari District, dated 19th March, 1931.

Report of the Police Officers Conference held at New Delhi from 5th to 12th February, 1927.

Report on the Disturbances in Purlakimedy, Vizagapatam and Goomsoor in 1832-36, by Russell G.E., Vol. II, printed by H. Smith, Fort St. George Gazette Press, Madras, 1856.

Ridsdale W, Second Report on the Indian Penal Code, Military Orphan Press, Calcutta, 1847.

OTHER PRIMARY SOURCES

Criminal Investigation Department Report, 1908 to 1919.

Government of India, Report of the Royal Commission on the Superior Civil Services in India, Government of India Press, Simla, 1924.

Government of Bengal Criminal Investigation Department, A Pamphlet on Gobinda Dom's gang of Hooghly-Burdwan declared under the Criminal Tribes Act (VI of 1924), Superintendent, Government Printing, Bengal Government Press, Bengal, 1942.

Handbook of Information on the Administration of the Province of Madras, printed by Superintendent, Government Press, Madras, 1947.

History of Police Organisation in India and Indian Village Police, published by the University of Calcutta with the permission of Government of India, University press, Calcutta, 1913.

Home Department Resolution No.1112-1120, dated 8th November, 1905.

Indian Arms Rules Committee Report Superintendent, Government Central Press, Simla, 1923.

Minutes of Evidence related to the Indian and Provincial Civil Services, printed in India, 1914.

Notes on Criminal Classes of Madras Presidency, Criminal Tribes Act No. XXVII of 1871, printed by the Government of Calcutta, Calcutta, 1897.

Observations on the Law and Constitution of India, printed for Kingsbury, Parbury and Allen, London, 1825.

Police Regulations, Bengal, 1915, Vol. IV, printed by Bengal Secretariat Press and published by the Bengal Secretariat Book Depot, Calcutta, 1915.

Police History and Directory, from the Annual Statements issued by the Department, Chicago Historical Association Files, India, 1916.

Police Officers Conference 5th to 12th Feburary, 1927, Report, Government of India Press, Delhi, 1927.

Royal Commission on Public Service in India, Appendix to the Report of the Commissioners, Vol. VII, India, 1914.

Royal Commission on Public Service in India, Appendix to the Report of the Commissioners, Vol. XIII, Police Department, London, 1915.

Rules for British officer's District Tours, Government of India Press, Simla, 1926.

Statutes, Acts and Regulations in Force in the Madras Presidency, Vol. I, published by H.S.Cunnungham and Co., 1876.

Second Report on the Indian Penal Code, Military Orphan Press, Calcutta, 1847.

The History of the Andhra Pradesh Police 1861-1961, published by Inspector General of Police Andhra Pradesh, Hyderabad, 1961.

The Andhra Pradesh Police Manual, Part-II, Annexures and Forms, issued by Inspector General of Police, Andhra Pradesh, Hyderabad, 1984.

The Madras State Discharge Aid Society, Tamil Nadu Archives, Madras, 1981.

The Law of Sedition in India, prepared under the Indian Law Institute, New Delhi, 1964.

Telegram No. 1800, dated 14th March, 1931, Home Department, Government of Madras.

GOVERNMENT ORDERS

G.O.No.739, Home, dated 7th June, 1861, Home Department, Government of Madras.

G.O.No.385, Judl., dated 25th February, 1896, Judicial Department, Government of Madras.

G.O.No.523, Home (Judl.), dated 5th March, 1917, Home (Judicial) Department, Madras Government.

G.O.No. I426, Home (Judicial), dated 15th June, 1918, Home (Judicial) Department, Government of Madras.

G.O.No.439, Home (Judicial), dated 16th February, 1920, Home (Judicial) Department, Government of Madras.

G.O.No.116, Judl. (Police), dated 13th March, 1923, Judicial (Police) Department, Government of Madras.

G.O. No.2107, L (General), dated 26th February, 1923, Law (General) Department, Government of Madras.

G.O. No.667, L (General), dated 26th February, 1923, Law (General) Department, Government of Madras.

G.O.No.171, Judl., dated 1st April, 1924, Judicial Department, Government of Madras.

G.O No. 502, Revenue, dated 31st March, 1925, Revenue Department, Government of Madras.

G.O.No.28, Judl., dated 15th January, 1926, Judicial Department, Government of Madras.

G.O.No.567, Home, dated 28th August, 1926, Home Department, Government of Madras.

G.O.No.28, Judl., dated 15th March, 1926, Judicial Department, Government of Madras

G.O.No.1386, L, dated 27th June, 1927, Law Department, Government of Madras.

G.O.No.467, Judl., dated 25th September, 1928, Judicial Department, Government of Madras.

G.O.No.172, Judl. (Ms), dated 28th March, 1928, Judicial Department, Government of Madras.

G.O.No.2412, Home, dated 9th May, 1928, Home Department, Government of Madras.

G.O.No.2412, Home, dated 9th May, 1928, Home Department, Government of Madras.

G.O.No.467, Home, 25th September, 1928, Home Department, Government of Madras.

G.O. No.2412, Home, dated 9th May, 1928, Home Department, Government of Madras.

G.O.No.354, Public (Police), dated 24th June, 1930, Public (Police), Department, Government of Madras.

G.O.No.275, A, (S-I) Public (Police) (Confdl.), dated 12th May, 1930, Public (Police) Department, Government of Madras.

G.O.No.275, A, (S-1) Confdl., Home, dated 4th May, 1930, Home Department, Government of Madras.

G.O.No.354, Public (Police), dated 24th June, 1930, Public (Police) Department, Government of Madras.

G.O. No.2169, L, dated 25th July, 1930, Law Department, Government of Madras.

G.O. No.354, Public (Police), dated 24th June, 1930, Public (Police), Department, Government of Madras.

G.O.No. 168, Public (Police) (Ms), dated 25th April, 1931, Public (Police) Department, Government of Madras.

G.O.No.765, Public (Police), dated 1st July, 1932, Public (Police), Department, Government of Madras.

G.O.No.600, Public (Police), dated 7th November, 1932, Public (Police), Department, Government of Madras.

G.O. No.2453, L, dated 10th November, 1933, Law Department, Government of Madras.

G.O.No.5421, L, dated 10th November, 1933, Law Department, Government of Madras.

G.O. No. 2930, Home, dated 28th October, 1936, Home Department, Government of Madras.

G.O. No.2930, Home, dated 28th October, 1936, Home Department, Government of Madras.

G.O. No.3565, Home, dated 7th September, 1937, Home Department, Government of Madras.

G.O. No.1026, Home, dated 12th March, 1937, Home Department, Government of Madras.

G.O.No.204, Home, dated 16th January, 1937, Home Department, Government of Madras.

G.O.No.294, Home, dated 2nd January, 1937, Home Department, Government of Madras.

G.O. No.21, Home, dated 3rd January, 1938, Home Department, Government of Madras.

G.O.No.6238, Home (Ms), dated 4th December, 1938, Home Department, Government of Madras.

G.O. No.2412, Home, dated 9th May, 1938, Home Department, Government of Madras.

G.O.No.5214, Home (Ms), dated 30th September, 1939, Home Department, Government of Madras

G.O.No.649, Home (Ms), dated 8th February, 1939, Home Department, Government of Madras.

G.O.No.5407, Home (Ms), dated 14th October, 1939, Home Department, Government of Madras.

G.O.No.6249, Home (Ms), dated 5th December, 1939, Home Department, Government of Madras.

G.O.No.2427, Home (Ms), dated 2nd May, 1939, Home Department, Government of Madras.

G.O.No.2617, Home (Ms), dated 11th May, 1939, Home Department, Government of Madras.

G.O.No.638, Home (Ms), dated 8th February, 1939, Home Department, Government of Madras.

G.O.No.717, Home (Ms), dated 10th February, 1939, Home Department, Government of Madras.

G.O.No.2617, Home (Ms), dated 11th May, 1939, Home Department, Government of Madras.

G.O.No.4225, Home (Ms), dated 7th August, 1939, Home Department, Government of Madras.

G.O.No.2407, Home (Ms), dated 1st May, 1939, Home Department, Government of Madras.

G.O.No.3905, Home (Ms), dated 19th July, 1939, Home Department, Government of Madras.

G.O.No.5273, Home (Ms), dated 4th October, 1939, Home Department, Government of Madras.

G.O.No.2041, Home, dated 28th April, 1941, Home Department, Government of Madras.

G. O.No. 664, Public (Confdl.), dated 21st March, 1941, Public (General) Department, Government of Madras.

G.O.No.2395, Home, dated 19th May, 1941, Home Department, Government of Madras.

G.O.No.644, Home, dated 3rd June, 1941, Home Department, Government of Madras.

G.O.No.2041, Home, dated 28th April, 1941, Home Department, Government of Madras.

G.O. No.768, Home, dated 5th April, 1943, Home Department, Government of Madras.

G.O.No.1014, Public, (General) Confdl., dated 9th April, 1943, Public (General) Department, Government of Madras.

G.O.No.7434-2, Public (General) Department, dated 6th March, 1943, Public (General), Department, Government of Madras.

G.O No.1013, Public (General) Department, dated 9th November, 1943, Public (General) Department, Government of Madras.

G.O. Ms. No. 2530, Public (Civil Defence) Department, dated 4th September, 1943, Public (Civil Defence) Department, Government of Madras.

G.O.No.3019, Home (Ms), dated 3rd September, 1945, Home Department, Government of Madras.

G.O.No.4376, Home (Ms) (Confdl.), dated 10th December, 1945, Home Department, Government of Madras.

G.O.No.2665, Home (Ms), dated 6th August, 1945, Home Department, Government of Madras.

G.O.No.151, Home (Ms), dated 16th January, 1945, Home Department, Government of Madras.

G.O.No.553, Home (Ms), dated 20th February, 1945, Home Department, Government of Madras.

G.O.No.4075, Home (Ms), dated 9th November, 1945, Home Department, Government of Madras.

G.O.No 784, Home (Ms), dated 10th March, 1945, Home Department, Government of Madras.

G.O.No.3024, Home (Ms), dated 19th October, 1945, Home Department, Government of Madras.

G.O.No.754, Home (Ms) (Confdl.), dated 27th Febrarury, 1945, Home Department, Government of Madras.

G.O.No 1353, Home (Ms), dated 28th April, 1945, Home Department, Government of Madras.

G.O.No.3470 Home (Ms), dated 29th September, 1945, Home Department, Government of Madras.

G.O.No 1830, Home (Ms), dated 9th June, 1945, Home Department, Government of Madras.

G.O.No.1951(Ms), dated 21st June, 1945, Home Department, Government of Madras.

G.O. No 4656, Home, dated 17th December, 1947, Home Department, Government of Madras.

G.O.No. 3701, Home, dated 6th October, 1948, Home Department, Government of Madras.

GOVERNMENT LETTERS

Letter No.F-78-28, Police, dated 15th June, 1926, from Government of India to all Local Governments and Administrations.

Letter No. 215/A R, dated 15th July, 1926, from Inspector General of Police to the Chief Secretary to Government, Judicial Department, Madras.

Letter No. 768/36 C-4, dated 21st October, 1936, from E.C Wood, District Magistrate, Vizagapatam, to the Inspector General of Police, Madras.

Letter No D-5741, dated 12th August, 1930, Political, Home Department, Madras.

Letter No. 2491-SB-32, dated August 17th 1932, from Inspector General of Police, Madras to the Chief Secretary to the Government of Madras.

Letter No. 900/Statl./36, dated 18th July, 1936, from Inspector General of Police, to the District Magistrate, Vizagapatam, Madras.

Letter No.1614-H, dated 24th July, 1935, from Major General Connor F.P., Surgeon General with Government of Madras, to the Joint Secretary to Government, Local Self-Government, Public Health Department.

Government of India letter No.E-78-26, Police, dated 7th January, 1927, to all Local Governments.

The Confidential Letter No. D. 8051/33, dated 1st December, 1933, from the Secretary, Government of India, to the Chief Secretary, Government of Madras.

GOVERNMENT ACTS

Government of Madras, Legal Department, The Madras District Police Act XXIV of 1859, printed by Superintendent, Government Press, Madras, 1937.

Government of Madras, Legal Department, The Criminal Tribes Act XXVII of 1871, Office of the Superintendent of Government Printing, Calcutta, 1897.

Government of Madras, Legislative Department, Scheduled District Act, 1874, Office of the Superintendent of Government Printing, Calcutta, 1895.

Government of Madras, Legislative Department, Act No.VI of 1943, printed by the Authority of the Governor of Madras by Superintendent, Government Press, Madras, 1945.

Government of Madras, Legislative Department, The Prisoners of 1971, Office of the Superintendent of Government Printing, Calcutta, 1894.

Government of Madras, Legal Department, Madras Act III of 1862.

Government of Madras, Legal Department, Madras Act VIII of 1867.

Government of Madras, Legal Department, India Act I of 1871.

Government of Madras, Legal Department, The Indian Penal Code Act 45 of 1860.

Government of Madras, Legal Department, Madras Regulation XI of 1816.

Government of Madras, Legal Department, Police Act No. XXXIV of 1859.

Government of Madras, Legal Department, Scheduled District Act 1874 XIV.

Government of Madras, Legal Department, Criminal Tribes Act 1921.

Government of Madras, Legal Department, India Penal Code Act XXIV of 1885.

Government of Madras, Legal Department, Prisoners Act XII of 1873.

Krishna Machariar and Srinivascharíar M, Madras Estates Land Act I of 1908, P.Varadacharary and Co., Madras, 1937.

Madras Motor Vehicles Taxation Act, Report for the quarter ending 31st March, 1941.

The Defence of India Act, 1939, published by Manager of Publications, Government press, Delhi, 1940.

The Madras Forest Department and Account Code, Vol. I, printed by Superintendent, Government Press, 1927.

The Unrepealed General Act VII of 1895, 1887, 1897, Vol. III, Government of India Central Publication Branch, Calcutta, 1929.

The Unrepealed General Acts, Vol. IV, Government of India Central Publication Branch, Calcutta, 1909.

The Criminal Tribes Act of 1911, Government of India, a collection of the Acts passed by the Governor-General of India in council in the year 1911, Calcutta, 1912.

The A.I.R. Manual, Unrepeated Central Acts, Civil and Criminal, Vol. III and XV, Fourth edition, 1979.

COLLECTOR'S STANDING ORDERS

Bhaskara Rao.T, Collector's Standing Orders of Krishna District, printed by Government Press, Madras, 1939.

Bennett, Collector's Standing Orders of East Godavari District, 1934, printed byGovernment Press, 1934.

District Magistrate's Standing Orders, Guntur District, printed by Superintendent, Government Press, Madras, 1931.

Mr Ry. Rai Bahadur, Collector's Standing Orders of Anantapur District, printed by Superintendent, Government Press, Madras, 1931.

Mr Ry. Rai Bahadur N Gopalaswami Ayyangar, Collector's Standing Orders of Nellore District, printed by Superintendent, Government Press, Madras, 1931.

Subhrahmanyan M.V. and A.C. Woodhouse, Standing Orders of the Collector of East Godavari District, Vol. II, printed by Government Press, Madras, 1941.

Subhahmanyan M.V., Collector's Standing Orders of the West Godavari District, Vol. II, printed by Government Press, Madras, 1941.

STATISTICAL APPENDICES

A Statistical Atlas of the Madras Province, 1940-41, published by Economic Adviser to the Government of Madras, Madras, 1949.

Madras District Gazetteers, Statistical Appendix for Nellore District, Madras Presidency, printed by Superintendent, Government Press, Madras, 1929.

Madras District Gazetteers West Godavari District, Vol. II, tables gathered for Police, Civil, Criminal and Jails, Statistics Appendix for West Godavari District, printed by Superintendent, Government Press, Madras, 1934.

Statistical Record of West Godavari District, 1934, printed by Superintendent, Government Press, Madras, 1934.

GAZETTEERS

Andhra Pradesh District Gazetteers, A Manual of the District of Vizagapatam in the Presidency of Madras, published by District Gazetteers, Hyderabad, 1994.

Andhra Pradesh District Gazetteers, A Manual of the Krishna District in the Presidency of Madras, Hyderabad, 1992.

Ayyar K.N.K., Madras District Gazetteers, Statistical Appendix, together with a supplement to the District Gazetteer, 1907 for Godavari District, Superintendent Government Press, Madras, 1934.

Francis W, Visakhapatnam District Gazetteers, Asian Education Services, Madras, 1992.

Francis W, Frederick Nicholson, C.S. Middlemiss and C.A. Barber, Gazetteer of South India, Vol. I, Mittal Publications, New Delhi, 1988.

Gazetteer of South India, Vol. II, Mittal Publications, New Delhi, 1989.

Gazetteer of South India, Vol. I, Superintendent of Government Printing, Madras, 1909.

Gazetteer of the Nellore District, Asian Educational Services, New Delhi, 2004.

Gazetteer of the Nellore District-1938, A-Volume, printed by Superintendent, Government Press, 1942.

Hunter W.W., The Imperial Gazetteer of India, Oxford University, Oxford, 1885.

Imperial Gazetteer-Coastal Districts, printed by the Government Press, Madras, 1909.

Imperial Gazetteer of India, published by Superintendent of Government Press, 1978.

Krishna Swamy Ayyar K.N., Madras District Gazetteers, Statistical Appendix, together with A Supplement to District Gazetteer (1907 for Godavari District), Madras, 1935.

Madras District Gazetteers, Guntur District, Vol. III, printed by Superintendent, Government Press, Madras, 1933.

Ramesan N, Andhra Pradesh District Gazetteers, Srikakulam, printed by Director of printing and stationery at Government Secretary Press, Hyderabad, 1979.

———, Andhra Pradesh District Gazetteers, Visakhapatnam, printed by Director of printing and stationery at Government Secretary Press, Hyderabad, 1979.

———, Andhra Pradesh District Gazetteers, East Godavari, printed by Director of printing and stationery at Government Secretary Press, Hyderabad, 1979.

———, Andhra Pradesh District Gazetteers, West Godavari, printed by Director of printing and stationery at Government Secretary Press, Hyderabad, 1979.

———, Andhra Pradesh District Gazetteers, Krishna District Gazetteer, printed by Director of printing and stationery at Government Secretary Press, Hyderabad, 1977.

Rajagopal. M.V., Andhra Pradesh District Gazetteer, Guntur, Secretariat Press, Hyderabad, 1977.

———, Andhra Pradesh Gazetteers, Nellore, printed by Andhra Pradesh at Government Central Press, Central Press, Hyderabad, 1977.

The Imperial Gazetteer of India, The Indian Empire, Vol. IV, Clarendon Press, Oxford, 1907.

Imperial Gazetteer-Coastal Districts, printed by the Government Press, Madras, 1909.

Imperial Gazetteer of India, Provincial Series, Superintendent of Government printing, Calcutta, 1909.

The Gazetteer of the Vizagapatam District, Asian Education Services, Madras, 1907.

MANUALS

Boswell A.C., Manual of the Nellore District in the Madras Presidency, Madras, 1873.

Carmichael D.F., Manual of the Vizagapatam District, Madras, 1869.

John A.C., Boswell Mes, Manual on the Nellore District in the Presidency of Madras, Government Press, Madras, 1973.

John Kelsall, Manual of the Bellary District, complied under the orders of Government, Lawrence Asylum Press, Madras, 1872.

Maclean C.D., Manual of the Administration of Madras Presidency, Vol. I, Asian Educational Services, New Delhi, 1987.

———, Manual of the Administration of Madras Presidency, Vol. II, Asian Educational Services, New Delhi, 1989.

———, Manual of the Administration of the Madras Presidency, Vol. III, Asian Educational Services, New Delhi, 1987.

Maltby T.J., The Ganjam District Manual, Lawrence Asylum Press, Madras, 1918.

Mackenzie Gordon, A Manual of Krishna District in the Presidency of Madras, New Delhi, 1990.

Manual for the Guidance of Police Officers, printed at the Military Orphan Press, Calcutta, 1865.

The Madras Prison and Reformatory Manual, Vol. II, printed by Superintendent, Government Press, Madras, 1939.

Sanjiva Rows, The All India Civil Court Manual, published by T.A. Venkasawmy and T.S. Krishnasawmy Row, Trichi and Madras, 1915.

Village Officers Manual, Vol. I, prepared under the orders of Government, printed by Superintendent, Government Press, Madras, 1893.

PROCEEDINGS

Andhra Pradesh Congress Committee Proceedings, 1937.

Madras Legislative Council Proceedings, Vol. VII, dated 22nd March, 1922.

Proceedings of the Indian Round Table Conference, dated 12th November, 1930 - 19th January, 1931.

RECORDS

Baramahal Records on Police and Justice Administration, printed by Superintendent Government Press, Madras, 1905.

Baramahal Records, Section XVI, Police, printed by Superintendent, Government Press, Madras, 1923.

Records of Fort St. George, selected documents series, 1900-1947, The Madras State Discharge Prisoner's Aid Society, issued by Commissioner of Archives and Historical Research, Tamil Nadu Archives, Madras Government, Madras, 1981.

GOVERNMENT CIRCULARS

Madras Police Department Circular No.310-S, 3rd September, 1921.

CENSUS REPORTS

Chandra Sekhar A, Census 1961, Andhra Pradesh District Census Handbook, West Godavari District, published by Government of Andhra Pradesh, Hyderabad, 1967.

Census of India 1931, Vol. III, Part III, Madras and Coorge, Madras, 1933.

Census of India 1931, Vol V-XIV, Madras, Part-I, Report by M.W.M Yeath, Madras, 1932.

Census of India 1951, Volume III, Part III, Madras and Coorge, Madras, 1953.

Census 1961, Andhra Pradesh District Census Handbook, West Godavari District, published by Government of Andhra Pradesh, 1967.

Venkateswaran S, Census of India 1951, Vol. III, Madras and Coorg, Part II- A, printed by Superintendent, Government Press, Madras, 1955.

SECONDARY SOURCES

PUBLISHED BOOKS

Aitchison C.U., *A Collection of Treaties, Engagements, and Sunnunds, related by India and Neighbouring Countries, Vol. VII*, Military Orphan Press, Calcutta, 1865.

Arnold, David, *Police Power and Colonial Rule: Madras, 1859-1947*, Oxford University Press, Delhi, 1986.

__________, *Looting, Grain Riots and Government Policy in South India*, Oxford University Press, Delhi, 1979.

Aggarwala R.C., *Constitutional History of India And National Movement,* published by S. Chand and Co. Pvt, Ltd., New Delhi, 1974.

Alan Watson, *The Making of the Civil Law*, Havard University Press, England, 1981.

Bhardwaj K.K., *Indian Police Administration,* National, New Delhi, 1978.

Baden B.H. Powell, *The Land Systems of British India,* Vol. III, London, 1963.

Bandita Devi, *Some Aspects of British Administration in Orissa (1912-1936)*, Academic Foundations, Delhi, 1992.

Bhatia H.S., *Origin and Development of Legal and Political System in India,* Vol - I to IV, Deep and Deep Publications, New Delhi, 1978.

Baker, C.J., *The Politics of South India 1920-1937,* Vikas Publishing House, New Delhi, 1976.

Basudev Panda, *Indian Bureaucracy*, Uppal Publications, New Delhi, 1978.

Baliga B.S., *Madras in the Struggle for Freedom*, Government Press, Madras, 1957.

Chattopadhyay Basudeb, *Crime and Control in Early Colonial Bengal, 1770-1860,* K.P. Bagchi and Co., Calcutta, 2000.

Chopra P.N., Puri B.N., Das M.N., A *Social, Cultural and Economic History of India,* Vol. II, published by S.G.Wasani for Macmillan India, Madras, 1974.

Dosagiri Rao, *Social Change and Political Development in East Godavari District 1875-1925,* Satyakrishna Publishers, Kakinada, 2003.

Devi Dayal Aggarwal, *CBI and Policing in India*, Kaveri Books, New Delhi, 2000.

Devendra Thakur and Thakur D.N., *Tribal Life in India,* Deep and Deep Publications, New Delhi, 1994.

Dodwell H.H., *The Cambridge History of India*, Vol. V, S. Chand and Company, Delhi, 1968.

David Levinson, *Encyclopedia of Crime and Punishment*, Vol. I, Sage Publications, New Delhi, 2002.

Edmund C. Cox, *Police and Crime in India*, published by Stanley Paul and Co., London, 1911.

Edwardes S.M., *Crime in India*, printed by Oxford University Press, Madras, 1924.

Fraser Tytler A, *Consideration on the Present Political State of India*, Vol. II, Kessinger Publishing, London, 1816.

George Smith, *The Geography of British India, Political and Physical,* publisher John Murray, Oxford University, 1882.

Giriraj Shah, *Encyclopedia of Crime, Police and Judicial System*, Vol. I, Anmol Publications, New Delhi, 1999.

__________, *Indian Police-A Retrospect*, Cosmo Publications, New Delhi, 1989.

__________, *State Policing in India*, Cosmos Publications, New Delhi, 1990.

Gouldsbury C.E., *Life in the Indian Police*, published by Chapman and Hall Ltd., 1912.

Ghose S.K., *Encyclopedia of Police in India*, Vol. III, published under the auspices of Law Research Institute, Calcutta, 1997.

Hirday Nath Kunzru, *The Public Services In India, Public Servants of India Society*, Allahabad, 1917.

__________, *Political Pamphlets-II*, The Public Services in India, Servants of India Society, Allahabad, 1917.

Henry Mories, *A Descriptive Historical Account of Godavari District,* Trubner and Co., Madras, London, 1878.

Henry J. Abraham, *The Judicial Process,* published by Delhi Oxford University Press, Bombay, Calcutta, Madras, 1962.

Henry Dodwell, *The Cambridge History of the British Empire*, Vol. VII, Part-I, Cambridge University Press, 1858.

James Vadackumchery, *National Police Commission*, Alph Publications, New Delhi, 1998.

__________, *Wounded Justice and the Story of Indian Police,* Kaveri Books, New Delhi, 2001.

John C. Weistart, *Police Practices*, Oceana Publications Inc., New York, 1974.

John J. Paul, *The Legal Profession in Colonial South India*, Oxford University Press, Delhi, Calcutta, Madras, 1991.

John Marriott and Bhaskar Mukhopadhyay, *Britain in India, 1765-1905, Justice, Police, Law and Order,* Vol. I, Pickering and Chatto, London, 2006.

Jagadisa Aiyer K, *The Criminal Rules of Practice 1931*, printed at the Nathan Press, 1931.

Khan S.A., *Power, Police and Public*, Vishal Publications, Kurukshetra, 1983.

Leitch Ritchie, *British World in the East*: A Guide, Vol –I and II, W. H Allen and Co., London, 1847.

Lucas J R, *On Justice*, Clarendon Press, Oxford, 1980.

Ludden David, *Peasant History in South India*, Oxford University Press, Delhi, 1993.

Lambrick H.T., *Sir Charles Napier and Sind,* Clarendon Press, Oxford, 1952.

Mishra, K.K. , *Police Administration in Ancient India*, Mittal Publications, Delhi, 1987.

Mehartaj Begum, *District Police Administration*, Anmol Publications Pvt Ltd., New Delhi, 1996.

Melville Lee W.L., *History of Police in England*, Methuen and Co., London, 1901.

Majumdar R.C., *The History of Culture of Indian People, Part-I*, British Paramountcy and Indian Renaissance, Bharatiya Vidya Bhavan, Bombay, 1963.

Mc. Setelvad, *Law and Culture*, Bharatiya Vidya Bhavan, Bombay, 1965.

Muttalib, *The Union Public Service Commission*, New Delhi, 1967.

Mahesh Prasad Tondon and Rajesh Tondon, *The Code of Civil Procedure*, Allahabad Law Agency Law Publications, Allahabad, 1982.

Mohd Abdul Waheed Khan, *A Brief History of Andhra Pradesh*, State Archives Government of Andhra Pradesh, Hyderabad, 1972.

Mohammad Mohabbat Khan, *Politics of Administrative Reforms*, Ashish Publication House, New Delhi, 1991.

Munshi K.M. and Diwakar R.R., *Law and Culture,* Bharatiya Vidya Bhavan, Bombay, 1965.

Maclean C.D., *Glossary of the Madras Presidency*, Asian Educational Services, New Delhi, 1982.

Naresh Chandrasen, *Administration in British India*, Gupta, New Delhi, 1976.

Orvill C Snyder, *An Introduction to Criminal Justice,* Text and Cases, Little, Brown and Company, New York, 1953.

Padala Rama Reddi and Padala Srinivasa Reddy, *The Andhra Pradesh Police Code*, Panchayat Publications, Hyderabad, 1995.

Ranjit Sen Gupta, *Management of Internal Security, Freedom from Fear*, Lancer Publications, New Delhi, 1992,

Ram Reddy G and Seshadri K, *Developing Society and Police*, Osmania University, Hyderabad, 1972.

Robert Eric Frykenberg, *Guntur District, 1788-1848, A History of Local Influence and Central Authority in South India*, Clarendon Press, Oxford, 1965.

Rushbrook Williams L.F., *India in 1923-24*, Central Publication Branch, Calcutta, 1924.

Ramaswami P.N., *Magisterial and Police Guide*, Vol. I and Vol. II, The Madras Law Journal Office, Madras, 1951.

__________, *Development of Criminal Law in India*, Madras Law Journal Office, Madras, 1951.

Rao P.R., *History of Modern Andhra*, Sterling Publishers Ltd., Delhi, 1993.

Sanford H Kadish, *Encyclopedia of Crime and Justice*, Vol. I, Law University of California, Berkeley, 1984.

Singha, Radhika, *A Despotism of Law, Crime and Justice in Early Colonial India*, Oxford University Press, Oxford, 1998.

Sharma S.R., *Evolution of Public Administration in India*, Central Book Depot, Allahabad, 1965.

Sarojini Regani, *Highlights of Freedom Movement in Andhra Pradesh*, The Ministry of Cultural Affairs, Government of Andhra Pradesh, Hyderabad, 1972.

Subba Rao K, *Social Justice and Law*, published by The Institute of Constitutional and Parliamentary Studies, New Delhi, 1974.

Srinivas Raghvaiyangar S, *Memorandum on the Progress of the Madras Presidency during the last 40 years of British Administration*, Asian Educational Services, New Delhi, Madras, 1988.

Swaran Lata, *Women in Civil Services*, Deep and Deep Publications, New Delhi, 1993.

Subodh Kapoor, The Indian Encyclopaedia, Cosmo Publications, New Delhi, 2002

Thurston E, *Castes and Tribes of Southern India*, Vol. II, Government Press, Madras, 1909.

Venkatarangaiya M, *The Freedom Struggle in Andhra Pradesh,* (Andhra) Vol. IV, The Andhra Pradesh State Committee, Hyderabad, 1974.

__________, *The Freedom Struggle in Andhra Pradesh* (1921-31) Vol. III, printed by the Commissioner Andhra Pradesh State Archives and Research Institute, Hyderabad, 1997, p.90-91.

Ved Kumari, *Treatise on the Juvenile Justice Act 1986,* The Indian Law Institute, New Delhi, 1993.

Walch G.T., *The Engineering Works of Godavari Delta*, Vol. I, Madras, 1896.

Who's Who Freedom Struggle of Andhra Pradesh, Vol. III, Hyderabad, The Ministry of Cultural Affairs, Government of Andhra Pradesh, 1982.

Winifred A, *The English Penal System*, Penguins Books, Victoria, 1957.

Wilson H.H., *Glossary of Judicial and Revenue Terms, and of all words*, W.M.H. Allen and Co., London, 1855.

JOURNALS

Ann Ewing, *The Indian Civil Service 1919-1924: Service Discontent and the Response in London and in Delhi*, printed in Great Britain, Modern Asian Studies, University of Cambridge, 1984.

Charles Richmond, *Control of Crime in India,* Journal of the American Institute of Criminal Law and Criminology, Vol. 4, published by Northwestern University, 1913.

David Arnold, *The Police and Colonial Control in South India* Social Scientist, Vol. 4, No. 12, (Judl., 1976), published by Social Scientist, pp. 3-16.

___________, *The Armed Police and Colonial Rule in South India*, 1914-1947 Modern Asian Studies, Vol. 11, No. 1, (1977), published by: Cambridge University Press, pp.101-125.

___________, *Dacoity and Rural Crime in Madras, 1860-1940*, Journal of Peasant Studies, 1979, published by Cambridge University Press, pp.140-167.

Das, Dilip K &Arvind Verma, *The Armed Police in the British Colonial Tradition: The Indian Perspective, Policing,* An International Journal of Police Strategies and Management, 1998, p.354-367.

Frank Carrington, *Speaking for the Police,* Journal of Criminal Law, Criminology and Police Science, Vol. 61, published by Northwestern University, 1970.

Hooja, *Police during the British rule*, The Indian Police Journal, 1861-1961, Centenary Issue, 1961.

Journal of Criminal Law, Criminology, and Police Science, Vol. 18, published by Northwestern University.

John Mc Cracken , *Aspects of the History of a Colonial Police Force,* The Journal of African History, Vol. 27, No. 1, published by Cambridge University Press, 1986.

John Robert, *Impact of Social Conditions on Country Police System in Rayalaseema District, 1550-1857*, Andhra Pradesh History Congress, Kadapa, 2007.

Lawrence W. Sherman, *Attacking Crime: Police and Crime Control, Crime and Justice,* Vol. 15, Modern Policing, published by the University of Chicago Press, 1992, pp. 159-230.

Lawrence W. Sherman, *Crime and Justice*, Attacking Crime: Police and Crime Control, published by the University of Chicago Press, 1992.

Madras Law Journal, Madras, 1945.

Murali Atlury, *Alluri Sitarama Raju and the Manyam Rebellion of 1922-*

1924 , Social Scientist, Vol. 12, No. 4, published by Social Scientist, 1984, pp. 3-33.

Marshall P.J., *British Society in India under the East India Company*, Modern Asian Studies, Vol. 31, No. 1, published by Cambridge University Press, 1997.

Peers, Douglas M, *Torture, the Police and the Colonial State in the Madras Presidency, 1816-55,* Criminal Justice History, 1991, pp.29-56.

Police Administration, Special issue of Indian Journal of Public Administration, Vol No. XXIV, Jan-March, 1978.

Rao S.V., *Police under the East India Company*, The Indian Police Journal, 1861-1961, Indian Police Centenary Edition, 1961.

Satadru Sen, *A Separate Punishment: Juvenile Offenders in Colonial India*, The Journal of Asian Studies, Vol. 63, published by Association for Asian Studies, 2004.

Sandria B. Freitag, *Crime in the Social Order of Colonial North India*, Vol. 25, published by Cambridge University Press, 1991.

Scott B. Cook, *The Irish Raj: Social Origins and Careers of Irishmen in the Indian Civil Service, 1855-1914,* Journal of Social History, Vol. 20, No. 3, published by Peter N. Stearns, 1980, pp. 507-52.

The Indian Law Reports (Madras Series) vol. XXXI, January, December, 1908.

The Madras Law Journal Volume-LXI, July-December, 1931.

The Law College Magazine, Vol. V, Febrarury 1930, Madras.

The Law College Magazine, Vol. I, September, 1926, Madras.

The Madras Law Times, Vol. XXIX, 1921, Madras.

NEWSPAPERS

Andhra Patrika, dated 2nd December, 1926.

The Hindu, dated 20th October, 1926.

The Hindu, dated 27th July, 1927.

The Hindu, dated 15th October, 1928.

The Hindu, dated 5th June, 1930.

The Hindu, dated 12th Apri,l 1930.

The Hindu, dated 23rd June, 1933.

The Hindu, dated 20th August, 1933.

The Hindu, dated 31st March, 1935.

Madras Mail, dated 11th August, 1936.

Index